The Psychology of Christian Character Formation

The Psychology of Christian Character Formation

Joanna Collicutt

scm press

Published in 2015 by SCM Press
Editorial office
3rd Floor
Invicta House
108–114 Golden Lane,
London
EC1Y 0TG.

Second impression 2019

SCM Press is an imprint of Hymns Ancient & Modern Ltd
(a registered charity)
13A Hellesdon Park Road
Norwich NR6 5DR, UK

www.scmpress.co.uk

Scripture quotations are from the New Revised Standard Version of the Bible,
Anglicized Edition, copyright © 1989, 1995 by the Division of Christian
Education of the National Council of the Churches of Christ in the USA.
Used by permission. All rights reserved.

On page viii, The Light of the World (1851–53) by William Holman Hunt is
from the chapel at Keble College, Oxford. Photograph by www.wikipedia.org
and used under a Creative Commons Attribution-ShareAlike 3.0 licence.

British Library Cataloguing in Publication data

A catalogue record for this book is available
from the British Library

978 0 334 05179 4

Typeset by Manila Typesetting Company
Printed and bound by
CPI Group (UK) Ltd, Croydon

Contents

Introduction   ix

Part 1: The Nature of the Endeavour   1
1 The F Word: What is Formation?   3
2 Growing up into Christ   13
3 The Character of Christ   29

Part 2: Insights from Psychology   43
4 Understanding Ourselves: From Temperament to Character   47
5 Understanding Ourselves: The Shape of Our Stories   62
6 How Growth Happens   76

Part 3: Cultivating the Fruit of the Spirit   91
7 Intimacy with the Holy Other: Taking the Lord's Prayer Seriously   97
8 Humble Power: Having the Mind of Christ   112
9 Heaven in Ordinary: Watching and Praying   125
10 Personal Coherence: Getting the Balance Right   142
11 Hospitality: Visiting and Welcoming   160
12 Compassion: Seeing, Feeling, Doing   177
13 Not Retaliating: Forgiveness and Repentance   194
14 Wisdom: Inhabiting Uncertainty with Confidence   213
15 Transformation: Embracing the Pattern of the Cross   230

Bibliography   241

Sources for Boxed Quotations   262

Index of Bible References   265

Index of Names and Subjects   271

In memory of Steph
Transformed from one degree of glory to another

Introduction

This is a book about psychology and faith but, unlike most books on psychology and faith, it is not primarily about how to give pastoral care to others. It takes seriously Jesus' saying about taking the log out of your own eye before you try and remove the speck from your neighbour's eye (Matt. 7.5/Luke 6.42). That is, it is about applying psychology to your own spiritual formation. It is essentially a psychological manual for Christian spirituality. However, because this involves the cultivation of virtues such as compassion and forgiveness, there are clear implications for relationships with others.

Several schools of psychology are drawn upon, especially positive psychology, developmental psychology, social psychology, clinical psychology and personality psychology. Cognitive psychology and object relations psychology also make an appearance. What these different psychologies have in common is a strong basis in empirical research, and throughout the book the degree of reliance that can be placed on their various claims is made clear. The aim is to equip the Christian disciple with well-grounded psychological insights and practical ideas that can support her spiritual growth, and may also resource her to help others. The book is written with Christian leaders or those training for leadership in mind, but it should also be helpful to all Christians who want to advance in the life of faith.

After a consideration of the nature of Christian formation in Part 1, Part 2 presents some relevant psychological accounts of the development of personality and character in some detail. Part 3 is the longest part, and is devoted to applying psychology to the task of developing a Christlike character, always recognizing that this is first and foremost a work of the Spirit. Each chapter begins with several quotations from the Bible (usually in the NRSV translation), and references to the Bible occur frequently throughout. The reader is therefore advised to have a Bible to hand. Voices from the history of the Church from earliest times up until the present day are also to be found in text boxes in each chapter. These are included as 'wise guides', and have been selected to highlight the fact that 'new' insights from psychology have usually been anticipated or have resonances in the Christian tradition.

In line with the book's practical emphasis, there are suggested exercises or activities at the end of each chapter, together with further recommended reasonably accessible reading. This, together with my relentless tendency to illustrate substantive points with 'homely anecdotes', reflects the fact that the book has grown out of many years of teaching students. Indeed, it could not have been written without their stimulation, challenging questions and wise insights. I would therefore like to acknowledge them: ordinands at Wycliffe Hall, St Mellitus College and especially Ripon College Cuddesdon; psychology undergraduates and postgraduates at Heythrop College; and my NHS clinical psychology trainees. I would also like to thank Ripon College Cuddesdon for giving me study leave to write this book, and Harris Manchester College, Oxford, for providing such a hospitable environment within which to research psychology of religion.

I have tried to write as clearly and coherently as I can, but I do not think this book is an easy read because it deals with complex issues, and stands at the interface of empirical psychology and Christian theology. It probably needs to be taken in bite-sized chunks. Each chapter builds on what has gone before (and the links are always clearly signalled), returning again and again to a relatively small number of key themes, aiming for their deeper appropriation by the reader through this recursive process. Like the Christian life that is its subject, the book gets progressively more demanding as it unfolds, but I hope and pray that it will also provide some correspondingly rich rewards.

PART I

The Nature of the Endeavour

I

The F Word: What is Formation?

My little children, for whom I am again in the pain of childbirth until Christ is formed in you.

Galatians 4.19

Now the Lord is the Spirit, and where the Spirit of the Lord is, there is freedom. And all of us, with unveiled faces, seeing the glory of the Lord as though reflected in a mirror, are being transformed into the same image from one degree of glory to another; for this comes from the Lord, the Spirit.

2 Corinthians 3.17–18

The use of the word 'formation' to describe the Christian life is a bit like Marmite. It is beloved of some and loathed by others, so much so that its appearance in conversation can serve as an identity marker,[1] indicating not only church tradition but also status; for it is part of the jargon of 'spiritual professionals'. For this reason alone, one can see why some might treat it with suspicion.

Yet aversion to the word 'formation' can arise from more than this. It has about it a slightly concerning resonance with the work of the sausage machine, which minces and mixes up meat and then literally forces it into a uniform mould to suit the requirements of the production company. Here 'formation' means violence, restriction, blandness and objectification. Something similar to this troubling picture of formation is seen in descriptions of spiritual renewal that allude to a potter moulding his clay.[2] Again there is a feeling of people being bashed about and broken before they are squeezed into a shape that is not of their choosing. Surely the Christian life isn't like this?

Indeed it is not. The image of the potter and the clay is to be found in the Bible, but not in passages that speak of the way God works in the life of the Christian. Instead it appears in the oracles that warn of God's judgement on Israel and of his wrath on the nations such as Assyria and Babylon (e.g. Ps. 2.9; Isa. 41.25; Jer. 18.6–7). The image is invoked by Paul in his letter to the Romans (Rom. 9.17–24) in the context of an argument about Jews and Gentiles, where he applies it to God's power over Pharaoh, crucially talking here of 'moulding' (*plassō*)[3] rather than 'forming' (*morphoō*). The image of the potter and the clay is used in each of these passages to assert the sovereignty and justice of the

---

1 For much more on identity markers, see Chapter 11.

2 See for instance 'Spirit of the Living God', Daniel Iverson © 1935 Birdwing Music.

3 This word can mean 'create', but its dominant meaning is 'manufacture'. It is used in the Greek Old Testament to describe the making of the material Adam before God 'inspirits' him with his breath (Gen. 2.7).

creator God in history, particularly in relation to corrupt and rapacious political regimes. It actually tells us little about Christian formation.

So if 'formation' isn't about breaking, bashing, melting, mincing, squeezing and moulding, what is it? In this opening chapter we will consider seven key character-istics of Christian formation that are vitally important to a proper understanding, but that can also be easily overlooked or forgotten. We begin with its context.

Formation happens in the context of cosmic transformation

In the ancient world *morphoō* was used to describe the mysterious unfolding development of a foetus. Notice how Paul uses the metaphor of childbirth when talking of formation in the passage from Galatians 4 that opens this chapter. This is a much more complex and organic metaphor than that of the sausage machine or potter's workshop, and it is the sort of image we should keep in mind when we think about 'formation'.

In our second opening Pauline passage, this time from 2 Corinthians 3, we find the word 'transformed' (*metamorphoomai*). In both New Testament Greek and English this word is made by taking the shorter word ('form' or *morph*) and adding a prefix ('trans' or *meta*), thus placing it in a broader context. Formation happens in the context of *trans*formation, a transformation that involves the whole created order (Rom. 8.19–21). There is a process of radical change afoot, and part of this process is the birthing and growing of something new.

The actual word 'transformation' doesn't occur very often in the New Testament. Perhaps this is because it is so fundamental to its message, so deeply embedded, so woven into its narrative that it doesn't need to be voiced explicitly. But the idea, if not the word, is everywhere. The message of the kingdom of God is one of radical transformation: the mustard seed, the yeast, being born again, the inversion of worldly values and priorities where the first are last and the last first. Moreover, the work of Jesus is in essence radical transformation: the turn-ing of water into wine, of want into plenty, of disease into health, of social exclu-sion into welcome, of sinner into saint, above all of death into life. This work is continued by the Spirit, marked definitively by the radical transformation of a group of cowering wretches into articulate and bold witnesses to Jesus at the first Pentecost. This brings us to perhaps the most important point about formation.

Formation is a work of the Spirit

'The Lord is Spirit', writes Paul in our second opening passage, as he concludes a complex section of a letter to the Corinthians where references to 'God', 'Christ' and 'the Spirit' tumble over each other. At one point in this section he describes Christian believers as letters written by Christ using the Spirit of God as ink (2 Cor. 3.2). Paul is emphasizing that the process of transformation of which his readers are a part is a special work of the One we now know as the third person of the Trinity – the Holy Spirit. In this sense the formation of the Christian can be said to be 'spiritual'.

It is important to be clear on this Christian meaning of the word 'spiritual' and also its close relative 'spirituality', for these words are, if anything, even more controversial and Marmite-like than 'formation'. 'Spirituality' is a term that has found increasing favour in western secular thought in recent years (Collicutt 2011a). It is the subject of a good deal of research by social scientists, some of which we shall explore in the course of this book. In this social scientific context, spirituality is understood to refer to certain aspects of human life: a concern with self-transcendence, a search for meaning and a sense of the sacred (Collicutt 2011b).

In more everyday usage the word 'spiritual' is often taken to refer to the immaterial aspects of life that cannot be directly observed or measured by science, such as particular altered states of consciousness or even a purported supernatural realm. Here the spiritual is set against the physical and the mundane. Spirituality is also sometimes seen as a facet of personal identity, so that an individual might be said to have a type of spiritual identity in the same way that she might have a type of sexual or occupational identity expressed in certain spiritual, sexual and occupational preferences and practices. Used in yet another way, spirituality may refer to a kind of talent or skill, with some individuals described as 'spiritual' in the same way others might be described as 'musical'. Finally, 'spirituality' can be a shorthand term for those aspects of religion that are perceived as positive (Pargament 1999; Selvam 2013).

Although this multiplicity of meanings can lead to some confusion, there is nothing inherently wrong with any of them; they each acknowledge important aspects of human lived experience. But that is the point. They are concerned with the *human* rather than the divine; and it is all too easy for this human-centred notion of spirituality to leach insidiously into Christian discourse.

While Christian spiritual formation may well involve self-transcendence, the finding of meaning and an increased sense of what is sacred or holy, these are not its primary aim. More importantly, Christian spirituality is not essentially experiential; not concerned exclusively with the immaterial aspects of life or a supernatural realm; not a set of preferences, practices or disciplines; and not the non-dogmatic, personal part of the Christian faith (McAfee Brown 1988, p. 25). Christian spirituality is simply what its name suggests: 'life in God's Spirit and a living relationship with God's Spirit' (Moltmann 1992, p. 83). Drawing on Paul (Rom. 12.1; 1 Cor. 6.9), Dallas Willard (1988, p. 31) rightly emphasizes the physicality of this relationship by describing it as one in which *embodied* human beings are alive to God in the *material* world *here and now*.

In summary therefore, Christian spiritual formation can be understood as the transforming work of the Spirit in every aspect of the life of the believer. This understanding leads to two interesting consequences. First, formation is seen to involve the *whole* of a person's life – embodied thinking, feeling, acting and being in relationship.[4] Second, as Paul asserts in our opening extract from 2 Corinthians, because of the nature of the Spirit, formation results in freedom.

---

4 This is not too far from the secular notion of spiritual well-being as 'holistic' (see e.g. Hawks 2004).

Formation involves liberation and cooperation

Contrary to the repressive and restrictive images of the sausage machine and potter, the Holy Spirit is a liberator. This is something Jesus emphasizes as he reads from the Isaiah scroll in the synagogue at Nazareth (Luke 4.18). The work of the Spirit is not to change a person into something she is not, but to enable that person to be truly and fully herself. The Spirit is, after all, also the authentic Spirit of truth (John 14.17; 15.26; 16.13).

But what does it actually mean to be fully oneself? Here an understanding of human psychology can be of help in articulating the ways in which we can end up trapped in inauthentic and dysfunctional patterns of behaviour that do not do us full justice. Sometimes these behaviour patterns are extreme and dramatically destructive of self and others. More often there is simply a chronic low level of dissatisfaction, expressed in semi-conscious awareness that 'this isn't really me' or 'I am stuck' or 'there's got to be more to my life than this'. Understanding ourselves better enables us to cooperate better with the Spirit's work of personal transformation and liberation.

Cooperation is a key aspect of the birthing that is formation. While there is no scope for meat to cooperate with the sausage machine or clay to cooperate with the potter, the process of birthing is a different matter; it will go better if the mother works with the midwife. More importantly, the conception of the foetus is the result of an act of cooperation between man and woman where mutual consent should be the norm. Notice the lengths to which Luke goes to make it clear that Mary was a willing, actively cooperating participant with the Spirit in the birth of Jesus (Luke 1.35; 1.38; 11.27–28). We might think of our intentional cooperation with God in the process of formation as our 'discipleship': just as a student is someone who is being educated and cooperates with the process by engaging in study, a disciple is someone who is being formed and cooperates with the process by engaging in discipleship.

This idea of cooperation is expressed even more clearly by Paul in Romans 8 where he says 'you did not receive a Spirit of slavery' (v. 15) and goes on to talk of 'the Spirit bearing witness with our spirits' (v. 16).[5] Here he brings together the idea of liberation with that of cooperation. By definition, those who are free cannot be forced to act. Their consent and cooperation are required:

> the Spirit does not take us over: we are not possessed or colonized. Instead, says Paul, the Spirit works in cooperation with our human spirit. I do not become Christ-like because Christ has somehow jackbooted his way into my life and taken it over. I become Christ-like by . . . cooperating with the Spirit in a jointly owned work of personal transformation. (Collicutt 2012b, p. 54)

---

5 Paul's use of the word *pneuma* (spirit) is the subject of much debate, and he clearly uses it in several different ways in different contexts. In Romans 8.16 it is probably best understood as the human will or disposition to act (as in Matt. 26.41).

Formation is then more than a work of the Spirit. It is a work of the Spirit with *our* spirits. It starts with God, but this is the God who chooses to work with – not on – human beings. So some of our human notions of spirituality touched on in the previous section, while not central and definitive, may turn out to be relevant to the endeavour after all.

Formation is for all of us

Notice how Paul talks about 'all of us' in our opening passage from 2 Corinthians 3. There is no sense anywhere in the New Testament that formation is only for Christian leaders or those with a formally recognized or ordained ministry. God is at work in the life of *every* Christian, and every Christian is to cooperate with the transforming work of the Spirit. In a similar way, every Christian is 'called' to ministry in the Church and the world. All Christians have vocations and all are participating in formation.

Of course the way this works out in detailed practice will differ between individuals. Christian leaders may need to pay attention to particular aspects of their life in God. If their ministry has a heavy teaching component, scholarship will be important. If their ministry involves leading worship, a focus on 'not getting in the way of God' will be vital. The demands of being a formal public representative of the institutional Church should also be faced. Above all there must be vigilance for and resistance to the temptation to think of oneself as 'special' (for more on this, see Chapter 8).

But none of this differs in any qualitative way from the formation of those not in leadership positions: 'there are varieties of gifts, but the same Spirit; and there are varieties of services, but the same Lord; and there are varieties of activities, but it is the same God who activates all of them in everyone' (1 Cor. 12.4–6).

Formation is happy and glorious

One of my precious memories from childhood summers is of my father singing while he shaved – quite a feat! – the opening song from the musical *Oklahoma!*, 'Oh what a beautiful mornin''.[6] This song is a joyful response to the 'bright golden haze' of the sun. My father sometimes changed the word 'beautiful' to 'glorious' as he sang, especially if it was his day off, and he anticipated the prospect of enjoying the sunshine outdoors.

Now the glory of the LORD is not traditionally something that calls forth joy. It is so bright that, like the sun, human beings cannot look on it. It is awe inspiring and sobering (see e.g. Exod. 33). But the New Testament asserts that because of Christ we have a new relationship with God's glory; anyone who looks on Christ sees the glory of the LORD (John 1.14; 14.9; 2 Cor. 4.4–6; Col. 1.25; Heb. 1.3) and lives to tell the tale. If this were not startling enough, in our

---

6 R. Rodgers and O. Hammerstein (1943).

passage from 2 Corinthians 3 Paul makes a further claim: Christians are themselves becoming 'glorious' – shining like stars (see also Phil. 2.15; Acts 6.15; 2 Thess. 2.14).

> For the glory of God is living man; and the life of man consists in beholding God. For if the manifestation of God which is made by means of creation, affords life to all living on earth, much more does the Revelation of the Father which comes through the Word, give life to those who see God.
>
> Irenaeus of Lyons (*c*.130–202 AD)

Our formation should make us want to sing out with joy, because through it we are granted the privilege of participating in the glory of God! As part of the transformation of the cosmos God is doing a work of glory in us, and our natural response should be one of joy and delight. Why? Because God himself[7] takes 'good pleasure' (*eudokias*) both in it and in us (Luke 12.22; Eph. 1.5, 9; Phil. 2.13). Our formation could be described as part of 'God's happy project' (Charry 2012, p. 247).

Given the circumstances of life and our varying moods and temperaments, we may not always, or even often, grasp the sheer happiness of this process of transformation; but we will all have at least fleeting moments where we are granted an insight into this reality, and we should make as much of them as we can. We will explore some ways of inhabiting happiness more fully in Chapter 10. In Chapter 15 we will consider the challenging issue of how happiness and glory might even emerge in the midst of suffering and adversity – a fundamental reality expressed by Jesus when he reframed the agony of his cross as his glory (John 12.21–28).

Formation is corporate

The corporate nature of formation is both easy and dangerous to overlook. We live in a highly individualist society. One way this is expressed is in the privatization of corporate 'religion' into personal 'spirituality' (Collicutt 2011a). It is common to hear people talking of 'my' or 'his' formation, but references to 'our' or 'their' formation are rarely heard. Yet to hive off the individual from the community in this way is a mistake. The formation of the individual only makes sense in the context of the formation of the faith communit(ies) of which that individual is a part.

---

7 Throughout this book the masculine pronoun is used to refer to God simply for ease of readership. It should not be taken to indicate a gendered concept of the divine.

The English language fails to distinguish between 'you' singular and plural, and so it is all too easy for us to receive biblical statements about the Christian life as statements about discrete individuals when they are in fact referring to the whole community. While the Bible in general and the New Testament in particular are deeply concerned with the stories of individuals, these should nevertheless be understood in a corporate context. Individuals are parts of a body, and they stand in relationship to other individual parts of this body and to the body as a whole. Following his statement on varieties of gifts, services and activities in 1 Corinthians 12, Paul says that these are all given for the *common good* (v. 7). This is typical of the New Testament approach to life in the Spirit and its concern with building up the body of Christ, which we shall consider more fully in Chapter 2.

The Christian life is all about community. After all, its foundational concept is stated in terms of a community: the 'kingdom of God'. This is a domain marked by peace, justice and social inclusion. Churches are social groups transfigured by the love of God; gatherings at which people are drawn together or networks through which people are connected. They are fluid and dynamic bodies that exist in some sort of relationship to the wider body that is the whole communion of saints, but which also have their own local identity as bodies. They are to varying degrees formally managed and subject to institutional organization and control, but they are most fundamentally simply the people(s) of God.

Each individual Christian has a *personal* life in the Spirit because he is a child of God. He also has a *collective* life in the Spirit because he is a member of the people of God, locally, nationally and cosmically. Moreover, he has an *interpersonal* life in the Spirit because he is the brother of other Christians in his community, sometimes taking on a particular role or ministry, but always being 'in a relationship' (as they say on Facebook) with his brethren.

It is in this complex context that individual and corporate formation takes place. It is personal, collective and interpersonal. Not only that, the body that is the Church is itself situated in a wider environment – 'the world', and it is this wider context that reminds us of the whole point of the Church's existence. Like Christ, who lived and died for the world, his body, the Church, exists for the world. It is part of the *Missio Dei*.

It is perhaps helpful here to remember Jesus' deceptively simple story of the mustard seed (Matt. 13.31–32 and parallels). The seed grows into a healthy tree through a process of deeply mysterious yet glorious transformation. The tree is an organic and complex whole of interdependent parts, whose branches must remain connected to the source of nourishment offered through the plant's vascular system if they are to flourish and bear fruit. However, unlike the true vine in John 15, the bearing of literal fruit is not the image used in this parable. These branches are fruitful in a different way: they reach out into the wider environment and serve its inhabitants. They are hospitable places for the birds of the air to make their homes. We have here in one short sentence a rich image of a flourishing, integrated community that is open to others.

This story gives two added dimensions to the notion of formation. The community is formed through relational *growth* (the topic of the next chapter); and in the process the peace, justice and social inclusion that are the mark of God's kingdom spill *outwards* from the flourishing community into the world. This more outward facing quest for social justice has not historically been seen as a central part of Christian spirituality (though it has a clear place in the life of some of the saints, such as Francis), but this is being reappraised by some (see e.g. McAfee Brown 1988; Shults 2006; Sandage 2012). We shall return to it in Chapters 11 and 12.

In this section the corporate and social nature of Christian spiritual formation has been emphasized. This is in tune with the coming of the Spirit on the first Christians when they were *all gathered together* (Acts 2.1). The Spirit came upon them as a group. Nevertheless, it is significant that the tongues of flame were individually divided. The Spirit thus acknowledged both the collective and personal identity of these folk. The body is made up of parts; both the parts and the whole are respected.

When Jesus said, 'where two or three are gathered in my name I am there among them' (Matt. 18.20), he was perhaps in part alluding to the events of Pentecost, but his statement is more general in scope. It claims that the very act of Christians gathering together or connecting with each other at any time and place invokes his presence.

This brings us to the most thorny question of all about formation. The Spirit is doing the forming, but who exactly is being formed?

Christ is formed in you

We return to the opening words of this chapter, the only place in the New Testament that actually talks of the Christian life as a formative process. Here Paul says something really quite surprising. It is *Christ* who is formed. The outcome of the formation process is that a Christian community becomes what it is; its true self, the body of Christ. Like childbirth, this is essentially a glorious and happy event; but that doesn't rule out pain along the way.

> The just man or woman lives in God and God lives in them just as they are in him, since every one of the just person's virtues gives birth to God and brings him joy.
>
> Meister Eckhart (1260–1328)

Paul's words may be understood most simply as a way of indicating that Christian communities should be conformed to the character of Christ.

However, there is more to it than this, evident in the theologies of Paul himself (see e.g. Rom. 8.10; Gal. 2.20), but also of other New Testament writers including Matthew, Luke and John: 'Truly I tell you, just as you did it to one of the least of these who are members of my family, you did it to me' (Matt. 25.40); 'I am Jesus, whom you are persecuting'(Acts 9.5b); 'I in them and you in me' (John 17.23a). There is a sense that through the formative work of the Spirit, Christian communities are to undergo a real 'ontological' change, to become not just Christlike (if this weren't astonishing enough), but in a deeply mysterious way to become Christ himself.[8]

Keeping this goal in mind saves us from falling into the error of thinking that formation is just about me becoming a better person. Of course this is part of it, but at heart it's a much more audacious project that involves whole communities being caught up into the Godhead, something referred to by the Eastern churches as *theōsis*.

> The one who can do good and who does it is truly God by grace and participation because he has taken on in happy imitation this energy and characteristic of his own doing good . . . God lifts up man to the unknowable as much as man manifests God, invisible by nature, through his virtues.
>
> Maximus the Confessor (580–662)

One way that the New Testament writers express this mystery is through the idea of 'growing up into Christ'. This is the subject of the next chapter.

---

8 For more on the biblical basis of this notion, see Collicutt 2012b.

Exercise

Return to the story of the mustard seed (Matt. 13.31–32); it's also instructive to read the slightly different version in Mark's Gospel (Mark 4.30–32). Reflect for a while on your 'life in the Spirit'. Then consider these 'wondering questions' from the Godly Play version (Berryman 2002, p. 120).

- I wonder if the person who put the tiny seed in the ground has a name?
- I wonder if the person was happy when he saw the birds coming?
- I wonder what the person was doing while the shrub was growing?
- I wonder if the person could take the shrub like a tree and push it all back down inside the seed?
- I wonder if the seed was happy while it was growing?
- I wonder where the seed was when it stopped going?
- I wonder if the birds have names?
- I wonder if they were happy to find the tree?
- I wonder what the tree could really be?
- I wonder if you have ever come close to this kind of tree?
- I wonder what the nests could really be?
- I wonder what this whole place could really be?

Further reading

Shults, F. L., 2006, 'Reforming pneumatology', in F. L. Shults and S. Sandage (eds), *Transforming Spirituality: Integrating Theology and Psychology*, Grand Rapids, MI: Baker Academic, pp. 39–66.

2

Growing up into Christ

Be perfect, therefore, as your heavenly Father is perfect.

Matthew 5.48

We must grow up in every way into him who is the head, into Christ, from whom the whole body, joined and knit together by every ligament with which it is equipped, as each part is working properly, promotes the body's growth in building itself up in love.

Ephesians 4.15b–16

Do not be conformed to this world, but be transformed by the renewing of your minds, so that you may discern what is the will of God – what is good and acceptable and perfect.

Romans 12.2

Beginning with the story of the mustard seed, the image of a healthy plant or tree is found throughout the New Testament, where it is used to describe the spiritual life of Christian communities. The plant is stamped with the divine DNA, planted by God, draws spiritual nourishment from connection with Christ (Luke 13.8; John 15.4–5) and bears the fruit of his Spirit (Gal. 5.22) – a 'harvest of righteousness' (Phil. 1.11).

The metaphor of the fruit-bearing tree is both highly evocative and very old; it may even be archetypal.[1] It opens the hymn book of ancient Israel. Here the psalmist describes the righteous man (or perhaps nation) as 'like a tree planted by streams of water, that yields its fruit in its season, and its leaf does not wither' (Ps. 1.3, RSV). Plant husbandry and its resultant harvest are also particularly marked in the teaching of Jesus, who was after all a country boy raised against a backdrop of seed time, growth and harvest in his native Galilee.

The fruit-bearing tree is a very helpful picture of the spiritual life, to which we shall return later in this chapter and throughout the book. However, like all metaphors, it is not complete in itself. One of its limitations is that plants don't move about much, and when they do, the movement is largely reactive; so the picture of a healthy tree or field of wheat cannot fully capture the dynamic, strategic and directional aspects of life in the Spirit.

Unlike Jesus of Nazareth, most of the writers of the New Testament were living in the more cosmopolitan and urban context of Graeco-Roman cities. Here they found themselves reaching for another metaphor to do justice to the new life that they had found in Christ: the healthy body that is fit to run in the civic

---

1 In the analytic psychological framework of C. G. Jung (1875–1961) an 'archetype' is a deep psychological structure that finds its way into the sacred stories and myths of all cultures.

games (see e.g. 1 Cor. 9.24–27). The body as a metaphor for community and political life was already well established in Roman intellectual culture through the writings of thinkers such Cicero and Livy, who were active in the century before Christ. As we know, the first Christian writers took this to new heights in their quest to communicate their experience of and vision for communities transfigured by the love of God.

In this chapter we will explore the image of the fit body as a way of setting out some of the contours of life in the Spirit, always remembering that this is one half of a finely balanced pair. The image of the fit body and the flourishing plant are *both* necessary if we are to understand the Christian spiritual life aright. Table 1 summarizes some of their similarities and differences of emphasis.

Table 1.

	The fit body	*The flourishing plant*
Overall quality	Dynamic	Static
Main task	Running a race	Being present
Encounter with God	Following	Receiving
Pattern of discipleship	Journey	Hospitality
Approach to evangelism	'Go and tell'	'Come and see'
Outcome of formation	Growing up into the likeness of Christ	Growing up to bear the fruit of the Spirit

Growing up and being perfect

The fit body and the flourishing plant each grows up. There is a sense of progress towards something that can be thought of in terms of both time and space. To grow up means to become fully mature in years; it also means to reach one's full stature.

The New Testament talks of this in terms of a concept that is frequently translated 'perfection' in English Bibles. This is a word set to strike discouragement into the heart; after all, 'nobody's perfect'. Even supermodels are subject to the Photoshop, even sports superstars make mistakes, even geniuses get it wrong sometimes; and we all mess up relationships. Yet at the end of the central section of the sermon on the mount, Jesus sums up his teaching on the life of faith with this impossible-sounding demand of his hearers: 'Be [you] perfect' (*Esesthe humeis **teleioi***) (Matt. 5.48).

It is helpful to look at the group of Greek words with the stem *tele* in a bit more detail. From this stem we get the English word 'teleology', which the *Oxford English Dictionary* defines as 'the study of ends or final causes' – in other words the goal or purpose of something. A system is described as 'teleological' if it is purposely working towards a goal. So in the context of the New Testament, the English word 'perfect' should be understood as meaning the state of having achieved a goal or completed a piece of work. In fact the most usual translation of *teleios* is 'complete', and another possible meaning is 'fully grown'. Perhaps 'perfect' gives a slightly misleading impression. To illustrate this, in the familiar quotations from the New Testament that follow I have replaced the 'perfect'-word with the word or phrase that seems to render the *tele*-verb most appropriately to the context:

The young man said to [Jesus], 'I have kept all these; what do I still lack?' Jesus said to him, 'If you wish to be complete (*teleios einai*), go, sell your possessions, and give the money to the poor, and you will have treasure in heaven; then come, follow me.'

Matthew 19.20–21

but [the Lord] said to me, 'My grace is sufficient for you, for power comes into its own (*teleitai*) in weakness.'

2 Corinthians 12.9a

It was fitting that God, for whom and through whom all things exist, in bringing many children to glory, should bring the pioneer of their salvation to fulfilment (*teleiōsai*) through sufferings.

Hebrews 2.10

Job done. (*tetelestai*)

John 19.30

Therefore grow up into conformity (*esesthe teleioi*) with your Heavenly Father.

Matthew 5.48

Bringing all of these shades of meaning together gives a picture of the Christian life that is one of purposeful growth to a full maturity marked by integrity and wholeness, with a view to the completion of a supremely important task. Or to put this more succinctly, the Christian life is 'telic'. We can understand the demand to 'be perfect' as one to grow up and focus on the job. This is of course still an enormous demand, but when stated in this way it helps us feel that we might at least be able to take a few first halting steps. The writer to the Hebrews, who is very concerned with the telic nature of faith, echoes this hope in lovely encouraging words drawn from the Psalms: 'Therefore lift your drooping hands and strengthen your weak knees' (Heb. 12.12).

The life of faith is like a race where we, the body of Christ, strain to reach a glittering prize. We need to keep ourselves fit for the job. In the next three sections we will start to look at how this might work out in terms of our psychology as individual members and as a whole body. We will then return to the question of what and where the prize might actually be.

Going for goals

It's not only the life of faith that is telic. Over the last three decades psychologists have turned their attention to the role that goals play in *all* parts of our lives, and they have found this to be a very helpful approach to understanding human motivation, well-being, individual differences and our sense of personal identity. This may at first glance seem surprising, and there is of course more to our personal identity than our goals, as we shall see in Chapters 4 and 5. Nevertheless goals are very important, and so in this section we consider the psychology of goals and the way they shape our personalities.

> You think you can identify a man by giving his date of birth and his address, his height, his eyes' color, even his fingerprints . . . But if you want to identify me, ask me not where I live, or what I like to eat, or how I comb my hair, but ask me what I think I am living for, in detail, and ask me what I think is keeping me from living fully for the thing I want to live for. Between these two answers you can determine the identity of any person.
>
> Thomas Merton (1915–68)

I first became aware of the psychological importance of goals when I was working with people who were recovering from accidents or illnesses that had left them very disabled. They could no longer pursue all their previous goals, at least in the way they used to, and this often left them feeling profoundly different, diminished and alienated. I found that in order for such people to reconstruct an authentic sense of self, close attention had to be paid to their personal goals, or to use Merton's words, 'what I think I am living for in detail' (McGrath and Adams (1999); Siegert, McPherson and Taylor (2004)).

In the 1990s psychologists Charles Carver and Michael Scheier advanced a theory that takes a systematic approach to understanding 'what I am living for in detail' (Carver and Scheier 1990, 1998). According to their theory our lives work at at least three different levels of goals. We each have a semi-conscious idea of the sort of person that we would like to be – our idealized self-image. This is expressed in terms of certain principles, which are in their turn expressed in action programmes. A less technical way of describing this is as who I want to be; rules for living this out; and what I actually try to do in order to keep to those rules, summarized in Figure 1.

For example, we might imagine a man who aspires to be 'a good father'. One rule for living this out could be 'make time to play with my children'. Not every man aspires to be a good father, but even among those who do the rules for living this out will vary: while one man might favour the rule 'make time to play with my children', another might favour the rule 'work hard to secure my children's financial future'. To complicate things further, two men who both favour the rule 'make time to play with my children' might try to keep the rule by doing completely different things: one might play football with his children every Saturday, the other might read them a bedtime story every night, as illustrated in Figure 2. These differences are likely to have their origin in the personal skills and preferences and the family and wider cultures of the two men.

Figure 1.

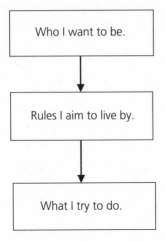

It is in the almost infinite variety of ideal selves, rules for life and expression of these rules in real behaviour that our individual differences play out. People vary as to which aspects of their ideal self are most important and in how they understand the expression of each of these. They also vary as to how rigidly they connect a particular rule for living with specific actions. For example, one man who is in the habit of playing football with his children might be devastated by an injury that prevents him from doing this: 'What kind of father am I who can't even play football with his kids?' Another might be much more flexible in his approach: 'This is a good opportunity to get out the model railway from the loft.' The first man sees football as a vital component of being a good father who spends time with his children; the second man holds to the same rule but

Figure 2.

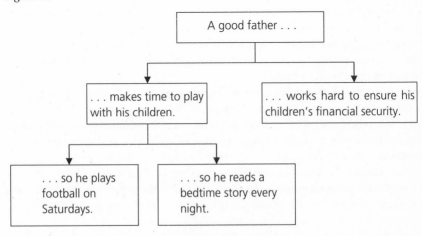

Figure 3.

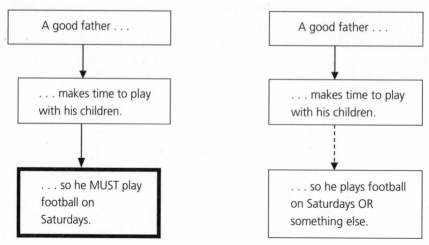

can see a satisfactory alternative way of expressing this in action. These different approaches are illustrated in Figure 3.

Much of the thinking that underlies this goes on at an automatic and tacit level. We have rules for being in the world and we assume that others share our rules, even though we don't usually state the rules openly – even to ourselves – until they are violated. This can lead to all sorts of misunderstandings and upsets because the same rule or principle can all too often be expressed in opposite actions. To give an example from my experience, I like to raise sensitive questions or proposals by sending an email, because I think it gives the receiver time to think about what I am saying without the demand of an instant response. In this way I believe I am abiding by the rule of being courteous and considerate. However, on occasion I have offended people by this approach: 'She didn't even have the courtesy to phone me up and ask me in person!' The people I unwittingly offended saw email as impersonal and lacking in care and therefore *dis*courteous. Again, two Christians from different traditions, both of whom try to live out the rule of deeply respecting Holy Communion, may express this by opposite actions: one may be a daily communicant, the other may purposely restrict receiving Communion to once a month (see Figure 4).

Carver's and Scheier's analysis of how our actions reflect underlying principles or rules, which themselves reflect the sort of person we want to be (or hope we are), helps us to understand something that happens in many settings but seems to be a particular bugbear of church life. This is the apparently disproportionate distress that can be caused by a very small change.

For example, introducing a new church coffee machine with flasks that are too heavy for a particular individual to use could have the unforeseen but shattering effect of undermining her assurance of her Christian identity (see Figure 5).

Figure 4.

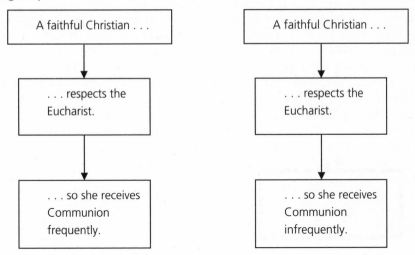

The goals that are most closely and rigidly connected to key aspects of 'who I want to be' (or hope I am) are the most important. We can tell which goals are most valued in our lives by how upset we get when they are thwarted. Sometimes we find ourselves wondering with surprise why we have 'over-reacted' to a trivial incident, and as we unravel our thoughts we find out new and sometimes enlightening things about our inner assumptive world.

Figure 5.

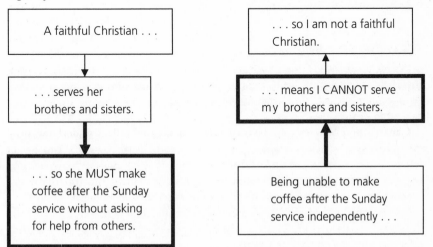

Goals and feelings

Carver's and Scheier's theory has much to say on the relationship between goals and how we feel; the different emotions we experience depend on how well we think we are doing in relation to our valued goals. This raises the question of how we measure our progress, and it appears that we mainly do this by comparing ourselves with others; that is, we set a norm for ourselves by looking around at our family, friends and colleagues.

If, in this light, we judge that we are on track to achieving a valued goal we will feel pleasurable anticipation or even excitement. When we achieve the goal, we will feel joy or contentment (for a while). If things get in the way of our making progress, we will get frustrated (a very common emotion and one experienced by most of us daily when our technology doesn't work). If it looks as if we are not going to achieve our goal, we will feel worried and anxious. If we think others are impeding our progress, we may feel angry. If we fail to achieve the goal altogether, we may well become discouraged or even depressed.

However, we can usually find ways to manage the disappointment of thwarted goals. Like the father who decides to switch from football to model trains, we can choose a different way of enacting our rule for living; or we may invest in a different rule. (For example, a man who has only limited access to his children as a result of divorce might direct his energy to earning more money to support them, as his previous rule of spending a lot of time with them can no longer be kept. In this way he can still see himself as a good father.)

We might even change aspects of our ideal self altogether. Most of us do this all the time in small ways, for instance when we manage our failure to attain our target weight loss by settling for an 'enlarged' ideal self: 'I'd rather be curvaceous and blooming than thin and haggard'. However, individuals vary in their ability to do this. People who are prone to depression seem to have particular difficulty in freeing themselves from the discouragement that comes from failed goals, and may need help to do so effectively.[2]

The perfect personality?

In the previous section the example of a father who chooses between earning money to support his children and spending time with them was used as an illustration. It is, of course, ridiculously oversimplified. Most fathers do both; and they have to balance the competing demands of home and work.[3] Most fathers are also husbands or partners, friends, sons, brothers, citizens and much more. The problem is that for most of us life is complicated. We have a multifaceted

---

2 This has been described as a kind of helplessness (Peterson, Maier and Seligman 1995) and can form a productive focus for cognitive therapy. For a Christian approach to this, see Williams, Richards and Whitton 2002; Procter and Procter 2012.

3 There is a lovely exploration of this in the 1989 Universal Pictures film *Parenthood* in which the character played by Steve Martin struggles to juggle the competing demands of family and work life.

ideal self played out in a whole complex of rules for living and stuff we are trying to do. Many of our goals are in tension with each other, and some are frankly incompatible. We experience this as conflict and stress. We might sometimes feel that we are falling apart as we are pulled in several different directions or we may become paralysed, unable to take action because what we do in one life area works against what we are trying to do in another life area. It can feel a bit like attempting to untangle a collection of hopelessly entwined balls of wool.

The psychologist Kennon Sheldon has described this situation of competing and conflicting goals as personal *incoherence*. My personality is coherent if all the different things I try to do generally fit well together and help each other along (horizontal coherence) and if they are clearly connected with my rules for living (vertical coherence). On the other hand, my personality is incoherent if the different things I try to do constantly pull against each other or are just a mishmash of random actions with no connection with my rules for living. Unsurprisingly, high degrees of personal incoherence have been found to be associated with psychological distress, whereas high degrees of personal coherence are associated with a sense of well-being (Sheldon and Kasser 1995).

Coherent goals are a sign of an integrated personality; yet there is more to the integrated personality than coherence. It's possible to have a coherent personality but still to be living a lie, to be well-ordered but inauthentic. Sheldon subsequently introduced a second concept: *self-concordance* (Sheldon and Elliot 1999) to address this issue. An individual has a high degree of self-concordance if her rules for living and the stuff she is trying to do bear a clear relationship to her ideal self. If what I do truly expresses who I want to be (or hope I am), I will experience deep contentment. If, for whatever reason, I feel a major mismatch, I will experience loss of confidence, alienation, perhaps even shame. Sometimes this can be positive, because it impels me to change a bad situation. Think of the story of the Prodigal Son. We are told that a young man from a good Jewish family ended up trying to eat pigs' leftovers. It's hard to think of anything less self-concordant, but the sense of discord seems to have helped, for at this very point 'he came to himself' (Luke 15.16–17) – remembered who he really was – and his behaviour changed accordingly.

His false life is, indeed, but one of the conditions of death or stupor, but it acts, even when it cannot be said to animate, and is not always easily known from the true. It is that life of custom and accident in which many of us pass much of our time in the world; that life in which we do what we have not proposed, and speak what we do not mean, and assent to what we do not understand; that life which is overlaid by the weight of things external to it, and is moulded by them, instead of assimilating them; that, which instead of growing and blossoming under any whole-some dew, is crystallized over with it, as with hoar-frost, and becomes to the true life what an arborescence is to a tree, a candied agglomeration of thoughts and habits foreign to it . . .

John Ruskin (1819–1900)

Figure 6.

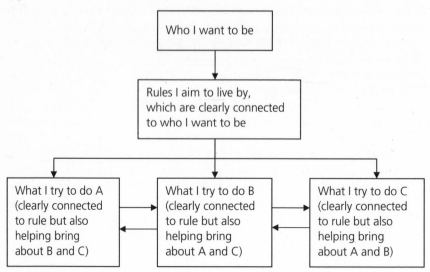

Taking all this together the integrated (coherent and self-concordant) personality can be summarized by Figure 6.

This is a picture of individual psychological health, integrity and authenticity that might equally apply to a community. Everything works in harmony together to promote the most fundamental goal of all – being who we are – and

Figure 7.

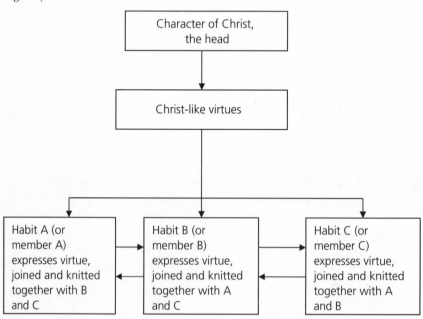

with it comes a deep sense of well-being. It is of course almost identical to the picture of the body presented in the passage from Ephesians 4 at the beginning of this chapter. This describes both the healthy Christian community with its many members and the healthy Christian individual with her many habitual attitudes and practices. Our task, with the help of the Spirit, is to work on ourselves and in active co-operation with others to become who we are, as individuals and communities. In this way Christ is formed in us.

This pattern for healthy, integrated and authentic Christian formation is summarized in Figure 7. It forms the basic framework for this book, which begins with the character of Christ (who we want to be), explores Christlike virtues (the rules we aim to live by), and wrestles with how these are to be lived out in habitual practices and attitudes (what we try to do). The presence of the arrows in this figure is important, for in the Christian life the connections between the individual parts and between the parts and the whole are not simply connections of meaning. The arrows here represent love 'which binds everything together in perfect harmony' (Col. 3.14).

Living the reality: becoming who you are

The fit body is growing up, becoming more and more Christlike. This upward direction is not accidental. It is a movement heavenwards. In his letter to the Philippians Paul talks about 'straining forward' towards a goal for a prize that he describes as *high* (*ano⁻*) (Phil. 3.13–14), and which he has earlier identified as 'gaining Christ', 'being found in him', 'so that I may obtain the resurrection from the dead' (vv. 8–10). This is all about being raised heavenwards with Christ. Paul is very clear that he personally hasn't got there yet (v. 12), but there is also a sense that this is his destiny – his true self. Elsewhere in the New Testament this upward heavenly trajectory is presented as the destiny of all Christians. Our true self is as Christ; our true home is with him in heaven. Christian growth is not about making ourselves good enough to go to heaven, but grasping fully the fact that because of Christ we are already set on a heavenly trajectory:

> So if you have been raised with Christ, seek the things that are above, where Christ is, seated at the right hand of God. Set your minds on things that are above. (Colossians 3.1–2a)

Jesus himself called the people he encountered to move heavenwards. Again and again we find him telling people to 'arise' or get up. Recall that the Prodigal Son's insight that 'this isn't me' is followed immediately by a decision to arise (Luke 15.17–18). In a previous book I noted that this 'involves a move from passive to active, from relaxed to alert, from weak to strong, from sick to well, from dead to alive, from "the world below" to "the world above" (John 8.23), and – perhaps most of all – from lowly to exalted status' (Collicutt 2009a, p. xiii). This upward movement to our full stature confers full human dignity upon us.

As we grow up we become Christlike, but we also grow towards Christ (as the flourishing plant grows towards the light), and in the end there is some sort of union with him. The phrase 'growing up into Christ' summarizes this mystery nicely. For Paul this growing up into Christ involves getting to know him better. This is more than head knowledge; it includes feelings of love and adoration, appropriating rules for living – what I am calling virtues – that express Christ's character, and getting on and doing them.

But how do we get to know Christ better?

Getting to know you

Read the Gospels

The most obvious way to get to know Christ better is to study the life of Jesus of Nazareth as told by the writers of the four Gospels. Despite this, there is a surprising degree of unfamiliarity with the Gospels among Christians. This is true across the board, but it is a particular feature of those traditions that place an emphasis on the saving work of Christ's death and resurrection. In these traditions the fact that Jesus died and was raised is far more important than details of his life or the circumstances of his Passion and death. Here 'seeking the things that are above' means fixing one's eyes on the glorious risen Christ, and so the human Jesus fades into the background.

Other traditions place more emphasis on the incarnation – the deep mystery of the eternal logos becoming flesh and blood. Yet often the incarnation becomes so important and attractive as a concept that it takes on a life of its own, even meriting its own adjective – 'incarnational'. The irony is that here too, as the focus on the idea of the incarnation increases, the human Jesus fades into the background.

But Christians don't assent to a set of ideas, we follow a person. The risen Christ whom we know through the Spirit is continuous with the human being Jesus of Nazareth who walked this earth; and if we want to know Christ better, we need to start with the witness to the life and death of Jesus that we find in the Gospels. These are not objective scholarly biographies in the modern sense. They are written with the clear purpose of communicating the important things that will help the reader or hearer come to know Jesus better; they are filtered through the stories of communities who loved, lost and still yearn for Jesus; and their authors are not dispassionate scholars, but people whose lives have been turned upside down by the Spirit. Knowing something about historical-critical approaches to these texts can actually help us see this more clearly and treat them with more respect, but can also enable us tentatively to draw out the core Jesus characteristics.[4] Therefore serious academic study of the Gospels should not be neglected.

---

4 For an interesting example of this, see Ellen Charry's analysis of the Sermon on the Mount where she draws out the core characteristic of Jesus' approach to piety as 'one that shifts attention from the act itself to the tone or style that accompanies it' (Charry 1997, p. 77).

However, there are (thankfully for some!) other ways to approach these texts that appeal to the imaginative rather than the scholarly human faculties. The best known of these is found in the spiritual exercises of Ignatius of Loyola (1491–1556). This is an approach to the Gospel narratives that Ignatius calls *Contemplazio*, but we would now term discursive meditation. It requires the person undergoing the exercises (the 'exercitant'), after prayerful preparation, to recall the story and then to enter it imaginatively. There is a strong emphasis on visualizing the scene as vividly as possible and embracing the emotions it evokes. For example, on contemplating the birth of Christ:

> To see the people, that is our Lady, and Joseph and the servant girl, and the child Jesus after his birth. Making myself into a poor and unworthy little servant, I watch them, and contemplate them, and serve them in their needs as if I were present and with all possible submission and reverence; and afterwards I reflect within myself for some profit.

> (Spiritual exercises First day, Second contemplation)

The exercitant is instructed to draw from this a response in the form of a prayer directed to the Christ she has encountered in the narrative, with the full expectation of consequent transformation in her life.

This practice of imaginative engagement with the Gospels enables a deep processing of Jesus material (not for nothing did Ignatius name his new brotherhood the *Compañia de Jesus*). It can be pursued outside of the context of a full 30-day Ignatian retreat, and many people find it highly beneficial to incorporate this kind of meditation into their regular devotions.

Contemplate Christ in prayer

Jesus taught his followers to pray like him and with him to our Father. Yet from earliest times some forms of Christian prayer have been directed very specifically to contemplating the person of Christ. This is rather different from the active imaginative engagement with Gospel material described in the previous section. Instead contemplation is 'actively passive', more like the focusing of a wordless gaze on our Lord and waiting upon him. This comes more naturally to some than others. It may be helped by a preparatory piece of poetry or music inviting Christ to be present in our life (I return again and again to *Mache dich, mein Herze, rein* from Bach's St Matthew Passion). It may also be helped by an icon,[5] picture or a candle to act as a symbolic reference point if our physical gaze wanders, but these are not necessary.

Sometimes this sort of contemplation may be supported by appropriate words, which can keep our attention fixed on Christ. The most common form of words used in this context is the Jesus Prayer:

---

5 Praying with icons is a spiritual discipline in its own right. For an introduction, see Jenkins 1998 and Williams 2003.

Lord Jesus Christ, Son of God, have mercy on me, [a sinner].

This is a very ancient formula based on the humble prayer of the tax collector commended by Jesus in Luke 18.13, but going further in asserting the Lordship of Christ and thus placing oneself firmly at the disposal of the Spirit (1 Cor. 12.3). Rooted in the words of the Jesus who walked this earth, it directs our attention upwards to the risen and glorified Christ. We adore him and come to know him in the way a baby comes to know its mother's face by gazing fixedly and adoringly on her.

Participate in the Lord's Supper

Whether we call it Mass, the Eucharist or Holy Communion, the gathering of the community around bread and wine is a profoundly Christocentric occasion. Here we remember a historical event from the life of Jesus – the Last Supper. Here we read a section of one of the Gospels that recalls the life of Jesus on this earth. As the one presiding says a blessing over the elements s/he re-enacts the historical practice of Jesus and recounts the acts of God in creation and in Jesus' life on this earth, his sacrificial death and his resurrection. The risen Christ is received in bread and wine, and the community, which is his body in that place, is re-membered in an act of corporate solidarity. Whatever our eucharistic theology, all Christians can agree that this is an event that gives us a unique chance to get to know Christ better.

One aspect of the Eucharist that has not been much emphasized in the western Church is the way that it draws the gathered community heavenwards. The Orthodox writer Alexander Schmemann (1921–83) writes:

the Eucharist is best understood as a journey or progression . . . [an] entrance into the risen life of Christ', for the Church is 'to follow Christ in his ascension to his Father, to make His ascension the destiny of man. (Schmemann 1963, pp. 27, 29)

This draws our attention to the importance of the *sursum corda* that signals the beginning of the Eucharistic Prayer in most traditions: 'Lift up your hearts: We lift them to the Lord.' The Lord's Supper tells the story of Jesus of Nazareth, and at the same time it points us, indeed pulls us, upwards to the risen Christ. If we can embrace this more fully, our knowledge of Christ will broaden and deepen.

By their fruits

If we want to become Christlike we need to get to know him. The practices of Bible-reading, prayer and corporate worship described in the previous section all have the capacity to help us here. But we are still left with a problem. How do we know if we have understood Christ aright? I may study the Gospels or contemplate Christ in prayer and encounter a holy Jesus who preaches purity of life and will have no truck with sexual immorality; you may encounter an edgy Jesus who welcomes the stigmatized outsider. In this light, I may emphasize the virtue of personal temperance whereas you may emphasize the virtue of humanity.[6] Following this through to our habits of life, I may decide to separate myself from certain people and cultures, you may decide to embrace them with open arms.

Or imagine that we both agree that 'speaking the truth in love' (Eph. 4.15a) is a Christlike virtue. I might see this as a mandate for brutal honesty in my relationships with others, simply informing them that 'I am saying this in love', whereas you might take it as a licence to tell white lies in order to keep the peace.

The history of the Church demonstrates that there are no simple answers to these dilemmas. As we have seen in this chapter, our reasoning from ideal self, through rules for living, to the stuff we try to do is largely tacit and determined by our own psychology or the cultural assumptions of our group. So it is as we try and behave in accordance with Christ. It is easy to project our own wants and needs on to the Christ we seek (Piedmont, Williams and Ciarrochi 1997); it is also easy for us to delude ourselves about our spiritual health and to collude with each other in group self-delusion (see Edwards and Hall (2003) for a systematic study of this).

This is why discernment is such an important issue in Christian formation. In the extract from Romans 12 at the beginning of this chapter, Paul talks of the Christian life as a process of mental transformation that gives us a vision for what the goal actually is and how God wants us to achieve it. The psychological goal theories that we have considered can help somewhat. They draw attention to our tendency to treat our idiosyncratic approach to life as absolute non-negotiable truth. They suggest that a healthy Christian individual or community is one whose growth is not distorted by an overemphasis on one virtue, habit or member at the expense of the others; that where these pull in different directions without any attempt at real integration – not the same as papering over the cracks – there will be stress and even fractures; that the connections between who we want to be, the rules we aim to live by, and the stuff we try to do should be kept well-oiled and transparent; and they give us a way of reading the distress that bubbles up in individual members whose function in the body is threatened or thwarted. These theories also offer a systematic framework for analysing the character of the human Jesus in terms of his virtues and habitual practices and attitudes (the topic of the next chapter), and thus help us to understand him aright.

But at the end of the day Jesus has left us with an image drawn from the flourishing plant, that reminds us that we are not simply out to win a prize (becoming as Christ) but to do a job (advancing the *Missio Dei*). He presents the process of discernment in a deceptively simple manner as both pragmatic and intuitive: 'You will know them by their fruits' (Matt. 7.16, 20). Like Christ, the bread of life, we should be good to eat and offer life to the world.

---

6 The virtues of 'temperance' and 'humanity' form part of the Values in Action classification system (Peterson and Seligman 2004), which is discussed in detail in Chapter 4.

Exercises

1 Recall two incidents – one where you found yourself unaccountably upset and another where you found yourself unaccountably delighted. Think about how the events related to the sort of person you want to be (or hope you are) or the rules by which you try and live your life. Did you learn anything new about yourself?

2 Think about these questions[7] and again reflect whether you have learnt something new about yourself:
   - Which areas of your life are most important to you right now?
     o Where I live and who I live with.
     o My personal independence.
     o My leisure, hobbies, and interests.
     o My work (paid or unpaid).
     o My relationship with my partner (or my prospects of finding a partner).
     o My family life (including those not living at home).
     o My contacts with friends, neighbours and acquaintances.
     o My religion or life philosophy.
     o My financial status.
   - Right now, what makes my life enjoyable, meaningful, and worthwhile?

3 In preparation for Chapter 3, and perhaps as the result of engaging with some of the practices discussed in the section 'Getting to know you', write a series of bullet points to summarize the way that you perceive the character of Jesus of Nazareth.

Further reading

Barrington-Ward, S., 2007, *The Jesus Prayer*, Oxford: Bible Reading Fellowship.

Emmons, R., 2003, *The Psychology of Ultimate Concerns*, New York: Guilford.

O'Brien, K., 2011, *The Ignatian Adventure: Experiencing the Spiritual Exercises of Saint Ignatius Loyola in Daily Life*, Chicago, IL: Loyola Press.

Silf, M., 1998, *Landmarks: Exploration of Ignatian Spirituality*, London: Darton, Longman & Todd.

Tomlin, G., 2009, *Spiritual Fitness*, London: Continuum.

---

7 From the Rivermead Life Goals Questionnaire and Interview (McGrath and Adams 1999).

3

The Character of Christ

Sir, we wish to see Jesus.

John 12.21b

Thomas said to him, 'Lord, we do not know where you are going. How can we know the way?' Jesus said to him, 'I am the way, and the truth, and the life. No one comes to the Father except through me.'

John 14.5–6

If we are to grow up into Christ, we have to start were we are. We are flesh and blood human beings inhabiting a particular place at a particular time. If we want to become like Christ, we have to start with the New Testament witness to Jesus of Nazareth, a flesh and blood human being who inhabited a particular place at a particular time. Of course we know that there is more to it than this, but the whole point of God becoming human in Jesus was to show us the way.

At one level this is easy to understand. Jesus is like the talented and diligent eldest son who shows his naughty and weak younger siblings how it should be done and helps them as they try to emulate him. He is the 'firstborn within a large family' (Rom. 8.29b), the 'pioneer and perfecter of our faith' (Heb. 12.2) and – sticking with the flourishing plant – a kind of 'first fruits' (1 Cor. 15.20, 23). Because Jesus was a human being like us, he showed that it is possible for all human beings to live a life that is fully pleasing to God; he also showed us the way to do it.

At another level the idea of Jesus the way is almost impossible to understand. This is because Jesus was like no other human being there has ever been. He was deeply strange and 'other'. He attracted large crowds of followers, but as they got to know him better he seemed to be too much to stomach for some (Mark 10.32a; John 6.66), for 'the road is hard' (Matt. 7.14). Peter found himself struggling, and Judas appears to have become disillusioned. In the end Jesus experienced overwhelming rejection.

We are at once attracted to and repelled by Jesus. We are attracted to all in him that draws out the best in us, but we are repelled by all in him that shows up the massive gulf between the divine and human perspective. The heated interchange between Jesus and Peter at Caesarea Philippi (Matt. 16.21–23) is instructive here, showing as it does Peter's horror-struck repulsion when the divine perspective is revealed to him, and Jesus' desperate fight to maintain this perspective in a context where it is being constantly undermined.

Jesus was handed over to crucifixion because of these human feelings of repulsion, and it is in this sense that we can each be said to be unwittingly complicit in his fate. This insight should not leave us stuck in hand-wringing misery; rather it should open our eyes to the extent of the gulf between the divine and human and cause us to fall down in wonder at the sacrificial love that set out to bridge it in Christ.

> The Word is flesh and is communicated in flesh . . . The Word re-forms the possibilities of human existence and calls us to the creation of new humanity . . . On the other hand: the Word is rejected and crucified by the world; only when we see that there is no place for the Word in the world do we see that he is *God's* word, the Word of the hidden, transcendent creator.
>
> Rowan Williams 1990, p. 181

So as we come to look at the Jesus of the New Testament we need to recall our tendency to project our wants and needs on to him, and to be suspicious if he always comes over as attractive, easy and accessible. We need to be aware that we may only get a series of glimpses rather than a full picture, and we need to be prepared for the possibility of surprise.

What follows is based on my reading of the Jesus material in the New Testament, mainly the Gospels, but also draws on passages in the epistles that seem to be referring to memories of Jesus of Nazareth. I have looked at the descriptions of Jesus' habitual practices and the attitudes that they convey, the way he is talked of by others, and I have drawn out some themes from them. Where it makes sense (and it doesn't always), I have expressed these themes in the language of virtue. I have also paid attention to Jesus' instructions to his followers to embrace these themes and emulate these virtues. In drawing out the themes I have paid attention to summary statements about Jesus' behaviour and also to repeated references to actions that form a pattern. I have focused on themes that can be identified in more than one strain within the Gospel tradition: Mark; the material common to Luke and Matthew (the 'double tradition'); the material unique to Luke ('L') or Matthew ('M'); and John (aware that John has a quite distinctive way of expressing and developing ideas that have their counterpart in the Synoptic Gospels).

This is not an attempt to reconstruct a 'historical Jesus'. It is instead a search for the imprint of Jesus on the memories of those who knew him – literally an impression; stories that sum up his way with people, phrases that reverberate, ways of looking at the world, emotions that make themselves felt. The picture that emerges is summarized in the statements below. Each of these core observations about Jesus forms the basis of one of the chapters in Part 3, in which we get to grips with the task of conforming to this aspect of his character.

- Jesus had a sense of deep intimacy with the Holy Other.
- Jesus exercised humble power.
- Jesus paid attention to 'heaven in ordinary'.

- Jesus achieved personal coherence by balancing competing demands in his life.
- Jesus showed hospitality.
- Jesus felt compassion.
- Jesus did not retaliate.
- Jesus taught wisdom.
- Jesus embodied transformation.

Jesus had a sense of deep intimacy with the Holy Other

In a 1917 book whose English title is *The Idea of the Holy*, Rudolf Otto (1869–1937), a German scholar of religions, described in detail the human experience of the divine using the word 'numinous'. The numinous calls up both intense fascination and tremendous fear in human beings. This mix of feelings has some resonance with the ambivalence evoked in us by Jesus discussed above. It is so foreign to usual human experience that Otto termed it *ganz Andere* – 'wholly other'. For human beings God is both wholly other and 'the Holy Other'.

The natural human response to the wholly other is awe, an emotion that has shades of fear and submission (Keltner and Haidt 2003). As mentioned in Chapter 1, we see this response to the felt presence of God throughout the Hebrew Bible (e.g. in Exod. 3.6; Isa. 6.5) and also in the New Testament (e.g. Luke 2.9; 5.8).

But Jesus himself was different. Perhaps the most characteristic thing about him was his deep sense of intimacy with God, expressed in his habitual practice of referring to God as 'Father' or *'Abbā*.[1] This Aramaic/Hebrew word has come down to us in the tradition in Mark's account of the agony in Gethsemane, the only Aramaic speech of Jesus that has been preserved, besides his characteristic 'Get up!' (*Talitha cum*) that we considered in Chapter 2.

Jesus appears to have been certain that he was the Son of God, and as such it was quite natural for him to address God as Father. His assertion that he was God's son was not simply the expression of a belief about his status, but of his *experience of divine parental affection and approval*. In the Synoptic Gospels this is conveyed in the accounts of Jesus' baptism (Matt. 3.13–17 and parallels). It is not entirely clear from these accounts whether the vision of the open heavens and the voice that declares Jesus to be God's beloved and pleasing son are seen and heard by the onlookers; their primary purpose is to assure *Jesus* of his identity.

John's Gospel is a little different. The baptism is not mentioned directly; instead Jesus' assurance of his intimate relationship with God as Father is conveyed and elaborated throughout (e.g. John 5.20; 14.10–13).

Jesus' concept of his own divine sonship seems to have extended to include his followers. He clearly instructed them to pray using the word 'Father' (Matt.

---

1 For a detailed discussion of the meaning of this word, see Barr 1988.

6.9; Luke 11.2). At several places in the Gospels God is referred to as 'Your father'. This is most prominent in Matthew's Gospel, where the phrase occurs a dozen times in the Sermon on the Mount and elsewhere; but it is also there in Luke (6.36; 12.30); Mark (11.25) and memorably in the appearance to Mary Magdalene in John (20.17).

Many of the first followers of Jesus appear to have taken this to heart. Addressing God as 'Abbā in prayer seems to have been an authenticating mark of charismatic intimacy in some early Christian communities (Rom. 8.15; Gal. 4.6).

Jesus exercised humble power

Jesus was a poor man of uncertain parentage who grew up in a humble family in a nondescript village. As we have seen, he came to believe that he was very special indeed – the favoured son of God. He was a poor and powerless man who believed that he was rich and powerful. If this was anyone else we might speculate that his life circumstances were so deprived and miserable that he dealt with them by escaping into a grandiose fantasy world, and indeed the charge of madness is a recurring theme in the Gospel narratives (see e.g. Davies 1995; Meggitt 2007).

But one of the many odd things about Jesus is the way that he lived out his self-perceived exalted status. He does come over as grandiose, especially in John 8 – who wouldn't, if they were claiming to have a hotline to God? But there is never any sense of the megalomaniac about him. Instead of demanding privileges that he might logically have viewed as his entitlement, a very common feature of gurus from all cultures (Oakes 1997), Jesus seemed to show a persisting concern to set such privileges aside.

This is explicitly worked through in the temptation narratives in Matthew and Luke. Whether or not one reads these as literal historical accounts, the more important issue is the nature of the dilemma that faced Jesus throughout his ministry on earth. He thinks he knows who he is, and some rules for living flow naturally from this sense of identity (see Figure 8).

Figure 8.

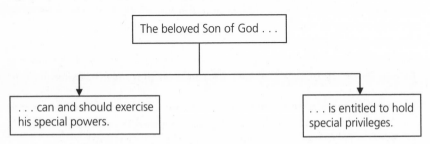

Satan then offers Jesus some plausible suggestions stated in an 'if then' format ('If you are the Son of God, then . . .') regarding the things he should try do to live out these rules (see Figure 9).

Figure 9.

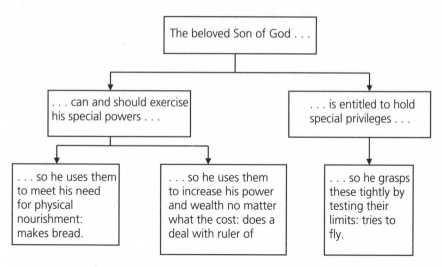

Jesus' response is given in the temptation narratives themselves but can also be seen to be worked out through the whole sweep of the Gospels (see Figure 10).

The evidence for this way of thinking in Jesus' life is first that he healed and spirituality liberated a lot of people. Second, the Gospels consistently describe his teaching and practice in relation to his mission in terms of service: 'the Son of Man came not to be served but to serve' (Matt. 20.28a; Mark 10.45a) and 'I am among you as one who serves' (Luke 22.27b). John, who has no temptation narrative, remarks in passing that Jesus chose to flee from a crowd who wanted

Figure 10.

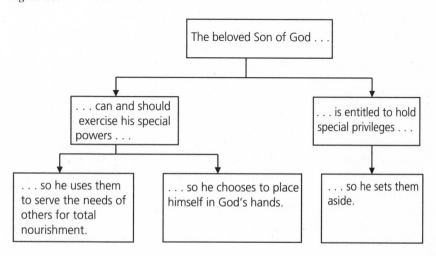

to make him king by force (John 6.15); and he presents Jesus' attitude to the use of power and status in the most beautiful account of the washing of the disciples' feet at the Last Supper (John 13.1–17).

There is a repeated thread in Jesus' attested teaching that his followers should also adopt an attitude of service (Matt. 20.25–27; 23.11; Mark 9.35; 10.43; Luke 22.26; John 13.15). They are God's beloved children but, like Jesus, they are to use their power to help others and to be prepared to set privilege aside.

Finally, in their depiction of the Passion and death of Jesus, each Gospel writer in his own way emphasizes the free and agonizingly difficult choice of Jesus to place himself in God's hands, entrusting himself to his Father in the darkest place of all.

The thing that spoke so powerfully to the first Christian communities from their memory of Jesus and their reflection on his actions with the benefit of hindsight, the thing that they felt impelled to communicate as a central part of his story, was this astonishing way of living out divine sonship, so different from the way of the Roman emperors who ruled them.

Jesus paid attention to 'heaven in ordinary'

As has already been noted, Jesus' teaching makes full use of the natural world. He told stories that drew on patterns of seedtime and harvest, domestic work practices, family relationships, social hierarchies involving honour, obligation and shame. Perhaps this is one reason that he attracted such crowds: his teaching had a kind of natural authenticity.

But behind this lies something else. In order to construct such stories, Jesus must have subjected the world about him to close and attentive observation. Much of the time these observations are neutral – this is simply the way the world is. Sometimes they are appreciative, expressing a deep sense of wonder: 'Look at the beautiful meadow flowers!'; 'Look at that amazing widow!' Before he was a teacher, Jesus was a watcher. He watched the physical world and he watched how people were with each other. He wasn't distracted by the big and obvious. He had an interest in the small and subtle. There is a focus on children for themselves (not as potential adults), in seeds and grains of wheat, in the mixing of yeast and salt into bread, in little birds, in a tiny coin given by a poor woman. There is an awareness that bad stuff happens to good people (Matt. 5.45; Luke 13.4), that pain can lead to joy (John 16.21), that death can bring life (John 12.24).

In all these circumstances Jesus sees the action of God. For him God does not act supernaturally on the world; God is at work in the natural world. To use a modern term, Jesus was a 'natural theologian' (Collicutt 2008b). He had a way of looking at the natural world and seeing it as a pointer to the divine.

As with the previous two characteristics, Jesus seems to have expected his followers to follow his example. They are to look carefully and to see things for what they really are or what they truly signify (e.g. Mark 8.17–18). Consistent with this, true perception is presented as a sign of spiritual advancement in the

New Testament as a whole. John gives great prominence to the appropriate reading of signs in his Gospel, and presents a very detailed and sophisticated account of the healing of the man born blind in Chapter 9 to ram this point home. Paul famously frames his final goal (the *teleion* of 1 Cor. 13.10) in terms of clarity of vision (1 Cor. 13.12).

Bound up with Jesus' concern that people look and see things aright is a repudiation of worry (Matt. 6.25, 28; 13.22; Mark 4.19; Luke 10.41; 12.22, 26; 21.34; 10.41). The worry words have the common stem *merimna*, and refer to the kind of thinking that preoccupies people so that they don't notice what is in front of their eyes. In modern psychology 'worry' refers to the cognitive aspects of anxiety – the tendency to go round and round in 'What if?' circles. It involves 'elaborative cognitive processing', something that is all well and good in its place but can cause problems if it gets out of control, winding us up to a fever pitch of anxiety. Its opposite is mindfulness.

Jesus' point is not so much that worry is a bad thing in itself (though it may be). He was not telling his followers to chill out, but to watch and pray. They are not to be distracted from paying attention to what is important, from looking around them and seeing things for what they are. Incidentally, this seems to be the main problem with wealth – it gives people more to worry about (Matt. 6.19 and parallels).

Jesus achieved personal coherence by balancing competing demands in his life

The Gospels give a glimpse of the multiple demands on Jesus, each pulling him in a different direction. There seem to have been family demands hinted at in some recorded tense exchanges (Matt. 12.46–47 and parallels; Luke 2.48; John 2.3–4; 7.1–5). There were demands from his disciples and friends (Matt. 16.22; Matt. 20.20–21 and Mark 10.35–37; John 11.21, 32). There were demands to justify himself made by his enemies and competitors (Matt. 16.1; Matt. 19.3 and parallels; Matt. 21.23 and parallels; Matt. 22.16–32 and parallels; John 8.1–11; 10.24). Most of all there were the demands of the crowds. The Gospels vividly communicate a sense of Jesus being squeezed from all sides and sucked almost dry by people who were desperate for his help: 'Master, the crowds surround you and press upon you' (Luke 8.45b); 'I noticed that power had gone out from me' (Luke 8.46b). Some people are so desperate that they break through the roof of the house Jesus is visiting (Mark 2.4 and Luke 5.17). At one point we are told that Jesus is in danger of being crushed by the crowds (Mark 3.9); they are so numerous that he preaches to people on shore from the safety of a boat (Matt. 13.2). John tells of an occasion when Jesus is pursued by people in boats; these are not those who want to follow his way but those who, like paparazzi with a celebrity in view, are hunting him down for their own ends (John 6.24–26).

However, the Gospel writers also take the trouble to spell out Jesus' response to these demands. He sets priorities, and he makes it clear that the demands of the family of origin can be given too high a place among these (Matt. 10.37 and Luke 14.26; Matt. 12.48–50 and parallels; Matt. 19.29 and parallels). Family obligations can even function as an excuse for inaction (Matt. 8.22 and Luke 9.60; Luke 14.20). Jesus extends the boundaries of those to whom he and his followers owe a family-like commitment, and this inevitably means that the family of origin has a less privileged position than it might normally expect. Jesus does not promote neglect of families (Matt. 15.4 and Mark 7.10; Matt. 19.19 and Luke 18.20; John 19.26–27), but he does challenge the place of the family in relation to the demands of the kingdom of God. For Jesus and his followers the first priority must always be the *Missio Dei*.

When it comes to advancing the wider *Missio Dei* by going out into the world beyond the family to teach, debate and heal, we are presented with a very characteristic pattern of engagement intentionally balanced with withdrawal. Periods of active engagement with people are followed by withdrawal to deserted places to be alone or to pray (Mark 1.35; Luke 4.42). All four Gospels present this in summary form in their account of the feeding of the 5,000 (Matt. 14.23; Mark 6.46; Luke 9.14; John 6.15), but Luke also reports that this was Jesus' habitual practice (Luke 9.18). Involvement in dangerous conflict is balanced by strategic retreat (Matt. 4.12; 14.13; 15.21 and Mark 7.2; Matt. 21.7; Luke 9.10; John 4.1–3; 7.1; 8.59; 11.54). Heavenly insights on the mountain top flow into goal-focused activity in the valley below (Matt. 17.1–18 and parallels). It may be that the periods of withdrawal provided rest and recreation or a kind of spiritual refuelling that sustained the periods of engagement. But it is also likely that they offered another perspective to counter the crushing demands of the world – an opportunity for recentring and the recalibrating of priorities. A third possibility is that the activities and encounters from the periods of engagement were offered up to God and thus transformed through prayer in the periods of withdrawal.

Besides this balance of withdrawal and engagement, we also see a hint of another balance: that between the telic and the 'paratelic'.[2] Much of the time Jesus appears to be about his Father's work, but there are occasions when he seems simply to be at play, enjoying a meal or a party. This is of course symbolic of the imminent eschaton; but notice that while John the Baptist's eschatology emphasizes punishment and is lived out through the practice of asceticism, Jesus' eschatology emphasizes redemption and is lived out through the practice of feasting.

Much has been made of Jesus' full experience of pain in this life. It is less frequently observed that the Gospels suggest that he experienced, indeed even relished, hedonic pleasure. Images of Jesus in the western Church have almost invariably depicted him as thin, if not emaciated. This does not sit easily with

---

2 The psychologist Michael Apter advanced the theory that human behaviour reverses between different and mutually exclusive motivational domains or modes. He used the term 'paratelic' to describe the playful mode of being fully in the present moment rather than driven by future or past concerns. Individuals are said to reverse between the paratelic and telic modes in different patterns and with varying degrees of insight and control (Apter 2001).

his reputation as an alleged 'glutton and a drunkard' (Matt. 11.19; Luke 7.34). Notice too that when he sends out seventy of his followers he tells them to eat (Luke 10.7), and that the action that most readily brought him to mind after his death was the sharing of food and drink (Luke 22.19; 24.30–31, 35; 1 Cor. 11.24; John 21.12). This brings us nicely to the next Jesus characteristic.

Jesus showed hospitality

The way Jesus showed hospitality is unusual. According to the Gospels, he didn't invite people round to his place; he invited himself to theirs. He was in the habit of being a guest in someone else's home rather than a host (e.g. Luke 10.38). In fact he didn't have a home into which he could invite people (Matt. 8.20; Luke 9.58). On only one occasion – the highly charged Last Supper – did Jesus act as host in the conventional sense of the word, and even then it was in a borrowed room. Jesus' habitual practice was to *receive* hospitality.

In our individualistic privatized society, with its gated communities, high hedges and double-locked doors, fear of intruding into the personal space of others, of looking as if we are angling for a free drink or meal, of making ourselves vulnerable by crossing the threshold into someone else's territory can all inhibit our impulse to visit or 'visit with' someone, especially if uninvited. The Gospels come from the very different world of the ancient near east, and they present taking the trouble to 'come under my roof' not as an intrusion, but as a mark of honour, respect and acceptance (Matt. 8.8; Luke 7.6; 19.5). In the song of Zechariah God is described as 'visiting' (*episkeptomai*) his people in Jesus (Luke 1.68). His people, in their turn, are expected to receive him.

Jesus seems to have seen hospitality for a prophet or teacher as part of the economy of the kingdom of God (Matt. 10.40–41; Luke 10.7), and this attitude continued in the Early Church (Rom. 12.13; Heb. 13.2; *Didache* Part 2 'On apostles and prophets'). This is an economy that trusts to goodwill, and thus makes its practitioners vulnerable. For goodwill can be ephemeral, and the welcome may not always be warm (Luke 7.44–46).

The biblical scholar John Dominic Crossan makes much of this intentional vulnerability in the itinerant ministry of Jesus that constantly seeks a welcome (see e.g. Crossan 1991). However, Crossan also points out that the homeless Jesus is in fact a host, because in the act of inviting himself to dinner with those who are not acceptable (as in the case of Zacchaeus) or in attracting unacceptable people into homes where he is a guest (as in the case of the woman who anoints him during a meal), he is declaring them worthy of a place at the table. As usual, these habitual practices of Jesus are communicated by both specific stories and general summary statements (Matt. 9.10 and parallels, 11.19; Luke 15.1–2).

Jesus' notion of hospitality is, like his notion of the family, extended beyond the normal boundaries. It is about a welcome that breaks down the barriers between in-group and out-group. All people – people on the margins of our society, people we don't like or against whom we bear a grudge, even people of other cultures[3] – are to be treated as if they were part of our in-group (Matt. 5.44–47 and Luke 6.27–36; Matt. 8.11 and Luke 13.29; Luke 10.25–37; John 4.9; 10.16).

Finally, the homeless Jesus seemed to have been rather good at hosting picnics (Matt. 15.15–21 and parallels; Matthew 15.32–38 and Mark 8.1–9; John 6.5–10; 21.12).

Jesus felt compassion

Although the Gospels describe the behaviour of Jesus in some detail, they rarely comment on his feelings. He is described as 'amazed' by the unbelief in his home town (Mark 6.6) and by the faith of the gentile centurion (Matt. 8.10 and Luke 7.9). However, this may be intended to communicate a mental state that is more cognitive – 'wondering' – than affective. Mark comments that Jesus 'loved' the rich young ruler (Mark 10.21), which is probably best understood as 'was rather taken with' or 'warmed to'.

As the Passion begins, Jesus describes himself as 'ardently longing' to eat Passover with his friends (Luke 22.15 NJB). There are also several points in the run-up to his betrayal and arrest when Jesus is described or describes himself in words best translated as 'sad and distressed' (Matt. 26.37), 'very alarmed and distressed' (Mark 14.27), 'in agony' (Luke 22.44) and 'troubled' (John 12.27; 13.21). These communicate a feeling of almost overwhelming inner conflict.

There is, then, clearly an understandable turning up of the emotional heat in the accounts of the last days of Jesus' life. However, once he reaches the decision to allow himself to be taken there is a deep sense of imperturbable calm.

But what of the earlier days of Jesus' ministry? Here we find one reference to Jesus' anger (Mark 3.5) at the lack of compassion shown to a man with a withered hand. This is a pointer to the fact that compassion is the emotion most consistently attributed to Jesus. He looks on those 'harassed and helpless' crowds who would make such demands on him, and he is moved with compassion (Matt. 9.36 and Mark 6.34; Matt. 14.14 and Mark 6.34; Matt. 15.32 and Mark 8.2). He looks on two blind men and on a woman who has just lost her only son, and he is moved with compassion (Matt. 20.34; Luke 7.13). The word used by the Synoptic writers is *splagchnizomai*. John uses the word *embrimaomai* to describe Jesus' response as he looks on the grief of those who have lost Lazarus (John 11.33, 38). Both words are deeply physical in tone, and carry with them a sense of indignation elicited by the sight of human suffering and need. When Jesus is described in this way, it is always in the context of his decisive and consciously willed[4] action to remedy a situation of hunger, grief or sickness.

---

3 The story of Jesus and the Syrophoenician woman depicts a gradual broadening of the limits of hospitality in the thought of Jesus. For a more detailed discussion, see Collicutt 2009a, pp. 26–37.

4 See Matthew 8.2 and parallels, which emphasize Jesus' choice and desire to heal.

The action taken by Jesus is usually to repair the immediate situation: feeding, raising the dead or gravely ill, healing demonized individuals and those with chronic health conditions or disabilities. However, there are also times when Jesus addresses the wider conditions within which such problems arise. He is critical of questionable contemporary interpretations of the *Torah* that inflict deprivation and suffering on older people (Matt. 5.4–6; Mark 7.11–13), married women (Matt. 5.31–32 and parallels) and widows (Mark 12.40 and Luke 20.47); and that prohibit doing good on the Sabbath (Matt. 12.11–12 and parallels; Luke 13.15–16). In a famous summary statement he declares 'Woe to you, scribes and Pharisees, hypocrites! For you tithe mint, dill, and cumin, and have neglected the weightier matters of the law: justice and mercy and faith. It is these you ought to have practised without neglecting the others' (Matt. 23.23 with parallel in Luke 11.42).

We see in this statement that Jesus' compassion for individuals arises in the context of his passion for justice across the whole system of which their lives are a part, a passion for the establishment of the kingdom of God.

Jesus did not retaliate

The ministry of Jesus has traditionally been associated with forgiveness (the release from debts or sins). Indeed, it appears that Jesus claimed divine authority to forgive sins (Matt. 9.6 and parallels; Luke 7.48). This seems to have been based on his sense of divine sonship, discussed earlier, and a conviction that a reconciliation was being effected between God and humankind. Out of this conviction comes the demand that people must live in accordance with the principle of mutual forgiveness if they are to benefit from divine forgiveness (Matt. 6.12–14 and parallels).

However, the link between Jesus and forgiveness is not as clear and simple as it first appears. While all the New Testament writers agree that the death and resurrection of Jesus dealt with sin, not all express this in terms of forgiveness, and only the Synoptic Gospels identify forgiveness as a key feature of the earthly life and teaching of Jesus. Of these, it is only Luke who uses forgiveness as the main lens through which to view the life of Jesus and the saving work of God. In contrast, forgiveness is mentioned just once in the whole of John's Gospel (John 20.23), when the gift of the Spirit is seen to impart the authority to forgive sins (see also Matt. 18.18). Notice also that in John's moving account of the reconciliation between Jesus and Peter (John 21.15–19) the transactional language of repentance and forgiveness is conspicuous by its absence; the conversation is all about love. Forgiveness is also not prominent in the writings of Paul (see Bash and Bash 2004 for a full consideration). All this should prompt us to look behind the word 'forgiveness' for something more fundamental and pervasive in the impression left by Jesus.

We find this in the attitude of not rendering evil for evil, and of actively embracing a stance of non-retaliation. This attitude, which is closely connected with love for enemies and may often, but not always, find its expression in the practice of forgiveness, is promoted across the whole New Testament. It forms a significant part of the Sermon on the Mount (Matt. 5.38–42), is advocated by Paul (Rom. 12.17; 1 Thess. 5.15) and, crucially, is traced back to the behaviour of Jesus himself (1 Pet. 2.23; 3.9).

Jesus takes up a stance of non-retaliation in heroic fashion following his agonizing conflict considered in the previous section. Each Gospel account highlights the fact that he chooses to place himself in the hands of his enemies and rejects the option of defending himself by force (Matt. 26.52–56; Mark 14.48–49; Luke 22.49–53; John 10.17–18; 12.27; 18.4–11). In doing this Jesus paradoxically seizes power, as do his followers when, by voluntarily turning the other cheek or going the extra mile they cease to be victims or slaves and become free and dignified human beings.

For Luke this attitude is summed up in Jesus' request that his Father forgive the Roman soldiers on crucifixion duty (23.34); the expectation that his followers are to follow suit is clearly laid out in the account of the death of Stephen (Acts 7.60).

Jesus taught wisdom

Jesus' passion for justice and his stance of non-retaliation may seem at odds with each other. However, like the telic and paratelic aspects of his life, they are successfully held together because they are invoked by him at different times as appropriate. This is characteristic of Jesus' discourse in all four Gospels. Jesus not only knows what should be done but is also exquisitely alert to *when* it should be done. He has a deep sense of *kairos* (the appointed or proper time), often using the word 'hour' to refer to key moments. There are many examples; two of the most striking are Jesus' words to his mother at the wedding of Cana: 'My hour has not yet come' (John 2.4) and his prayer to his Father in Gethsemane: 'he . . . prayed that, if it were possible, the hour might pass from him' (Mark 14.35).

In Mark's Gospel Jesus' move from passionate active ministry into quiet passivity as 'the hour' indeed approaches is particularly clear (see Vanstone 1982 for a detailed analysis), but it is there in all four Gospels. The non-retaliative Jesus of Holy Week had previously shown himself perfectly capable of causing trouble by overturning tables in the temple and driving out the moneylenders (Matt. 21.12 and parallels; John 2.14–15), and according to John, he used a whip to do it! For Jesus, like Qoheleth, the author of Ecclesiastes, 'there is a time to break down and a time to build up' (Eccl. 3.3b).

This sensitivity to context and timing pervades the thinking and practice of Jesus. Knowing which mode of response is called for by a particular situation or 'hour' is a mark of the wise person. Such wisdom is vital for effective functioning in the military, political, business, medical, performative, agricultural and culinary spheres.

Jesus' wisdom is also evident in his teaching. Like many purveyors of wisdom before and after him, he uses pithy proverbial sayings, for example 'beware of wolves in sheep's clothing' (Matt. 7.15), to convey deep and complex truths. These are especially evident in the double tradition of Matthew and Luke. Jesus is also a master of paradox, and the use of stories, parables and parabolic statements to express and hold contradictions in creative tension is one of his most distinctive features (Crossan 2008). Paradox is itself deeply connected with wisdom because it acknowledges that a situation can be viewed from more than one, sometimes contradictory, perspectives and enables us to inhabit these perspectives simultaneously.

Jesus of Nazareth was the ultimate wise man. For Paul Christ is the wisdom of God (1 Cor. 1.24), and Christlike wisdom is a sign of maturity in his followers (1 Cor. 2.6).

Jesus embodied transformation

Paradox may be wise but it is also unsettling and sometimes threatening. We can deal with a paradoxical statement by rejecting it as nonsense or contradiction so that our existing beliefs and assumptions about the world or ourselves remain intact. Alternatively we can allow the paradox to stimulate a reappraisal of these beliefs and assumptions, so that they develop and grow or, more radically, get turned upside down. Paradox can result in transformation.

If there is one word that sums up the life of Jesus of Nazareth it is 'transformation'. As we noted in Chapter 1, his teaching is shot through with images of transformation; the Sermon on the Mount begins with a set of promises of radical transformation – the Beatitudes – which are programmatic for what follows. Jesus' encounters with individuals result in lives that are utterly transformed. The definitive miracle attested in all four Gospels is that of the transformation of five loaves and two fishes into food sufficient to feed a multitude. This all takes place against the background of a steadily beating theme: loss is transformed to gain and death to life (Matt. 10.39; 16.25; 19.17, 29 and parallels; Luke 15.32; John 6.51; 11.25; 12.24–25).

Above all, the accounts of the risen Jesus give an impression of someone who was the same yet profoundly different; who had gone through a shameful judicial execution and come out the other side vindicated and glorious, thus transforming the whole process. The death and raising of Jesus embody and fulfil the teaching and practice of his life. The risen Christ is the first fruit of the cosmic transformation worked by God.

This brings us full circle back to Christian formation, something that, as argued in Chapter 1, happens in the context of this cosmic transformation. We are to be formed in accordance with the character of Christ and as such are to become agents of transformation.

In this chapter, which concludes Part 1 of the book, I have presented an analysis of the character of Christ. Of course he will not be reduced to or hemmed in by the categories I have laid out. However, they help map the territory as we embark on the quest of growing more like him. We now need to turn our attention to ourselves in order to understand what personal resources and limitations we each bring to this task. This is the topic of Part 2.

"He who follows Me, walks not in darkness," says the Lord. By these words of Christ we are advised to imitate His life and habits, if we wish to be truly enlightened and free from all blindness of heart . . . Now, there are many who hear the Gospel often but care little for it because they have not the spirit of Christ. Yet whoever wishes to understand fully the words of Christ must try to pattern his whole life on that of Christ.

Thomas à Kempis (1380–1471)

Exercises

Reflect on the following questions:

- Does the account of Jesus of Nazareth presented in this chapter resonate with my own perception? Are there points of dissonance? Is this account complete, or would I want to add something?
- Do I find it easier to connect with Jesus as God who became human or as a human being who turned out to be divine?
- If I am honest, are there things about Jesus that trouble or even repel me? How do I handle these?

Bring all of these reflections to God in prayer.

Further reading

Collicutt, J., 2012, *When You Pray: Daily Reflections for Lent and Easter on the Lord's Prayer*, Oxford: Bible Reading Fellowship, pp. 6–31.

Duff, J. and Collicutt McGrath, J., 2006, *Meeting Jesus: Human Responses to a Yearning God*, London: SPCK.

Theissen, G., 1987, *The Shadow of the Galilean*, London: SCM Press.

Insights from Psychology

We have already encountered some psychology in Chapter 2, when we explored the relationship between goals and personality. However, this was really to set the scene for a consideration of the character of Christ, the head of the body.

In the Christian life it is always important to look at Christ before we consider ourselves. Nevertheless, self-awareness is a key part of Christian formation; Jesus' charge of hypocrisy directed at the religious leaders of his day is essentially an accusation of poor self-awareness – a lack of insight into their own behaviour and motives. In Part 2 we will use the approaches and findings of contemporary psychology to help us develop more insight into what makes us tick, both those human attributes that tend to work with the *Missio Dei* and those that have a habit of getting in the way of God.

Psychology is the 'scientific study of the behaviour and mental processes of human beings in interaction with their environment, or to put it less technically, the study of people' (Collicutt 2010c, pp. 1–2). It is therefore concerned with human behaviour, human thought processes, human emotions and human relationships. We should not forget that the 'psych' part of psychology is related to the Greek *psuchē* and that the early German-speaking psychologists – most notably Sigmund Freud – were concerned with the *Seele*, both of which can be translated 'soul'. Present day empirical psychology may seem a long way from the Christian theology of the last 2,000 years, yet both aspire to understand the human 'soul'.

The relationship between psychology and theology or faith can work itself out in a number of different ways:

- Psychology of religion: using the methods and assumptions of secular academic psychology to study the ways people act, think, feel and relate when they are 'doing' religion, (e.g. studying the relationship between personality and churchgoing).
- Psychology and theology in creative dialogue:
  - Offering different and complementary perspectives on the same topic (e.g. forgiveness) to give an enriched description.
  - Using the insights of one to advance the agenda of the other (e.g. using attachment theory to give a more sophisticated account of divine love).
- Psychology serving the churches: the Church using the findings of secular academic or applied psychology as part of its practical toolkit (e.g. incorporating cognitive therapy techniques into pastoral ministry).
- Theistic or Christian psychology: the enterprise of constructing a faith-based discipline of psychology, whose methods and assumptions are distinct from 'mainstream' secular psychology.

In this book there will be elements of all these ways of relating the disciplines, with the exception of the final one.[1] The psychology used here is secular. This

---

1 The reasons for this need not detain us, but the interested reader can access a robust discussion on theistic psychology in the 2013 special issue of *Christian Psychology* 7:1, pp. 5–70, available online.

does not mean that it is hostile to faith, but that the explanations it constructs to account for human behaviour do not involve God; it leaves that task to theology.

In Part 2 the agenda is to use this secular psychology to understand ourselves better and then to bring this understanding to the task of formation. This is largely 'psychology serving the churches'. In Part 3 more of a two-way dialogue between psychology and theology develops, and some insights from psychology of religion are brought to bear. However, these are always at the service of the main agenda, which is the advancement of spiritual growth.

Further reading

Johnson, E., 2010, *Psychology and Christianity: Five Views*, Downers Grove, IL: InterVarsity Press.

Jonte-Pace, D. and Parsons, W. B., 2001, *Religion and Psychology: Mapping the Terrain*, London and New York: Routledge, especially chapter 1.

Watts, F., 2002, *Theology and Psychology*, Aldershot: Ashgate, especially chapter 1.

4

Understanding Ourselves: From Temperament to Character

Then Peter and the other disciple set out and went towards the tomb. The two were running together, but the other disciple outran Peter and reached the tomb first. He bent down to look in and saw the linen wrappings lying there, but he did not go in. Then Simon Peter came, following him, and went into the tomb. He saw the linen wrappings lying there, and the cloth that had been on Jesus' head, not lying with the linen wrappings but rolled up in a place by itself. Then the other disciple, who reached the tomb first, also went in, and he saw and believed.

John 20.3–8

Jesus answered, 'The first [commandment] is, "Hear, O Israel: the Lord our God, the Lord is one; you shall love the Lord your God with all your heart, and with all your soul, and with all your mind, and with all your strength."'

Mark 12.29–30

It is something of a truism to observe that we are all different. The amazing extravagance of creation is marked by more than diversity of types; each individual of a given species is unique. This becomes increasingly evident on ascending the phylogenetic scale. We can't detect significant differences between a pair of flies, but anyone who has kept even a pet budgerigar will be convinced that no two birds are the same (Matt. 12.29; Luke 12.6), and when it comes to cats and dogs, the point is unarguable. We each have our own unique personality – the thing that makes me 'me'.

In the next two chapters we will consider the many different factors that work together to make us who we are. In this chapter we look at the basic building blocks of personality, connecting with some of the theories on goals from Chapter 2. In Chapter 5 we will look at how these building blocks are woven together with our early experience of parental care and with significant events across our lifespan, to make the stories that we tell about ourselves and that others tell about us.

Temperament: our biological heritage

Temperament is the characteristic phenomena of an individual's emotional nature, including his susceptibility to emotional stimulation, his customary strength and speed of response, and the quality of his prevailing mood, these phenomena being regarded as dependent upon his constitutional make-up. (Allport 1961, p. 34)

When I was growing up, 'Blue Peter guide dogs' were a regular fixture on children's television. The purchase and training of these dogs were funded by thousands of metal foil milk bottle tops collected by viewers. From time to time the selection of the latest puppy would be shown on air. A gentleman from the dog training centre would examine each puppy in a litter to ensure that it was healthy. Then he fired a starting pistol quite close by to see how they would react. Some would jump, others would whimper, some would ignore the sound. He would usually select a puppy that looked up but stayed calm, on the basis that this showed the appropriate 'temperament' for guide dog work. The assumption was that individual differences in disposition are present and detectable in puppies at birth or at least shortly after.

As it is with dogs, so is it with people. Individual differences between babies are evident from the earliest days of life. This should be of little surprise to those of us who are parents. It was established to the satisfaction of the scientific community in the 1970s as the result of pioneering work by Stella Thomas, Alexander Chess and colleagues (Thomas, Chess, Birch, Herzig and Korn 1963; Thomas and Chess 1977). This group carried out close observations of babies and extensive interviews with their parents through the 1950s and 1960s and followed them up to see if the individual differences that they showed in their infancy persisted through childhood into adult life. On the basis of their work they came up with nine dimensions of temperament, which they took to be biologically hardwired, giving the child a kind of temperamental signature that is hers for life.

This early work has been built on by Mary Rothbart and her colleagues, who have used the more sophisticated methods and greater knowledge of neurobiology that have become available since the 1970s. This group has studied children across a number of cultures (for a review, see Rothbart, Ahadi and Evans 2000) and has been able to reduce the initial nine dimensions to three core stable dimensions of temperament that are evident in infancy and childhood:

- Degree of extraversion/surgency (active and responsive, preference for intense stimulation and ease in social situations).
- Degree of negative affectivity (a tendency to sadness, discomfort, anger, fear, frustration and difficulty in being soothed).
- Degree of effortful control (preference for low intensity stimulation, self-controlled behaviour, focused attention and sensitivity in perception).

The first two of these dimensions bear a very close resemblance to two aspects of human personality that have come up again and again in the work of different researchers throughout the twentieth century, and which are usually labelled 'extraversion' and 'neuroticism'. Both of these dimensions are thought to have a biological basis.

Extraversion may reflect the resting level of arousal in the brain (Eysenck 1967) and sensitivity to reward through the fine tuning of certain dopamine[2]-

---

2 Dopamine is one of several brain chemicals that transmit messages between nerve cells. It plays a significant part in the brain systems that underlie reward-based behaviour and the control of movement.

based brain circuits (Panksepp 1998; Panksepp and Biven 2012). It is thought that individuals who score high on measures of extraversion have a relatively low resting level of brain arousal; they therefore feel a need for stimulation in order to increase their arousal levels. They are also particularly susceptible to reward, and they make active attempts to seek it out; exciting social encounters and risky leisure activities usually do the trick for them. On the other hand, individuals who score low on measures of extraversion have a relatively high resting level of brain arousal. They are not naturally disposed to seeking intense pleasure; exciting social encounters or risky leisure activities are likely to make them uncomfortably over-aroused.

The separate dimension of neuroticism is thought to reflect the reactivity of brain centres concerned with fear and avoidance and possibly also with frustration (Eysenck 1967; Gray 1982; Panksepp 1986). Individuals who score high on measures of neuroticism have a reactive nervous system – are what my mother used to call 'highly strung'. Those who score low have a relatively unreactive or stable nervous system.

To summarize and simplify: extraversion is about how much you need social contact and are attuned to pleasure, which you will tend actively to seek out (other things being equal); neuroticism is about how easily you find yourself getting upset by challenge, from which you will tend to withdraw (other things being equal).[3]

It's important to emphasize three things about extraversion and neuroticism (hereafter referred to as 'E' and 'N' respectively):

1 These are not two ends of the same dimension; they are two *independent dimensions*. An individual is not either extraverted or neurotic. Instead each of us will show a degree of E *and* a degree of N.
2 These dimensions arise from biology. They have high heritability, indicating that genetics plays an important part (Eysenck 1990), though it is likely that the physical conditions of pregnancy and childbirth also contribute. They are thus rather like height and hair colour in being to a large extent 'given'.
3 Following on from this, it makes no sense to blame or congratulate someone for being constitutionally extraverted or neurotic (or their opposites – introverted and stable). In this respect we are what we are.

Personality traits: the expression of temperament in patterns of thinking and doing

As we have seen, temperament is based in our characteristic ways of feeling and reacting to pleasurable or challenging stimulation. These play out in habitual ways of being in the world, which can best be understood through the lens

---

3 For a full exploration of the relationship between E, N and emotions, see Verduyn and Brans 2011.

of 'personality traits'. Personality traits are summary statements of the ways that people behave in the area of human relationships. In the academic study of personality the traits are constructed using a 'psycholexical approach'. This approach assumes that consistent patterns in people's behaviour are reflected in the language of their culture. Systematic analysis of the way that words describing human qualities cluster together can then yield some basic dimensions. From these personality traits are identified.

This is a massive undertaking that has been repeated many times since the mid twentieth century with increasing degrees of sophistication as information technology has advanced. In its last decade a final consensus was reached among personality psychologists as to the core personality traits that emerge from the psycholexical approach, and they turn out to include E and N. This is reassuring, because it indicates that the biological approach and the psycholexical approach converge, and this makes it more likely that we are talking about 'real' human qualities. The core personality traits identified by the psycholexical approach have come to be known as the 'Big Five' (McCrae and Costa 1990), with the acronym OCEAN, which stands for:

- Openness (the tendency to be open to and curious about unusual ideas and aesthetic and emotional experiences).
- Conscientiousness (the tendency to be dutiful, disciplined, organized and reliable).
- Extraversion (the tendency to be energetic, assertive, sociable, talkative and seeking stimulation).
- Agreeableness (the tendency to be co-operative and helpful – 'oiling the wheels').
- Neuroticism (the tendency to experience unpleasant emotions such as anxiety).

We have already seen that E and N have their origins in some basic temperamental dispositions that can be observed in infancy. This seems also to be the case for conscientiousness and agreeableness (Rothbart, Ahadi and Evans 2000), though it's less clear for openness. There is evidence that all of the Big Five dimensions, not just E and N, have a moderate to high degree of heritability (Loehlin, McCrae, Costa and John 1998). They are also fairly stable across the lifespan, though not completely unchanging (Soldz and Vaillant 1999; Srivastava, John, Gosling and Potter 2003). The Big Five have been found to apply across many different languages and cultures (McCrae, Costa, Del Pilar, Rolland and Parker 1998). In addition, they are capable of subsuming most other systems of personality classification, for example the Myers-Briggs Type Indicator (see e.g. Furnham 1996). So it seems that these personality traits, which describe our general dispositions to think and act in certain ways, also have a strong basis in our biology.

An individual is assessed formally on the Big Five by completing a complex personality inventory, the NEO-PI,[4] which must be administered and

---

4 Costa, P. and McCrae, R., 1992, *NEO PI-R Professional Manual*, Odessa, FL: Psychological Assessment Resources, Inc.

interpreted by a qualified professional. However, there are also shortened indicative assessments, some of which are included in the suggested activity at the end of this chapter.

We might be tempted to think that there's not much point in knowing about our personality traits because, like our shoe size, we didn't choose them and we can do little if anything to change them. Yet it's extremely important to know one's shoe size; it makes the difference between a life blessed by healthy feet and a life of pain and foot pathology. In the same way, although for the most part we can do little to change our basic personality traits, we can manage our lives much more effectively if we understand them. Understanding something of the personality traits of others may also make us less likely to judge them. We will look at this in more depth in Chapter 10, but for now here is an example.

In Chapter 3 I argued that because Jesus showed hospitality, we can consider it as a Christlike virtue. That is, 'to show hospitality' can be considered one rule for living out conformity to the character of Christ. But it is not clear exactly how this rule for living might express itself in the nuts and bolts of what I actually try to do. It may be that I belong to a church culture that interprets this rule as having a continuous open house, with folk constantly dropping in for a meal or a bed unannounced, as summarized in Figure 11.

Figure 11.

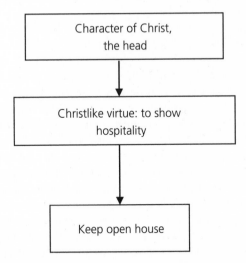

Now if I am the sort of person who scores high on E, this would actually suit my need for stimulation and social intercourse rather well. It would come naturally. But what if I am the sort of person who scores low on E? This would be torture. I might force myself to do it in order to comply with the norms of my group, but I would be miserable and also quickly become exhausted from the effort. I (and others) might see me as grudging and deficient in the Christian virtue of hospitality, or worse – unloving. I might feel guilty at my inability to live up to the standard of Christ in this area when other Christians seem to find this easy.

However, if I know that I am low on E (or in other words introverted), and accept that this is how God has made me, I might be a bit kinder to myself. I might look more creatively and confidently at ways of expressing the virtue of hospitality (see Figure 12).

Figure 12.

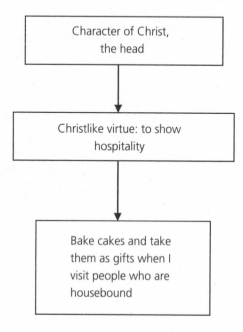

This example is actually very relevant to the process of formation of Christian leaders. There is evidence that clergy and other Christian leaders tend to be low on E (Jones and Francis 1992; Francis, Penson and Jones 2001). Yet often the roles expected of them are framed in a way that emphasizes a high degree of sociability, and this can be a major source of stress (Francis and Rodger 1994). We will look at how this might best be managed in Chapter 10.

Our temperament, expressed through our personality traits, tells us something of the 'how' of personality. The goals to which we aspire tell us the 'why'. All Christians have the same 'why' (conformity to Christ), but we may differ with respect to the 'how'. This is part of the glorious diversity of creation.

The account of Peter and the beloved disciple at the tomb from John 20 that opens this chapter illustrates this nicely. Peter is one of the few characters depicted in the New Testament about whom we have enough information to make educated guesses in the area of temperament. He seems unquestionably to be high on E. The beloved ('other') disciple gives the impression of being lower on E. He is also traditionally thought to have been the youngest of the Twelve, so was perhaps lithe and fleet of foot. He outstrips his companion physically and gets to the tomb first, but then stops and considers (as he does shortly after when he sees the linen wrappings); Peter, on the other hand, rushes straight in. Both have the same 'why' or ultimate goal – they want to find Jesus; but their 'hows' are quite different, and we may observe, complementary.

We are blessed with a diversity of voices in the New Testament, and this includes no less than four Gospels. At first this may seem rather a luxury. In fact it is necessary, for the story of Jesus is told through different temperamental lenses. Peter's version is traditionally recorded most directly in Mark's Gospel, a fast paced, exciting thriller. The beloved disciple's version is traditionally to be found in John's Gospel, a deeply reflective, slow-paced work, with little in the way of thrills and spills. Both are true. Both offer valuable, indeed priceless, perspectives on Jesus.

'Other things being equal': taking the situation into account

The psychologist Martin Seligman uses a lovely phrase: 'a psychology of rising to the occasion' (Seligman 2002, p. 12). This draws an important point to our attention. If we want to know how somebody will behave at any particular point in time, we need to know the situation or occasion. Even the most neurotic of us can be a hero if our child is in danger; even the most agreeable young woman can turn into a 'bridezilla' as the big day approaches. That is why my definitions of E and N above include the caveat 'other things being equal'. Other things aren't usually equal.

This obvious point struck psychologists rather late in the day with the publication of Walter Mischel's book *Personality and Assessment* in 1968. Mischel argued that situations are at least as important as personality traits in predicting how people actually behave, and his arguments have been confirmed by many subsequent studies (e.g. Mischel and Shoda 1995). We are deeply social beings and we conform to the expectations of our groups, as the infamous Milgram experiments on obedience to authority figures demonstrate.[5] The behaviour of individuals at a job interview or ministerial selection conference is more likely to be influenced by the situation than their inherent temperament.

However, it is in the *interaction* between situation and temperament that the stuff of personality is formed. We come into the world with certain temperamental 'givens', but we find ourselves in certain situations, often repeatedly, and it is the mix of these that determines our individual personal development. Understanding the importance of situations and occasions, and the complex way they interact with temperament, can help us guard against a rather common and dangerous tendency: that of typecasting ourselves and others.

---

5 In a series of experiments (e.g. Milgram 1965), Stanley Milgram was able to demonstrate that ordinary volunteers could be induced to inflict what they believed to be painful electric shocks on other volunteers simply because they were instructed to do so by an authoritative research officer.

There is something in our make-up that renders us particularly prone to thinking in terms of prototypes. When I was working in an NHS neurology unit, I noticed that nursing colleagues would often identify a newly admitted patient with a previous patient who had shown similar symptoms or behaviour; they would remark 'She's a Mrs X'. Thinking about the newly admitted Miss Y as a version of a prototype seemed to help them get to grips with the challenge of managing her care; what had worked for Mrs X would probably work for Miss Y. But I always wanted to, and occasionally actually did, cry out (much to my colleagues' amusement), 'No she's not. She's herself!'

Prototypes can be helpful, but they do not mirror nature, which tends to continuous variation along dimensions rather than division into discrete types. Consequently prototypes don't do us justice and can often hem us in. I well remember my shock when a pleasant-seeming young woman who had been chatting to me for a few minutes at a conference drinks reception suddenly announced, 'I'm going to my room now. I'm an introvert and I can't tolerate too much social intercourse.' She turned on her heel and swept from the room leaving me on my own with my mouth open. Knowing something of our temperament, especially our levels of N and E is very helpful, but it should never serve as an excuse for neglecting common courtesy nor, more importantly, doing what is required in the life of faith. As someone with low E, I may be liberated to find that Christian hospitality does not entail keeping open house. Nevertheless, if there is a flood in my village, and I live on a hill, I should be prepared to take people in.

This is one reason why typological models of personality – and indeed of gender – are ultimately deficient. Types can give a sense of certainty that can provide a kind of security – 'I'm an X'. But this can set up in us an expectation of conformity to the X prototype when perhaps God has other plans for us (Amos 7.14–15).

Aptitudes and skills

As we have seen, we all differ in our temperament and personal style. We also differ in our aptitudes – our abilities to acquire domain-specific skills such as languages, mathematics, music, memory-based knowledge, logical reasoning or sport. Aptitudes are rather like the dimensions of temperament, but they could be said to refer to the 'how well' of personality rather than simply the 'how'. Like temperament, there is a strong genetic component to our aptitudes (Vinkhuyzen, van der Shuis, Posthuma and Boomsma 2009). Again this confirms our everyday impression that being good at certain things runs in families; although family cultures and values often enhance the effect of genetic endowment so that a mix of nature and nurture is at work. This is because, unlike temperament, we can do something about our aptitudes: if we know we have them and are given the right opportunity, we can nurture them into full-blown skills.

For example, my mother was an excellent pianist, and I showed quite an aptitude for music from an early age. But this aptitude was formed into a full-blown

musical skill through my mother's insistence that I took music lessons and practised my instruments. My son is now a skilled cellist. He had an aptitude, but I
also gave him opportunities and encouragement – quite vigorous at times! – to
develop this aptitude into a skill.

My maternal uncle was a very skilled violinist. However, my mother was not
sure that music ran in their family in earlier generations; her parents had no
remarkable musical prowess, and she was anyway quite hazy about her father's
background. This week, after trying for several years, I finally managed to trace
his parentage. I came across the marriage banns of my great, great grandfather
who was born in the 1830s, and was astonished and touched to read his occupation given as 'musician'. My mother and I had nurtured our children's musical
aptitude, but it seems that it was first of all a gift from a long-dead generation.

This short section on aptitudes, biological givens that develop into skills if
they are valued and cherished, is included because it has something to say to us
about the main concern of this book: character. We cannot change our temperament (though we can manage it), but we can build up our character strengths.
These are aspects of our personality that sit somewhere between temperament
and aptitude, and it is to these that we now turn.

Strengths of character

A person who is high on E and low on N may develop into a 'fearless' personality; someone who rushes into danger without thinking too hard about the
consequences and who feels little in the way of anxiety. This should not be
mistaken for bravery. A person who is low on E and high on N may develop
into an 'avoidant' personality; someone who is so keenly aware of danger and
so troubled by anxiety that she rarely departs from her usual settled and limited
routines. This should not be mistaken for cowardice.

Bravery is the overcoming of fear in order to do the right thing. Cowardice is
succumbing to fear and thus failing to do the right thing. Bravery is a character
strength that involves the management of fear. If I feel no fear, I have no opportunity to display bravery. If I feel much fear, bravery will be a great challenge,
but it is one to which I may rise. This reminds us of the fact that people who are
neurotic can nevertheless show extraordinary bravery. Neuroticism is a given
personality trait (that expresses temperament); bravery is a character strength
that can be nurtured and developed.

It is only in recent years, with the advent of the positive psychology movement, that psychologists have turned their attention to character strengths. The
positive psychology movement developed at the turn of the twentieth century
as a reaction against the preoccupation of many schools of psychology at that
time with human failure, dysfunction and misery (Seligman 1999). However,
this preoccupation with the negative isn't the monopoly of professional psychologists. It appears to be built into human nature. In an interesting and comprehensive review that places this negative bias in an evolutionary context, Paul
Rozin and Edward Royzman (2001) note in passing the asymmetrical nature of

the Christian cultural narrative of the Fall and redemption. They observe that quite a small act in the Garden of Eden led to the entry of evil into the world yet a very large redemptive act was required of Christ, and that the churches feel compelled to continue with activities designed to keep evil at bay.

This disproportion appears illogical, yet it seems that it is psychologically plausible. Historically, Christians have not had difficulty in believing in Original Sin, but they have had great difficulty in being convinced that sin really has been dealt with. As an example of how this pervades Christian culture, consider this passage from Chapter 3 of Paul's letter to the Romans, which is reproduced here first in the NRSV translation as it appears in English Bibles and second with the punctuation as it appears in the Nestle-Aland Greek text based on the earliest manuscripts:

[21]But now, irrespective of law, the righteousness of God has been disclosed, and is attested by the law and the prophets,
[22]the righteousness of God through faith in Jesus Christ for all who believe. For there is no distinction,
[23]since all have sinned and fall short of the glory of God;
[24]they are now justified by his grace as a gift, through the redemption that is in Christ Jesus

But now apart from law, the righteousness of God has been disclosed and is attested by the law and the prophets, the righteousness of God through faith in Jesus Christ for all who believe.
For there is no distinction, since all have sinned and fall short of the glory of God they are now justified by his grace as a gift through the redemption that is in Christ Jesus.

Notice how the division into verses and the moving of a semicolon in the English text (also there in the KJV) subtly foregrounds the sin and unbalances what was originally a beautifully symmetrical sentence moving towards a positive conclusion. It is easy for us to believe that things are bad or that it can take very little to make things turn bad. It is much harder for us to see and be assured of the good or that goodness can be sustained (see also Baumeister, Bratslavsky, Finkenauer and Vohs 2001).

At a more concrete level Rozin and Royzman (2001) note that there are far fewer words in English (and other languages) for pleasurable than painful feelings; pleasant than unpleasant emotions; human strengths than human deficiencies. You only have to switch on the nightly television news to be aware of our bias as a society to attend to the negative.

One of the ways the positive psychology movement has addressed this issue has been to develop a catalogue of human strengths. In a playful mood its authors, Christopher Peterson (1950–2012) and Martin Seligman, named this catalogue 'Un-DSM-I'. In doing this they were parodying the increasingly elaborate and unwieldy Diagnostic and Statistical Manual of the American Psychiatric Association (DSM-V), whose aim is to catalogue and classify every aspect of human psychopathology. The 'Un-DSM-I' was finally published under the title

Character Strengths and Virtues (Peterson and Seligman 2004), and the system it set out is now referred to as the 'Values in Action' (VIA).

Like the psychologists who identified the Big Five using a psycholexical approach, Peterson and his colleagues focused on the words people use to refer to character strengths, and looked at how these cluster together. They already had a good idea of what they meant by a 'character strength'; it was somewhere between a personality trait and an aptitude, and it was *virtuous*: 'a subset of personality . . . on which we place moral value' (Peterson and Park 2009, pp. 26–7).

Peterson and colleagues examined representative writings from the philosophical and religious traditions of the world, initially Athenian philosophy, Buddhism, Christianity, Confucianism, Hinduism, Islam, Judaism and Taoism (Dahlsgaard, Peterson and Seligman 2005); and later extended this to include African traditional religions (Park, Peterson and Seligman 2006; see also Selvam and Collicutt 2012). The aim was to come up with a set of valued human attributes that are ubiquitous across cultures.

Strict criteria were used to identify character strengths in a text. These included the requirements that the personal quality in question should:

- be seen to contribute to the flourishing of self or others;
- be morally valued in its own right, not dependent on its outcome;
- not diminish others in the vicinity when it is displayed;
- not have an opposite that could be phrased in a positive way;
- be manifest across a range of behaviours and situations and show some stability over time;
- be distinct from other strengths in the classification and not decomposable into them;
- be embodied in consensual cultural paradigms (myths, parables, wisdom sayings, role models);
- be evident in the institutions and rituals of a culture that are aimed at cultivating and sustaining it.

The result consisted of 24 character strengths.

Peterson and his colleagues arranged these character strengths in six groups, which they termed 'virtues'. The use of this term is in some ways misleading because the word 'virtue' has become so strongly associated with Virtue Ethics[6] in the field of moral philosophy. It's important to be clear that Peterson and his colleagues were not moral philosophers, and the VIA is not promoting a particular ethical system. It simply records patterns of behaviour that are recognized across many cultures as expressing valued human characteristics. The VIA 'virtues' are little more than heuristic devices that place the many character strengths in some sort of order. Indeed, subsequent psychometric research has shown that, while the VIA character strengths are robust concepts, the VIA

---

6 This is an approach to moral philosophy that locates morality in personal qualities rather than in actions or their consequences; see e.g. McIntyre 2007.

virtues are weaker. This is not a problem for us, because this book is organized around the Christlike principles set out in Chapter 3, not the VIA virtues. Our primary interest in the VIA is the character strengths (and this is also in line with most researchers in this area). This is indicated in Table 2, which sets out the VIA in full, by placing the character strengths in bold type.

Table 2.

Virtue	Character strength
Wisdom and knowledge	**Creativity**
	Curiosity
	Judgement
	Love of learning
	Perspective
Courage	**Bravery**
	Perseverance
	Honesty
	Zest
Humanity	**Love**
	Kindness
	Social intelligence
Justice	**Teamwork**
	Fairness
	Leadership
Temperance	**Forgiveness**
	Humility
	Prudence
	Self-regulation
Transcendence	**Appreciation of beauty and excellence**
	Gratitude
	Hope
	Humour
	Spirituality

The big achievement of the VIA is the framework and vocabulary it offers for talking about and researching human strengths. Many psychometric measures have been devised for each character strength. Hundreds, if not thousands, of research papers have been published within this framework, which attempt to delineate more clearly what it means to show a particular character strength and, following from this, how such strengths can be nurtured or thwarted. We will draw on much of this research in Part 3 as we pursue the idea of cultivating the fruit of the Spirit.

At a practical level it is fun to complete strengths assessments such as the VIA (several other similar measures have now been developed); the result is a personal profile of 'signature strengths' that is stated entirely in positive and encouraging terms. As noted earlier in this section, we do not have a well-developed vocabulary for describing strengths or a well-established habit of talking about them (particularly in Britain!). To illustrate: one of my students plus spouse completed the VIA assessment as part of an assignment. The wife expressed surprise that she had scored highly on 'creativity'. Her husband was not at all surprised, and he told her that creativity was the most characteristic feature of her personality. She asked him why he hadn't mentioned it to her before, and he replied that he had not had the occasion, conceptual framework or vocabulary to do so until the VIA had provided them.

This seems to be highly relevant to a ministry of encouragement. We cannot encourage ourselves and each other in our formation unless we have a way of noticing, thinking about and describing good character. We cannot offer adequate prayers of thanksgiving for our brothers and sisters unless we have an appropriate vocabulary. Furthermore, in seeking to develop good character it is easier to aspire to something that is clearly articulated rather than vaguely stated.

In general, the ethos and precision offered by positive psychology is very encouraging because it enables us to see ourselves and others differently and instils a 'can do' attitude. Focusing on weaknesses and negatives only inhibits action, it does not inspire, as the parable of the talents makes clear (Matt. 25.24–25). Insights from positive psychology can inform the process of conforming to the character of Christ. This is the Spirit's work but, as Jesus reminds us in the words from Mark's Gospel at the beginning of this chapter, it is an enterprise to which we must bring our *strength*.

> Grace is not opposed to effort, it is opposed to earning. Earning is an attitude. Effort is an action. Grace, you know, does not just have to do with forgiveness of sins alone.
>
> Dallas Willard (1935–2013)

Is it really OK to celebrate human strengths?

Some of the discourse of positive psychology jars with the traditional Christian habit of self-denigration. Some might argue that human beings are so deeply part of a fallen creation that our characters are tainted, so that all our apparent strengths are distortions of the good, leading us only to repeated cycles of exploitation and violent conflict to which history bears witness. Others might point out that the Christian gospel asks us to deny ourselves and lose our lives (Matt. 16.24–25 and parallels), not accentuate the positive. Still others might want to focus a ministry of encouragement on the mighty works of God manifest in human weakness, not on human strengths.

While there is clearly truth in all these positions (some of which will be pursued further in Chapters 8 and 9), they need to be set alongside the fact that we have been created in the image of God (Gen. 1.26–27). Like our aptitudes, the seeds of our character strengths appear to be grounded in our biology (Steger, Hicks, Kashdan, Krueger and Bouchard 2007), and it is justifiable to see them as a gift of creation that, like the gift of music, art or dance, carry something of the divine image. Just as we might thank God for people's aptitudes in the academic, artistic or sporting spheres, or take delight in the physical beauty with which they have been endowed, so we can thank God for their – and our own – curiosity, bravery, humour, love of learning and so on. Like the bread and fish on the Galilean hillside, we bring these gifts of creation to the formation process so that, through the transforming work of the Spirit, we may bear good fruit. But if we are to do this, we need first to recognize what we have.

> It is sufficient that the Seeds of [benevolence] be implanted in our Nature by God. There is, as is owned, much left for us to do on our own Heart and Temper; to cultivate, to improve, to call it forth, to exercise it in a steady, uniform Manner. This is our Work: this is Virtue and Religion.
>
> Bishop Joseph Butler (1692–1752)

Conclusion

In this chapter we have looked at some of the human givens we bring to the process of formation: our temperament, which is unlikely to change but can be managed; our aptitudes, which can be nurtured into skills or left undiscovered or undeveloped; and our character strengths – what we might consider 'virtuous aptitudes'. Martin Seligman, the founder of the positive psychology movement, considers a meaningful life as one in which we identify our signature strengths and use them 'in the service of something larger than you are' (2002, p. 263). Here we return again to the goals discussed in Chapter 2. In order to understand ourselves we need to know about more than our human givens. We need to understand our values, goals and ultimate concerns. As we have already noted in this chapter, we also need to understand the key situations and events from the past that have shaped us. Only then will we have a sense of the overall shape of our story, to which we turn in the next chapter.

Exercises

1 If you are interested in seeing how you score on the Big Five, the websites below offer anonymous assessments (though they will store the numerical data for their own research):
   • www.personalitytest.org.uk
   • www.psychometrictest.org.uk/big-five-personality
2 You can also explore your character strengths using the VIA and other similar systems:
   • www.viastrengths.org
   • www.authentichappiness.org
3 Another way of identifying your strengths is to think of a time when you were at your best. Write a detailed account of what was happening and draw out your strengths from that. Alternatively, think of someone who 'gets' you and appreciates you and try and articulate what it is you think s/he sees in you that others don't. Ryan Niemiec (see Further reading below) suggests that, having made yourself more *aware* of one or more character strengths, you should *explore* in much more detail the ways it shows itself in your daily life, the impact that exercising this strength has on you and others and how it feels if you are not able to exercise this strength. Having done this, you should intentionally *apply* the strength in an imaginative way each day.

Further reading

Cain, S., 2013, *Quiet: The Power of Introverts in a World that Can't Stop Talking*, London: Penguin.

Linley, P. A., 2008, *Average to A+: Realising Strengths in Yourself and Others*, Warwick: CAPP Press.

Niemiec, R., 2013, *Mindfulness and Character Strengths: A Practical Guide to Flourishing*, Göttingen: Hogrefe.

5

Understanding Ourselves:
The Shape of Our Stories

Guard me as the apple of the eye; hide me in the shadow of your wings.

Psalm 17.8

Even though I walk through the darkest valley, I fear no evil; for you are with me; your rod and your staff – they comfort me.

Psalm 23.4

My God, my God, why have you forsaken me? Why are you so far from helping me, from the words of my groaning?

O my God, I cry by day, but you do not answer; and by night, but find no rest.

Psalm 22.1–2

In this chapter we will look at personality not so much from the perspective of personal qualities such as traits and aptitudes, but in terms of narrative. We begin by looking at how we may carry what we have learnt from our earliest relationships into our adult life, weaving particular repeated patterns into the tapestry of our story. We then look more broadly at what this process of weaving actually involves.

As we reflect on our past, especially our relationships with our parents, it is important to remember three things. First, while our early experience may influence our adult personality quite strongly, it does not *determine* it. As with our temperament, we can't change what happened, but we can take it into account and manage it, and we don't need to be imprisoned by it. It is one factor among several that come together to make us who we are, and there is always room for change. Second, unless we have a contemporaneous continuous audio-visual recording of our early life (and we don't), we can't be 100 per cent sure what actually happened. Our memory for our childhood is not completely reliable; it can be particularly prone to suggestion from others and to distortion through our own cognitive biases (Hardt and Rutter 2004). Once I have a view of how things are, for example that my mother was 'cold', I will tend to recall events that confirm my view. Third, while it is of some importance to know the historical factors that contributed to who I am now, these may have little relevance for my further development into the person I hope to be. This is certainly the case in psychological therapy where a distinction is often drawn between what got you to where you are and what is keeping you there. Psychotherapeutic work may need to take the first into account, but its main focus is – or should be – on the second.[1]

Attachment theory

Attachment theory is probably the most researched, well-known and influential psychological theory today. It is prominent in the fields of education, social work, parenting, psychotherapy, animal psychology and increasingly in religious studies. It is associated with two founding figures, John Bowlby (1907–90) and Mary Ainsworth (1913–99), and was developed in the aftermath of the Second World War.

The war had brought massive dislocation of populations across Europe and beyond. Children had been separated from parents as refugees or evacuees, and many children were orphaned. Along with this, the revelation of the full horrors of the Third Reich and the degree to which ordinary people seemed to collude with it, led to a renewed interest in the formation of adult personalities: are some types of people more prone to collude with such regimes than others, and does early experience play a part in this? Women had gained significant freedoms during the war years, taking on jobs that had previously been the province of men and finding a place for themselves outside the domestic sphere. With the return of peace there was a regrouping, so that the nuclear family became for a while intensely idealized, especially in Britain and the USA. The issue of the appropriate place for women was raised; people posed the question of whether children suffered irreversible psychological damage if their mothers worked outside the home and delegated their care to others. It was in this context that attachment theory emerged (Bowlby 1951).

John Bowlby trained as a psychiatrist and psychoanalyst, initially working with the object relations[2] analyst Melanie Klein. However, he moved away from the psychoanalytic approach. Among his difficulties with psychoanalysis was the way it tried to explain people's behaviour solely in terms of what was going on inside their heads and largely ignored the effect of actual events in their lives. Furthermore, classic psychoanalysis holds that individuals pass through a series of psycho-sexual stages and that in order to grow up they need to leave the previous stages behind them; return to a previous stage is seen as regressive and unhealthy. Bowlby wasn't convinced of this; he thought that patterns established in early life can re-emerge in a *healthy* way in adulthood (e.g. the use of baby talk between lovers). Also at this time the discipline of ethology (the study of animal behaviour under natural conditions) was emerging. This naturalistic approach, deeply steeped in evolutionary theory, was quite different from the clinical approach of the psychoanalysts, and it greatly attracted Bowlby.

---

1 In classical psychoanalysis the past and present are seen as so inextricably linked that this distinction is not drawn strongly, if at all. However, this is not representative of most psychotherapeutic approaches.

2 Object relations theory will be explored in Chapter 11.

He thought that the insights of ethologists, such as those of Konrad Lorenz (1903–89) into bonding between baby ducks and geese and their parents, might be relevant to the bonds formed between human infants and their parents.

Separation and the safe haven

Bowlby's theory of attachment grew out of work he undertook with his colleague James Robertson (1911–88), which involved detailed observation of the effect of hospitalization on young children. In the 1950s hospital visiting was very restricted, even in children's wards. This was the cause of acute distress that seemed to lead to persisting change in the affected children (Robertson and Robertson 1989).

Bowlby and Robertson identified three phases in the child's reaction to separation from her parents, most pronounced in children between about six months and three years of age:

- Protest (the child searches fruitlessly for the absent parent and screams in distress).
- Despair (the child appears to give up the search for the parent and lapses into a more profound type of distress characterized by withdrawal and apathy).
- Detachment (the child seems superficially more content but loses interest in the parent and remains detached when reunited).

On the basis of these findings, the results of a series of highly controversial experiments on the effects of maternal deprivation in rhesus macaque monkeys (Harlow 1958; van der Horst, LeRoy and van der Veer 2008), and further research of his own, Bowlby developed the idea that human beings and many other animals have a basic drive to maintain proximity to our 'primary caregiver' (usually the mother). Bowlby argued that this drive is as important for our survival as the drives of hunger and thirst, but instead of being about food and drink it is about security. Just as hunger and thirst call forth food- and drink-seeking behaviour, this drive[3] calls forth what he termed 'attachment behaviour'.

So the protest that a young child makes on initial separation from her primary caregiver is a sign that attachment behaviour has been activated but cannot be shut off; it is an expression of 'separation anxiety' (Bowlby 1959). Anyone who has fruitlessly attempted to comfort another parent's toddler while on crèche duty will be very familiar with the separation anxiety that is expressed so robustly in the protest phase. It is entirely healthy. Under normal circumstances these days we do not come across the despair and detachment phases (though I have seen it in our cats when we left them in a boarding cattery for

---

3 We now know that attachment behaviour is underpinned by the complex interplay of several neurobiological systems, so it isn't as simple as thirst or even hunger. Nevertheless the analogy remains helpful.

rather too long). We might think of the despair and detachment phases as a kind of giving up the search, an emotional version of the metabolic shutting down that happens as starvation advances and hunger ceases to be relevant.

Just as hunger and thirst are assuaged by food and drink, which give a feeling of deep satisfaction, separation anxiety is assuaged by cuddles and caresses, which give a feeling of deep peace and security. Just as food doesn't only assuage hunger but also gives us pleasure, so the emotional warmth – and felt bodily warmth – involved in attachment gives rise to positive feelings of affection, not simply the relief of negative feelings of anxiety. Attachment is therefore the first context in which we experience love.

Bowlby argued that attachment behaviour is vital for the survival of the young child, mammal or bird, because it gives access to protection from predators. He described the function of the primary caregiver as a 'safe haven' – somewhere to run and hide under wings or skirts or atop shoulders. Attachment behaviour is thus a mark of perceived vulnerability, and it would therefore be predicted that it will persist into adulthood in those who feel vulnerable, or that it will re-emerge at times of crisis. This is precisely what is found. When things are very tough for us we literally cling to those with whom we are intimate and who we think can do us good. It's not unusual to hear adults say ironically but with a grain of truth, 'I want my mummy!' or 'I want to go home!' when life is getting too much.

The phases of response to separation that Bowlby and Robertson observed in children who were too young to understand that their parents would eventually return are also a feature of the responses of adults to the death of a loved one whom they *know* will not return (see e.g. Parkes 2010). Both are a kind of mourning.

Attachment styles and the secure base

Bowlby arrived at the idea of a human need for security as a result of his studies on childhood separation. Some years earlier in the USA the psychologist Mary Ainsworth (née Salter) had been investigating the role of security in contributing to healthy psychological adjustment in the developing child. She had come up with the idea of the 'secure base' (Salter 1940), a concept that she was later able to elaborate through detailed naturalistic observations during her time living in Uganda due to her husband's work. Ainsworth had worked with Bowlby in London for two years prior to going to Uganda, and from that time their research became closely linked.

Ainsworth's particular contribution was in identifying *individual differences* in the quality of infant–mother interaction. Her work in Uganda was based on observations of how infants used their mothers as a secure base from which to explore their environment, and the quality of reunion after short separations. She was able to identify three broad patterns of attachment. Some infants cried little and seemed content to explore in the presence of their mother; others cried frequently, even when held by their mothers, and explored little; and a third group appeared indifferent to their mothers. While, in the light of Chapter 4, we might think that these differences were based on differences in the infants' temperaments, Ainsworth's research indicated that maternal sensitivity to the subtle signals provided by the infants was what accounted for the differences.[4] Highly sensitive mothers who enjoyed the process of breast feeding had securely attached infants; less sensitive mothers had insecurely attached infants (Ainsworth 1967).

Subsequent more detailed and systematic research in Baltimore confirmed and extended the Ugandan findings. The sensitivity of mothers in harmonizing and meshing their behaviour with that of their infants in the first three months of life predicted the security of the attachment shown by the infants, both at the time and at nine to twelve months of age. In addition, this early sensitivity of mothers predicted the reunion behaviour shown by the children at one year of age in a laboratory test known as the 'strange situation'. In this situation the child is in a playroom with his mother; they are then joined by an unfamiliar female; the mother then leaves briefly and returns; then both the mother and the unfamiliar female leave the infant alone; finally they both return.

This standard situation enables observation of the way infants use the presence of the mother to give them confidence in exploring and playing in an unfamiliar environment, sticking closer to her in the presence of a stranger. It also enables observation of separation and reunion behaviour. From this Ainsworth and her colleagues were able to develop an experimentally based system of classification of attachment patterns (Ainsworth, Blehar, Waters and Wall 1978), which is now in widespread use:

- Secure attachment (the infant explores and plays confidently in the presence of the mother, shows separation anxiety when she leaves but is easily and rapidly soothed by the mother on her return).
- Anxious avoidant insecure attachment (the infant does not explore and play in the presence of the mother, avoids or ignores her and appears indifferent to her return following a short separation).
- Anxious ambivalent insecure attachment (the infant is clingy and reluctant to play or explore far from the mother, and is not easily soothed on her return, even kicking or swiping at her).

Not all children fitted this classification and later a fourth category, that of 'disorganized attachment', was added (Main and Solomon 1986). Some of the children who fall in this category clearly do so because of experiences of parental abuse and neglect.

This research is of course important in relation to the well-being of children, but it is also relevant to our concern with formation, because it seems that we

---

4 More recent work suggests, however, that one of the things that can affect the sensitivity of mothers to their infants is the temperament of the infant (van den Boom 1994). If this is true then we can envisage a vicious circle where a mother is less sensitive to her difficult infant who then becomes more difficult due to her insensitivity. Nevertheless, the overall major predictor of infant attachment style is the behaviour of the primary caregiver.

carry these early patterns of relating to our caregivers into our adult lives. Our readiness to trust others, the demands we make on others, our fear of rejection or abandonment by others all have their origin in the attachment and separation experiences of our infancy and childhood.

Attachment across the lifespan: internal working models

As a psychiatrist, Bowlby was extremely interested in the effects of childhood experiences on an individual's subsequent psychological development and ultimate mental health. He famously asserted that healthy psychosocial development requires that a child experience a 'warm, intimate, and continuous relationship with his mother (or permanent mother-substitute) in which both find satisfaction and enjoyment' (Bowlby 1959, p. 11).

Bowlby's theory is most fully expressed in his trilogy *Attachment and Loss* (Bowlby 1969; 1973; 1980). A key idea he develops here is that of the 'internal working model' (IWM). This is a personal representation of the world of social relationships that the child constructs on the basis of her early experience with her caregivers. The IWM represents others as more or less trustworthy, dependable, benevolent, accessible and so on. It also represents self in relation to others as deserving, lovable, of value, socially competent and so on. The IWM acts like a lens through which the growing child sees all other relationships, and this influences how she behaves. Although Bowlby talked of the IWM in psychological terms, more recent research indicates that its development corresponds to identifiable (though not necessarily irreversible) physical changes in the brain (see e.g. Schore 2001).

Adult relationships, for example with friends, adult parents, lovers or a spouse, are not attachment relationships, because the element of security-seeking is not dominant. They may involve deep affection or love, and at times, as we have seen, attachment may become a part of them; but they are generally more equal and reciprocal than those of parent and infant (Ainsworth 1993). Nevertheless, we approach these relationships with the IWMs we have established in the context of our early attachment relationships, and they can sometimes wreak havoc.

One aspect of our IWM that seems to be important is that of self-esteem. There is evidence that children who were securely attached as infants and toddlers enter middle childhood with more positive views of themselves and others (Kerns 2008). Conversely, death of a parent in early childhood is a risk factor for the development of depression in later life, with low self-esteem and a sense of failure – 'I couldn't make Mummy stay' – as mediating variables (see e.g. Harris, Brown and Bifulco 1990).

Our assumptions about others are also an important part of our IWM. If I believe people to be inherently untrustworthy, and I form a relationship with a trustworthy man, I may be so insecure and clingy or so controlling that he eventually confirms my assumption by violating my trust. Or I may find intimacy impossibly difficult because I have a working model of the world as a place where my attempts at intimacy are likely to be rejected. Or I may be simply so ravenous for affection that I see every relationship as a possible way of meeting my hunger, but am rejected as 'too high maintenance' by friends or potential lovers who do not want the job of re-parenting another adult.

However, the good news here is that IWMs are not set in stone; understanding ourselves better can be the first step towards modifying our IWMs.

Human resilience: love will find a way

The attachment system turns out to be reasonably flexible. Infants can easily bond to individuals other than the biological mother, and indeed seem to form attachments to more than one familiar individual. This will most often be to father, grandparents or older siblings. In her Ugandan studies Ainsworth noted that infants formed ready attachments to their fathers despite the fact that they saw them relatively infrequently, and she put this down to the *quality* of the interaction, which could often involve 'tenderness or intense delight' (Ainsworth 1967, p. 352). However, the number of attachment figures is not limitless, usually being around three or four, and there is normally a clearly identifiable 'favourite'.

The continuity of the relationship is important, but this doesn't mean that the primary attachment figure has to be available all the time, especially after the age of three years, when children begin to understand and remember the intentions of their caregivers to return following an absence. Repeated contact with an individual who gives high quality care and who appears emotionally invested in the child seems to be the important thing (Cassidy 2008).

It is also the case that adverse experiences in infancy can be ameliorated by later relationships in which a degree of caregiving takes place. Bowlby suggested that mentors, priests, pastors or therapists may often take on this function (Bowlby 1988), and attachment theory is now woven into many psychotherapeutic approaches (e.g. Holmes 2001). A good deal of low-level re-parenting goes on in marriage (Matt. 19.5; Mark 10.7–8), and the role of pets as surrogate attachment figures is beginning to be better understood (Julius, Beetz, Turner, Kotrschal and Uvnäs-Moberg 2013).

Attachment to God

It is perhaps not surprising that psychologists have applied attachment theory to the study of how individuals and communities relate to God. In the 1990s I drew heavily on attachment theory in a book on the Christian basis of self-esteem (McGrath and McGrath 1992/2001), and the same year saw the publication of a seminal article by the psychologist of religion, Lee Kirkpatrick (1992).

Kirkpatrick made it clear that he was not trying to reduce religion to attachment behaviour or to explain God away.[5] Instead he was posing the more subtle question of whether the human attachment system colours our experience of the divine and influences the way we express this in our religious practice. If attachment pervades all our human relationships, it makes sense that it would play a part in our relationship with God.

You make me think of a little child that is learning to stand but does not yet know how to walk. In his desire to reach the top of the stairs to find his mother, he lifts his little foot to climb the first stair. It is all in vain, and at each renewed effort he falls. Well, be this little child: through the practice of all the virtues, always lift your little foot to mount the staircase of holiness, but do not imagine that you will be able to go up even the first step! No, but the good God does not demand more from you than good will. From the top of the stairs, He looks at you with love. Soon, won over by your useless efforts, He will come down Himself and, taking you in His arms, He will carry you up to his kingdom never again to leave him. But if you stop lifting your little foot, He will leave you a long time on the ground.

Thérèse of Lisieux (1873–97)

As soon as attachment is brought into conversation with faith it becomes apparent that this will be a fruitful dialogue. This is rather more true for the Abrahamic religions than for Far Eastern faiths. It is particularly true for Christianity, for our faith story is framed in terms of separation from and reunion with our divine parent. Beginning with the events of Genesis 3 the Bible is saturated with attachment and separation images: the rock of ages (Ps. 27.5; 89.26); the true vine (John 15.5); the mother hen (Matt. 23.37 and Luke 13.34); the Good Shepherd (John 10.4–5); the Prodigal Son who separates himself from the one who could do him good and literally attaches (*kollaomai*) himself to a useless source of security (Luke 15.15). This last example is often presented as a story of a parent and child who have fallen out and become reconciled, whereas it is more fundamentally the story of a parent and child who become separated and are reunited.

Kirkpatrick observed that people of faith try to get close to their God, and they do this by reaching upwards. Mountains are considered sacred, places of worship are tall buildings reaching heavenwards, and worshippers raise their hands aloft in prayer. This is reminiscent of the infant who raises her arms, hoping

---

5 That is, he was not repeating Feuerbach's and Freud's claim that belief in a God who is an idealized version of our own father means that God is nothing but an illusory wish-fulfilment (see e.g. Freud 1928).

to be lifted high out of danger in a secure parental embrace. God is treated as a safe haven who can protect against the perils of this life, but is also a secure base who gives believers confidence to venture out into the world. Christians even address God as 'Father'.

Kirkpatrick also pointed out that faith can intensify at times of crisis (see also Pargament 2001). This, as we have seen, is characteristic of attachment behaviour – when we are in trouble we all tend to reach out to loved ones, and some of us reach out for God. Consider this popular worship song by Brian Doerkson:

Faithful one, so unchanging
Ageless one, You're my rock of peace
Lord of all I depend on You
I call out to You, again and again
I call out to You, again and again

You are my rock in times of trouble
You lift me up when I fall down
All through the storm
Your love is the anchor
My hope is in You alone.[6]

The undoubted connection between attachment and faith led Kirkpatrick to wonder if individual differences in our childhood attachment relationships might be expressed in adult life as individual differences in the way we relate to God. This question has given rise to an enormous body of research across the world that is still in progress (for reviews see Kirkpatrick 2004; Granqvist, Mikulincer and Shaver 2010). The findings are complex, but there seems to be reasonably good support for the theory that divine attachment can work in two ways: our relationship with God can correspond to the secure relationship we experienced with our primary caregivers or our relationship with God can compensate for the insecure relationship we experienced with our primary caregivers.

An individual who has grown up securely attached and who later comes to an adult faith is likely to find in God a warmth, availability and intimacy that *corresponds to* what he enjoyed with his parents as he grew up. If the family is Christian, he will have learnt and internalized Christian teaching. So the head knowledge and the heart knowledge come together. Such individuals often say that they have not had a conversion experience, but that God has always been a presence in their lives who has gradually become more real over the years.

In contrast, an individual who has grown up insecurely attached and who later comes to an adult faith is likely to find in God a warmth, availability and intimacy that *compensates for* what he was denied by his parents as he grew up. The family's teaching may be rejected, because the head and heart knowledge

---

6 © Mercy/Vineyard Publications. Reproduced with permission.

have not come together. Such individuals often report intense and dramatic conversion experiences. (If the family is Christian, the conversion may be to another denomination or sect.) These individuals have a much more emotionally charged faith, with a more vivid sense of gratitude for what they have gained. They come to God more aware of their own neediness.

Something of the quality of this compensation-based spirituality is captured by Joseph Scriven's famous hymn 'What a friend we have in Jesus', one verse of which is reproduced below:

Are we weak and heavy laden, cumbered with a load of care?
Precious Saviour, still our refuge, take it to the Lord in prayer.
Do your friends despise, forsake you? Take it to the Lord in prayer!
In His arms He'll take and shield you; you will find a solace there.

Scriven (1819–86) had a tragic life. He became estranged from his family of origin due in part to his increasing involvement with the Plymouth Brethren. He lost his fiancée to drowning on the night before their wedding and then lost a second fiancée to pneumonia. He was – unsurprisingly – troubled with depression throughout his life and drowned under mysterious circumstances. Yet through all of this, or perhaps because of it, he was clearly a holy man who brought much comfort to others through his ministry of service, and untold comfort to many through the hymn he penned. It touches profound attachment needs.

Reflecting on our own attachment histories

Whenever I teach attachment I find that my students become very emotionally engaged. Sometimes there are tears. We all have our own joyous and painful stories from childhood, and we also want to ensure that we are doing or have done the best for our children. On encountering attachment theory, mothers who have placed their children in day care and fathers who have sent children away to boarding school may feel guilty or get defensive. Those whose teenagers are playing up may wonder if it is their fault for being insensitive when they were babies and toddlers. Women who suffered postnatal depression wonder if they have messed their children up for life by being emotionally unavailable at a key time.

Those who have had a gradual awakening to God with no highly charged conversion experience may feel dull and inferior to those who have had dramatic emotional conversions, wondering if their own faith is just an uncritical replication of that of their parents. Those who have had dramatic conversions may wonder if this is just a sign of their emotional needs.

The key word to notice here is 'just'. I came to my marriage carrying expectations based in my experience of my father, but the relationship is not *just* about that. We come to God with our attachment histories, but the relationship is not *just* about that.

This is primal territory and is bound to call up feelings, but there is little place for blame or guilt here. Understanding my childhood relationship with my mother has helped me to see why, while I am relatively high on E, people often describe me as 'reserved'. It helps me to see that relationships have at times gone wrong for me due to my reserve, and it allows me to consider the possibility of being different with people. It would be quite wrong to blame my mother for this legacy; she had her own backstory, as do we all. Indeed, I perhaps wouldn't enjoy the delights of divine compensation as I do if I wasn't just a bit too self-contained.

Human beings are resilient creatures, and God works by transforming loss to gain. Most children survive the mistakes of their parents and many go on to flourish (Kagan 2013). This can even be true for some very neglected or abused children (though the damage wrought by neglect and abuse should never be minimized). It is helpful in this context to recall Donald Winnicott's famous term 'the good-enough mother' (Winnicott 1957). As we are engaged on a path of conformity to the character of Christ, it is even more important for us to recall that the infancy and childhood of Jesus himself were marked by shame, geographical dislocation, trauma, parental loss and family tensions that, like the wounds of his crucifixion, were gloriously transformed.

Our early relationships do not determine the future course of our lives absolutely. This is because we are not passive recipients of life events. We take the events and do something with them; we make and re-make stories. Sometimes these stories are self-destructive; sometimes they are transformative and redemptive (McAdams 2006).

This is my story: from schema to script

A 'schema' is a mental structure consisting of rules and assumptions by which we represent the world and through which we look at the world. Bowlby's IWM is one sort of schema that focuses on attachment relationships, but an individual will have far more schemas than this. We have schemas about all sorts of things besides attachment; for example we have schemas about the physical nature of the world, which would include assumptions like 'objects always fall downwards'.

It seems that human beings have a strong tendency to express their schemas as scripts (Tomkins 1987). Scripts contain information about *sequences* of events and the causal links that bind these events together to form a chain. So, for example, our ideas of gravity easily cohere around the *story* of Isaac Newton and the falling apple.

Stories have a particular form of script (Bruner 1990). They are organized around a temporal sequence ('once upon a time', 'and then, and then'), moving or pointing towards a perfect completion ('they all lived happily ever after'). Stories refer to particular happenings rather than general ideas. They are highly teleological, featuring protagonists who have agency and choice. They are worth telling because they impart news; they do this by conforming to a convention for the most part but departing from it in certain respects that give the story its point. Stories are told, heard and repeated, and they tend to get elaborated and enriched. Think of the story of a group of wise people who come from the east to visit the infant Jesus in Matthew 2. Over time these have turned into three kings who even have names and particular ethnicities: the Oriental Caspar, the African Balthazar and the European Melchior. This sort of telling, hearing and enriching is a highly social process that is embedded in culture.

Finally, and most importantly, telling and hearing stories make meaning: 'Beyond dispositional traits and characteristic adaptations, human lives vary with respect to the integrative life stories, or personal narratives, that individuals construct to make meaning and identity . . . storytelling shapes self-making' (McAdams and Pals 2006, pp. 209–10).

The psychologist Dan McAdams has written widely on the way our personality is essentially a story that gets told (see e.g. McAdams 1996). It is a story that brings together our temperament, our goals (he refers to these as 'characteristic adaptations' in the above quotation), our aptitudes and character strengths, and the events and relationships that we have experienced. Our story guides us through life and is revised as necessary in the light of events and new situations.

In order to tell our story we need to use our memory.[7] Certain key memories, often to do with attachment, can become 'self-defining' (Singer and Salvoley 1993); Jesus' experience at his baptism, considered in Chapter 3, is an excellent example. Furthermore, our memory is usually 'helped along' by those with whom we share our story. Stories are thus not so much solitary recollections but 'coconstructions' (Pasupathi 2001) that are formed from conversations. The story we tell depends on the occasion, the audience, what questions they ask, which themes seem to interest them, and all sorts of cultural expectations on their and our parts. The question of 'Who am I?' is addressed through a subtle process of negotiation. In the Christian context this seems to be particularly clear in narratives of conversion and vocation. Sometimes acceptance in a Christian community is dependent on a particular sort of conversion testimony. Admittance to the religious life or recognized public ministry is dependent on an oft-rehearsed story shaped around calling.

> Great is the power of memory, an awe-inspiring mystery, my God, a power of profound and infinite multiplicity. And this is mind, this is myself. What then am I, my God? What is my nature? It is characterized by diversity, by life of many forms, utterly immeasurable . . . Here I am climbing up through my mind towards you who are constant above me. I will pass beyond even that power of mind which is called memory, desiring to reach you by the way through which you can be reached, and to be bonded to you buy the way in which it is possible to be bonded.
>
> Augustine of Hippo (354–430)

The fact that stories are socially constructed doesn't at all mean that they are lies, but it does mean that if we aspire to authenticity we should treat our stories as

---

7 This is one reason why dementia can be so devastating: it robs us of the ability to tell our story (Collicutt 2012a).

provisional accounts of ourselves (and most of us have several possible stories that could be told). It can be good for us to have conversations with critical friends from outside our Christian micro-culture, who can offer us an alternative story from the one that may have become comfortable through the consensus of our circle. One of the reasons I value the company of atheists and people of other faiths is the perspective it gives me on my story. It is also important that we tell our story to and with God in prayer. Pilgrimages and silent retreats, where we step away from our familiar social and physical context, can help greatly in this, allowing us to return and re-appropriate our story afresh.

The practice of the *Examen* is also particularly valuable in this respect. This is part of the Ignatian spiritual exercises already mentioned in Chapter 2, though it probably predates Ignatius of Loyola and can be profitably undertaken on its own. It is essentially a way of cultivating attentiveness to the work of God in the world and awareness of how the way we behave can be aligned or at odds with this. It should always be carried out in an attitude of prayer rather than a mental exercise. It begins with giving thanks for the gifts of the day and then moves into a review of the day. This includes reflection on personal motives and feelings, consideration of what habits energized or drained you, how God helped you and how you hindered God from helping you, and a turning to Christ to request transformation of life.

This telling of our own story to ourselves and God reminds us that storytelling is a deeply spiritual activity. Stories touch all the aspects of human spirituality identified on page 5: as we have seen, stories help us in our search for meaning, and faith stories allow us to engage with the sacred. Less obviously, stories can offer us the possibility of transcending our present situation by showing us that things don't have to be the way they are now: we can remember a different and better past or envisage a better future because our story is not yet complete (Williams 1982). God's story is one of liberation; he repeatedly calls his people to remember that story and so have hope for the future. The Prodigal Son seems to do this when he recalls his story as someone who once had bread aplenty in his father's house; it offers him an alternative course of action from just staying put with the pigs (Luke 15.17).

It is then no accident that Jesus told stories and that the 'Christ event' has been transmitted to us through four stories. The fact that God reveals himself through story, and particularly through story that is rich in attachment themes, reflects the way that he accommodates himself to human capacities. More than that, it is a vehicle for his gracious offer of a restored relationship. For we are given the opportunity to be part of God's story, even to co-construct the story in conversation with him. To conform to Christ is not simply a matter of acquiring virtue, important though this is; his story is to become our story and our story his story.

Exercise

Reflect on the following questions:

- As you look back over your life, what would you say were your 'self-defining memories'?
- Think about your relationship with your 'primary caregiver(s)'. Reflect on the gifts you have received and the unhelpful baggage you carry. Offer both back to God.
- What adjectives would you use to describe your intuitive image of God? Do you think this intuitive image relates to your experience with your 'primary caregiver(s)'? How is it different?

Further reading

Bowlby, J., 1988, *A Secure Base: Clinical Applications of Attachment Theory*, London: Tavistock.

Bowlby, J., 2005, *The Making and Breaking of Affectional Bonds*, London: Routledge.

Gallagher, T., 2006, *The Examen Prayer: Ignatian Wisdom for Our Lives Today*, New York: Crossroad.

Hughes, G., 2008, *God of Surprises*, London: Darton, Longman & Todd.

Kirkpatrick, L., 2004, *Attachment, Evolution, and the Psychology of Religion*, New York: Guilford.

Nouwen, H., 1994, *The Return of the Prodigal Son: A Story of Homecoming*, London: Darton, Longman & Todd.

6

How Growth Happens

Now on that same day two of them were going to a village called Emmaus, about seven miles from Jerusalem, and talking with each other about all these things that had happened. While they were talking and discussing, Jesus himself came near and went with them, but their eyes were kept from recognizing him. And he said to them, 'What are you discussing with each other while you walk along?' They stood still, looking sad. Then one of them, whose name was Cleopas, answered him, 'Are you the only stranger in Jerusalem who does not know the things that have taken place there in these days?' He asked them, 'What things?' They replied, 'The things about Jesus of Nazareth, who was a prophet mighty in deed and word before God and all the people, and how our chief priests and leaders handed him over to be condemned to death and crucified him. But we had hoped that he was the one to redeem Israel. Yes, and besides all this, it is now the third day since these things took place. Moreover, some women of our group astounded us. They were at the tomb early this morning, and when they did not find his body there, they came back and told us that they had indeed seen a vision of angels who said that he was alive. Some of those who were with us went to the tomb and found it just as the women had said; but they did not see him.' Then he said to them, 'Oh, how foolish you are, and how slow of heart to believe all that the prophets have declared! Was it not necessary that the Messiah should suffer these things and then enter into his glory?' Then beginning with Moses and all the prophets, he interpreted to them the things about himself in all the scriptures.

As they came near the village to which they were going, he walked ahead as if he were going on. But they urged him strongly, saying, 'Stay with us, because it is almost evening and the day is now nearly over.' So he went in to stay with them. When he was at the table with them, he took bread, blessed and broke it, and gave it to them. Then their eyes were opened, and they recognized him; and he vanished from their sight. They said to each other, 'Were not our hearts burning within us while he was talking to us on the road, while he was opening the scriptures to us?' That same hour they got up and returned to Jerusalem; and they found the eleven and their companions gathered together. They were saying, 'The Lord has risen indeed, and he has appeared to Simon!' Then they told what had happened on the road, and how he had been made known to them in the breaking of the bread.

While they were talking about this, Jesus himself stood among them and said to them, 'Peace be with you.'

Luke 24.13–36

In Chapter 2 we looked at the process of psychological and spiritual growth, and we saw that growth involves becoming more fully ourselves across all aspects of our lives – achieving authenticity and integrity. We considered the importance of having personal goals that are self-concordant and coherent if authentic integrity is to be achieved. For the Christian individual and community, however, authentic integrity is not enough; our authentic integrity must express Christ. The true self to which we aspire is a Christlike self. In Chapter 3 we explored what it might mean to be Christlike (and we will continue to pursue this in Part 3). In Chapter 4 we saw that we each bring different temperamental dispositions, aptitudes and character strengths to this process of becoming more Christlike, and that this is good, reflecting the diversity of creation. In Chapter 5 we saw that we can, and most often do, frame this process as a story. In their tone and style our stories reflect our temperament, aptitudes and character strengths. In their self-defining memories they also incorporate our significant relationships and life events. Above all they incorporate our goals, for they are themselves highly teleological in form: they have to have a point. Stories are, as we have seen, organized around time, but they also have a directional aspect: when someone tells a long, rambling story we may say to ourselves, 'Where is he going with this?'

Here we move into another dimension: that of space. While the life of faith is often conceived as a story with a point, it is equally often conceived as a journey with a destination. The destination is Christ – we are becoming like Christ and are going deeper into Christ – but, as we saw in Chapter 3, the route itself is Christ and, as we saw in Chapter 5, the story of the journey is Christ's. No biblical narrative illustrates this better than that of the Emmaus Road. Here Christ is a travelling companion, critical friend, host and the subject of the discussion. The two disciples are raised to their full stature ('get up'), and they become more like Christ through the telling of their story, which is now also his story. They then meet Christ again at their final destination.

In this chapter we will look at spiritual growth by returning to goals, recalling that the life of faith involves goal-*directed* behaviour; it has a route and destination. So one way of understanding growth is as progress along the route and towards the destination.

Setting out

> [P]rayer consists of attention. It is the orientation of all the attention of which the soul is capable towards God.
>
> Simone Weil (1909–43)

If we are journeying rather than wandering, we need to be facing in the right direction. We need to be facing God-wards. Some people would say that the essence of prayer is the intentional positioning of ourselves so that we face God. The psychologist and spiritual director Barbara Roukema-Koning defines human prayer as '[p]erforming acts which actualize a state of being oriented towards a reality perceived as sacred or ultimate' (2007). This definition captures not only the active nature of prayer, but emphasizes that the doing is aimed at being and that this being is orientated in a particular direction. Prayer is a kind of setting of the compass.

Elsewhere, I have described *Christian* prayer as an 'intentional stance': 'When we pray in Christ's name, we are placing ourselves under his authority and protection and taking up an intentional stance that is in accordance with his nature' (Collicutt 2012b, p. 14).

There is here an attempt to face towards God, so that we can attend to his voice, lift our eyes heavenwards and align ourselves with his purpose. The idea of standing is also important, as it indicates the stretching of the self and rising to the occasion discussed in Chapters 2 and 4. This attitude of facing Godwards can and should be cultivated. It begins with a basic instinct that is closely related to attachment – 'keep your eye on the one who can do you good' – but can develop into a habit of gratitude that sees the current situation as a divine gift, as is the whole of life.

We give thanks to God because, in the words of the Book of Common Prayer, it is 'very meet, right, and our bounden duty'. However, recent research suggests that it may also be in our own interests (Rosmarin, Pirutinsky, Cohen, Galler and Krumrei 2011). Because Christians are called to give thanks to God in all circumstances (1 Thess. 5.18), there are limitless opportunities for us to develop the character strength of gratitude, a strength strongly associated with a sense of well-being (Seligman 2002).

Jesus' habitual practice of setting his compass was to look up to heaven and give thanks or to bless (Collicutt 2012b, p. 26). Prayers of thanksgiving and blessing are essentially an act of attributing events to a good God (Watts 2001). They express faith in God's sovereignty in good times and bad and thus invest life with meaning (Phillips 1965).

Teaching a child to pray 'God bless Mummy . . .', and so on, is therefore not a bad way to set her on the life of faith. Each new day or phase in the Christian life should begin with taking up an attitude of gratitude. This means deciding to look at life in a certain way, not trying to conjure up a certain emotion; for gratitude is not primarily a feeling but a way of construing events (Roberts 2004; 2007, p. 146). It may find expression in the formal Benedictus of traditional Morning Prayer or in more simple words such as those of John O'Donahue: 'I bless the night that nourished my heart . . . All that is eternal in me welcomes the wonder of this day' (O'Donahue 2007, p. 27).

The Sermon on the Mount sets out the way the Christian life is to be orientated and, as already noted in Chapter 3, it begins with a 'position statement'. It is no accident that this position statement takes the form of a hymn of *blessings* (Matt. 5.3–11).

The long and winding road

Thinking of life as a journey along a route to a destination may lead us to wonder about the nature of the route. Images abound: a journey to a peak in the prime of life and then 'over the hill' to a second childhood;[1] an ordered ascent on a ladder or staircase (as in the words attributed to St Thérèse in Chapter 5); the 'straight and narrow'; a circle where the end meets the beginning.

Jesus describes his way as a 'hard' road that leads to life (Matt. 7.14), but says little more than this. However, the Gospels are full of stories of journeying and roads, not least Jesus' own journey to Jerusalem, which he approached in a highly focused, goal-directed way (Luke 9.51). These journeys are very rarely in a straight line; they are full of diversions, there is often some backtracking and, as in the journey to Emmaus, the destination sometimes changes. A key feature of many of these journeys is turning or returning. It is absolutely clear that the way of Christ cannot be followed by setting the compass and then going into automatic-pilot mode. The disciple needs to be constantly alert for twists and turns, and branches that depart from the easy route (Matt. 7.13; see also Exod. 3.3 and Luke 10.31–34).

Perhaps this is why the main image for Christian conversion is that of turning. The verb that is usually translated 'to repent', *metanoeō*, literally means 'to change one's mind', and carries with it a sense of turning away from something. The 'something' is usually not stated,[2] but when it is it seems to refer an immoral or wicked *way* of life (2 Cor. 12.21; Acts 3.26; 8.22). As well as turning away, the New Testament describes conversion as a turning *to* something – *epistrephō*. Again this 'something' is rarely made explicit, but *metanoeō* and *epistrephō* are occasionally combined (Acts 3.19; 26.20), and then it is made clear that the turning is towards God (see also Acts 15.19).

Thou must abhor [Worldly Wiseman's] turning thee out of the way; yea, and thine own consenting thereto; because this is to reject the counsel of God . . . The Lord says, 'Strive to enter in at the straight gate,' the gate to which I send thee; 'for strait is the gate that leadeth unto life, and few there be that find it.' From this little wicket-gate, and from the way thereto, hath this wicked man turned thee, to the bringing of thee almost to destruction: hate, therefore, his turning thee out of the way, and abhor thyself for hearkening to him. Second, Thou must abhor his labouring to render the cross odious unto thee; for thou art to prefer it before the treasures of Egypt.

John Bunyan (1628–88)

---

1 This is Shakespeare's image in the famous speech that begins 'All the world's a stage, And all the men and women merely players.' *As you like it.* Act II, Scene VII.

2 In the light of traditional Christian baptismal promises it is particularly noteworthy that the phrase 'repent of sins' is not to be found in the New Testament.

This turning from and to is perhaps most characteristic of dramatic conversion, but in a more subtle way it is part of the ongoing Christian life (Luke 17.4; Gal. 4.9). When Jesus describes people as having faith, it is always because they have turned to him with a trusting attitude (Matt. 8.10; 9.2, 22, 29; 15.28 and parallels; Luke 7.50; 17.19). So coming to faith involves turning, and the life of faith involves continual turning. Sometimes this is a small turn, sometimes it is 180 degrees back the way we came, as with the Road to Emmaus and the Return of the Prodigal. In this case some remembering of the place we have left or the person we have been is part of the process. But when we return we find that the situation we left, or the person we were, is the same but different. We don't and can't replicate it; instead we re-appropriate it in a new way.

This is perhaps what Jesus is referring to in his conversation with Nicodemus (John 3.1–8) when he talks of a spiritual birth that is like but not like our natural birth, and elsewhere when he makes the demand that his followers become *as* a little child (Matt. 10.15 and parallels). It seems then that the trajectory of the life of faith has something of the spiral about it. Images of straight roads and ladders do not do it justice. A spiral staircase might be nearer the mark, but it would have to be highly convoluted. Perhaps the image of a three-dimensional labyrinth[3] is the nearest we can get.

This spiral motion fits quite well with some influential contemporary secular models of psychological development, which see it as recursive. These understand child cognition as proceeding through a series of stages; as the end of one stage is reached movement to the next can only occur by reworking of the present stage in the light of the next and carrying it forward in a new way. This going back and reworking thus integrates one stage into the next (Case and Okamoto 1996; Fischer and Bidell 1998).

Faith development is not like child cognitive development to the extent that it does not seem to proceed in a sequence of identifiable stages that occur in an invariant order. It is a much more variable and less ordered animal. But it is like child cognitive development in terms of the *processes* that are at work (Coyle 2011), some of which will be considered in more detail shortly. Returning to the old in the light of the new seems to be one of these processes. In a more philosophical context this has been described as a 'second naïveté' (Ricoeur 1967).

It is obvious that turning and returning entail a change of direction. This brings with it a change in perspective. Turning means looking at things differently:

> For this people's heart has grown dull, and their ears are hard of hearing, and they have shut their eyes; so that they might not look with their eyes, and listen with their ears, and understand with their heart and turn (*epistrephō*) – and I would heal them. (Matt. 13.15/Isa. 6.10)

---

3 The spirituality of the labyrinth, whose origins are very ancient, has made something of a comeback in recent years. For more details, see Bloos and O'Connor 2002 and Welch 2013.

As this rather disturbing passage indicates, changing perspective – and therefore turning – does not come easily. The ability to see things from an alternative perspective is something that is achieved relatively late by the developing child. The Swiss psychologist and epistemologist Jean Piaget (1896–1980) famously described young children as egocentric. He did not mean by this that children have a moral difficulty in being unselfish, but that they have a cognitive difficulty in seeing that there is any view other than their own. In order to see alternative perspectives we have to be able to carry out mental rotations and transformations, and this makes too many demands on the capacities of the young child. For example, when my nephew was about three or four years old, he could tell me that he had a sister but he just wasn't sure if his sister had a brother or indeed who that might be.

The experiment on which Piaget based his conclusion that children are egocentric is called the 'three mountain experiment' (Piaget and Inhelder 1948/1956). The child sits in front of a three-dimensional model of three mountains. A doll is placed in various positions in relation to the scene; the child is then shown a number of pictorial views of the scene as if from various angles, and is asked which one corresponds to what the doll can see. Piaget and Inhelder found that children below the ages of eight or nine tended to choose the picture that corresponded to their view rather than the doll's.

Like many of Piaget's experiments, this has been repeated under more carefully controlled conditions and it has been found that children younger than eight can then succeed at the task (Borke 1975). *Given the right conditions*, even children as young as four appear to be able to understand not only that there may be more than one visual perspective on a scene but that different people may hold different beliefs about a situation (see e.g. Wimmer and Permer 1983). However, as with most of Piaget's work, the basic point about how human beings think remains secure. Often we do not have the right conditions to transcend egocentricity: when our capacities are limited by illness or fatigue, when the social and linguistic demands are too great, or out of sheer laziness we default to an egocentric setting. This seems to be particularly the case when we feel anxious, vulnerable and threatened (Savage and Boyd-MacMillan 2010). While children may be rather less egocentric than Piaget originally thought, it seems that adults are often *more* egocentric than he had hoped (Royzman, Cassidy and Baron 2003). We may need help in transcending egocentricity. We can, nevertheless, also help ourselves.

Turning around

We can set up conditions that make it more likely for us to see alternative perspectives. Most obviously we can seek a different physical perspective through a holiday, pilgrimage or retreat. However, shifting perspective is also a basic aspect of the practice of prayer. In this section we briefly consider two types of prayer that assist in the turning process: intercession and mindful contemplation.

Intercessory prayer, for people known to us or for the situation facing the wider world, shifts the spotlight of our attention. It's the mental equivalent to 'getting out more'. We can do this in an intentional way by reading the stories of individuals and communities who are in need across the globe and by trying to align ourselves with their perspective for a while. Prayer letters and diaries are hugely helpful here, but the daily newspaper should not be overlooked; reading the newspaper can be a spiritual activity.

This turning outwards isn't simply a psychological technique for self-improvement, it is fundamental to the nature of intercessory prayer. The primary meaning of the Greek word *entugchanō*, usually translated 'to intercede', is 'to turn'. When we pray for others we turn outwards and take their perspective, and then we turn again, bringing them with us in a Godward movement (Ramsey 2008, p. 14), joining in with a movement of the Spirit (Rom. 8.27) and the risen Christ (Heb. 7.25). This has quite a different feel from asking God to do something (though there is of course a place for this).

Intercessions can also be made in a spirit of gratitude. On page xx we encountered the Ignatian practice of the *Examen* and noted that it always begins with an act of thanksgiving. Several writers have drawn connections between Ignatian spirituality and positive psychology, particularly in the area of cultivating gratitude (Zagano and Gillespie 2006; Carson 2013). Focusing on the strengths of others helps us to pray for them in an appreciative as well as a compassionate way. This is also true for ourselves. We can shift our perspective on a situation quite effectively and simply by counting blessings rather than rehearsing burdens (Emmons and McCullough 2003), and these blessings include our natural character strengths: 'God I thank you that you have given X the strength of kindness and that you have given me the strength of creativity for use in the service of your kingdom' is a long way from 'God I thank you that I am better than X in the following ways . . .' (cf. Luke 18.11–12).

Contemplative prayer offers the opportunity for a different kind of turning: the reappraisal of our position, a kind of resetting of the compass. It does this through its embrace of mindfulness. We will look at mindfulness in much more detail in Chapter 9; here it is sufficient to note that it involves an intentional turning aside from our normal ways of thinking and doing. There is for a while a letting go of engagement with goal-directed striving and a moving into the paratelic mode of being in the present moment. Mindfulness runs like a thread through the Christian contemplative tradition, particularly evident in the way that the Jesus Prayer became incorporated into the practice of using the whole body in Christian meditation from the fourth century onwards. In mindful contemplative prayer there is an emphasis on pausing to receive God rather than striving to follow his way, something more in keeping with the image of the healthy plant than the fit body.

A mindful attitude allows the individual to be a critical friend to himself, freeing him from the uncritical friendship of self that leads to complacency and the critical enmity with self that leads to depression. As noted on page xx, depression is associated with over-rigid and overly high investment in certain goals, and a consequent vulnerability to feelings of disappointment, failure and entrapment. Mindfulness enables progress towards goals to be appraised in a more detached manner. This perhaps explains why mindfulness – removed from its faith context – has become an important component of the psychological treatments recommended for depression (Segal, Williams and Teasdale 2013; NICE 2009); it can loosen the ties to the perspectives that bind us.

Turning is an important part of mindfulness in the therapeutic context. Individuals are encouraged to break the habit of turning away from pain or fear and instead to turn towards it and greet it – to 'turn turn toward and approach painful experiences with kindness' (Segal, Williams and Teasdale, 2013, p. 292). One interesting and perhaps unexpected result of this seems to be a turning outwards from self so that the perspectives of others are taken on more readily (Condon, Desbordes, Miller, DeSteno 2013).

Where contemplative prayer is truly mindful, setting aside preoccupations with evaluative judgements about self and others, it can put the right conditions in place for turning from a settled way of seeing ourselves, the world and God.

So sometimes we may be highly engaged with the needs and qualities of others through intercessory prayer; at other times it will be right for us to disengage from this and float free in contemplative prayer for a while. Both types of prayer help in the process of turning and shifting perspective. Intercession helps shift the perspective from me to others; contemplative prayer raises my eyes to the horizon and so shifts the focus from this part of the journey to its ultimate destination in God, allowing me to re-evaluate my priorities in its light.

In the life of faith such shifts in perspective are often achieved gradually and slowly, as the turning of a great cruise liner opens up new vistas little by little. This is what seems to be happening to the blind man in Mark 8.24 and the (same?) man born blind in John 9. However, sometimes we experience shifts in perspective that are so sudden and extreme that it is appropriate to refer to them as epiphanies. This describes well what happens to Cleophas and his companion at the breaking of the bread. Epiphanies are one kind of self-defining memory, significant markers along the way of life, and it is therefore worth exploring them further.

Epiphanies: seeing things differently

The psychologist and philosopher James Pawelski sees epiphany as a general class of experience that might be divisible into a number of types:

> sudden intuitions that burst into our normal, everyday experience like revelations. They carry with them a sense of clarification, which seems to allow us to understand things in their true nature. Such epiphanies are like bolts of lightning on a dark night that brilliantly illuminate everything in a single, instantaneous flash. There are many different kinds of epiphanies. They can be religious, philosophical, romantic, aesthetic, or of some other type. (Pawelski 2007, p. 135)

One of these other types is the epiphany of the scientist:

> Faith . . . emerges through a process of enlightenment that enables the disciple to see things in a new way. The religious model of faith is thus not so . . . very different from the experience of a great scientist (Charles Darwin again comes to mind) who has all the facts at his or her disposal and comes to see in them something that has been missed by others. These insights often feel

inexplicably 'given' – epiphanies – rather than consciously attained intellectual objectives. (Collicutt 2008a)

The most systematic empirical work on epiphanic experiences has been conducted by the clinical psychologists William Miller and Janet C'de Baca, whose interest in this area arose from their work with people recovering from alcohol dependence. In a series of interview and questionnaire studies on a sample of the healthy general public they were able to delineate the circumstances and characteristics of these experiences, together with their perceived consequences in the lives of those who underwent them (Miller and C'de Baca 1994; 2001). Miller and C'de Baca actually use the term 'quantum change' to describe what they intriguingly call the 'landscape'; this covers a group of experiences that are extraordinary, surprising, vivid, discontinuous with everyday experience, benevolent in tone, call up profound emotion and seem to open a 'one way door' to a changed way of life (p. 17).

Within this experiential landscape two main types of quantal change emerge. The first is an utterly new way of thinking about a problem or issue that comes in an 'Aha' moment and carries with it a profound conviction of truth. This seems similar to the sorts of insights people sometimes achieve in the context of counselling and psychotherapy (see also Watts and Williams 1988, pp. 70–4). A classic description of this sort of insight in a religious context is given by John Wesley, with its clear allusion to the Emmaus Road:

> In the evening I went very unwillingly to a society in Aldersgate Street, where one was reading Luther's preface to the Epistle to the Romans. About a quarter before nine, while he was describing the change which God works in the heart through faith in Christ, I felt my heart strangely warmed. I felt I did trust in Christ, Christ alone, for salvation; and an assurance was given me that He had taken away my sins, even mine, and saved me from the law of sin and death. (John Wesley (1738))

The second type of quantal change is more mystical in character. In his Gifford Lectures, William James (1842–1910) described the 'four marks of mystical experience'[4] as 'ineffability' – defying expression and description; 'noetic quality' – giving a sense of revelation of the truth; 'transiency' – not sustainable for long and not extendable at will,[5] and 'passivity' – not biddable but more like a gift (James 1902, pp. 380–2). James thought that such experiences are relatively common, but they only become significant in exceptional cases when an individual incorporates the experience into his life with a resulting change in behaviour. Miller's

---

4 James' approach, which treats mysticism as a universal psychological phenomenon, has subsequently been criticized as insufficiently contextual (see Nelstrop, Magill and Onishi 2009, pp. 1–20, for a helpful account). However, the evidence is strongly supportive of his general position (Hood, Hill and Spilka 2009, p. 262).

5 Notice how the disciples on the Road to Emmaus beg Jesus to stay but cannot in the end hold him.

and C'de Baca's research indicates that this happens more frequently than James supposed. In what follows I use the term 'epiphany' to refer to both the insightful and the mystical quantum changes identified by Miller and C'de Baca.

One of the features of epiphanies is a kind of 'joining up of the dots', a seeing of links between oneself and the universe and between different aspects of the universe. This infuses the whole experience, and indeed life itself, with great significance. This integration may seem to come out of nowhere (as in August Kekulé's famous dream, which led to his discovery of the ring structure of the benzene molecule), or it can be helped along by insights offered by another person. This is precisely what Jesus does on the Emmaus road as he systematically sets out for the disciples connections between the events of Holy Week and the Hebrew Scriptures.

This joining up of the dots experience indicates that our schemas[6] are reorganizing themselves and connecting with each other. This can happen at any point in the lifespan, but it is particularly characteristic of adolescence. Throughout childhood the individual's schemas are becoming more differentiated and sophisticated. As she enters her teens she becomes ready to bring separate schemas together to form a more abstract and integrated way of seeing and being in the world. This involves the application of 'formal operational thinking' (Inhelder and Piaget 1958), and also her rapidly developing competence in more social and practical thinking (Staudinger and Pasupathi 2003).

These cognitive changes happen at the same time as the young person's body undergoes dramatic changes and the prospect of approaching adulthood comes ever closer. This is a liminal place. The young person is naturally disposed to try to make sense of her life so far and to set herself up for the future by searching for an overarching script or framework. This might be philosophical, scientific, romantic or religious. The process of latching on to this script or framework is often marked by the experience of epiphanies: 'Suddenly everything fits together!'

It is during adolescence that we achieve the cognitive wherewithal to ask big existential questions: 'Who am I?' (cf. Luke 2.49); 'Am I worth anything?'; 'What is the right way to live?'; 'Does life have any meaning or purpose, and is this purpose benevolent – is there hope?' (Baumeister and Muraven 1996). These questions are returned to and reworked periodically for the rest of our lives (Baumeister 1992), especially at liminal periods such as childbirth or retirement; and the reworking may well be punctuated by epiphanies: 'Suddenly everything fits together in a new way!'

Miller's and C'de Baca's research on adults indicates that their epiphanies often arose in the context of a background of trauma or desperate personal circumstances (see also Lambert, Stillman and Fincham 2013), and indeed the adolescent search for significance may be intensified by trauma, loss or adversity (see e.g. Batten and Oltjenbruns 1999). Such experiences prompt a very particular existential question: 'If the world is the way I thought, how could *this* happen?' – precisely the issue that was troubling the pair on the Emmaus Road.

---

6 Recall from Chapter 5 that these are mental structures consisting of rules and assumptions by which we represent the world and through which we look at the world.

Reorientation through disorientation

To explain the connection between trauma and epiphanies we need to recall that epiphanies are a sign of schema reorganization. During childhood and adolescence schemas are relatively fluid and adaptable. As we enter adulthood we tend to settle on a view of the world and to take up a settled place in the world; our schemas become more fixed.

In many ways this is healthy. We couldn't get on with our lives and meet all our responsibilities in the adult world of work if we were stopping all the time to agonize about life's big questions or inhabiting a Walter Mitty world of alternative possibilities for ourselves. But there is no doubt that we lose something in the process:

> For children many experiences are new, and every day can be an adventure. As adulthood is reached . . . the opportunity for . . . major schema reorganization in response to anomalous, strange, or intriguing experience in everyday life is reduced . . . life becomes less exciting but more predictable and secure. Much can be done on 'automatic pilot', and therefore much can be done. (Collicutt 2009b, p. 94)

In his account of child cognitive development Piaget identified two key processes. The first is 'assimilation', where the child masters the world by fitting it into her existing schemas (for example, 'It's OK to cut hair because it always grows back'). The second is 'accommodation', where the child changes her existing schemas in the light of her encounter with the realities of the world (for example 'Oh dear! Dolls' hair doesn't grow back'). Piaget held that child cognition advances through the interplay of these two processes in adaptive balance. However, once our adult schemas are settled there is far less need for us to accommodate ourselves to the world; we operate largely in assimilation mode. This makes us naturally resistant to turning and changing perspective.

This is where trauma comes in. It forces adults into accommodation mode. The developing child's constant accommodation to the realities of the world mean that his life is punctuated by many mini-traumas as his provisional schemas reach their limits: he is often in tears. The fundamental nature of adult psychological trauma is similar but more dramatic: it shatters *well-established* schemas (Janoff-Bulman 1992). The things we believed to be true, our grounds for hope, our assumptions about the way the world works are, like the twin towers of 9/11, at one fell swoop lying in pieces at our feet.

Trauma thus has the capacity to destroy us, and there is no doubt that many people who have experienced trauma suffer severe and lifelong mental health problems (Gradus, Qin, Lincoln, Miller, Lawler, Sørensen and Lash 2010). Nevertheless, most people seem able to regroup following one-off trauma in adult life and, most interesting of all, some people show significant psychological growth in the aftermath of trauma (see e.g. Linley and Joseph 2004; Joseph 2009). In a landmark book entitled *Trauma and Transformation*, Richard Tedeschi and Lawrence Calhoun labelled this phenomenon 'post-traumatic growth' and asserted that its first principle is that of schema change (Tedeschi and Calhoun 1995, p. 78). Schemas are shattered by trauma but, given the right conditions, this can be an opportunity for the pieces to be reconstructed into a view of reality that does it far better justice than what went before.

Tedeschi and Calhoun (1995) trace the process of post-traumatic growth through a number of phases. First there is the event and a response of unmanageable distress, incomprehension and ineffective action. Then follows a period of rumination about the event, with much questioning of existing schemas. During this phase the support of others is crucial; they offer solidarity and can be the source for alternative perspectives. If all goes well, the event starts to become comprehensible in terms of revised or new schemas connected with existing beliefs; emotions feel manageable, and effective action re-emerges.

Here we find that we are back again on the Emmaus Road. Two people are fleeing the scene of a trauma that has shattered their hopes for the redemption of Israel. They are ruminating together on the events when they are joined by a stranger who offers both the solidarity of fellowship on the way and an alternative perspective that can pick up the pieces and connect everything together. Then they experience an epiphany that leaves them energized and full of hope. They see things differently, and they turn.

Tedeschi and Calhoun suggest that, as well as the initial growth, there is also a longer-term phase of internalization of what has been learnt into a life narrative: 'Growth occurs when the trauma assumes a central place in the life story' (1995, p. 85). This story will be marked by wisdom and the kind of hope that takes human suffering and limitation into account. Central to this is the embrace of paradox.

We too have turned and returned to Chapter 3, where I described Jesus as the master of paradox who embodies transformation. Progress along his way involves setting our compass Godwards and embracing gratitude, being open to new perspectives, taking the time to reset our compass, and realizing that our greatest leaps forward may happen during liminal periods or in the aftermath of trauma and adversity. As the way is full of twists and turns a leap forward is rather more like spinning around. There may well be massive disorientation before reorientation happens (Brueggemann 2002) and, while this is going on, we may feel sick at heart.

The largely secular psychology of child and adult development that we have touched on in this chapter is perhaps more in accord with the way of Christ than we might have expected. There is, for example, acknowledgement that the transformation of suffering is one way – perhaps the only real way – to life. There is also an acknowledgement that we should not travel this way alone. What is understandably missing from such secular approaches is the recognition that the way of life leads to God and that our travelling companion must be the risen Christ. He is the one who, through the Spirit, and sometimes unrecognized, sets us aright when we take a wrong turn, opens our eyes to see things differently, joins up the dots for us when things don't make sense, picks us up when we fall down, and holds us when the process of turning makes us dizzy. He is the one who breaks bread with us, and at the end greets us with the words 'Peace be with you.'

Christ be with me, Christ within me,
Christ behind me, Christ before me,
Christ beside me, Christ to win me,
Christ to comfort and restore me.
Christ beneath me, Christ above me,
Christ in quiet, Christ in danger,
Christ in hearts of all that love me,
Christ in mouth of friend and stranger.

Attributed to Patrick (fifth century),
translated Cecil Frances Alexander

Exercises

1 A popular exercise that has come out of the positive psychology movement is that of the 'gratitude letter'. Think back over your recent or distant
life to someone who has helped you but whom you never really thanked
(for example, a teacher, youth leader, a family member or just a friend or
acquaintance). Sit down and write them a thank-you letter. This will help
you develop an attitude of gratitude, but the evidence also shows that
people are delighted to receive such letters, partly because it shows them
in tangible form that they have made a difference in this life.

2 Repeat the exercise from Chapter 4 on becoming aware of and exploring
a character strength, but this time apply it to someone you know. Apply
your knowledge by giving thanks for this person in prayer and/or finding
an opportunity to express your appreciation directly to him/her.

3 Try and draw a trajectory for your life of faith, placing markers signifying
epiphanies, encounters with wise guides, and so on along the way. Reflect
on how far back you had to go to find the beginning and the shape your
journey has taken so far.

4 Go on a 'prayer walk', stopping at various points to offer up a silent prayer
for the place you have paused. Reflect on the change in perspective you
have experienced. If, for whatever reason, walking is difficult, try doing this
in imagination.

Further reading

Brueggemann, W., 2007, *Praying the Psalms: Engaging Scripture and the Life of the Spirit*, Eugene, OR: Cascade Books.

Lewis, C. S., 2009, *The Horse and His Boy*, London: HarperCollins.

Loder, J., 1989, *The Transforming Moment*, Colorado Springs, CO: Helmers & Howard.

Thompson, J. and Thompson, R., 2012, *Mindful Ministry: Creative, Practical and Theological Perspectives*, London: SCM Press, pp. 23–44.

Welch, S., 2011, *Every Place is Holy Ground: Prayer Journeys through Familiar Places*, Norwich: Canterbury Press.

PART 3

Cultivating the Fruit of the Spirit

Live by the Spirit, I say, and do not gratify the desires of the flesh. For what the flesh desires is opposed to the Spirit, and what the Spirit desires is opposed to the flesh; for these are opposed to each other, to prevent you from doing what you want. But if you are led by the Spirit, you are not subject to the law. Now the works of the flesh are obvious: fornication, impurity, licentiousness, idolatry, sorcery, enmities, strife, jealousy, anger, quarrels, dissensions, factions, envy, drunkenness, carousing, and things like these. I am warning you, as I warned you before: those who do such things will not inherit the kingdom of God.

By contrast, the fruit of the Spirit is love, joy, peace, patience, kindness, generosity, faithfulness, gentleness, and self-control. There is no law against such things. (Galatians 5.16–23)

The image of spiritual fruit is used by Paul in his letter to the Galatians in order to contrast the life of faith with two alternatives. The first is life under the law. The Christian's habits and rules for living flow naturally from her new identity in Christ through the action of the Spirit. In contrast, the individual who is still operating under the law has habits and rules for living that are attempts to maintain identity through keeping a code. These rules and habits are then, says Paul, contrived works (Gal. 3.5), no longer necessary now that Christ has come (Gal. 3.24). They might be morally worthy, but if they do not flow from a relationship of trust with Christ they are ultimately futile.

This account of life in the Spirit versus life under the law is summarized in Figure 13. The figure does not feature Paul's language of Judaism, circumcision and *Torah*, but instead uses generic language. This is because I understand Paul's criticism of the Judaism of his day to be a special case of a general criticism of religion (a point to which we shall return in Chapter 11).

Figure 13.

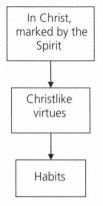 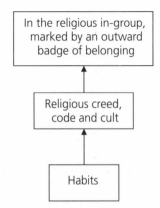

The second alternative with which the life of faith is contrasted is life 'in the flesh' (see Figure 14). In the New Testament the word translated 'flesh' (*sarx*) is sometimes used to mean human nature in a relatively neutral sense, but more often it refers to the lower or darker side of human nature, and this is how Paul uses it in Galatians. In this context the important thing is the *moral valence* of the rules and habits. The fruit of the Spirit are clearly good. The works of the flesh are bad. Note that, as with the law, these are works and not fruit, indicating that Paul sees them as in some sense unnatural. Ironically it is as if the utterly human life of the flesh is actually less than human, an impoverished or *unnatural* life. To quote Alan Bennett, 'when people say they are only human, it's because they have been making beasts of themselves'.[1]

Life in the Spirit, on the other hand, is genuinely human (Wright 2010, p. 27), because this is the Spirit of *Christ*, the only truly human being (1 Cor. 15.21, 45). So Paul's famous list of the fruit of the Spirit – which is indicative rather than exhaustive – is used in the context of an argument in which he is repudiating two opposite extremes: the futility of a type of religiosity that emphasizes dogma and practice at the expense of a relationship of trust with God *and* the destructiveness of a moral licentiousness that promotes hedonism and 'doing what comes naturally' whatever the cost to others.[2]

Here, as throughout his letters, Paul is walking something of a tightrope. He is emphasizing that as we turn to Christ in faith we will naturally be disposed through the Spirit to develop Christlike virtues, and that one of the things that Christ has freed us from is the oppression of rule-bound religion. But he is also aware, apparently from bitter experience, that we need to keep turning or we may slip back into the destructive habits of the flesh. We need discernment to

Figure 14.

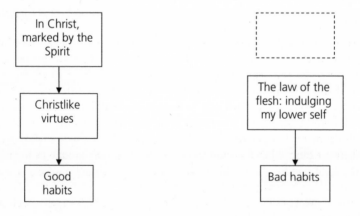

---

1 Alan Bennett and Malcolm Mowbray, 1984, *A Private Function*, Handmade Films.

2 In Chapters 7 and 8 of his letter to the Romans, Paul elaborates his argument, at points coming close to identifying the law with the flesh in a way that need not detain us here.

perceive which virtues to embrace and which habits to foster, and we need discipline to carry this through:

> Theologically speaking, Christian formation is the work of the grace of God. Practically speaking it requires the intentional care of pastoral leadership and the willingness of the believer to allow God's grace to be transforming. The constant exhortation throughout [the New Testament epistles] attests to the challenge that Christian formation poses to other lifestyles. Christian excellence requires concentration of mind and heart. (Charry 1997, p. 53)

This tension between allowing an organic and ultimately mysterious process to do its work and taking some responsibility for helping it along seems to me to be well summed up in the phrase 'cultivating the fruit of the Spirit'. This paints a picture of formation as a kind of horticultural or perhaps agricultural pursuit in which, like the flourishing plant, we bear fruit, but also, like the fit body, actively participate in the enterprise.

The *process* of cultivation is as important as its outcome for, as we saw in Chapter 6, Christian growth happens along the way to the destination. The psychologist of religion Kenneth Pargament captures this point well when he defines religious spirituality as 'the search for significance in ways related to the sacred' (2001, p. 32); the *way* that the search for ultimate meaning is conducted is what make the quest distinctive. At the very least this means that our attempts at cultivation should be prayerful attempts.

In the following chapters we will look in turn at the nine core characteristics of Jesus identified in Chapter 3, and for each of them articulate some rules and practices that may help foster conformity to this aspect of his character – help in cultivating this particular fruit. As we are all different, a good degree of self-awareness, informed and enhanced by some of the material from Part 2 of this book, will be important in guiding how we apply this material.

However, working on developing self-awareness should never turn into an exercise in navel-gazing. Its purpose is to enable us to place our properly identified resources at the disposal of God, and to pay attention to aspects of our individual and corporate personalities that habitually get in the way of God. As a counterpoint to the practice of self-awareness we should recall that the research on mindfulness tells us that too much self-awareness can sometimes be a bad thing, dragging us downwards or inwards so that we cease to see the bigger picture. There are times when it is more appropriate for the left hand to be unaware of what the right hand is doing (Matt. 6.3). An excessively self-conscious attitude to formation can be one of the things that gets in the way of God. The American children's writer Laura Ingalls Wilder (1867–1957) puts this rather well in one of her autobiographical novels:

> I don't believe we ought to think so much about ourselves, about whether we are bad or good . . . . – it isn't so much thinking, as – as just knowing. Just being sure of the goodness of God. (Ingalls Wilder (1941), pp. 11–12)

Connected with this, it will be important to recall that Christian formation is a corporate endeavour. Individual rules of life and habitual practices take place in the broader context of a community. The individual should be attentive to the well-being of this community as well as to his own, and should also be aware of the way that the community helps or hinders him and others in the life of faith.

Steven Sandage helpfully suggests five characteristics of a community that is likely to foster healthy Christian formation (Sandage 2006). First, formation is passed on through the medium of relationships, so the community leaders need to recognize this in the ethos they promote. Second, formation is facilitated through good quality 'apprenticeships' with mentors, teachers and spiritual guides, and such relationships should be encouraged and monitored. Third, the community may be treated as an attachment figure, and it should therefore be able both to hold and to let go. Fourth, transformation is best supported within a community culture that wisely and intentionally faces contradiction and encourages change. Finally, these processes of formation and transformation are best rooted in communities that remain in place in a generative rather than stagnant way, so that they can be a continuing resource for the revisiting the old in the light of the new, as discussed in Chapter 6.

Bearing all this in mind, we now move on to consider material that I hope will help us in the main task of formation: the imitation of Christ.

Further reading

Plante, T., 2012, *Religion, Spirituality, and Positive Psychology: Understanding the Psychological Fruits of Faith*, Santa Barbara, CA: Praeger.

7

Intimacy with the Holy Other:
Taking the Lord's Prayer Seriously

He said to them, 'When you pray, say: Father.'

Luke 11.2a

And because you are children, God has sent the Spirit of his Son into our hearts, crying, 'Abba! Father!'

Galatians 4.6

For you did not receive a spirit of slavery to fall back into fear, but you have received a spirit of adoption. When we cry, 'Abba! Father!' it is that very Spirit bearing witness with our spirit that we are children of God.

Romans 8.15–16

For this reason Jesus is not ashamed to call them brothers and sisters, saying, 'I will proclaim your name to my brothers and sisters, in the midst of the congregation I will praise you.' And again, 'I will put my trust in him.' And again, 'Here am I and the children whom God has given me.' Since, therefore, the children share flesh and blood, he himself likewise shared the same things . . . For it is clear that he did not come to help angels, but the descendants of Abraham. Therefore he had to become like his brothers and sisters in every respect.

Hebrews 2.11b–14a, 16–17a

The first aspect of Christ's character that we are called to emulate is his intimacy with the Holy Other – the God whose name cannot be spoken and who identifies himself only as 'I AM WHO I AM' (Exod. 3.14). In this area of formation, cultivating is strongly bound up with realizing: we need to realize that we are the beloved children of this God if we are to cultivate an intimate relationship with him; conversely, intentionally relating to God as our good parent will help us to realize that he is just that.

This is something of a tall order, to put it mildly; after all, we're only human (with a disturbing tendency to make beasts of ourselves), and God is God. The first thing to realize, then, is that it is precisely because we are *only* human that the eternal logos became *fully* human in Jesus of Nazareth. In doing this he not only showed that human beings can be intimate with God, but restored the conditions for this intimacy.

We are made in the image of God (Gen. 1.26), created to be in relationship with him, and our turning to him is, like the turning of the Prodigal Son, a kind of remembering of this; an attraction to someone to whom we already have a deep, if unconscious, connection. One way of understanding the work of Christ is as reminding us of something we had forgotten, a retrieval and reclamation of our true story.

> For God, the Creator of the universe and King of all, who is beyond all being and human thought, since He is good and bountiful, has made humanity in his own image through his own Word, our Saviour Jesus Christ; and He also made humanity perceptive and understanding of reality through its similarity to Him . . . [to] rejoice and converse with God, living an idyllic and truly blessed and immortal life. For having no obstacle to the knowledge of the divine, it could continuously contemplate in its purity the image of the Father, God the Word, in whose image it was made, and could be filled with admiration in grasping divine providence towards the universe.
>
> Athanasius of Alexandria (298–373)

As we saw in Chapter 3, Jesus repeatedly did exactly this – reminded his followers that they were children of God and exhorted them to behave as if they were. This seems to be an enormously presumptive claim, but Jesus makes it easier for us to grasp by taking an indirect approach.

Jesus our brother

As he went about Galilee, Jesus proclaimed a straightforward message of the Fatherhood of God, encapsulated in the words of the prayer that he gave his followers; but he also approached this idea obliquely via the related message of the 'Jesus brotherhood'. Jesus' followers are his brethren:

> While he was still speaking to the crowds, his mother and his brothers were standing outside, wanting to speak to him. Someone told him, 'Look, your mother and your brothers are standing outside, wanting to speak to you.' But to the one who had told him this, Jesus replied, 'Who is my mother, and who are my brothers?' And pointing to his disciples, he said, 'Here are my mother and my brothers! For whoever does the will of my Father in heaven is my brother and sister and mother.' (Matthew 12.46–50)

It is somewhat easier to see Jesus as our big brother than to see God as our Father. For a start, it's just easier to see Jesus, because no one has ever seen God (John 1.18). It is also easier to form an attachment relationship to a flesh and blood human being who has come close to us than to an invisible transcendent God. Recall that attachment is expressed in proximity seeking; so at its most basic level this simply means turning to or reaching out to Christ.

In the discussion of attachment theory in Chapter 5 we saw that younger siblings often form attachment relationships to older siblings. This is a pattern that could be identified in child evacuees and refugees in the aftermath of the Second World War, when attachment theory was beginning to develop. Later research confirmed that an older sibling can be a very effective attachment figure. We see this today with a new generation of children in Africa orphaned by AIDS, famine and war: if you stick close to an older sibling, there's a good chance you'll be all right.

Once we are prepared to entertain the idea of Jesus as our big brother, the next step is to realize that Jesus is God's beloved son, who himself enjoys a secure attachment relationship with his divine parent. As we have seen, a sense of deep intimacy with God based around secure attachment is something that seems to have pervaded Jesus' life. After his death the first Christians, if not already convinced, now saw his resurrection as irrefutable proof of this identity (Rom. 1.3).

If Jesus is God's son, it is then simple logic that we, his brethren, are ourselves children of God. This is a highly intuitive and plausible notion. Several years ago my niece, aged seven at the time, interrupted an agnostic adult conversation about the afterlife with the words, 'I know I'm going to heaven, because my aunty is a personal friend of Jesus – so there!' She understood that it's your connections that count.

Because Jesus is fully human, we can claim him as our brother, as the extracts from Hebrews 2 at the beginning of this chapter indicate. We don't have to make the audacious claim that God is our Father; Jesus has done that for himself. Our attachment to Jesus means that God's parenthood is automatically conferred on us.

Intentionally focusing on the fact that Jesus is our brother is one way that we can remember that we are children of God.

The brotherhood of Christ also starts to show us how we can let God be our parent, the topic of the rest of this chapter. Here again, human sibling relationships can be instructive. I was by no means perfect as big sister, but I had something in common with our brother, Christ. I trod the difficult way first, acted as a mediator when relations with parents were tricky, was a confidante, a model to emulate and a hand to hold in times of trouble. In other words I helped my sibling to grow up.

> Thanks be to you, our Lord Jesus Christ,
> for all the benefits which you have given us,
> for all the pains and insults which you have borne for us.
> Most merciful Redeemer, Friend and Brother,
> may we know you more clearly,
> love you more dearly,
> and follow you more nearly,
> day by day.
>
> Richard of Chichester (1197–1253)

Letting God be our parent

We grow up to resemble our earthly parents – sometimes despite our best efforts! – because we are their biological offspring. So it is with our heavenly parent. Our transformation into the likeness of the triune God is fundamentally an organic work of the Spirit that is something like an unfolding of our genetic endowment as children of God. Yet good parents will give us more than their genes: they give a relationship marked by intimacy; an identity and name that reflects our formal status as their child; material inheritance rights as their heir. We need actively to receive these good things from God by fully engaging with all aspects of the parental relationship: through cultivating intimacy; living up to our status; looking forward in hope to our inheritance.

Of course, without the work of Christ and the continuing help of the Spirit this would itself be impossible for us. As indicated above, there is a theological issue with the distance and otherness of God. However, and perhaps of more importance, there is a corresponding psychological issue: we are constitutionally unable to trust God as a good parent.

The events of Genesis 3 depict a loss of the primordial harmony described in the text-box quotation from Athanasius; a loss of our grasp on the 'divine providence towards the universe'. With the eating of the fruit of the tree of knowledge of good and evil, Adam and Eve become aware 'that the world, including oneself, *is* good or evil depending on whether one sees it with or without God' (Beier 2010, p. 136); that is, they discover the need to hold on to God for dear life through fear of evil, rather than simply to enjoy being with him. But for some reason, possibly the serpent's insinuation that God is unloving and not to be relied upon (Gen. 3.1), Adam and Eve are not able to turn to God for help with this new sense of exposure and separation anxiety. Instead they try to deal with it themselves and indeed *hide* from God in shame (Gen. 3.10). The irony is that it is out of their fear of losing God that the relationship is broken.

The work of Christ, especially his heroic act of filial trust as he prays in his own garden, restores this relationship. However, we also need to do our part. In Chapter 8 we will address the issue of shame. Here we focus on the practice of intentionally approaching God as a good parent.

Cultivating intimacy

Attachment

God longs for us to have a secure attachment relationship with him; to gather us under the shadow of his wings, to be our safe haven and secure base, but like an insecure and ambivalent infant, we pull away or approach in half-hearted fashion (Matt. 23.27; Luke 13.31).

The existential predicament of the human race is that it finds it difficult to trust in the goodness of God. While this is a universal aspect of being human, we will each experience it differently. As we saw in Chapter 5, our attachment histories with our own parents and other events in our life will colour, intensify or ameliorate our mistrust of God. Here I am not talking about what we think about God, but what we *feel* about God. We may gladly assent to the proposition that God is good and to be trusted, but we may not feel it in our heart. It's important then to remember that this is as likely to reflect individual differences in our psychology as differences in our spiritual advancement – something we will consider more fully in Chapter 8.

One obvious area of potential difficulty is the use of the metaphor of fatherhood to depict our relationship with God, together with the deeply ingrained Christian practice of addressing God as 'Father'. We do not share the patriarchal societal norms of Jesus' day. Children increasingly grow up without a father. We are more aware than ever that there has always been a significant minority of fathers who neglect or abuse their children physically, sexually or emotionally. My experience in pastoral ministry has led me to conclude that his can affect our conception of God as father in precisely the two ways that Kirkpatrick suggests (correspondence and compensation). Some people who have experienced absent, neglectful or abusive fathers are turned off or traumatized by the fatherhood of God: for them if God is a father, they want none of him. Others with similar childhood experiences find in God the father they wish they could have had. Their experience of the divine father somehow heals their memories of their earthly father.

In this context it may be helpful to reflect on the childhood of Jesus, and in particular the emergence of his consciousness of the world and of himself. Jesus' full humanity was not just about his having a physical body but also about his having human psychological processes. Just as his developing physique depended on the food he ate and the exercise he took, so his developing consciousness depended on his relationship with his human caregivers and his experience with the world about him.

The child's sense of self develops in large part in relation to his parents, in this case Mary as mother and Joseph as an ambiguous adoptive father, who had his own biological children. Luke's account of the incident in the Temple (Luke 2.41–50) is the only biblical reference to the childhood of Jesus, and its central point is the ambiguous position of Joseph in relation to Jesus' sense of identity. After this Joseph essentially disappears from the biblical narrative. There is no longer even a proxy father. Jesus is known not as Jesus son of Joseph but plain Jesus of Nazareth.

What must it have been like for Jesus to grow up presumably in a secure relationship with his mother but an ambiguous relationship with an adoptive father (not to mention step-siblings) who is then off the scene as his adulthood approaches? We can of course only speculate, but it is not inconceivable that as Jesus' relationship with God developed, both correspondence and compensation processes were at work to good effect: God was for him like Mary, and God was for him providing something that Joseph could not. Perhaps Jesus was humanly primed to trust God because he had experienced Mary as trustworthy. Perhaps he was hungry for filial intimacy with God, because the identity of his true father was mysterious, and he lost his proxy father at a crucial time in his growing up (see e.g. Capps 2000; van Os 2007).

The little we know of the early life and possible family dynamics of Jesus provide us with a way of realizing that he is in solidarity both with those of us who have experienced secure parenting *and* with those of us who have no father or mother, whose parents are unknown, were neglectful or abusive. The conditions within which Jesus came to the insight that he was God's son show that access to an intimate attachment relationship with God is not only on offer for those who have the secure psychological histories that enable them to recognize it, but also, and perhaps above all, for those who have the broken psychological histories that make them yearn for it. Of course, the way Jesus is God's son is not the same as the way we are God's children; it is unique. Yet the mystery of the incarnation is that his realization of a filial relationship with God makes it real for us too (Gal. 4.3–6).

We are like Jesus of Nazareth in that we are human. We are unlike him because he was divine. We are also unlike Jesus because we are not first-century Galilean Jews. In order for us to appropriate his intimate relationship with God we may need to connect with its deep psychology rather than its surface culture-bound expression. God was for Jesus his primary attachment figure, perhaps initially experienced through the love of Mary but later quite distinct from her in his mind. For Jesus God was the ultimate safe haven and secure base. Jesus had an internal working model (IWM) of his relationship with God that can be summed up as 'I am beloved, and God is well pleased with me'. It so happened that given Jesus' particular cultural and personal location this was best expressed in terms of masculine parental care.

For many of us this continues to make good sense: God is our heavenly Father. However, some of us may be helped by realizing that Jesus' message is not about patriarchy but about the intimacy and dependency of attachment and other affectional bonds. We need to be able to approach God with an attitude that allows us to love him and to receive his love, care and protection. It may mean searching for a way to address him – or her – that doesn't get in the way of this. I knew a woman who found the word 'God' so hard and unyielding that she replaced it with 'Love' whenever she talked of the divine. I thought this was rather a good idea, and at times I have tried it myself. Another way is to take Jesus' instructions on prayer literally and to address God as 'Abbā. This is an easy sound to make (our son called me 'Baba' for a while before he learnt to say 'Mum'), it has little in the way of psychological and cultural baggage, yet is a direct link to the human Jesus and, according to Paul, a mark of the indwelling of the Spirit.

We also need to pay some attention to our IWMs. Jesus' proclamation of the good news (e.g. Mark 1.15) can be understood as 'turn and embrace this IWM: You are beloved of God, and he is pleased with you.' For many of us, a familiarity with the idea of the wrath of God and our sense of our own sin or inadequacy make this a difficult message to hear. But we must dare to believe it. The New Testament understands the wrath of God as his righteous anger that will be expressed on the Day of Judgement against those who wilfully harm his people by exploitation, abuse or peddling misinformation. It is not God's fundamental starting attitude to humanity: this is instead an attitude of love that treats us as if he is pleased with us even when we don't look very worthy of this approval (Rom. 5.6–8).

If we can move towards believing that God loves, even likes, and is pleased by us, we might find that we are able to approach him with a greater degree of confidence and less ambivalence. This message first understood and proclaimed by Jesus – that God is really a loving and trustworthy attachment figure to whom we can dare to run with open arms and with whom we can conquer the world – is hammered home by Paul in a rightly famous passage from his letter to the Romans:

> What then are we to say about these things? If God is for us, who is against us? . . . Who will separate us from the love of Christ? . . . in all these things we are more than conquerors through him who loved us. For I am convinced that neither death, nor life, nor angels, nor rulers, nor things present, nor things to come, nor powers, nor height, nor depth, nor anything else in all creation, will be able to separate us from the love of God in Christ Jesus our Lord. (Romans 8.31, 35, 37–39)

Affection

> A mother may interact with her infant as caregiver, as playmate, and/or teacher. All these facets characterize that particular relationship, but perhaps only one of them – the caregiving component – is directly related to the protective function . . . [of] . . . attachment. (Ainsworth 1993, p. 37)

There is more to our love relationship with our parents than the security provided by effective attachment. There is affection, joy and delight. Recall from Chapter 5 that Ainsworth wondered if the 'tenderness and intense delight' of the Ugandan fathers in her sample formed part of the glue of their children's attachment to them. God has not simply saved us *from* something, he has saved us *for* a relationship of tenderness and intense delight. While this is a key part of attachment relationships, it is also there in other affectional bonds with friends, teachers, colleagues and lovers.

It is worth pausing here to consider the nature of joy. In his sermon to the Athenians Paul asserts that joy is, like the seasons that lead to a good harvest, an aspect of the natural world that points to the goodness of God (Acts 14.17). Psychologists are agreed that joy is indeed one of a very few primary universal emotions along with fear, anger and sadness (Panksepp 1998, p. 46; and see e.g. Ekman 1992). However, they have tended to focus their research not so much on joy as on the related concepts of pleasure, happiness and mirth, from which it should be distinguished.

Happiness – often referred to as 'subjective well-being' by psychologists – is an enduring mood state (Diener 2000), whereas joy is a more short-lived emotion. Pleasure – often referred to as 'hedonia' by psychologists – is strongly related to restoring a physiological imbalance (Panksepp 1998, p. 82),[3] whereas joy is not (Vaillant 2008, p. 125). Finally, mirth/hilarity, the subjective component

---

3 We luxuriate in pleasure from food when we are hungry, drink when we are thirsty, stimulation when we are bored, sleep when we are tired, cool when we are too hot, warmth when we are cold, and sex when we are tense or frustrated.

of humour (Ruch 1993), can look rather like joy but it is not the same; it's possible to experience joyless mirth.

Joy is fairly easy to recognize but hard to define and measure. It seems to have a number of aspects. First, it appears to be strongly connected with libido – the life force. Young creatures in particular can give off a sense of real joy simply at being alive and being part of life. There can also be a sense of apparently effortless mastery about it; sometimes birds seem to be darting and swooping through the air for sheer joy. As young children jump and splash in rain puddles, they exude joy. Adults too can experience joy from doing something 'just because I can'.

Sweet Infancy!

O Heavenly Fire!

O Sacred Light!

How fair and bright!

How Great am I

Whom the whole world doth magnify!

O heavenly joy!

O Great and Sacred Blessedness

Which I possess!

So great a joy

Who did into my arms convey?

Thomas Traherne (1638–74)

But there is more to joy than this. It appears to be a profoundly social emotion. Years ago, when our son was nearly two, I sat him in his high chair to await lunch in the kitchen while I went to hang out some washing to dry in the garden. Our daughter was just a few weeks old at the time, and she was also in the kitchen asleep in her baby chair. As I returned from the garden I heard laughter. I wondered if the radio had turned itself on. Then I entered the kitchen and an astonishing sight met my eyes. The two infants were looking at each other and taking it in turns to make each other laugh. They showed no interest in my return at all. The air was full of the joyful chuckles that are so delightfully characteristic of the very young. They had made their first real connection.

'Joy is all about connection with others' (Vaillant 2008, p. 124). This is often a physical connection. In the young this may involve cuddling, handling and romping with adult caregivers and with each other in rough and tumble (RAT) play. Here joy is expressed in mutual smiling and often also laughter. This may not be confined to the human participants. The physiological psychologist Jaak Panksepp has carried out a fascinating series of experiments which involved stroking and tickling rats to induce joy and then observing the changes in brain chemistry that resulted. He claims that these rats make very characteristic 'ultrasonic vocalization patterns' (Panksepp and Burgdorf 2003) – that is, they laugh.

Secure attachment relationships are built when parents facilitate the experience of joy in their infants (Jones 1995, p. 87). Joy is often the expression of reunion after parent–child separation, played out from very early in the relationship through the universal and mysteriously hilarious game of peek-a-boo and later as hide and seek. These games not only build tolerance of separation anxiety in the child but also lay down a store of joyful reunion experiences. For parents these little reunions can be a re-experience of the joy they first felt on the emergence of their wanted infant into the world. Up until that point her presence has been felt but not fully revealed, and her safe arrival has been keenly anticipated but not taken for granted. Personally, I have never experienced joy that equalled the moments shortly after the birth of my children.

The Hebrew Bible is full of joy and rejoicing, and this continues into the New Testament (for a comprehensive and detailed account see Chan 2012). Its use here resonates strongly with the psychological themes considered above. Perhaps its definitive occurrence is when, filled with the Holy Spirit, Jesus rejoices at his intimacy with his Father (Luke 10.21–22); here Luke depicts relations between the different persons of the Trinity as suffused with joy. Elsewhere, joy is most often expressed at reunion (e.g. Matt. 28.8; Luke 15.32; 24.41, 52; John 16.22; 20.20; Acts 15.3; 1 Cor. 16.7; 2 Cor. 7.7; Phil. 2.28, 29; 2 Tim. 1.4; 2 John 1.12) or at the finding or revealing of a great treasure (e.g. Matt. 13.20, 44; Luke 1.14; 15.6, 9; 1 Cor. 13.6; 1 Pet. 1.8). There is also a kind of joy that expresses triumph as spiritual goals are achieved (recall Carver's and Scheier's model of affect and goals on p. 20), or pride, as the harvest of the gospel is made manifest in the lives of Christians (e.g. John 4.36; 8.56; Acts 11.23; Rom. 16.19; 2 Cor. 13.9; Phil. 4.1; Col. 2.5; Heb. 12.2; 3 John 12). Joy is to be found in the fellowship of community; rejoicing is promoted as an inherently social activity (e.g. John 3.29; Rom. 12.15; 1 Cor. 12.15; 2 Cor. 1.24; Phil. 2.18; 1 John 4.4).

It is thus clear that the first Christian communities, secure in their identity as children of God, were marked by strong affectional bonds consolidated through the intentional taking of delight in others (John 15.10–11). It is nearly impossible to generate feelings of joy when we are down, but it is possible to be intentional about taking delight in others, and feelings of joy can then often arise and take us pleasantly by surprise (especially if others respond with joy). This is a practice parents learn when presented with scribbles or tatty presents by their small children. What starts as something simulated and effortful mysteriously becomes genuine and natural. Our decision to take delight opens us to receive the gift of joy.

The notion of delight reminds us that the context of joy is often play (Frijda 1994). As Ainsworth demonstrated in her strange situation experiments, we can only play when we feel secure (Vaillant 2008, p. 129). In Proverbs Chapter 8 we are presented with a picture of God at play with Wisdom (hokmâ), his child or helper who prefigures Christ, and in whom he takes delight (Prov. 8.30). The game they are playing is that of creation. Wisdom responds to God with delight and she goes on to rejoice in the created world and to take delight in human beings (Prov. 8.31). The whole sweep of God's creative activity is marked by joy; what's more God seems to be having fun. The work of God is also his play.[4]

We are perhaps used to the idea that God graciously invites us to be co-workers in his mission. We do this through our ministry but also through our prayers of intercession and thanksgiving, which join with the work of Christ, the great high priest (recall p. 82). Less familiar is the idea that God also invites us to be his play-mates. We do this by rejoicing with the community of Christians and the wider world that is his creation, by having fun in prayer and worship and by giving due care to our own creative impulses so that they flourish and grow. In this respect we are joining with the play of Christ, the Wisdom of God.

Just as in a healthy relationship with a parent, the life of prayer can be thought of as moving between phases of work for God, rest in God and play with God (see Figure 15). We pray to join in with the *Missio Dei*; as an expression of our attachment relationship to God; and for the sheer joy of it.

Of course, sometimes prayer will feel almost exclusively like work: there will be times when we find it difficult to rest in God; and play may seem out of the question because of our own mood or circumstances or because God seems to be playing at hiding. We will return to the balance between these in Chapter 10; for now it is enough to appreciate the wonder of a God who invites us to be intimate with him in play, even RAT play (Gen. 32.24–30).

'Oh, children,' said the Lion, 'I feel my strength coming back to me. Oh, children, catch me if you can!' He stood for a second, his eyes very bright, his limbs quivering, lashing himself with his tail. Then he made a leap high over their heads and landed on the other side of the Table. Laughing, though she didn't know why, Lucy scrambled over it to reach him. Aslan leaped again. A mad chase began. Round and round the hill–top he led them, now hopelessly out of their reach, now letting them almost catch his tail, now diving between them, now tossing them in the air with his huge and beautifully velveted paws and catching them again, and now stopping unexpectedly so that all three of them rolled over together in a happy laughing heap of fur and arms and legs. It was such a romp as no one has ever had except in Narnia; and whether it was more like playing with a thunderstorm or playing with a kitten Lucy could never make up her mind. And the funny thing was that when all three finally lay together panting in the sun the girls no longer felt in the least tired or hungry or thirsty.

C. S. Lewis (1898–1963)

---

4 For an extended consideration of God's playful joy at creation, see Fretheim 2012.

Figure 15.

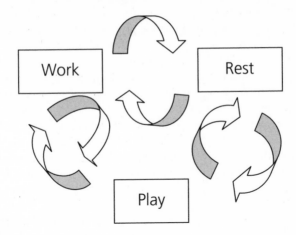

Work

Rest

Play

Living up to our status

Jesus tells his followers that God is their father, that they should address him as such in prayer and approach him with an attitude of expectation that they will receive what is due to them as his children. In this he raises human dignity very high.

Because the relationship is utterly secure and the love of our heavenly parent is unconditional, we can hold out our hands with confidence that they will be filled with the good things that God knows we need (Matt. 6.7–8, 25–32; 7.7–11; Luke 11.11–13; 12.22–30; John 16.23), rather than hiding them behind our backs in fear of a smack. This is reflected in the structure of the Lord's Prayer, where a very simple request for bread on a daily basis rightly follows an assertion of God's greatness, but makes no reference to our own deservingness:

> It is striking that only . . . quite late in the Lord's Prayer, is a mention made of the fact that we have sins that require forgiveness. It follows rather than precedes expressions of intimacy, praise, welcome for the kingdom and a request for food. How different from many of our church services! (Collicutt 2012b, p. 149)

How different, too, from Anglican collects, which in their eagerness to emphasize the grace of God are so often prefaced by lengthy assertions of our unworthiness.

Yet the gospel tells us that because of Jesus we do not need to grovel before God. There will be times when we fall to our knees in awe and wonder at his majesty; nevertheless he continues to raise us up so that we can stand in his presence (Rom. 5.2; Jude 24). It may be helpful in this light to reflect on our posture when we pray (Mark 11.25) or receive communion.

As we turn to God in prayerful expectation as his children we also turn away from other things that are not concordant with the dignity of our status for, as discussed in Chapter 6, *metanoia* is a continual process. After our request for

Figure 16.

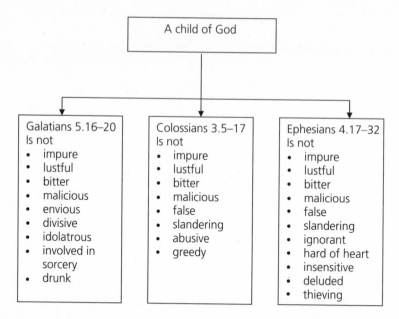

A child of God

Galatians 5.16–20 Is not	Colossians 3.5–17 Is not	Ephesians 4.17–32 Is not
• impure • lustful • bitter • malicious • envious • divisive • idolatrous • involved in sorcery • drunk	• impure • lustful • bitter • malicious • false • slandering • abusive • greedy	• impure • lustful • bitter • malicious • false • slandering • ignorant • hard of heart • insensitive • deluded • thieving

bread in the Lord's Prayer, we ask for forgiveness for the occasions on which our behaviour has failed to express our true identity in Christ. The New Testament provides us with several remarkably consistent summaries of the things a child of God should avoid,[5] which include attitudes as well as actions. These are summarized in Figure 16.

Growing up into Christ, our big brother, involves a constant stripping away of that which is not worthy of him yet has a tendency to cling to us (Heb. 12.1). There are two areas of life that the New Testament presents as particularly problematic. First there is pleasure, which can sometimes turn from healthy appreciative savouring of our God-given physicality into an addictive quest for the next hedonic fix – a kind of counterfeit joy. Christians are by no means immune from addictions; the fact that the Lord's Prayer itself contains an appeal for protection against temptation is an indication of this. However, there is evidence that spiritual practices, some of which are considered later in this book, and the support of a community of faith can both guard against the development of addictions (Cook 2004) and help overcome them (Leigh, Bowen and Marlatt 2005).

---

5 This book does not deal with the management or elimination of problem behaviours using specific techniques. Its focus is almost exclusively on building strengths. Often the building of positive behaviour leads to a natural decline in problem behaviour, but sometimes problem behaviour will need to be targeted directly. The approach taken will depend on the nature of the behaviour and the past history and current situation of the person who is troubled by it. It is therefore not possible to be prescriptive about which approach to take. Various combinations of prayer with spiritual direction, psychological therapy and even medication may be necessary.

Second, there is the tongue, which can spread evil intentionally or cause unintentional hurt through speaking before thinking (James 3.5–10). These days the tongue extends into email and social media. Christians now need to think and pray, 'Is this worthy of Him? Is this worthy of me?' not only before we speak but before we text or Tweet. This is an area that can helpfully come under the scrutiny of the *Examen*, discussed in Chapter 5.

Growing up

Letting God be our parent does not mean that we have to remain stuck in an infantile relationship with him. We depend on God for our very being, but he also gives us freedom and autonomy even though we are his creatures. Unfortunately, it's generally quite easy for us to remain stuck in outmoded ways of relating, especially to our parents, or to regress under certain circumstances. I have experienced something of this. Whenever I returned to my parents' home, even when I was in my forties with children of my own, I found myself resuming the behaviour of a teenager; I raided the larder freely and at random, bickered with my sibling about control of the television channels and called to my mother to adjudicate between us.

The psychiatrist Ana-Maria Rizzuto makes the point that we need to update our mental representations of our parents and our relationship to them throughout our life, and that this usually happens as part of healthy development (rather as a computer automatically updates its software functions if we let it). She argues that this is also true of our 'God representation'[6] (Rizzuto 1979, p. 200), but that many people do not allow this process to occur. Thus God is relegated to a fond memory of the nursery, someone to whom we may quite rightly return in times of liminality or crisis, but not an ongoing part of our adult lives.

Here again Jesus comes to our aid. Indeed, it could be argued that this is one way he saves humanity. Jesus doesn't just show us that we can be secure in our dependence on God; he also shows us that it is possible to approach our divine parent adult-to-adult[7] and, more than this, he shows us how to do it.

Jesus begins his prayer in Gethsemane with the first words of the Lord's Prayer, 'Abbā (Mark 14.36). This is the great and final crisis of Jesus' life and ministry. He turns in distress to his primary attachment figure, throwing himself (Matt. 26.39; Mark 14.35) or kneeling (Luke 22.42) down on the ground in anguish. But he also does something else: as in the temptation, he questions, reflects and then – again in the words of the Lord's Prayer – makes a free and considered decision to align himself with God's will. Finally he gets up and

---

6 Rizzuto uses objects relations theory rather than attachment theory as her organizing psychological framework; but in the language of attachment theory she is saying that our parents are more than the providers of our early IWMs, important as this is.

7 This phrase is drawn from the psychotherapeutic theory of transactional analysis (Berne 1964).

exhorts his disciples to do the same (Matt. 26.46 and parallels). Here Jesus returns to a relationship with his Father that grew out of his childhood and adolescent needs and which he has reworked throughout his ministry; but he now re-appropriates it as a fully mature adult. A key part of this is his coming to an understanding of God's ultimate purpose for him so that he can make it completely his own.

Elsewhere Jesus describes a similar process in relation to Christian disciple-ship (John 15.15). This is not simply about proximity seeking and blind fol-lowing, but about sharing the divine mind: 'As we share in the knowledge of Jesus, we experience the faithfulness of the divine Spirit as an intimate presence that holds us, loves us, and draws us into the knowledge of the Father' (Shults 2006b, p. 85).

How are we to work this out in our lives? There is something here about discernment and critical questioning, both within ourselves and with the help of others. It will involve wrestling in prayer – arguing with God; but also wrestling in scholarship. Our faith should not be the one area of our lives that is a thinking-free zone. No matter what our academic abilities, the call of the Christian is continually to engage as intelligently as she can with Scripture and the theological riches of the tradition; like Mary of Bethany who chose the better part, to think the gospel through.

Claiming our inheritance: the strange nature of this attachment bond

It is no accident that Jesus fully apprehends the mind of his Father in the context of the anguish of Gethsemane. This is where the profoundly 'other' nature of the divine perspective, the thing that makes Jesus very nearly as repellent as he is attractive, reveals itself most fully. The way that we attach ourselves to Christ is by walking his way of suffering and death.

The Lord's Prayer asks that we be spared affliction; we are not to seek it out in a bid for self-improvement. Nevertheless, the New Testament as a whole is clear that if unavoidable affliction comes it is to be greeted not just with stoical resignation but with joy (Matt. 5.12; 6.23; 16.20; John 16.20–24; Acts 5.41; 2 Cor. 6.12; 8.2; Phil. 2.17; 4.10–13; Col. 1.24; 2.17; James 1.2; 1 Pet. 1.6, 8; 4.12–13). Our attachment to Christ that begins by turning to him, is strength-ened by suffering with him, empathetically or literally. Here insights from the psychology of post-traumatic growth, the mindful practice of turning towards pain in greeting, and the psychology of attachment and affection are brought together in a radical and totally unexpected way. Our joy can flourish not only in good times, but even more so in adversity precisely because this brings us closer to Christ, and because we see through it to the ultimate transformation of all things (Roberts 2007).

This extraordinary and paradoxical joy both expresses and claims the reality that it is only through the death and resurrection of the incarnate God that we have been redeemed as his children. We were brought to glory because the pio-neer of our salvation was brought to fulfilment through sufferings (Heb. 2.10).

Our inheritance is glorious, but we obtain it through sticking close to our big brother, making his story of self-denial, suffering and death in some way our own (Matt. 16.24–25 and parallels; Rom. 8.17). This begins for us all with our baptism (Rom. 6.3), but each of us will live and die it out differently. In the next chapter we begin our exploration of this hard road to glory by addressing the Christian virtue of humility.

Exercises

1 Reflect on your place in your family of origin. Does this impact on your ability to see Jesus as your brother?
2 Experiment with using alternative names to address God in prayer, with the aim of getting over any barriers there might be to intimate discourse with God.
3 Look hard at the way you take pleasure and the way you talk to and about others directly and on social media. Is there anything that needs attention?

Further reading

Barton, S., 2013, *Joy in the New Testament*, Cambridge: Grove Books.
Collicutt, J., 2012, *When you Pray: Daily Reflections for Lent and Easter on the Lord's Prayer*, Oxford: Bible Reading Fellowship, pp. 33–90.
Rizzuto, A.-M., 1979, *The Birth of the Living God: A Psychoanalytic Study*, Chicago, IL: Chicago University Press.
Vaillant, G., 2008, *Spiritual Evolution*, New York: Random House.

8

Humble Power:
Having the Mind of Christ

Let the same mind be in you that was in Christ Jesus, who, though he was in the form of God, did not regard equality with God as something to be exploited, but emptied himself, taking the form of a slave, being born in human likeness. And being found in human form, he humbled himself and became obedient to the point of death – even death on a cross.

Philippians 2.5–8

I therefore, the prisoner in the Lord, beg you to lead a life worthy of the calling to which you have been called, with all humility.

Ephesians 4.1–2a

Love is the fundamental Christian virtue – the first 'fruit of the Spirit' (Gal. 5.22), that which 'binds everything things together (Col. 3.14) and gives us life and growth (Eph. 4.16). Nevertheless, love must find its expression in action, and the life and death of Jesus shows us that the virtue of humility is a necessary condition for the expression of love. To have the mind of Christ is to have an attitude of humility: 'I am gentle and humble in heart' (Matt. 11.28b).

Yet the words 'humble' and 'humility' do not sit easily in our contemporary culture. They sound archaic, speaking out of feudal or class-dominated societies where people were expected to know their place. Thanks to Dickens' depiction of Uriah Heep in his novel *David Copperfield*, the word humble has come to be associated with servility, creepiness and inauthenticity. Moreover, in the light of twentieth-century psychological insights into the destructive nature of low self-esteem, expressions of humility have often been seen as signs of mental pathology.

So as we come to examine the nature of humility (first in the person of Christ and second as a Christian virtue), we need to keep in mind the dangers of mis-understanding its nature, misreading ourselves and others, or simply missing this most elusive of qualities.

'There is a Redeemer – and it's not you'

This sentence is one of the most helpful things I have ever heard said to a group of ministers in training. When I in my turn quote it, I have found that it is invari-ably greeted with a laugh of recognition by the audience who see in themselves the tendency to think that Christians can, indeed have to, do what Jesus did. But it's not our job to save the world. God has done this already in Christ. Of course, it *is* our job to participate in the working out of this salvation – in the

Missio Dei. In the same way, although our humility is both inspired by and a participation in the humility of Christ the eternal logos, it also differs significantly from it.

So what is the nature of Christ's humility? The ancient Christian hymn quoted by Paul in the letter to the Philippians (2.6–11) is a song of praise that sets out the humility of Christ in some detail as a prelude to and a necessary condition for his exaltation. This hymn is theologically complex (and a compelling illustration of the fact that our most sophisticated theology happens not so much in studies and libraries but in the context of worship). It presents Christ's humility as having three parts: first, he did not treat 'equality with God' as 'something to be exploited' (v. 6); second, he 'emptied himself, taking the form of a slave' (v. 7); finally, he 'humbled himself and became obedient to the point of death – even death on a cross' (v. 8). The Greek words translated by the NRSV as 'something to be exploited', 'emptied himself' and 'humbled' each have a range of meanings and have therefore been much debated by scholars. It is worth spelling out these meanings in more detail as this gives added depth and colour to the picture being painted by the hymn:

- *harpagmos* – something to grasp or hold tight to; booty to be taken; something to use for one's own advantage.
- *emauton kenoō* – to give up or lay aside what one possesses; to strip; to disempower; to empty; to invalidate.
- *tapeinoō* – to make ashamed, to humiliate, to take a lowly place.

The humility of the incarnation is thus expressed in Christ's

- *attitude* to his divinity; he wears it lightly.
- *free choice* to set aside his entitlement, specifically his entitlement to be served, in order to take on a role of service.
- *ultimate willingness* to take on the shame of the world in the humiliating nature of his death.

This makes it clear that our humility is not a simple replication of Christ's humility. We don't have any divinity to set aside; we are not entitled to be worshipped or served; above all, it is not our job to take on the shame of the world in order to redeem it.

On the other hand there is a connection between Christ's humility and the calling of all Christians. After all, Paul uses this hymn (which would presumably have been well known to his audience) precisely to say 'Look at him – go and do likewise!' And in John 13 we are told that Jesus himself washes his disciples' feet first as a parable in action expressing the divine humility of the incarnation – the setting aside of one garment, the putting on of another associated with service, the actions of a slave; but second as an example to his followers: 'For I have set you an example, that you also should do as I have done to you' (John 13.15).

The question then arises as to what it is that Christians are called to wear lightly, what it is we are called to set aside in order to take on a role of service, and whether there is any sense in which, or any circumstances under which, we might be called to bear shame. It is at this point that psychology becomes relevant; for it seems that we are called to sit lightly to questions of self-worth, to set aside the ego and, as an inevitable part of this, to engage with issues of shame in ourselves and others.

'Because I'm worth it': the snares of low self-esteem, pride and narcissism

On the face of it being humble looks something like low self-esteem because both seem to share the idea that 'I am of little account'. On the other hand a boastful attitude – what I will call 'pride' – looks rather like narcissism because both seem to share the idea that 'I am important'. However, things are not always as they seem, and the situation is in fact more complicated than this (it's summarized in Figure 17 on page 119). For instance, you don't have to be a psychologist to recognize that for some people self-important behaviour is a defence against feelings of low self-esteem.

Human beings in many different cultures seem to be obsessed with issues of self-esteem,[1] both as individuals and communities. To varying degrees and in varying ways the question, 'Am I/are we good enough?' permeates our psychological life. A concern with self-esteem seems to be part of the human condition,[2] and it could be argued that our readiness to doubt our own worth is a defining aspect of fallen human nature. If true, this would of course be deeply ironic: our belief that we are no good would then not be an expression of insight into our sin but instead be an *aspect* of that sin. It's worth giving this a good deal of thought: our conclusions on it will affect the way we preach, teach, pastor and pray.

In the field of psychology and psychiatry, study after study has demonstrated a link between positive self-esteem and indicators of well-being. Positive self-esteem, often expressed in confident self-assertion, is associated with psychological resilience, optimism and good scholastic and vocational performance; negative self-esteem, often expressed in denigration and envy of others, is associated with depression, anxiety, eating disorders, violence, substance abuse and poor scholastic and vocational attainment (see e.g. Mann, Hosman, Schaalma and de Vries 2003). The cause and effect relationship is complex: for example, if your self-esteem is low you may be more likely to be drawn into a violent relationship and this relationship may in its turn make your self-esteem lower. Nevertheless, the fact that such vicious cycles can be broken simply by targeting and building up an individual's self-esteem confirms that it is a significant *cause* of human behaviour and not just a consequence of it.

People differ in their resting levels of self-esteem. The reasons for this are not fully understood, but the most important factor seems, as we have seen, to be a secure sense of being loved unconditionally – something that is usually laid

---

1 The terms self-esteem and self-worth are often used interchangeably.
2 But see Heine, Lehman, Markus and Kitayama 1999 for a counter-argument.

down through our childhood experiences at the hands of our parents and other caregivers. A child who has been treated with consistent warmth and intimacy and who has been able to rely on her caregiver – be it mother, father, nanny or older sibling – to be available when needed, is more likely to grow up with positive self-esteem (Kernis 2003; Mikulincer and Shaver 2004). As already discussed in Chapter 5, there seems to be a sort of compelling emotional logic that says 'S/he was there for me, so I must be worth being there for' and conversely 'S/he abandoned me so I must be worthless.' This connection between parental presence and a sense of self-esteem is clearly part of the joy contained in the notion of *Immanuel*. If God is with us we feel that we are worth being with.

If we don't feel a deep and assured sense of worth, we still have to get through life, so we find ways of managing our self-doubt or even self-loathing. Not all these ways are helpful.

Defensive pride: I'm better than he

Self-esteem can be enhanced by more external factors, such as having a place of honour or popularity in one's social group due to birth or marital status, prowess at a valued skill or personal charm. Being wealthy or making one's mark in the world can also help. Such things are not bad in themselves, but the danger is that if we have an insecure sense of belonging and being loved unconditionally, we will invest too highly in these external sources of self-esteem, will grasp them too tightly – something that is emotionally effortful and humanly costly (Crocker and Park 2004).

This grasping can take the form of a destructive competitiveness; the way I assure myself that I am good enough is that I am better than he. I may do this by 'boasting' – constantly harping on about my achievements, wealth, social connections and so on, but also by denigrating the achievements of others. This kind of defensive 'pride' is empty and fragile and all too common:

> The Pharisee, standing by himself, was praying thus, 'God, I thank you that I am not like other people: thieves, rogues, adulterers, or even like this tax collector. I fast twice a week; I give a tenth of all my income.' (Luke 18.11–12)

So the mark of healthy self-esteem is the ability to sit lightly to these external sources of worth and the need to feel superior to others. Healthy positive self-esteem turns out to be rather like humility. Both are based in an assurance of being loved *unconditionally*.

Explicit low self-esteem: I'm not like them – nothing I do will amount to anything

Rather than boasting, we may simply express our feelings of low self-esteem directly. When we feel like this we don't try or expect to achieve success because it seems impossible, and anyway we don't think we deserve it. When good things happen they are downplayed or attributed to chance rather than our own skill or worth:

> The one who had received the one talent went off and dug a hole in the ground and hid his master's money . . . 'Master, I knew that you were a harsh man, reaping where you did not sow, and gathering where you did not scatter seed; so I was afraid, and I went and hid your talent in the ground.' (Matthew 25.18, 24–25a)

Both defensive pride and explicit low self-esteem direct our attention to ourselves. The first is expressed in thoughts such as 'It's not true that I'm no good – look at my achievements! I'm better than they'; the second is expressed in thoughts such as 'I don't care what you say – I'm no good! I'm worse than they.'

We may wonder why anyone would persist in this sort of self-denigrating habit with all the unpleasant feelings that can accompany it. The answer seems to lie in the fact that it also has some hidden advantages (sometimes referred to as 'secondary gains'). While it may make us miserable to focus on our own worthlessness, at least this can provide some sort of certainty in a world of relationships that may otherwise be chaotic. It is also a good way of staving off demands, and it rarely fails to invoke well-meant sympathetic responses from others who tell us that we are indeed worth something.

Then the enemy tries with a second weapon, that is boasting or vainglory, giving a person to understand that there is much goodness or holiness within them, and setting them in a higher place than they deserve.

If the servants of the Lord resist these arrows by humbling themselves, refusing to agree that they are such as the enemy suggests, then he brings along the third weapon which is false humility. Thus when he sees the servants of the Lord so good and so humble that they think all they do to be of no use, concentrating on their weaknesses and not on any kind of self-glorification, even while doing what the Lord commands, then he insinuates into these people's thoughts that if they disclose some gifts that God Our Lord has given them . . . they are sinning through another sort of vainglory since they are talking of their own glory. He tries to get them not to speak of the good things received from their Lord, so that they are of no benefit to others, nor to themselves . . . In this way, the devil by making us humble tries to lead us into false humility, that is into an exaggerated and perverted humility.

Ignatius of Loyola (1491–1556)

The stories of the praying Pharisee and the talents, like all Jesus' stories, present us with stereotypes rather than nuanced portraits of real individuals. This is because Jesus is not doing biography but instead using his characters as exemplars of ways of being in the world. It is then important to understand that the world is not divided into people who are proud and people with explicit low self-esteem, but that these are instead pathways we can all take at times, though some are clearly more prone to them than others. Even the most healthy-minded of us can have moments of excessive self-doubt or overly ambitious striving. We all need to be aware of the dangers of straying too far down such pathways. If we wish to tread the path of humility, we need to wear our self-worth lightly.

There is one other pathway that we need to avoid: this is the way of narcissism.

Narcissism: I am special

Narcissism refers to a psychological condition in which the individual believes that s/he is special and therefore entitled to special privileges; is above the rules that apply to ordinary mortals. Narcissism is a relatively rare but highly destructive condition. Its causes are poorly understood (Otway and Vignoles 2006), but may be related to parental over-involvement, excessive praise and a lack of boundaries, so that the child comes to believe that he is loved only because of his special qualities. As we saw in Chapter 3, it is precisely because Jesus is special that the New Testament presents his main temptation not as low self-esteem or pride but narcissism:

> Then the devil took him to the holy city and placed him on the pinnacle of the temple, saying to him, 'If you are the Son of God, throw yourself down; for it is written, "He will command his angels concerning you," and "On their hands they will bear you up, so that you will not dash your foot against a stone."' . . . And Peter took him aside and began to rebuke him, saying, 'God forbid it, Lord! This must never happen to you.' But he turned and said to Peter, 'Get behind me, Satan! You are a stumbling block to me.' (Matthew 4.5–6; 16.22–23a)

While very few of us will be full-blown narcissists, many of us may have some tendency to think we are special – to believe our own publicity. This becomes more of an issue as we become more senior in our profession of choice or advance in our social circle. If you ever find yourself thinking indignantly, 'Don't they know who I *am*?!', take it as a sign that you have started to stray from the path of humility on to the path of narcissism.

The fear of shame and the power of love

Satan tests Jesus in the area that he thinks he will be most vulnerable – the temptation to narcissism – but Jesus successfully resists that temptation, both in the desert and in his exchange with Peter at Caesarea Philippi. Jesus is able to embrace the path of humility described in the Philippians hymn. He can do this because he is secure in the unconditional love of his heavenly Father with whom he has a warm and intimate relationship and who – until that devastating moment on the cross – has been a reliably felt presence in his life. At his baptism Jesus receives a special assurance that he is loved and *after that* an assurance that he is worthy (Matt. 3.17

and parallels). This is not performance-related love. Jesus is not loved because he is pleasing; he is loved for who he is – 'my Son' – and so he is pleasing.

When we are confident that we are loved unconditionally, we are able to be honest with our beloved about our weaknesses and faults. When we go wrong, we will want to own up to the fact and make the relationship right. In the context of a secure relationship guilt can be a healthy emotion (Hood 1992). It can develop into contrition (Roberts 2007, p. 104), prompting us to admit our failing and to do something about it so that reparation and reconciliation can take place. Guilt can – and often should – feel very unpleasant, it may include the fear that our loved one will be angry or hurt, but it should not include the fear that the relationship will end.

On the other hand, when we are insecure in a relationship, feeling that we are loved only on certain conditions, we may be compelled to hide our weaknesses and faults lest their exposure brings the relationship to an end. Or we may wallow in an exaggerated sense of our own unworthiness, pre-empting any signs of rejection from our beloved by rejecting ourselves: 'You can't say anything worse to me than I've already said to myself.' Here feelings of shame rather than guilt will predominate: we either try to hide that of which we are ashamed, or shame ourselves in a bid to inoculate ourselves against the effects of being shamed by our beloved.

It is highly significant that the Philippians hymn talks of the humiliation of Christ and the shameful nature of his death. The hymn is in two symmetrical parts, the first half charting the incarnation, the central point being marked by humiliation and shame; the second half charting the transformation of shame to glory in the raising of Christ from the dead and to the heavenly places. The relentless message of the New Testament[3] is that in Christ God has dealt with the human tendency to shame and, as argued in Chapter 7, given us access to a relationship with the Father that is like his own – warm, intimate and reliably present – and in which we can be assured that we are 'good enough'.[4] This is a relationship where we may often feel guilt but will always be assured of forgiveness, and where there is no place for shame.

The conditions for humility are a sense of being loved unconditionally; just as 'perfect love casts out fear' (1 John 4.18), perfect humility casts out shame (see Figure 17).

Yes, but . . .

All this sounds positive and reassuring. All we have to do is to realize how much God loves us just for ourselves, and we will be able to embark on the humility path with joy. It's true. Yet that first step – realizing how much God loves us –

---

3 See for example Luke 1.48,52 (it's not often noticed that this refers to the humiliating circumstances of Jesus' conception for Mary) and also Romans 5.8; 8.1; 9.33; 10.11; Philippians 3.21; Hebrews 2.11; 12.2.

4 While Winnicott uses this phrase to refer to parenting quality, it is also a helpful psychological way of approaching the theological concept of the justification by faith: in reaching out to God we realize the fact that we are 'good enough'.

Figure 17.

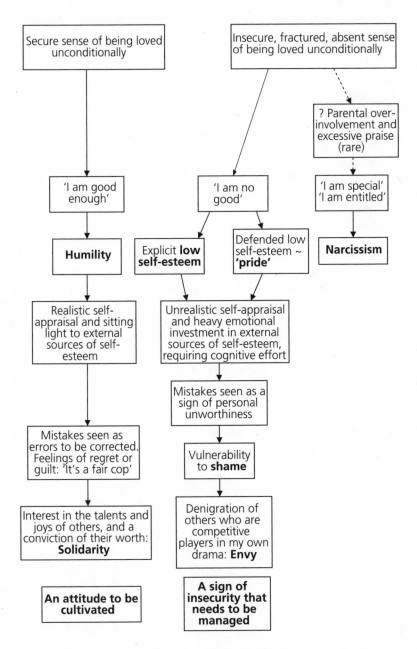

is very difficult for many of us through no fault of our own. In Chapter 7 we began to explore the issue of knowing and assenting to the theory, but having a heart understanding that may lag a long way behind this head understanding. A colleague of mine once told me about a church service in which the minister tried an experiment. First he asked the congregation to raise their hands if they thought God loved them. There was a rapid and unanimous positive response to this. Then he asked them to raise their hands if they thought God *liked* them. This time the response was slow and uncertain, and many people kept their hands down. This congregation knew the right answer to a question phrased in familiar church language, they just had not appropriated it fully as a felt reality. They knew that they were supposedly 'good enough' but wondered if they were actually 'likable enough'.

There is a gap between our theological rhetoric and our lived experience.[5] The fact is that people who are depressed, who have had abusive, neglectful or un-reliable parenting, who have suffered trauma and bereavement, may find it very hard to have faith in the unconditional love of God, no matter how hard they try. This sort of thing isn't fixed by simply reading more books on theology. However, some secular psychological approaches such as cognitive therapy and mindfulness (of which more in Chapter 9) can help with destructive habitual patterns of thinking about the self (Fennell 2009; Pepping, O'Donovan and Davis 2013).

Most fundamentally a felt lack of divine love has to be addressed within the love of Christian communities – the body of Christ – in which the individual occupies a valued place. As Shults and Sandage wisely point out (recall p. 96), this is a long – indeed lifetime – game of commitment and care through thick and thin, yet it has the potential to bear great fruit. The person who feels loved is able to take on genuinely humble service for the greater good after the pattern of Christ.

It is also within the community of the Church and beyond that the second strand of Christian humility – the setting aside of the ego – plays itself out.

Me, myself and I: setting aside the ego

Christlike humility involves wearing our self-worth lightly, not considering it something to be grasped. This means that we will not be preoccupied with our-selves and with the task of shoring up our self-esteem or defending our identity. Humility involves feeling sufficiently secure in our sense of who we are to set this aside, forget it, even to be prepared to lose it in the interests of something greater:

> For those who want to save their life will lose it, and those who lose their life for my sake, and for the sake of the gospel, will save it. (Mark 8.35)

---

5 There is a lot of evidence from the field of cognitive psychology and neuroscience that there are at least two ways of knowing something that are underpinned by separate pathways in the brain and that can operate largely independently of each other (see e.g. Teasdale and Barnard 1993; Graf and Masson 2013).

The word here translated 'life' is the Greek word *psuhē*, whose most common meanings are 'self' or 'inner life'.[6] We might understand this as referring to the ego – the conscious sense of our identity as a fully functioning autonomous human person. Each of us is entitled to an ego. The call to humility can then be understood as a call voluntarily to put our ego aside; to remove it from centre stage. In confirmation of this, psychologists who study humility have identified this correct placing of the ego as its hallmark:

> Although humility frequently is equated with a sense of unworthiness and low self-regard, theoreticians view true humility as a rich, multifaceted construct that entails an accurate assessment of one's characteristics, an ability to acknowledge limitations, and a 'forgetting of the self.' (Tangney 2000, p. 70)
>
> [B]eing able to let go, e.g. quiet, one's ego . . . is an important quality of a true humility. (Niemiec 2013, p. 56)

Those of us who have had the blessings of good parenting and easy temperaments are likely to have developed well-defined and healthy egos. We will have a fairly clear sense of what it is that we are being called to set aside, the self we are called to forget. Others of us who have not been so fortunate may have fragile and wobbly egos; we may lack a clear sense of who we really are or a fully articulated sense of whether we even have a distinct identity. Here some continuing attention to consolidating a sense of identity, perhaps through counselling or therapy, is appropriate. Yet even under these more difficult conditions we can still aspire to place our ego in the right place in relation to God – not to make an idol of our search for identity and human agency. We are entitled to our ego, but we are also called to put it into perspective. One of the things that can help most with this is to look outwards from our own needs to the needs of others. In the run-up to his quotation of the hymn on the humility of Christ, Paul writes: 'Let each of you look not [only] to your own interests, but also to the interests of others' (Phil. 2.4). Many have found that as they start to focus on the needs of their community their sense of self has been oddly and unexpectedly strengthened and authenticated, rather than weakened. For our sense of identity and agency is not something that lives inside our heads but rather something that emerges and grows out of the context of our relationships with others: 'I am because we are.'

It is in the context of community needs that the forgetting of self makes sense. This is true of all Christian virtue. The objective is not to become more holy as an individual by denigrating or obliterating the self; it is to build up the community in love by ensuring that obstacles to this are managed. It so happens that chief among these obstacles is our tendency to be preoccupied with ourselves. Just as Christ set aside his divine status not for the sake of it but in order to take the form of a slave, the Christian is called to place her ego correctly in order to serve the community well. The important thing then is to have a realistic sense of what it is we bring to the community.

---

6 Also 'soul' – recall p. 45.

Being realistic: 'Is there anybody musical here? Then come and help shift this piano!'

> What then is the essence of humility? We believe that humility involves a nondefensive willingness to see the self accurately, including both strengths and limitations. (Peterson and Seligman 1995, p. 463)

In that run-up to the Philippians hymn, Paul also encourages his readers to regard others as better than themselves (v. 3). This is an attitude that we might describe as 'unassuming'. In his letter to the Romans, Paul emphasizes that it is a *realistic* appraisal of our personal qualities, not neurotic self-denigration, that is important:

> For by the grace given to me I say to everyone among you not to think of yourself more highly than you ought to think, but to think with sober judgement, each according to the measure of faith that God has assigned. For as in one body we have many members, and not all the members have the same functions so we, who are many, are one body in Christ, and individually we are members one of another. (Romans 12.3–5)

It's crucial to notice that the pattern of humility that is being laid out here is one that focuses on others, that recognizes the importance of their strengths, not one that devalues our own. We are not called to think of ourselves as worse than others; we're called to forget ourselves as we delight in others. We are also called not to think ourselves too important to take on apparently menial tasks. A worshipping community will be failed equally by the professional organist who will not lower himself to play the humble church instrument as by the amateur pianist who dare not expose herself to the risk of humiliation by attempting to play it. In both cases the community loses the gift of music.

One mark of a servant attitude is a willingness to own up to our aptitudes and skills, not in the falsely self-deprecating manner that is the special talent of the English (saying 'I play a little tennis' when I am county champion); nor in a boastful attention-seeking manner that takes no account of the talents of others; but with realism and as an offering of a resource for the greater good. This is a benevolent kind of pride that we might refer to as 'dignity'. Our service should dignify rather than humiliate us.

Being realistic about ourselves, our strengths and weaknesses, emerges naturally from a sense of realism about our place in the cosmos, and particularly from a coming to terms with our own mortality. The word 'humility' is after all related to the word 'humus', which means soil. We are from the earth and to the earth our bodies shall return. A flower fades and drops but the plant continues to grow; a sheep dies but the flock lives on. Our earthly lives are a small and passing part of something much bigger. This perhaps explains why older people who have experienced death at first hand and are living in their own end times often have a sense of greater realism. I certainly have become more realistic about my place in the cosmos since losing both my parents in recent years.

One way of nurturing this realism is through 'humour', another word with the same root as 'humility'. Humour is a double-edged sword (Collicutt and Gray 2012). Its primary purpose is to offer an alternative view so that what we think is important or settled is seen to be trivial or questionable. It can be used to humiliate and bully. But it can also be used to liberate us from the prison of taking ourselves too seriously. If we want to wear our self-esteem lightly then we need to lighten up and learn to poke some gentle fun at ourselves.

> If there be skilled workmen in the monastery, let them work at their art in all humility, if the Abbot giveth his permission. But if anyone of them should grow proud by reason of his art, in that he seemeth to confer a benefit on the monastery, let him be removed from that work and not return to it, unless after he hath humbled himself, the Abbot again ordereth him to do so.
>
> Benedict of Nursia (480–543)

Embracing shame

Shame is bad. As argued in Chapter 7, it is possible to understand the fundamental sin of Adam and Eve as arising from shame. It wasn't so much that they disobeyed God but that they misunderstood his nature, and so were not able to own their disobedience, being compelled to hide in self-conscious shame.

> Being faln into sin before we were redeemed we had no power to love God, not to believ in him, nor to endeavor our Happiness, not to prize his Works nor to adore his Godhead, or rejoice in him. For seeing our selvs hated of God and destined to Eternal Torments, (as Adam did when he fled away to hide him self among the Trees of the Garden) we could not chuse but hate him, and being Carried away by the vanities and follies of the World we had no sence. But an infinit change was wrought when Gods Redeeming love was discovered.
>
> Thomas Traherne (1638–74)

God has dealt with sin and shame in the life, death, raising and vindication of Christ. Shame has no part in the redeemed life. Yet shame continues to haunt the life of this world, and there may be times when Christians are called to live out the kingdom of God by standing in solidarity with those who are shamed. Because of Christ we know that we have nothing to be ashamed of, but we may on occasion have to bear shame that is imputed to us because of our association with stigmatized groups. Here the dignity of service lies deeply hidden within its shameful context. If I am called to ministry among people convicted of child sexual abuse, it is almost inevitable that I will share in part of their shame. Again, in these circumstances I am not inviting shame as a masochistic act of self-improvement; rather I am willing to risk shame and humiliation for the sake of the kingdom.

This focus on the kingdom begins with a way of looking, not just at ourselves but at the world around us, and is the subject of the next chapter.

Exercises

1   Reflect on the unconditional love of God for you. Remember that 'Abraham was old and Jacob was insecure and Joseph was abused as a young man and Moses stuttered and Gideon was poor and Rahab was immoral and David had an affair and Elijah was suicidal and Jeremiah had depression and Jonah ran away and Naomi was a widow and John the Baptist was eccentric and Peter was impulsive and Martha worried all the time and Zacchaeus was a crook and Thomas had doubts and Paul had poor health and Timothy was timid . . .',[7] and yet God used them.

2   Be ready to own and name your personal strengths identified in Chapter 4 and to think through how you might use these in the service of Christ.

3   Consider laughing at some of your cherished ideas and habits, or at least framing them in a humorous way. (Imagining what teenage offspring might make of them is always helpful here.) Think about times when an apparently humiliating mistake you have made was transformed by God into an unexpected opportunity or blessing.

4   Meditate on Psalm 8 and its paradoxical consideration of human significance.

Further reading

Cherry, S., 2010, *Barefoot Disciple: Walking the Way of Passionate Humility*, London: Continuum, especially Chapter 4.

Collicutt, J., 2009, *Jesus and the Gospel Women*, London: SPCK, pp. 38–56.

Dearing, R. and Tangney, J., 2006, *Shame and Guilt*, New York: Guilford.

McGrath, J. and McGrath, A., [1992] 2001, *Self-esteem: The Cross and Christian Confidence*, Leicester: InterVarsity Press.

Pattison, S., 2001, *Shame: Theory, Therapy, Theology*, Cambridge: Cambridge University Press.

Worthington, E., 2007, *Humility: The Quiet Virtue*, Philadelphia, PA: Templeton Press.

---

7 Sermon on Maundy Thursday 2012 delivered in Christchurch Cathedral, Oxford by Rt Revd John Pritchard, Bishop of Oxford.

9

Heaven in Ordinary:
Watching and Praying

And behold, the LORD passed by, and a great and strong wind tore into the mountains and broke the rocks in pieces before the LORD, but the LORD was not in the wind; and after the wind an earthquake, but the LORD was not in the earthquake; and after the earthquake a fire, but the LORD was not in the fire; and after the fire a still small voice.

1 Kings 19.11b–12 (NKJV)

Look at the birds . . . consider the lilies . . . do not worry, saying, 'What shall we eat?' or 'What shall we drink?' or 'What shall we wear?' . . . But seek first the kingdom of God and His righteousness, and all these things shall be added to you. Therefore do not worry about tomorrow, for tomorrow will worry about its own things. Sufficient for the day is its own trouble.

Matthew 6.26a, 28b, 31, 33–34 (NKJV)

In Chapter 7 I suggested that Jesus had an IWM of his relationship with God that can be summed up as 'I am beloved, and God is well pleased with me'. In Chapter 8 we saw how this sense of being worthy and loved unconditionally shows itself in Christ's perfect humility, and explored the ways we too can live this out. In this chapter we will consider another IWM: Jesus had an IWM of the world as a place to which the kingdom of God was coming ever nearer; a place that was itself full of signs of the kingdom. He looked at the world in a particular way, and he asks us to emulate his way of looking.

The Gospels tell us that people were continually demanding a sign from Jesus to give credibility to his message and a clue to his identity (e.g. Matt. 16.1 and parallels). It seems that they were wanting something like the fire that Elijah called down from heaven in his dispute with the prophets of Baal (1 Kings 18). In the Synoptic Gospels Jesus consistently refuses this demand for supernatural pyrotechnics, simply alluding to his resurrection as the sign that will put an end to the need for signs. Instead he keeps telling people to use their eyes to see that his way of life authenticates him (Matt. 11.4–6; Luke 7.22–23), and explicitly likens this ability to reading the natural world:

When it is evening, you say, 'It will be fair weather, for the sky is red.' And in the morning, 'It will be stormy today, for the sky is red and threatening.' You know how to interpret the appearance of the sky, but you cannot interpret the signs of the times. (Matthew 16.2–3)

The one unequivocal sign reported in the Synoptic Gospels is that given to the shepherds. Nothing could be less spectacular or more mundane and natural: a baby wrapped in cloths lying in a manger (Luke 2.12).

John's Gospel does describe some of Jesus' actions as 'signs' (e.g. John 2.11), but these are always acts of service that are highly theologically loaded, rather than dramatic tricks executed for effect. Jesus' discourse on these signs of his identity and work is couched largely in natural categories such as water, bread, light, shepherding, cereal and fruit-growing (John 4.10; 6.35; 8.12; 10.7, 11; 12.24; 15.1). The significance of these categories should have been apparent to his audience because, while natural and mundane, they draw heavily on ways of speaking about God already well-established in the Hebrew Bible, especially in second Isaiah (see Ball 1996 for a full consideration).

These natural categories, alongside several others such as housekeeping, parenting and managing a business, are present throughout the parables of Jesus. Yet despite these homely features, the parables are not primarily designed to make complex and abstract truths more easily accessible by the use of simple illustrations (Duff and Collicutt McGrath 2006). They are more like riddles that can conceal as well as reveal (Matt. 13.10–13). The overall message is consistent across all four Gospels: the natural world is capable of disclosing the things of God, but in order for it to do so it must be read aright, and more than this, read 'unnaturally'. This is because nature is ambiguous (McGrath 2008).

Here we have a fascinating parallel with Scripture, something that has long been noted in the Christian tradition of the 'two books' (Harrison 2001; Fiddes 2013). The Bible can reveal God if read aright, but it can also appear opaque or – worse still – is vulnerable to misreading and misuse, as history makes clear (see e.g. Jones 2008; Kille 2004). The same is true for the natural world. Both the book of nature and the book of Scripture seem to require the 'eye of faith'.

> The whole of this sensible world is like a book, written by the finger of God, being created by His power. And the individual creatures are like symbols or letters that are not invented in an arbitrary way by man, but ordained according to the will of God in order to demonstrate his wisdom. But it is also so that if an illiterate person saw the book lie open he would not recognize the letters; he will then be like a foolish and soulless person who does not realize that which is of God and who sees in the visible things only the exterior face of creation without understanding its interior reasons. But the spiritual man, who shows discretion in all things, will grasp the wonderful wisdom of the Creator from within by considering the beauty of His works from the outside.
>
> Hugh of St Victor (1096–1141)

Is natural theology legitimate?

In Chapter 3, I described Jesus, perhaps controversially, as a natural theologian. Natural theology rests on the idea that the created order is capable of disclosing

God, and that 'by nature' – that is, just by being human beings – men and women have a certain degree of knowledge of God and awareness of him, or at least a capacity for such awareness (Barr 1993, p. 1). Yet the whole enterprise of natural theology has been questioned by many, particularly within the western Protestant tradition that emphasizes that the natural world is fallen, as is the human capacity to interpret it (see e.g. Moore 2010). On this account Jesus, who was not tainted by the Fall, was capable of seeing God aright in nature, but the rest of humanity is not. We must instead rely on the Word of God witnessed to by Scripture and interpreted by the Church.

The debate is complex and beyond the scope of this book, but it should be clear to the reader that the approach taken here, which tries to bring natural and social sciences into conversation with Christian theology, is based on the conviction that natural theology *is* legitimate. This conviction itself arises from the biblical witness to Jesus. His teaching shows that nature as well as Scripture can point to God, and moreover requires us to look at the natural world in this light. Jesus also reminds us that Scripture can be as problematic as nature if it is not read with the eye of faith (John 5.39).

A man that looks on glass,
On it may stay his eye;
Or if he pleaseth, through it pass,
And then the heaven espy.

George Herbert (1593–1633)

To see a World in a Grain of Sand
And a Heaven in a Wild Flower,
Hold Infinity in the palm of your hand
And Eternity in an hour.

William Blake (1757–1827)

Unlike the detractors of natural theology, Jesus didn't seem to see the fallen character of worldly systems as an obstacle to their signifying the divine (Matt. 7.11; Luke 11.13; Luke 13.1–3; Luke 16.1–9; 18.3–8). Furthermore, Paul's speech to the Athenians (as recorded by Luke) is clearly based on the idea of a natural and worthy human desire for God expressed even in idolatry; one that gropes towards him and may yet find him (Acts 17.22–28). At the beginning of the letter to the Romans Paul writes that God's nature was evident in creation long before the coming of Christ, for those who had eyes to see it (Rom. 1.20).

Of course it is true that God is utterly other and distinct from his creation, not just in the way that he is, but in the *fact* that he is; everything else is dependent on him for existence. Yet it is still possible, by introducing the idea of analogy,[1] to understand the created order as having an existence that is recognizably similar to God's existence, while at the same time being profoundly different. The similarities between the natural world and God allow it to respond to him with a degree of recognition, a felt sense of correspondence. The differences prevent it from fully connecting with him – that is, until he comes to inhabit the created order himself. In the incarnation God stands in solidarity with human beings and enlightens them by saying, 'Try looking at it this way' (John 1.9). But more than that, he gives us something really worth looking at – himself (John 1.14, 18):

> The divine light of the *logos* allows us to 'see' the created order in the proper way, so that human limitations in discerning the divine might be overcome. Yet Christ, as the Word incarnate, does more than illuminate and interpret the created order. He is the one who enters into that order, thus transforming its capacity to point to God. And there is more: Christ himself discloses the nature and glory of the hitherto invisible God in a human person. The disclosure of the glory of God thus comes through nature, not above nature. The enfleshed Word of God makes God known to humanity in and through the natural order. (McGrath and Collicutt 2008, p. 173)

If we are to take the incarnation seriously, we must understand that Christ will reveal himself in the natural order and through our natural capacities. We need to play our part in reading the two books aright by co-operating with the Spirit in developing the eye of faith. The rest of this chapter will explore several ways in which we might do this, particularly with regard to the Book of Nature.

Insight and the psychology of visual perception

One of the features of religious epiphanies discussed in Chapter 6 was the achievement of insight. Religious faith is fundamentally about insight into the divine rather than beliefs about the divine (contra Dawkins 2006); more like perceiving than knowing. Perception brings with it a deep conviction of truth in a way that belief about something that has not been directly observed cannot. Job sums this up well in his response to his epiphany (which is actually a theophany). Notice too how, in relation to the discussion on perspective in Chapter 6, this insight leads Job to view his previous perspective negatively:

---

1 An analogy draws out similarities between two different entities. Here it is used in a very specific way as an 'analogy of being', an idea that has its origins in the thought of Erich Przywara (1889–1972) and is taken up in the natural theology of Hans Urs von Balthasar (1905–88).

I have uttered what I did not understand, things too wonderful for me, which I did not know . . . I had heard of you by the hearing of the ear, but now my eye sees you; therefore I despise myself, and repent in dust and ashes. (Job 42.3b, 5–6)

Understanding the nature of the quest to see aright may be helped by knowing something of how human beings naturally go about seeing the world,[2] and so this section gives a basic account of the highly complex process of visual perception, focusing on three aspects. These will provide a structure for reflection on how our natural perceptual faculties work both for and against the eye of faith, and can inform practices aimed at supporting spiritual insight.

Perception is about sense-making

The act of perceiving involves making sense of information that is picked up by our sensory organs. In the case of visual perception the information is provided by the light-sensitive cells in the retina that lines the inside of each eye. It detects variations in light intensity and wavelength across the visual field.

Healthy eyes are necessary for vision; however, they are not sufficient. This is because all perception relies on activity in the brain, to which the sensory organs are connected by nerves. Information from each retina travels to the brain via the optic nerve. When this information reaches the primary visual cortex at the back of the brain the cells here have a first go at making some sense of it. These cells are specialized to draw out features, such as orientation, shading and edges. Figure 18 illustrates the way this process compels us to see certain patterns of light and dark as overlapping solid shapes. It requires a good deal of effort for us to set this natural way of seeing aside and instead see the basic configuration of light and dark – what's 'really there'.

Figure 18.

---

2 Much of what is covered in this section is presented in more detail in Collicutt 2008a.

Cells in an adjacent brain area then draw out even more complex features, such as three dimensional shape, colour and movement. This enables me, for example, to identify that there is a spherical object, orange in colour, of a certain size and with a shiny pitted surface, ahead of me and to my left.

This information about the physical appearance of the environment is in its turn matched to schemas that hold existing knowledge about the possible *meaning* of certain physical configurations; for example that a spherical object, orange in colour and of a certain size, with a shiny pitted surface, is a fruit that is good to eat. This meaning-making happens further forward in the brain through the activity of cells in the temporal cortex. Only when all the information has been brought together in this way can perception – identifying an orange – be said to have happened.[3]

Because perception is a process of matching incoming data to stored schemas, an easy way to think about it is as a multiple-choice examination question with the schemas as the possible answers. As sensory information comes in, the brain does not ask 'What's this?'; instead it asks 'Is this an a, b or c?' ('Is this a pyramid, a cube or a sphere? Is this sphere an apple, an orange or a tennis ball?') Just as with multiple-choice questions, this method is quick and efficient but it doesn't always do full justice to the incoming data. The system may have to distort or oversimplify to achieve a fit.

However, sometimes the fit between the incoming data and the available schemas is so poor that a 'none of the above' multiple-choice option is needed. This allows for the development of new schemas: 'It's life, Jim; but not as we know it.' I can recall going through something like this when faced with my first baked whole aubergine on a school trip to Italy in the early 1970s: was it a fish, a big slug, a small rodent, a blighted potato or something even weirder? This example illustrates the fact that many of our schemas are culturally constrained. We see the world through multiple lenses shaped by personal history, family and local or national culture; my food schemas were definitely British.

This brings us to the next point about perception.

Perception is egocentric, concerned with action, and modulated by emotion and motivation

We see things from a point of view. The information provided by the retina only covers its field of vision; it doesn't provide a panorama. Therefore, as discussed in Chapter 6, we are always operating from a perspective, and one with limitations. This understanding of perception is paralleled at a cultural and philosophical level by the pluralist approach to knowledge of the late modern and postmodern eras, which has largely replaced the Enlightenment notion of 'objectivity'. Human beings are now understood to be participants in rather than observers of nature, always operating from a position and with an agenda, though often unawares. Thus qualitative social-science research, which sits very

---

3 Assigning a name to this fruit that is good to eat is an entirely separate process, as those of us of riper years are only too well aware.

much within this paradigm, requires its practitioners to articulate and own their position as part of good practice (see e.g. Finlay and Gough 2003); not to say 'This is how things are'; rather, 'This is the view from here.'

Research in cognitive neuroscience has demonstrated that the brain represents the physical and social world not only from our perspective, but in an idiosyncratic form that relates to our personal needs and coded in terms of our potential *actions* on a 'need to know' basis (see e.g. Arbib 1991). I don't carry a detailed Ordnance Survey map of my home town in my head; I just know *how to get* to and from the places I frequent. I don't know where that orange is in terms of some abstract system of Cartesian coordinates; I know where it is *in relation to me* so that I can work out *how and if I can reach it.*

My teenage attempt to identify the aubergine was also concerned with action; I needed to assimilate the object perceptually if I was going to work out whether it was safe to ingest it physically. In a similar vein, we persuaded our son to try sweetcorn for the first time by calling it 'yellow peas'; once it fitted into the 'pea' part of his 'good to eat' schema, he was prepared to put it in his mouth.

Emotion and motivation are also important in perception. There is a large literature that indicates that our perception is often distorted to fit with our hopes and wishes (Balcetis and Dunning 2006) and is particularly susceptible to our concerns, anxieties and fears (Bar-Haim, Lamy, Pergamin, Bakermans-Kranenburg, van Ijzendoorn 2007). Anxious individuals may have a lower threshold for identifying neutral stimuli as threatening; they may scan the environment for the presence of the particular things that disturb them (a feature of post-traumatic stress disorder); or may find it difficult to calm down once they have realized that there is actually no threat to them. If our perceptual system detects threat, we become alert and aroused, and we devote a significant amount of attention to dealing with the source of threat, perhaps by taking steps to avoid or escape it, but most often by ruminating and worrying. We start to see and think about the world almost exclusively in terms of our physical or psychological survival, and we have little attention left for other, perhaps more important, matters.

Perception pays attention to significance

This brings us to the final point about perception. Because we can't see everything all of the time, we have to choose what we look at; that is, we have to direct our attention, rather like a torch or spotlight (Posner 1980). We can direct our attention quite broadly to get an overview, or we can choose to focus down on something. We can even switch attention across several activities. However, we don't have limitless capacity, and so we have to allocate our attention according to certain priorities. The fundamental thing that drives this is personal significance: 'What's in it for me?' This may relate to long-term agendas about personal development or survival (Matt. 19.16); or it might relate to an acute concern (Luke 15.8).

So not only do we occupy a position, we can influence the view from that position by the way we deploy the light of our attentional torch. This is how we impose our agendas.

All the features of perception that we have considered in this section are entirely natural and arise from our evolutionary history, presumably because they have good survival value. Nevertheless, the fact that they are part of our fleshly human endowment means that they may at times make us blind or inattentive to the things of God (Matt. 16.17, 23). The next section explores some ways we might place our perception at the disposal of God by trying to look and direct our attention aright.

Paying due attention

Resisting premature sense-making: from awe to wonder

In Chapter 6 we saw that there is a connection between trauma and epiphanies because trauma forces us to accommodate to a different reality by shattering our schemas; as it were removing all our multiple-choice options and forcing us to come at the world afresh. In fact trauma is the most dramatic example of a whole class of experiences that challenge our tendency to make sense of, and thus master, the world. In 2003 Dacher Keltner and Jonathan Haidt advanced the theory that such experiences call up feelings that are variants of one prototypical emotion: awe.[4] Awe is an intense emotion that is characterized by a difficulty in comprehension combined with feelings of surprise, amazement and the like. Keltner and Haidt suggested that, depending on the circumstances in which it arises, awe may be 'flavoured' with fear, aesthetic appreciation, admiration, moral elevation or a sense of the uncanny. But, they argue, fundamentally awe is a response to something very big that makes us feel small and insignificant and that, crucially, we cannot fit into our existing schemas. We experience awe because our usual process of sense-making has been suspended, and we are stopped in our tracks. This theory has generated a good deal of further research, which has largely supported it (see e.g. Shiota, Keltner and Mossman 2007).

There are aspects of the natural world that have the capacity to evoke awe. I experienced this once when I drove into a freak tornado in the middle of the Cotswolds. I didn't know that it was a tornado until it was reported on the television news later the same day. In fact I wasn't aware that a tornado could happen in Britain. I was completely awe-struck by the scale and strangeness of the weather and had to stop my car and simply stare, as did all the other motorists around me. Afterwards I was incapable of communicating the experience adequately, merely mumbling things like 'The sky was green, and it touched the ground.'

---

4 Trauma and awe are also related. Recall the 'shock and awe' tactics of the US military command during the second Gulf War.

We know that encounter with the grandeur or beauty of the natural world is also often the occasion for mystical experiences (Hood 1977; Hardy 1979), and it seems that the great cathedrals were designed to evoke awe in a similar way, perhaps with the intention of facilitating mystical encounter with God.

If we recall William James' description of the psychological form of mystical experiences as ineffable, noetic, transient and passive (see p. 84), we can see that it has much in common with Keltner's and Haidt's analysis of awe. Both mystical and awe states are ineffable: we do not have the language to do justice to them because they do not fit our existing schemas. Both can be noetic: as our schemas break down we are forced to deal with something more like raw data rather than an interpretation of it, and this brings a sense of reality breaking in. Both are transient: it's impossible to abandon schema-driven perception for long without going mad (as we shall see below). Both involve a sense of passivity: we have seen that our perceptual schemas are concerned with action; if we are not able to use them we are likely to feel passive, even frozen to the spot.

It is possible to have a mystical experience without invoking the idea of God, but throughout history people have associated mysticism with the divine, valuing and cultivating mystical states as a way of connecting with God (Nelstrop, Magill and Onishi 2009). This raises the question of whether it is desirable to cultivate awe as a means of transcending the limits of our perceptual system so that we might encounter God in and through the world about us. This was a question that greatly exercised the Victorian art critic John Ruskin (1819–1900), who incidentally was very concerned with the construction of his own 'cathedral', the Oxford University Museum of Natural History. For much of his life Ruskin promoted the practice of trying to cultivate awe in response not only to the dramatic and exceptional, but also to the everyday, as a way of seeing heaven in ordinary – a kind of mundane mysticism which he thought could bring one closer to God. He of course did not use the language of schema, assimilation or accommodation; but he was clearly working with very similar ideas.

> To be receptive to the highest truth, and to live therein, a man must needs be without before and after, untrammelled by all his acts or by any images he ever perceived, empty and free, receiving the divine gift in the eternal Now, and bearing it back unhindered in the light of the same praise and thanksgiving in our Lord Jesus Christ.
>
> Meister Eckhart (1260–1328)

Ruskin essentially wanted to lose any sense of the wood and concentrate on each and every tree in it. In his *Modern Painters III* he enjoined his readers to set aside the way they had been taught to look and instead to look 'properly' by concentrating on every detail of a scene without trying to make it fit some preconceived notion of its relation to a greater whole, rather as one might try to do with Figure 18.[5] For Ruskin, schemas are like a veil that stops us fully seeing God's glory in creation. His aspiration was to abandon schema-driven process-ing and to shine the torch of attention into every nook and cranny of the visual world. The abandonment of schema-driven processing is also a feature of the apophatic tradition in Christian spirituality, which asserts that God can only be encountered through unknowing, and whose dominant image is that of a cloud that obscures as well as enlightens (cf. the fourteenth-century English text *The Cloude of Unknowing*). There is clearly a connection here with Ruskin's almost fanatical attraction to the works of Joseph Turner (1775–1851).

This is not the place to enter into a detailed analysis of Ruskin's thought, but it seems that he was on to something. Intentionally setting aside schema-driven perception has the potential to give us a deeper connection with, or at least a fresh perspective on, the created order, to read it differently. It may open up a space where we can, like Elijah, hear the 'still small voice' that is not, after all, in the wind, the earthquake or the fire:

> Time was (when I began drawing) that . . . I cared for nothing but oaks a thousand years old split by lightning or shattered by wind . . . *Now*, there is not a twig in the closest-clipt hedge that grows that I cannot admire, and wonder at, and take pleasure in and learn from . . . Now this power of enjoy-ment is worth working for, not merely for enjoyment, but because it renders you less imperfect as one of God's creatures – more what He would have you, and capable of forming – I do not say truer or closer, because you cannot *approach* infinity – but far *higher* ideas of his intelligence. Whether to attain such as an end, you cannot by a little determination spare a quarter of an hour in a day, I leave to your conscience. (Ruskin 1894, pp. 147–8)

Intensely focusing on a natural object in this way from time to time, contemplat-ing it in detail, bringing to conscious awareness the fact that it was made by God (cf. Ps. 139.14), can be a good spiritual practice, especially if carried out in the context of prayer and thanksgiving. However, the idea that one can automati-cally access 'total reality' by doing this is misleading.

It is sobering to recall that Ruskin eventually rejected his Christian faith and moved into what has been described as a kind of nature paganism (Drury 2000, p. 174). His mental health also broke down while he was still in his fifties. The precise nature of his condition is not clear (Kempster and Alty 2008), but it was marked by vivid and disturbing visual hallucinations, and thought disorder that reflected the complete breakdown of schema-driven processing that is so charac-teristic of psychosis (Hemsley 2005). Ruskin's attempt to look aright went very badly wrong, perhaps because he was trying to fix his gaze on that which we

---

5 In his autobiography, Ruskin describes a quasi-mystical experience that arose in the con-text of his reflection on nature as co-composer with the artist. He had made 'careful light and shade pencil study' of a piece of ivy wound around a tree stump, aiming 'to draw what was really there! . . . I had [until then] never seen the beauty of anything, not even a stone – how much less a leaf!' (Ruskin 1907, pp. 105–6).

are only capable of glimpsing momentarily. To quote T. S. Eliot, 'human kind Cannot bear very much reality'.[6]

Perhaps we should accept the fact that we 'see a through a glass, darkly' (1 Cor. 13.12, KJV), and be content with glimpses of reality when they break through, rather than straining to see the whole picture. This may mean cultivating an openness to the unexpected and a tolerance of ambiguity and partial information; fixing on neither the wood nor each individual tree, but instead being highly aware of the provisionality of our perception.

Here the notion of 'wonder' becomes important. Wonder can refer to something very like awe: marvelling at miraculous signs and wonders (John 4.48). But it can also mean to ponder, doubt or question. A tornado filled me with awe; an aubergine made me wonder. We should welcome awe, but cultivate wonder.

Wonder is inherent in science (Deane-Drummond 2006): after all, a falling apple made Isaac Newton wonder; a boiling kettle made George Stephenson wonder; smallpox-resistant milkmaids made Edward Jenner wonder. Unlike the violence of trauma and the overwhelming nature of awe, wonder gently opens us to that which requires further question (Miller 1992). When we wonder we allow something to niggle at us, resisting the attempt to smooth it so that it fits our expectations but, as it were, saying, 'Hang on a second . . .'. Instead of trying to set our schemas aside entirely or clinging to them defensively, we bring them to the table to be re-examined in the light of what niggles us, prepared to have them changed.

Informed systematic wondering is a definitive aspect of scientific method, as the title of one of the most famous works on philosophy of science, Karl Popper's *Conjectures and Refutations* (1963) makes clear. Here the scientific theories are the schemas that are constantly re-examined and reshaped in the light of niggling findings from empirical studies. The experience of wonder – the sense not that you know the answer but that you are, however obliquely, engaging with reality – is said to be a key motivator for working scientists (Deane-Drummond 2006). Indeed, scientists sometimes talk about their work as a kind of worship. Their awareness of nature's scope and complexity, much of which still remains beyond their conceptual and empirical reach, moves their wonder from questioning into intense appreciation (Boden 1985; see also Ps. 8.3–4). There is in this attitude a deep kind of humility; a recognition that there is always more to reality than the sense we make of it. Taking science seriously is one way of cultivating wonder.

As noted earlier, the riddle-like nature of the parables of Jesus means that they evoke this sort of wonder; they open up rather than close down the mind. It may help us to read them intentionally searching for the niggle and using this to set ourselves wondering. Seeing the glory of the Lord is as much about wondering at the ambiguity of nature and the paradox of Jesus as it is about falling down in wonder as our senses are flooded in a mystical experience. In this context it is helpful to compare and contrast Isaiah of Jerusalem's dramatic encounter with the LORD, full of awe and wonder (Isa. 6), with the child Samuel's subtle

---

6 'Burnt Norton' (1935). From *Four Quartets*.

encounter with the LORD in the dim lamplight, full of wondering and openness (1 Sam. 3). As we have seen, children seem to be particularly good at wondering (Berryman 1991), and this is often the first step in seeing aright.

The famous painting *The Light of the World*[7] by William Holman Hunt (1827–1910) is based on Revelation 3.19. It depicts Christ standing in the dark with a dimly glowing lamp in his hand, knocking at a door (see p.viii). Here we have the idea that human beings must attend to the voice of Christ and open the door so that he can come in and gently enlighten us. We cannot see aright without his light, but in order to receive its illumination we need first to open our minds: to wonder.

Opening up the perspective: managing worry

Sadly, wonder can easily become worry; turning things over in our mind can easily become obsessive rumination. Worry is not good for our psychological or spiritual health because it so often distracts us from what is important. This insight is shared by nearly all faith traditions, and over the centuries they have come up with the practice of contemplative meditation as a way of addressing the issue. Contemplative meditation is 'a family of techniques which have in common a conscious attempt to focus attention in a non-analytical way, and an attempt not to dwell on discursive, ruminating thought' (Shapiro 1980, p. 14).

In recent years mental health practitioners have seen the wisdom in this and have incorporated some principles of contemplative meditation into mindfulness therapy, which has been shown specifically to reduce ruminative thinking (Ramel, Goldin, Carmona and McQuaid 2004). Mindfulness was originally introduced into the therapeutic context in the late 1970s by Jon Kabat-Zinn (1982), an American physician and molecular biologist, and has been developed into a therapeutic approach to a wide variety of health conditions (Grossman, Niemann, Schmidt and Walach 2004).

Mindfulness is practised in order to develop certain habits of mind, with a view to reducing reactive modes of thinking and feeling (for example, responding to a twinge of pain with, 'Oh no! → I'm going to get one of my headaches → I'll miss that meeting, and I will let everyone down yet again → Why does this always happen to me? → I'm so sick of my life!') and instead cultivating curiosity (for example, 'That's interesting; there's a slight pain in my head . . . there's also a breeze on my face from the open window . . . the carpet is blue and has a stain on it . . . my shoe is pinching somewhat . . .'). Increasing general awareness of the body – rather than obsessing about particular physical symptoms – is supported through the use of simple breathing techniques.

All of this is conducive to kindly wonder rather than angst-ridden worry. Practitioners of mindfulness talk of its giving a sense of intimacy with the self

---

7 This painting was highly appreciated by Ruskin, who wrote a letter to *The Times* on 5 May 1854 defending it against its largely negative reception by contemporary critics.

through detachment from inessential accretions: I am not my headache script, and as I let it go, I may gain a better sense of who I am.

Mindfulness has been found to have five related but distinct facets (Baer, Smith, Lykins, Button, Krietemeyer, Sauer, Walsh, Duggan, Williams 2008):

- Observing: noticing and attending to sensations, thoughts and feelings, without becoming absorbed in their content.
- Describing: labelling experiences with (neutral) words.
- Not judging: taking a non-evaluative attitude towards experiences.
- Acting with awareness: attention to the present moment.
- Non-reactivity: allowing thoughts, sensations and emotions freely to enter or leave awareness, treating them as passing events of the mind.

Kabat-Zinn first discovered these principles in the context of meditation practices that are part of the Buddhist eightfold path to enlightenment. However, mindfulness therapy is not the same as faith-based meditation, and it is not inherently Buddhist. It is about the promotion of a particular type of consciousness that fully inhabits the present moment. Nevertheless, because of its association with Buddhism, many Christians have been cautious, if not frankly suspicious about embracing it.

This is a shame, because the principles of mindfulness are very much there in the Christian tradition. The mindful practice of managing unwanted thoughts and passions, not by engaging with them or trying to suppress them, but by a measured detachment from them in order to turn more fully Godwards, comes up repeatedly and through a range of traditions in the history of Christian spirituality. We have already noted Jesus' instruction not to worry. He also advised against premature judgement (Matt. 7.1 and Luke 6.37; Matt. 13.24–30).

The Desert Fathers and Mothers spent much time in solitude and developed practices for dealing with impure thoughts and feelings that assailed them. Some of these practices emphasized non-reactive thinking. For example, Makarios the Great (c.300–91) is reputed to have said: 'Meditate on the Gospel and the other Scriptures, and if an alien thought arises within you, never look at it but always look upwards, and the Lord will come at once to your help' (Ward 1975, p. 37).

Here we see that the practice of meditation is firmly centred on Christ, as it always is in the Christian tradition. This is also evident in the development of the practice of *hesychasm* in the Eastern Orthodox Church.[8] *Hesychasm* is a type of contemplative meditation that involves the cultivation of a deep inner stillness, which is achieved by considering thoughts, feelings and bodily sensations in a detached manner, and setting imagination and discursive thought aside. Over time this was combined with particular postures – often the foetal position was taken up – and slow, deep breathing aimed at anchoring attention by reducing arousal (Watts and Williams 1988, p. 78). These practices were

---

8 This is recorded in the *Philokalia* (literally 'Love of beautiful things'), a four-volume anthology of the spiritual writings of the Eastern Church between the fourth and fifteenth centuries. There are several translations available.

never mistaken for prayer, but were seen more as a kind of ground clearing that readied the soul to receive God; so *hesychasm* was described as the 'the birth of prayer' by John of Damascus (675–749). However, as it was placed under the authority and protection of God by the incorporation of the Jesus Prayer into the practice of breathing, it essentially became a form of prayer (Ware 2000).

Mindfulness can refer to a general attitude beyond the formal practice of contemplative meditation (see Thompson and Thompson 2012 for an interesting application to contemporary Christian ministry). One obvious application is in the reading of Scripture, and it seems that this is being increasingly embraced in the practice of *Lectio Divina*.

Lectio Divina ('divine reading') refers to quite a diverse range of approaches whose origins are ancient and obscure but probably lie in the Jewish practice of meditating on the *Torah*. Central to these approaches is reading the Bible with the expectation of encountering God. This is an exact parallel to the idea of reading creation considered earlier; both rest on the belief that Christ both inhabits and interprets the 'text', be it Scripture or nature.

It may seem rather obvious that we should approach the Bible expecting to encounter God, but because of the danger of misreading it we need to cultivate the eye of faith here also. One way to do this is by rigorous and transparent exegetical and hermeneutic techniques, brought under the discipline of the community of the Church. Indeed some, beginning with the Church Father Origen (185–234),[9] would say that study informed by such techniques is a necessary part of the practice of *Lectio Divina* (e.g. Wansbrough 2010, p. 172). However, the practice goes beyond this, aiming for a deep personal appropriation of the text through, in the words of Benedict of Nursia (480–547), a 'listening of the heart'.[10]

Following Guigo II[11] (1140–93), *Lectio Divina* is now usually divided into four phases: reading, meditation, prayer, contemplation. The text is read carefully and, if necessary, repeatedly. It is then studied, with particular attention to contextualizing it and connecting it with other parts of Scripture. This should take the individual or group to the limits of their understanding and engender a sense of wonder and humility. At this point prayer for enlightenment is offered and then a more contemplative approach to the text begins. Guigo seems to have had something rather like Ruskin's schema-free processing in mind, for he emphasizes that this contemplation brings only fragmentary glimpses of reality, at one point remarking 'The eye of the human heart has not the power to bear the shining of the true light.'

Nowadays the contemplative phase of *Lectio Divina* is conducted rather more like mindfulness. Discursive and analytic thinking is set aside and the text is contemplated with a kindly curiosity that does not privilege any particular part. Attention eventually will come to rest on a phrase that does not have to be analysed but can instead be received as a gift and treasured. This will lead to a different way of seeing, which may perhaps – though not necessarily – result in

---

9 For more details on Origen's approach, see Shin 1999.
10 Prologue to the Rule of St Benedict; multiple translations available.
11 *Scala Claustarium*, Letter to Gervase. See College and Walsh 1978.

new ideas, working through feelings or taking action. As with mindfulness, there is often a deepened sense of intimacy with the text, the self and the world; and a more vivid awareness of the presence of God in all of these (Painter 2012).

I have sometimes used this approach in preparing sermons, especially when I reach the limit of my analytic and discursive thinking. For example, I recently had to preach on the story of the paralysed man (Mark 2.1–12). This is a passage I have studied in depth. It is a fascinating Synoptic parallel, with interesting variants on the words used to describe the bed and the roof. It has a hidden very high Christology, with its allusions to Christ's heavenly pre-existence. It is an important text on the relationship between faith and forgiveness. It has much to say about friendship. There are all sorts of questions about the man's diagnosis. However, when I moved into the prayer and contemplation of *Lectio Divina*, one single and completely unexpected phrase came to my attention: 'go to your home' (Mark 2.11b). I set aside all the other possibilities and instead preached my sermon on the nature of home and homecoming. It felt the right thing to do and, as it turned out, it met the needs of my hearers well.

Shining the light: noticing the right things

This example of the practical impact of *Lectio Divina* brings us to the final aspect of seeing aright. We welcome awe, cultivate wonder and manage worry not as ends in themselves, but in order to notice the right things about ourselves, others, the world and God. We do not trip out or chill out; we watch and pray. It is, then, no accident that as *hesychasm* developed, it incorporated into its prayerful stillness a practice of vigilant watchfulness called *nepsis*.

Mindful wondering opens the eyes to the light of Christ, the ears to the voice of Christ, the heart to the touch of Christ. It is an invitation for Christ to drive our attention, directing its torch according to his priorities. These priorities are not arcane or complicated, but are clearly and simply expressed across the New Testament. They concern bringing the marginal into the centre of the attentional field (Luke 19.5) and looking for and appreciating the image of God in others (Matt. 25.40), together with his footprint in creation.

In order to do this our natural 'What's in it for me?' agenda has to be set aside (Phil. 2.4). This has already been considered in Chapter 8 with regard to self-esteem and identity. We need to approach situations not in the light of self-seeking but, as the second of the Bible passages that begins this chapter indicates, seeking the kingdom. This means being prepared to look out for that which has no relevance to our own interests.

This is not easy, even for Christians. Some years ago I attended a church meeting whose guest speaker was an eminent national figure. Several of those present eagerly manoeuvred their way into his vicinity during the reception. In doing this they trod on the toes of the church cleaner, who happened to be standing in their way, and one nearly knocked her over. They literally did not notice her. They were not being intentionally boorish; indeed they would have been upset to think they had hurt her. They were just not seeing aright. We are called to look out for the small and lowly. This includes children; recall that the sign given to the shepherds was a baby. We are also to notice the stranger; the newcomer, the foreigner or the one who is different. This is not to scapegoat or exclude; on the contrary it is the first step in the practices of hospitality (of which more in Chapter 11) and compassion (of which more in Chapter 12).

I once saw a beautiful example of this kind of noticing in the late Archbishop Robert Runcie. We were both passengers on a Mediterranean cruise ship whose cabin staff and crew were largely made up of Filipino men and women. They were pleasant, unobtrusive, and smiled a lot. We passengers hardly noticed them; that is, except for Lord Runcie. He took the trouble to get to know several of the staff by name, asked them about their families back home, showing great interest in baby photos and the like, and commiserated with them about their long period of separation from their loved ones. Once I noticed that he noticed them, I started noticing them too. When we arrived at a port, instead of looking out for 'the sights', I looked down at the portholes of the staff quarters deep in the bowels of the ship and saw their joy when extended family members turned up on the quayside. I saw that their smiles could hide grief. I saw their dignity and the pride they took in their work. It all made me wonder.

Sometimes what we are looking at appears unremittingly dark or ugly. Here we are to keep looking, an attitude to perception described by Ruskin as 'gazing without shrinking into the darkness' (1860, Part 9, 2). We are to keep asking 'Where is God in this?' or 'How might God's light be shone into this?', always remembering that the most beautiful one was not seen aright:

> He had no form or majesty that we should look at him, nothing in his appearance that we should desire him. He was despised and rejected by others; a man of suffering and acquainted with infirmity; and as one from whom others hide their faces he was despised, and we held him of no account. (Isa. 53.2b–3)

Finally, and above all, we are to notice love, especially sacrificial love; for where love is there is God. Love can happen in very unexpected places and between odd couples and groups, turning ugliness into beauty; so we need to look beneath the surface in order to recognize it. Often love happens in relationships between humans and animals, something of which Saint Francis of Assisi, who certainly knew how to look, was well aware.

One of the great privileges of being an Anglican priest is being invited into people's lives to bless their relationship with loved-ones, sharing their love expressed as joy at weddings and baptisms or as grief at funerals. Recall from Chapter 6 that blessing is essentially saying, 'Yes! This is of God!' Blessing is a kind of noticing, and noticing is a kind of blessing – a shining of the light of Christ.

Exercises

1 Find a quiet place, sit comfortably, close your eyes. Notice what it feels like to be you in your body. Notice the physical sensations as they come and go, but don't stop to pay attention to any particular one. Notice the feeling of the chair that supports you, the sounds in the room or outside, the smells and the air on your face. Welcome these sensations, pleasant and unpleasant, hospitably, but don't try and hold on to them. Do this for just five minutes as a kind of 'mindfulness taster'. You may wish to move into a time of prayer after this.

2 Choose a parable of Jesus and read it as if with a niggle detector (Matt. 21.35–37 is a good example of a niggle). Pause at the niggle, resisting the urge to smooth it over. Does this open up new avenues of thought or questions for you?

3 Even if you think you are no good at art, choose an everyday object such as a stone, a leaf or twig, a piece of fruit, and draw it in as much detail as you can. Make a mental note of the things you noticed in this exercise that you hadn't been aware of before. Offer these back to God in praise.

Further reading

Adam, D., 2012, *Occasions for Alleluia*, London: SPCK.

Bennett, Z., 2013, *Using the Bible in Practical Theology*, Farnham: Ashgate, Part II, pp. 53–105.

Hay, D., 2006, *Something There: The Biology of the Human Spirit*, London: Darton, Longman & Todd.

Sacks, O., 2011, *The Man who Mistook His Wife for a Hat*, London: Picador.

van der Hart, W. and Waller, R., 2011, *The Worry Book: Finding a Path to Freedom*, Nottingham: InterVarsity Press.

Watts, F. and Williams, M., 1988, *The Psychology of Religious Knowing*, Cambridge: Cambridge University Press, pp. 75–90.

Williams, M., Kabat-Zinn, J., Teasdale, J. and Zindel, S., 2007, *The Mindful Way through Depression*, New York: Guilford.

10

Personal Coherence:
Getting the Balance Right

Indeed, the body does not consist of one member but of many. If the foot were to say, 'Because I am not a hand, I do not belong to the body', that would not make it any less a part of the body. And if the ear were to say, 'Because I am not an eye, I do not belong to the body', that would not make it any less a part of the body. If the whole body were an eye, where would the hearing be? If the whole body were hearing, where would the sense of smell be? But as it is, God arranged the members in the body, each one of them, as he chose. If all were a single member, where would the body be? As it is, there are many members, yet one body.

1 Corinthians 12.14–20

I have learned to be content with whatever I have. I know what it is to have little, and I know what it is to have plenty. In any and all circumstances I have learned the secret of being well-fed and of going hungry, of having plenty and of being in need. I can do all things through him who strengthens me.

Philippians 4.11b–13

My child, eat honey, for it is good, and the drippings of the honeycomb are sweet to your taste. Know that wisdom is such to your soul; if you find it, you will find a future, and your hope will not be cut off.

Proverbs 24.13–14

In Chapter 2 we saw that a perfect personality, be it of individual or community, is marked by coherence and self-concordance; all the different things I try to do generally fit well together and help each other along so as to enact my rules for living, which in their turn reflect the person I want to be (or hope I am). This is likely to involve a degree of intentional balance, not just in relation to prayer, as discussed in Chapter 7, but across the whole of life. As the passage from 1 Corinthians that opens this chapter indicates, a well-balanced life does not emphasize one aspect at the expense of others.

A balanced life is fit and flexible, able to respond appropriately to change. Like a well-balanced supermarket trolley, it can be steered in the right direction without relentlessly pulling off course down avenues of its own making. A balanced life promotes resilience – something to which we shall return in the final chapter of this book – because it has a range of resources that can share the strain if required (Gal. 6.2), and may feed and repair each other, thus also promoting coherence. These are some of the reasons that a disciplined balance between, work, rest and holy play is a feature of many monastic rules.

Balance is also a feature of Christian doctrine, with imbalance often the defining feature of heresy (see e.g. McGrath 2009, pp. 92–3). Christ is not more human than divine, nor more divine than human. God is not more Father than Son than Spirit, but three co-equal persons. God is not more merciful than he is just, nor more just than he is merciful; the eschaton is now and not yet. It can be argued that the poise and balance of doctrine are designed to prevent the distortion of truth by attempts to hold or grasp it. Thus well-balanced doctrine is essentially humble. Well-balanced lives are also more likely to be humble because no one aspect is grasped too tightly.

> Idleness is the enemy of the soul; and therefore the brethren ought to be employed in manual labour at certain times, at others, in devout reading. Hence, we believe that the time for each will be properly ordered by the following arrangement; namely, that from Easter till the calends of October, they go out in the morning from the first till about the fourth hour, to do the necessary work, but that from the fourth till about the sixth hour they devote to reading. After the sixth hour, however, when they have risen from table, let them rest in their beds in complete silence; or if, perhaps, anyone desireth to read for himself, let him so read that he doth not disturb others . . . Let such work or charge be given to the weak and the sickly brethren, that they are neither idle, nor so wearied with the strain of work that they are driven away. Their weakness must be taken into account by the Abbot.
>
> Benedict of Nursia (480–543)

Detachment

In Chapter 8 the humble life was described as one that sits lightly to external sources of self-worth. In Chapter 9 a mindful attitude that does not grasp at passing thoughts or feelings, but instead treats them with a measured detachment, was seen to be a feature of contemplative prayer. There is thus a relationship between balance and detachment.

It is important to understand that detachment is an intentional strategy. Notice that in the second of our opening passages, this time from his letter to the Philippians, Paul says that he has *learnt* detachment – to be content in all circumstances. We are all familiar with the natural tendency to avoid or dissociate from things that make us feel uncomfortable by looking away and keeping our distance. This can happen either consciously or unconsciously as a way of managing anxiety. Detachment is different; as practitioners of mindfulness emphasize, it is an intentional noticing of such things as they arise, but at the same time relinquishing the tendency to respond with anxiety. The problem is that we can kid ourselves that we are being detached when in fact we are engaging in defensive dissociation. Here, advice from others who know us well, such as good friends or a spiritual director, is invaluable in discerning which process is really at work. One clue is that true detachment should lead us to care more – not less – about important issues: the priest and Levite who passed by on the other side were dissociating themselves from the situation of the injured man; the Samaritan was detached from preoccupation with risk of contamination or of violent attack and was thus able to respond with compassion.

The Christian tradition of detachment, which is perhaps most developed in the Carmelite spirituality of Saint John of the Cross (1542–91) and Saint Teresa of Ávila (1515–82), is not pursued for its own sake, but in order to promote loving attachment to God. In this, like the other Abrahamic faiths, it differs from Far Eastern traditions, most of which view detachment as a state of consciousness in which the individual is freed from the suffering caused by desires and attachments, in order to achieve impersonal cosmic union. The practice of Christian detachment is a complex and multilayered process, and we will pursue it, especially its more painful aspects, in more depth in Chapter 15. Here we simply note that it is part of higher attachment agenda, and so the two processes of detachment and attachment are held in a delicate balance.

> The natural desires hinder the soul little, if at all, from attaining to union, when they are not consented to nor pass beyond the first movements (I mean all those wherein the rational will has had no part, whether at first or afterward) . . . But all the other voluntary desires . . . must be driven away every one, and the soul must be free from them all, howsoever slight they be, if it is to come to this complete union; and the reason is that the state of this Divine union consists in the soul's total transformation, according to the will, in the will of God, so that, there may be naught in the soul that is contrary to the will of God, but that, in all and through all, its movement may be that of the will of God alone.
>
> John of the Cross (1542–91)

As we saw in Chapter 3, if we are to model our lives on that of Jesus, we will also be required to strike a balance between withdrawal, which offers us the opportunity for detached consideration of events, and passionate engagement with them. Detachment may help us to see more clearly which issues are worth our passion so that we can reset our priorities, but as we reconnect with the issues themselves, passion may overcome us, and then we cease to be detached. We should not grasp at the things of this world, but we should be engaged with it (John 17.15–16). This is particularly the case with righteous anger. The situations that require us to become engaged may also make us seem unbalanced or even deranged (Mark 3.21–22), both to ourselves and others. This is quite complicated: we are called to be fundamentally integrated and well balanced; but this fundamental stability should, like a roly-poly doll, give us a greater capacity to wobble in a way that may look quite alarming at times. To put it another way, our basic sanity may be expressed in our capacity to go mad on occasion.

The long account of the healing of Lazarus beautifully illustrates the interplay between Jesus' withdrawal to reflect on events in a detached manner (John 11.5–6, 14–15); his passionate engagement with events and people (11.33–38) and his attachment to his Father (11.41–42). His ability to know when different psychological modes should be deployed is an aspect of his wisdom that we are called to emulate. However, before we can know when, we need to know how. We need to develop self-awareness of our different ways of being, so that we can inhabit them fully, manage the shifts from one to another and the overall balance between them.

The good life

Martin Seligman offers one approach to this in his analysis of the good life (Seligman 2002; see also Seligman, Parks and Steen 2004; Sirgy and Wu 2009). He suggests that the good life is made up of the pleasant life (experiencing pleasure regularly); the engaged life (experiencing a high degree of engagement with satisfying activities); and the meaningful life (experiencing a sense of connectedness to a greater whole or higher purpose).[1] Seligman draws on the Aristotelian distinction between *hedonia* (pleasure) and *eudaimonia* (gratification), suggesting that while *hedonia* can be obtained from the passive receipt of a physical experience such as sunshine on the skin, a massage or an ice cream, *eudaimonia* requires psychological engagement and is strongly related to the achievement of a valued goal – to which he gives the rather grandiose term 'noble purpose' (2002, p. 112). Seligman argues that *hedonia, eudaimonia* and meaning are all important for the good life; attention should be paid to each, and to establishing an appropriate balance between them.

The wisdom books of the Hebrew Bible are concerned with the question of how to live the good life. They contain themes that closely correspond to both *hedonia* and *eudaimonia*, Ecclesiastes being more hedonic and Proverbs more eudaimonic in tone. This literature is realistic and pragmatic and pays attention to context. There is, for example, an acknowledgement that *eudaimonia* may be unattainable in life circumstances or social conditions marked by a lack of any personal control (such as enslavement or peasantry);[2] happiness and meaning can then be most appropriately enhanced by focusing on moments of hedonic pleasure (Newsom 2012, p. 134). This may also be the case for certain health conditions such as dementia, where a 'spirituality of the present moment' is to be both valued and cultivated (Jewell 2011, p. 182). The present moment

---

1 Seligman has little to say about detachment; he is much more interested in engagement. If pressed he would probably locate detachment within the meaningful life. This is because it is a way of setting aside spurious sources of gratification in favour of authentic gratification achieved by connection with a higher source of meaning.

2 But see the work of Victor Frankl for the alternative idea that attitudinal – rather than behavioural – *eudaimonia* may still be achieved under conditions of intense deprivation (Frankl 1946/59).

is framed as an unappreciated treasure by the poet and priest, R. S. Thomas (1913–2000) in his poem *The bright field*, where it is described as the pearl of great price of Jesus' parable (Matt. 13.46).

Seligman's notions of the pleasant (hedonic) and engaged (eudaimonic) life form a counterpoint to the attitude of detachment discussed in the previous section and to be found in many of the classic writings on Christian spirituality. They are to be held in balance with it. We will therefore explore the pleasant and engaged lives[3] further before returning to the practices of cultivating personal authenticity and balance that were so characteristic of Jesus.

The pleasant life: zest and savouring

Some people seem to have a zest for life. The VIA system described in Chapter 4 identifies zest as a character strength that expresses courage; it is essentially an enthusiasm and willingness to engage fully with life at the limits of our capacity. For people high on E this might typically be seen in the social domain; for people low on E it might be seen in more solitary pursuits. Evidence suggests that zest is associated with general life satisfaction and, more specifically, can transform work to vocation (Peterson, Park, Hall and Seligman 2009).

Closely related to zest is the skill of savouring. Savouring is a kind of focused appreciation of a positive experience through intentional eager anticipation (Luke 22.15), being fully in the moment, and reminiscing so that the positive feelings are rekindled (Bryant and Veroff 2007). Savouring can apply to any positive experience, but perhaps it is most characteristic of hedonic pleasure. My father, who could be grumpy and pessimistic at times, nevertheless had a highly developed capacity to savour the basic pleasures of this life. He would anticipate a good meal by lurking in the kitchen as it was being cooked, sniffing the air like a Bisto Kid; he would revel in the act of eating, and if it was a special occasion, would take a photograph of the table set with good food; afterwards he would describe all but the most mundane repasts as 'The best meal I've had in my life – bar none!' (until the next one). This capacity to savour made him very good company; somehow he could draw others into his simple, almost childlike, enjoyment. In this respect, he was rather like Jesus (Matt. 11.19; Luke 7.34).

My father's savouring was thus deeply hospitable (something we will explore more fully in Chapter 11); and indeed one well-recognized aspect of savouring is the desire to share the experience: 'Come on in – the water's lovely!' Moreover, because savouring involves attentiveness to God's gifts in creation, it also has the potential to develop into the appreciative wonder discussed in Chapter 9 and through this into a kind of worship (though the potential error of mistaking the gift for its creator must be borne in mind).

Savouring the moment also seems to have an effect on more enduring mood states. While we feel happier when nice things happen to us, it appears that this

---

3 We will not pursue Seligman's notion of the meaningful life in detail as it adds little that is distinctive to a theological analysis of the 'noble purpose' of the Christian.

relationship is intensified by savouring those things. A person who savours their few good experiences is likely to be happier than a person who has more good experiences but does not savour them (Jose, Lim and Bryant 2012).[4]

The way that savouring appears to work to enhance zest, building happiness and drawing others in, is a good example of the 'broaden-and-build' principle of positive psychology. This principle was established by Barbara Fredrickson (see e.g. Fredrickson 2001). Essentially it states that negative emotions such as fear and shame lead to a narrowing of the range of options; attention is focused on fight, flight or freezing like a rabbit caught in the car headlights. In contrast, positive emotions such as joy lead to an expanded field of cognition and action; possibilities are opened up rather than closed down. If the individual acts on these possibilities she is likely to have more 'can-do' experiences,[5] which in turn will build her skills and self-confidence. This principle is supported by the findings of many studies that have demonstrated a link between positive emotions and creative problem solving and also, crucially, an increased ability to connect well with other people (see e.g. Fredrickson 2004). As we saw in Chapter 8, negative emotions turn us in on ourselves; positive emotions overflow outwards.

In Chapter 7 we considered the playfulness and joy of God and noted its link with divine creativity. It seems then that God is the ultimate exemplar of the broaden-and-build principle. This is especially evident in his grace: God's generosity to us is an expression of overflowing positive feelings of joy and tender loving kindness (what the Hebrew Bible calls *ḥesed*):

> [T]he dynamic of the whole Godhead is outward and overflowing, hospitable and welcoming. It is from God's fullness that we receive 'grace upon grace' . . . In prayer we also give praise to God, and this too can be seen as a joining in with his work . . . God's creative and sustaining fullness overflows, so that it is possible for us to be caught up in it, into a giant and joyful 'Yay!'. (Collicutt 2012b, pp. 76, 79)

When we cultivate zest by savouring pleasurable moments we energize rather than drain both ourselves and our communities, we are well on the road to praising God, and we reflect something of the divine nature.

The engaged life: flow

According to Seligman, there is more to the good life than healthy hedonic pleasure. There is the sort of active engagement in relationships and projects in which one becomes pleasurably absorbed in the endeavour, both at the time and in retrospect as one reflects on what has been achieved. This type of experience, which he calls 'gratification' (*eudaimonia*), happens in the context of skilled creative activity, competitive sport and well-managed and rewarding personal relationships.

---

4 It may well be that the relationship is two-way: perhaps if you are happy you may be more disposed to savour, and if you are more disposed to savour this will make you happier.

5 The technical term for this is 'self-efficacy' (Bandura 1997).

Some time before the positive psychology movement emerged, one American psychologist, Mihaly Csikszentmihalyi, was already carrying out research into pleasurable absorption in skilled activities. He identified a distinct psychological state that he named 'flow' (Csikszentmihalyi 1975; 1990), whose antithesis is boredom. Just as boredom leads to alienation, flow leads to deeper engagement.

Csikszentmihalyi argues that there are both biological and psychological answers to the 'Why?' of human behaviour. For example, we eat food in order to fuel, build and repair our bodies (biological[6] explanation), and we eat food because it satisfies us and tastes good – it's rewarding (psychological[7] explanation). A very basic law of psychology, articulated by the behaviourist B. F. Skinner (1904–90), is that if we do something, and it is rewarding (or rewarded), we are more likely to do it again. The converse of this is the principle that if you want to know what someone finds most rewarding, simply look at what she does most of (Premack 1959).

According to Csikszentmihalyi, flow is a rewarding experience that makes us repeat goal-directed behaviours in such a way that they become increasingly effective, and so we develop skill. While the early stages of acquiring a skill can be fraught with frustration, there comes a point when everything comes together and we begin to experience a sense of mastery that makes us want to persevere, not because we think we should, but because it is starting to feel like fun:

Flow is a subjective state that people report when they are completely involved in something to the point of forgetting time, fatigue and everything else but the activity itself. It is what we feel when we read a well-crafted novel or play a good game of squash or take part in a stimulating conversation. The defining feature of flow is intense experiential involvement in moment-to-moment activity. Attention is fully invested in the task at hand, and the person functions at his or her fullest capacity. (Csikszentmihalyi, Abuhamdeh and Nakamura 2005, p. 600)

I believe God made me for a purpose, but he also made me fast. And when I run I feel His pleasure.

Eric Liddell (1902–45)

The features of flow appear to be very consistent across work and leisure, and the brain changes associated with flow are beginning to be explored (Weber, Tamborini, Westcott-Baker and Kantor 2009). Flow is found to emerge where there is a good match between perceived challenges and existing skills (a sense of being moderately but not excessively stretched), clarity about what needs to be done, and timely feedback on progress. Ongoing adjustments in the level of skills or level of challenge within the activity maintain flow, keeping attention

---

6 This is a 'distal' explanation, looking at the ultimate purpose of the behaviour.
7 This is a 'proximal' explanation, looking at the immediate purpose of the behaviour.

totally absorbed. During flow, thinking, feeling and acting are unified, generating an experience that feels fluent and coherent (Csikszentmihalyi 1988; Nakamura and Csikszentmihalyi 2002).

> A Native Health and Innocence
> Within my Bones did grow.
> And while my God did all his Glories show
> I felt a vigour in my Sense
> That was all Spirit:
> I within did flow
> With Seas of Life like Wine;
> I nothing in the World did know
> But 'twas Divine.
>
> Thomas Traherne (1638–74)

I encountered a lovely example of flow this week in a man who was building a stone wall for us in our garden. He told me that he was trained as a bricklayer, but that simply laying uniform bricks on top of each other was a 'mindless' way of occupying oneself. His face lit up as he described the challenge of fitting our pile of irregular stones together, exclaiming 'It's like a jigsaw – it gives me so much satisfaction to see it completed. I've really enjoyed this job – the time just flew by.'

In summary, flow involves:

- Intense and focused concentration on what one is doing in the here and now.
- Merging of action and awareness.
- Loss of reflective self-consciousness.
- A sense that one can control one's actions.
- Distortion of temporal experience (time may seem to pass very quickly).
- Experience of the activity as intrinsically rewarding.

Flow is thought to support the development of skill, because as the individual improves he will need to stretch himself just a little bit further in order to achieve the rewarding flow experience. Moreover, flow is not confined to individuals; it is something that can be experienced by groups. One of the most characteristic situations in which flow can occur is in jazz ensembles whose skilled improvisation draws them into a seamless unity and draws the listener in to be part of their endeavour.

Flow is also closely related to play (see Hay and Nye 2006); we feel it when we do something as an end in itself, are deeply absorbed, have fun, and find that our competence has increased. In the spiritual classic *Love's Endeavour, Love's Expense*, W. H. Vanstone (1923–99) describes the creative play of two adolescent boys who, bored during a half-term holiday, took up his suggestion of making a model of a familiar area of countryside using a rather unpromising collection of stones, twigs, plaster and paint:

> By the end of the day they had something which they wanted to show me. Something was beginning to take shape. Next morning they came early; and thereafter for three days they worked with remarkable intensity and concentration, without thought to mealtimes or the lateness of the hour . . . the placing of each stone and twig was a matter for careful discussion . . . Some stones and twigs and details of plaster-work proved 'difficult': they had possibilities but would not easily 'come right' . . . the full possibility of each fragment must be discovered and tried in relation to other fragments. As the model grew and became of greater value, each step in its creation became of greater moment and was taken with greater intensity of care . . . Having expended to the full their own power to make, they became the more attentive to what the model might itself disclose. (Vanstone 1977, pp. 31–2)

Here we see a beautiful depiction of flow. Vanstone also draws out a link with attentiveness and goes on to reflect on the balance between action and attentiveness, working and waiting, that was so characteristic of the creative endeavours of these youngsters. This is a theme he would develop in his later book *The Stature of Waiting* (1982), which focuses on this balance in the life of Jesus.

The lack of reflective self-consciousness that is characteristic of flow states (losing oneself in the activity) is a feature of skilled performance; the tightrope walker who starts to think about what his legs are doing is likely to fall. It is also a feature of mindfulness; both flow and mindfulness are incompatible with rumination or worry. But there are also differences between mindfulness and flow, and it may be helpful to think of them as two sides of the same coin. Mindfulness seems to be associated with a distinctive pattern of brain activity (see e.g. Farb, Segal, Mayberg, Bean, McKeon, Fatima and Anderson 2007; Siegel 2007). It is a practice aimed at the setting aside of elaborative cognitive processing through taking a wondering observer stance in relation to the present moment. Flow cannot be practised as such. It instead arises as a by-product of absorption in masterful action that naturally inhibits elaborative cognitive processing, often emerging after a period of unrewarding struggle with an activity that feels meaningless, boring or difficult. It can therefore feel more like a gift that takes one by surprise. So while we might associate mindfulness with deep calm, flow can involve a kind of quiet excitement. Nevertheless, in their different ways both mindfulness and flow enable us to transcend our worries and preoccupations.

The authentic life: recognizing fruit of the Spirit

We have seen that flow states are marked by a unity of thinking, feeling and acting that feels fluent and coherent, 'joined and knit together by every ligament working properly' (Eph. 4.16).

Flow states are also marked by intrinsic motivation – carrying out the activity for its own sake because I want to do it for my own sake. The activity thus expresses something of who I am or who I am becoming. It seems that being in flow on a regular basis may be a sign of that 'perfect personality' that was described on page 22 as one in which all the different things I try to do generally fit well together and help each other along (horizontal coherence), are clearly connected with my rules for living (vertical coherence) and bear a close relationship to the person I want to be or hope I am (self-concordance).

There is something about authentic identity here. When Eric Liddell describes his experience of flow in running, he sees it as a sign of his being most fully the person God created him to be. When I am being true to myself, there will be flow; when I am not, there will, in the words of Ignatius of Loyola, be 'sharpness, noise, and disquiet'.

Some writers have seen a particular connection between flow and aspects of Ignatian spirituality (Csikszentmihalyi 1988; Zagano and Gillespie 2006). The Society of Jesus has always been a movement that emphasizes action at least as much as contemplation, and its founder was a soldier. From its beginnings it has offered young men a life with a degree of engagement, of being caught up with a greater endeavour, that parallels the military. Ignatius' account of the experience of 'consolation' that is a mark of the activity of the Spirit also bears some similarity to flow. Flow is deeply connected with authenticity, as we shall see in the next section, and in the Ignatian tradition. 'Spiritual consolations will always be experienced in the person's heart as the more natural, more fitting, deeper, truer experience . . . to a person's authentic inner core' (Horn 1996, p. 146):

> I give the name 'consolation' to every increase of hope, faith and charity, to all interior happiness that calls and attracts a person towards heavenly things and to the soul's salvation, leaving the soul quiet and at peace in her Creator the Lord.
>
> With those who go on from good to better, the good Angel touches the soul sweetly, lightly and gently, like a drop of water going into a sponge; and the evil touches it sharply and with noise and disquiet, as when the drop of water falls on the stone . . . The reason for this difference is the disposition of soul, either contrary or similar to those spirits . . . when the disposition is similar, they come in quietly, as someone comes into one's own home opening the door. (Ignatius of Loyola (Spiritual Exercises 316, 335))

We return now to the question of individual differences in the expression of Christian virtue. As we saw in the introduction to Part 3, Paul describes these as fruit of the Spirit in his letter to the Galatians. There is no choice for the Christian; she is required to cultivate this spiritual fruit. But she does have some choice as to how she expresses the fruit in her behaviour and, given Jesus' strong condemnation of hypocrisy and exhortation to intrinsically motivated holiness (e.g. Matt. 6.1–18), she should seek for authenticity. Given that flow is a mark of authenticity, she should expect to be experiencing flow on a reasonably regular basis.

In Chapter 4 we explored the example of different ways of expressing the virtue of hospitality. Here this approach is applied to the first three fruit of the Spirit from Galatians 5.22: love, joy and peace.

Love

'Love is a many-splendored thing.' In his 1960 book *The Four Loves*, C. S. Lewis famously divided love into unconditional charity, *erōs* (romantic love), *philia* (friendship) and *storgē* (familial or kin affection). Lewis' charity essentially corresponds to the *agapē* of the New Testament, whose characteristics are helpfully spelt out by Paul in 1 Corinthians 13.4–7: *agapē* is not motivated by self-interest (it has no hidden agenda); it has an enduring quality in the face of adversity and rejection; it is based on truth rather than delusion or ignorance (e.g. Luke 7.39), yet looks for the best in people and situations. Above all, *agapē* is sacrificial (John 15.15; see also Rom. 5.8), and in Jesus' statement that this type of love can be shown to friends, we see that *agapē* is potentially a part of all types of love, rather than a special separate category.

Having said all this, there is still a great degree of potential for individual differences in the expression of *agapē*. Some people may be effusive in their shows of affection, being generous with hugs and kisses; others may find it easier to send a card with appreciative or encouraging words; others may be particularly good at selecting just the right gift that makes the receiver feel known and understood; others may be more practical in their approach. I well recall our son telling me that he knew his father loved him, not because of the sorts of things he said, but because 'He does stuff like waiting in the rain for the AA man that time when I pranged the car, so that I could go home to get dry.'

There is a kind of love called maintenance,
Which stores the WD40 and knows when to use it;
Which checks the insurance, and doesn't forget
The milkman.

U. A. Fanthorpe (1929–2009)

We should do what we can (Mark 14.8). Notice how Jesus, ever attentive to love, sees authentic *agapē* in the sacrificial gift of ointment from the woman who anoints his feet (Luke 7.47), where others see only vulgar histrionics (Collicutt 2009a, pp. 117–21). It is possible for us to do love our way and let others do love their way.

Joy

Joy should not be confused with extraversion. This is an easy mistake to make because joy is most usually seen in social situations of reunion or the celebration of group solidarity. It is often expressed through laughter, even shouting and screaming. In the context of worship the notions of 'joyful' and 'happy-clappy' may seem interchangeable.

But joy (*chara*) is a fruit of the Spirit, a virtue and not a personality trait. As we saw in Chapter 7, the New Testament writers describe Christian joy as an emotional attitude to be cultivated. It is therefore important to ask the question of how joy might be expressed by those who are not naturally sociable, such as people who are low on E, some people with conditions on the autistic spectrum or even people who are living with depression. Joy is relational, but its relationality may be equally about quiet one-on-one connection as about loud group partying, as the stories of the early Christian hermits make clear:

> There was in the Cells an old man called Apollo. If someone came to find him about doing a piece of work, he would set out joyfully, saying, 'I am going to work with Christ today, for the salvation of my soul, for that is the reward he gives.' (Ward 1975, p. 36)

The solitary runner, who feels God's breath propelling her as her skill increases and she gains a sense of mastery, can experience deep spiritual joy. The meticulous and eccentric lone mathematician, who sees complex patterns in numbers and gains a window into the mind of his Creator, can experience something similar. The shy and lonely middle-aged woman who finally finds love in the arms of another may simply express her joy in a mysterious smile.

Even the person who is going through dark emotional times may be briefly touched by joy or may practise the spiritual discipline of taking intentional delight discussed on p. 115. For such individuals, joy can be more like an idea that gives a glimmer of hope in an otherwise bleak situation rather than a felt emotional reality here and now.

The point is that, like love, there are different ways of doing joy.

Peace

The New Testament idea of peace (*eirēnē*) arose in the context of the *Pax Romana*, with its strong cultural imperative to 'keep the peace'; a unified Roman Empire with an absence of repeated civil warfare was seen to be in the greater interests of all. There is no doubt that this sort of thinking influenced the New Testament writers. However, Christian peace is not a pragmatic political policy but a theological principle. It arises out of a gospel whose fundamental message is that there is peace between God and humankind (Luke 2.14). This peace comes through a cosmic reconciliation that has been effected through Christ (Col. 1.20). It is then a fulfilment of the vision of *shālôm* to be found in the Hebrew Bible (see e.g. Zech. 8; Isa. 64.17–25/Rev. 21.1–4). This is a vision of deep well-being and a harmony of all things held together by the love of Christ (Col. 1.17).

Peace is a key marker of the kingdom of God (Matt. 5.9; Rom. 14.17). The body of Christ is a body that tends to be in flow – where everything works together in harmony for the common good. So peace is not primarily about rest; it is more about a kind of integrated wholeness that means that our actions flow, and that our rest is one that comes out of security and satisfaction rather than exhaustion.

Peace is also a process; notice how Jesus talks of 'peace*makers*' (*eirēnopoios*) in the beatitudes and is described as 'making peace through the blood of his cross' in Colossians 1.20. The peace of Jesus is a peace that comes out of torment (John 14.27; 16.33), even while it is based in his secure attachment to his Father. Jesus also stands in the prophetic line in which peace is closely connected with truth-telling about stuff that matters deeply and is therefore likely to engender conflict (Matt. 10.34ff.). Peace is not about the avoidance of conflict or the maintenance of the status quo at any cost (Jer. 6.14).

It therefore seems that the spiritual fruit of peace and its making can be expressed in stillness and waiting; in holding a situation and calming conflict; in holding one's tongue for the greater good; in speaking out to name what is wrong or to challenge a lie; in adopting a way of life that silently but powerfully and influentially subverts what is wrong; in exhorting others to address an issue; in making a stand on something that has the potential to divide a community and, as in healthy cell division, enables that community to grow. What it can never be is putting a lid on conflict and hoping it will go away.

The way that peace is done will depend on the situation, and this must always be underpinned by prayer. However, it is clear that some of us are more naturally disposed to holding and soothing, others to naming what is wrong. Some of us find peace in strenuous mental or physical work, others in silence and stillness.

Just as in the case of love and joy, it is possible to do peace differently; but because peace-making is a complex process we need to be very alert to the fact that we may think we are making peace when we are simply doing what comes naturally. Some of us – especially those high on E – need to manage the fact we have a tendency to promote needless conflict in the name of truth-telling because conflict excites and stimulates us. Others – especially those high on N – may need to manage the fact that we avoid necessary conflict in the name of peace-keeping because conflict frightens us.

The prejudices of church cultures

The tendency to confuse Christian virtues with certain types of emotion or with certain personality traits is regrettably rather common in church cultures. In this they mirror some attitudes of secular culture, for example the high value placed on extraversion (Cain 2013), and the use of 'neurotic' as a pejorative term. In other respects church cultures can depart from secular norms, placing less value on rationality and more value on the emotions.

There is, however, quite a lot of variation in the 'personality profile' of church communities: some are quiet and contemplative, some active and expressive, some cool and cerebral. This is not a problem in itself. Indeed, it is to be expected. It does, however, become a problem if a church community understands its particular culture as the normative or unique way of expressing the fruit of the Spirit. Here the link between rules for living and what people are expected to do to enact those rules are overly rigid (and often unstated); for example, the assumption that the virtue of joy must be expressed by smiling all the time.

In some circles the practice of silence is confused with the virtue of attentiveness; in others spiritual growth is seen in terms of a particular type of relationality marked by intense and nuanced emotional expression. Generally in church life there is an increasing tendency to frown upon rational thought and scholarship as 'the wisdom of the world' (1 Cor. 1.20), especially where this involves a scientific approach to qualities that are asserted to be 'unmeasurable' or 'mysterious'.[8] Yet this is to confuse that which is marvellous and sublime (to which our response should be wonder) with that which we do not understand because of our factual ignorance or conceptual vagueness – to which our response should be an effort to attain clarity (Bennet and Hacker 2003, pp. 242–3). Rationality and scientific enquiry are not inherently unspiritual:

> When wonder is based on pure ignorance or on error and illusion, it must fade in the light of understanding. Science is therefore opposed to superstition. But understanding may lead in turn to a new form of wonder, which cannot be so easily destroyed. (Boden 1995, p. 392)

Where individuals do not fit the dominant culture of their church they may be judged harshly simply for being themselves: for her activism, his anxiety, her preference for solitude, his tendency to 'tell it how it is', her love of book learning and so on. But our call is to be conformed to Christ who will enable each of us to be most fully herself, and this is not necessarily the same as being conformed to the culture of our church community.

One of the things that has really opened up the understanding of this point in recent years has been a growing awareness of the valuable qualities and ministries of people with special needs in Christian communities. The case of people with conditions on the autism spectrum is especially instructive here. These people have a particular need for structure, routine and predictability that makes them highly reliable but apparently lacking spontaneity in their worship; yet they often have a deep spirituality. Their relationships with others are complicated by the fact that they do not read non-verbal clues and non-literal communication easily, so they may come over as socially inept and tactless; yet it is obvious that they are capable of great love (see Memmott 2009).

The balanced life

Different church communities have different 'personality profiles', but all are part of the exquisitely balanced body of Christ. Within each church community there are many different individuals who have the capacity to contribute

---

8 For example, 'number-crunching disciplines bear little relation to questions of transcendence' (Carmichael 2003, p. xxii).

uniquely to its rich diversity and whose interests need to be held in balance by the community's leaders. This is also true within the life of each individual.

Much of this relates to timeliness. As we saw in Chapter 5, the faith stories and journeys of individuals and communities have a temporal dimension. Different ways of being and doing are appropriate to different times. This mirrors the account of creation in Genesis 2, which is broken into periods of days, and in which God rests. God does not rest because he is tired but because he has finished his work, and it is timely to pause and relish the satisfaction of a job well done. An awareness of the significance of God's timing lies behind the sanctification of time by the Jews, most obviously focused on the keeping of the Sabbath. It is also an important part of the sanctification of time in the Early Church through the Liturgy of the Hours (Rumsey 2003; 2008), and the ordering of the Church's liturgical year, marked by its periods of feasting, fasting and mundanity. These structures and practices can be hugely helpful in freeing us from being stuck in one particular way of being, and in prompting an intentional shift to restore some balance. However, the very fact that Jesus took such a flexible approach to Sabbath observance should warn us that here, as in the discussions in previous sections, the important thing is the principle (godly balance) rather than the specifics of the way it is worked out (Matt. 12.7–12 and parallels). It is possible to be imprisoned by the liturgical calendar (Gal. 4.9–10).

Work, rest and play

In this chapter and the previous one we have looked at different types of engagement and detachment, which correspond roughly to the notions of work, rest and play introduced in Chapter 7. All are necessary for the healthy Christian

Figure 19.

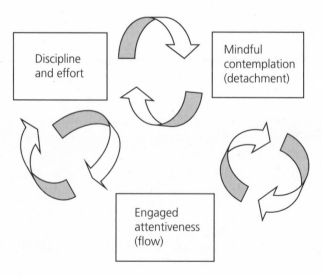

life, which may move between them minute by minute, hour by hour and day by day (see Figure 19).

Our life in all its parts is marked by each of these ways of being and doing, and each can be prayerfully savoured. Our effort, our contemplation and our creativity can be offered to God in anticipation at the start the day; thanksgiving for tasks achieved and unanticipated blessings received (including the blessing of physical pleasure) can be given at the end of the day. This pattern of anticipation in advance and reflection in retrospect (holy savouring) is a feature of the corporate daily prayers of all traditions. Retrospective reflection is also, as we have seen, to be found in a more intense form in the practice of the *Examen*.

It is worth reflecting on the relative balance of these three ways of being and doing across a day or a week in one's life. There should be a balance between contemplation and action; between detachment and engagement; between hard slog and flow. For example, if our paid occupation or course of study is all slog and no flow, we are likely to be deeply unsatisfied. Likewise, if our Christian ministry does not play to our temperament and strengths but instead requires us to act in a way that is not self-concordant, we are likely to feel at odds with ourselves, drained and discouraged.

However, we should not expect a slog-free life. Flow emerges from disciplined practice (the arrows in Figure 19 are two-way), so if we do not ever step outside our comfort zones and stretch ourselves, we are unlikely either to experience flow or to grow. Second, we are part of a wider community in which sacrificial love is required of us. Sometimes we have to bite the bullet and do that which does not come naturally, perhaps because a job needs to be done and there is nobody else to do it (recall from Chapter 8 that a willingness to offer oneself in such circumstances is a sign of humility); perhaps simply out of courtesy (recall from Chapter 4 the introverted young woman who made it clear that my company was onerous to her). It helps, nevertheless, to develop our self-awareness in this area, as the self-discipline and effort required is likely to tire us, and we may need to manage this by scheduling some personal rest or recreation.

Seeking and dwelling

Over a longer period we may, as individuals or communities, need to consider the balance between times of seeking that can involve intense transformative change, and times of dwelling that allow for consolidation and conservation of spiritual gains (Wuthnow 2000; Pargament 1996). This parallels the balance between the image of the fit body and the flourishing plant on page 14, and also the different phases of the process of peacemaking discussed earlier in this chapter. Some of us are more habitually accustomed to, or temperamentally given to, spiritual seeking, and some more to spiritual dwelling (Batson, Schoenrade and Ventis 1993; Pargament, Koenig and Perez 2000). So we may need to ensure that we are not simply adopting our default setting without regard for its appropriateness to our context. It is important not to impose our current phase on others who may be at a different point in their journey. Personally, I know that

I am a 'seeker' by temperament and can sometimes force this on to those whose current need is simply to dwell.

There is always a danger of seeking turning into aimless spiritual wandering and of dwelling turning into complacency or even spiritual boredom (Shults and Sandage 2006, pp. 34–5). This is an area where a critical soul friend may be able to give us good advice. We can also help ourselves – keeping a spiritual journal enables us to review our lives, notice the phases and draw out any patterns so that we can learn from them. If it looks as if we have become so static that there is a danger of stagnation, intentional disorientation and reorientation through pilgrimage may be a good means of remedying this. If it looks as if we have been on a very steep spiritual learning curve, we may need to build some undemanding stability and routine structure into our practice of prayer. If we have been church hopping (or shopping), committing to attending a single church for a set period, regardless of whether it's 'doing anything for us', is a good discipline. If we have become overly comfortable in one church community, a few weeks visiting a church of a different tradition or with a different demography may stretch us. This will open us to 'the other' – something on which Jesus was an expert, and the topic of the next chapter.

Exercises

1 Choose an everyday experience – such as eating a meal, having a bath, walking the dog – and savour it. Don't rush into it, but spend some time in pleasurable anticipation. While it is happening, appreciate the delights of the moment. Afterwards, share your enjoyment by describing it to someone else.

2 Try and identify an activity or situation in which you have experienced flow. Remember that during flow your mind will not wander, because you are totally involved with what you are doing; you will not be aware of bodily aches and pains or hunger; you are oblivious of your wider surroundings and have a sense of timelessness; you feel as if you are seamlessly joined to what you are doing. Thank God for it. Make sure that you find opportunities to engage in this activity or enter this situation on a fairly regular basis. On the other hand, if it already dominates your life rather like an obsessive addiction, consider laying it aside for a while as an act of spiritual discipline.

3 Construct a rule of life for yourself that builds in a good balance of work, rest and play. Look at your prayer life in terms of these categories also.

4 Reflect on an occasion when you may have misjudged an individual or community because they were 'doing the fruit of the Spirit' differently from you.

Further reading

Brueggemann, W., 2014, *Sabbath as Resistance*, Louisville, KY: Westminster John Knox Press.

Buchanan, M., 2006, *The Rest of God: Restoring Your Soul by Restoring Sabbath*, Nashville, TN: Thomas Nelson.

Csikszentmihalyi, M., 2008, *Flow: The Psychology of Optimal Experience*, New York: Harper Perennial.

Kellenberger, J., 2012, *Dying to Self and Detachment*, Farnham: Ashgate.

Seligman, M., 2002, *Authentic Happiness: Using the New Positive Psychology to Realize Your Potential for Lasting Fulfillment*, New York: The Free Press, Part I, pp. 3–121.

Vanstone, W., 1982, *The Stature of Waiting*, London: Darton, Longman & Todd.

II

Hospitality:
Visiting and Welcoming

And the Word became flesh and lived among us.

John 1.14a

When Jesus came to the place, he looked up and said to him, 'Zacchaeus, hurry and come down; for I must stay at your house today.' So he hurried down and was happy to welcome him . . . Then Jesus said to him, 'Today salvation has come to this house, because he too is a son of Abraham. For the Son of Man came to seek out and to save the lost.'

Luke 19.5–6, 9–10

When they had gone ashore, they saw a charcoal fire there, with fish on it, and bread. Jesus said to them, 'Bring some of the fish that you have just caught.' So Simon Peter went aboard and hauled the net ashore, full of large fish, a hundred and fifty-three of them; and though there were so many, the net was not torn. Jesus said to them, 'Come and have breakfast.' Now none of the disciples dared to ask him, 'Who are you?' because they knew it was the Lord. Jesus came and took the bread and gave it to them, and did the same with the fish.

John 21.9–13

Contribute to the needs of the saints, practise hospitality.

Romans 12.13 (RSV)

Let mutual love continue. Do not neglect to show hospitality to strangers, for by doing that some have entertained angels without knowing it.

Hebrews 13.1–2

Listen! I am standing at the door, knocking; if you hear my voice and open the door, I will come in to you and eat with you, and you with me.

Revelation 3.20

The ministry of hospitality can be about seeking or about dwelling. The image of the fit body is one in which the good news of Christ is communicated by seeking out and coming near to people where they are – by visiting them (Luke 10.1–11). The image of the flourishing plant, on the other hand, is one of a welcoming dwelling place; the birds of the air find a home in its branches. Here the good news of Christ is communicated by saying 'come and see' (John 1.39).

The New Testament word usually translated 'visiting' (*episkeptomai*) contains an element of seeking out.[1] When we visit someone at home, we get a much fuller picture of the whole person. We know where he lives; we gain an insight into

---

1 This verb is used in Acts 6.3 to describe the seeking out of men of good character to become the first deacons.

his tastes and interests; we get to meet or see evidence of his wider family, including beloved pets; perhaps start to piece together a backstory. When I was working as a clinical psychologist, I always found that doing a home visit changed my perception of an individual; s/he turned from patient into person. This was partly because of all the contextual information that I was able to gather, but also because the power dynamic in the relationship changed. In the hospital office or ward I was in charge and in control; any welcoming that was to be done was my job. In the individual's home these roles were reversed. Accepting the offered cup of tea was a crucial part of this dynamic. (There is something of this in Jesus' request for a drink from the woman of Samaria in John 4.) Visiting is about looking properly at the person and risking something by entrusting ourselves to his goodwill.

Welcome is the other side of this coin. Luke's Gospel tells the story of Martha, who welcomed Jesus into her home (Luke 10.38). The word that is translated 'welcomed' by the NRSV (*hupedechomai*) literally means 'received' (and this is how it is translated in the KJV). We have 'reception rooms' in our homes, the idea being that these are the areas into which we welcome our guests. In English the word 'receive' can also mean to hear or understand a message: 'Are you receiving me?' Here reception involves attentive listening. This is a point made by Henri Nouwen, who describes attentive listening as 'a form of spiritual hospitality' (Nouwen 1997, p. 85). The story of Martha and Mary seems to turn on this dual understanding of reception. It is full of irony: Martha welcomes Jesus into her home, but she is too preoccupied with elaborative cognitive processing to welcome him into her mind; this is left to her sister Mary who, in her engaged attentiveness, chose the 'better part' (Luke 10.42). Welcoming is about listening attentively to the other person and risking something by opening our personal space to her.

So hospitality is about looking properly and listening attentively, and is therefore, perhaps unexpectedly, connected with much of what we considered in Chapter 9. It is also about risk and edginess, because the Bible places a special emphasis on hospitality to strangers and foreigners, those whom we don't know well, those who are 'other' (Deut. 10.19; Matt. 5.46–47 and Luke 6.32; Luke 14.12–14; Matt. 25.38).

Let all guests who arrive be received as Christ, because He will say: 'I was a stranger and you took Me in'. And let due honour be shown to all, especially to those 'of the household of the faith' and to wayfarers . . . When the guests have been received, let them be accompanied to prayer, and after that let the Superior, or whom he shall bid, sit down with them. Let the divine law be read to the guest that he may be edified, after which let every kindness be shown him . . . Let the Abbot pour the water on the guest's hands, and let both the Abbot and the whole brotherhood wash the feet of all the guests . . . Let the greatest care be taken, especially in the reception of the poor because Christ is received more specially in them . . .

Benedict of Nursia (480–543)

In this chapter we will explore both the visiting and welcoming sides of hospitality in more depth.

Visiting

Visiting, both literally and metaphorically, is about seeing our host more fully. This means getting beyond our stereotypes; seeing the person as she is rather than as we think she should be; and seeing her potential.

Crossing the threshold: getting beyond stereotypes

Stereotyping is a natural psychological process. Like the use of schema-driven perception, it saves mental effort; we can make a quick decision based on minimal information with a reasonable chance that the decision will be correct. It can be highly efficient and effective.

But stereotyping is a double-edged sword. Some years ago I was sitting in our front room and glanced up briefly from my reading to see an unmarked white van pull up across the road. Half a dozen men of south Asian appearance with pieces of paper in their hands jumped out and went off in different directions. I remarked to our daughter, 'The Dial-a-Curry people are here again.' She immediately took me to task for racism, pointing out that these men might have been, for example, postgraduate social science students on a research exercise that involved questionnaires. A few seconds later a Dial-a-Curry leaflet dropped through our front door. I had, as it turned out, been correct, and at one level my stereotype had served me well. Nevertheless, our daughter was right: stereotypes of that sort stop us from looking properly at an individual or group and can lead to prescriptive beliefs that they should not step beyond the stereotype we have assigned to them. Stereotyping oils the wheels of prejudice.

Stereotyping is one of the ways we maintain the distinction between in-groups and out-groups. It seems that human beings are naturally tribal, with a tendency to form social groups that stand in power and status relationships to one another. The first systematic studies to demonstrate this were carried out by Muzafer Sherif (1906–88) and Carolyn Sherif (1922–82) on boys[2] attending summer camps in Connecticut (Sherif, Harvey, White, Hood and Sherif 1988). These, now (in)famous, studies showed how easy it was to establish bonds between boys of one group and prejudice towards those in another group, which could be ratcheted up to outright hostility under conditions of competition for limited resources. We saw in Chapter 5 that, following the Second World War, social scientists tried to develop explanations for the widespread collusion of the ordinary German population with the Third Reich. Following in the steps of Sherif, Henri Tajfel (1919–82) worked to provide at least part of an answer to this problem. Tajfel was a Polish Jew who had spent much of the war as a

---

2 It is interesting that all the early experiments in this area involved exclusively male participants. It is quite likely that there are gender differences in the way social identity is expressed; there are some theoretical reasons to expect more fluid boundary related behaviour in females.

German prisoner. He lost nearly all his family in the Holocaust, and after the war he became active in Jewish relief organizations. He then studied psychology and devoted his academic career to the investigation of inter-group relations.

Tajfel carried out a series of laboratory-based experiments involving teenage boys, each of whom was assigned to a group on an essentially arbitrary basis (his score on a computer task). The boys never met the other members of their group, who were only identified by numbers. The experiment demonstrated the remarkable ease with which each boy was prepared to discriminate against members of another fictitious group – again only identified by numbers – by allocating them less money in a simulated task (Tajfel 1970). There was obviously no history of conflict or competition for scarce resources between the groups, and no interpersonal dynamics at work. The mere fact that each boy believed that he belonged to one group (his in-group) was sufficient to invoke discrimination against the other (his out-group).

Tajfel and his colleague John Turner went on to develop social identity theory, which holds that people form group affiliations because these provide them with a source of both personal identity and self-esteem (Tajfel and Turner 1979). The groups we belong to tell us something about who we are, and we may feel that we have some kudos from being part of the group.[3]

Affiliation to a social group contributes to an individual's identity: 'I'm an Englishman.' It also consolidates the identity of the group: 'This group is composed of Englishmen.' This process of identity-giving is made more powerful where the group is positively distinctive (or even elitist), so that there is a natural (downward) comparison with other groups. This means that identity may often be stated in terms of negatives: 'I don't drink coffee – I take tea.' The whole process seems to be intensified if the group feels under threat, perhaps because it perceives itself to be in an alien environment: 'I'm an Englishman in New York.'[4]

Social identity is therefore not value-free. It plays itself out in ethnocentrism – the preference for all aspects of one's group over others, and behaviour that favours this group over others. As it is important to be able to recognize the members of one's group, identity markers that can effectively differentiate between groups become important. In addition to habits (such as 'taking tea'), these may involve aspects of appearance such as clothing, the assent to certain key beliefs, or forms of speech and language. Notice how, as the perceived threat to British society from radicalized forms of Islam has increased, debates around the wearing of the *hijab*, the teaching of 'British values' and the use of English have become more prominent. We feel the need to know who is 'in' (and thus for us) and who is 'out' (and thus against us).[5]

---

3 While the relationship between group affiliation and identity is well supported by much subsequent research (Brewer and Gardner 1996), the relationship between group affiliation and self-esteem is rather more complicated (see e.g. Aberson, Healy and Romero 2000). Nevertheless, it can be taken as a general rule of thumb that a sense of having a place in a group gives us dignity as well as meaning.

4 Sting 1987.

5 Identity markers of this sort can be used to police boundaries. A very clear – and horrific – example of the use of a linguistic identity marker to do just this is to be found in Judges 12.5–6, where in-group members are identified by their ability to pronounce *shibboleth*.

Evaluative stereotypes come into their own here: our ideas about 'us' and 'them' are reduced to a collection of identity markers.

The formation of in- and out-groups usually centres on issues of culture, geography and ethnicity. There is, however, no doubt that the process is intensified when religion is brought into the picture. As social psychologists explored the nature of prejudice following the Second World War, they were shocked to discover that religious faith was one of the strongest predictors of whether an individual held attitudes of ethnic or other types of cultural prejudice (the more religious the individual the more prejudiced s/he is likely to be). This relationship, first identified among American Christians, has proved to apply to all faith traditions across many countries of the world (Hunsberger and Jackson 2005).

The psychologist who first identified this relationship and then went on to try and explain it was Gordon Allport (1897–1967). He summarized the irony of the situation in these famous words:

> The role of religion is paradoxical. It makes prejudice and it unmakes prejudice. While the creeds of the great religions are universalistic, all stressing brotherhood, the practice of these creeds is frequently divisive and brutal. The sublimity of religious ideals is offset by the horrors of persecution in the name of these same ideals . . . Some people say the only cure for prejudice is more religion; some say the only cure is to abolish religion. (Allport 1954, p. 444)

The connection between religion and prejudice seems to be more marked where faith is expressed through group affiliation rather than individual spirituality (Batson, Schoenrade and Ventis 1993; Scheepers, Gijsberts and Hello 2002). This should not surprise us, because wherever there is a strong sense of group identity and solidarity, this seems to be achieved at the price of an increased propensity to out-group hostility. Human nature[6] is prone to deepening friendship by uniting against a common enemy:

> What crucified Jesus, first metaphorically and then literally, was the human drive to form a club and keep out non-members. It is the most human and harmless of tendencies, without which human society would be impossible. Yet it is also the most demonic and destructive of forces, repeated again and again in the human race's long tale of hatred and malice and genocide. (Barton 1999, p. 10)

It was not long after the establishment of social identity theory as a dominant approach in secular psychology that biblical scholars realized that it could be a helpful lens through which to view some of the controversies in the New Testament (see e.g. Esler 2000; Horrell 2002; Tucker 2011). I would go further and say that the issue of social identity is arguably *the* key issue in the New Testament, and its main point of tension with the Hebrew Bible. Allport's reflection on the paradox of religion that can both redeem and destroy humanity is directly paralleled in Paul's reflection on the *Torah* which can bring both life and

---

6 This corresponds to use of the word 'flesh' in its more neutral form discussed on page 93.

death (e.g. Rom. 7.11–13), and his total aversion to the Jewish identity marker of circumcision that dominates his letter to the Galatians.

Paul understood, apparently better than any of the other apostles, that the saving work of Jesus is fundamentally about breaking down the barriers between in- and out-groups, offering a social identity that is not achieved at the cost of out-group hostility. This notion of *cost* is important. We sometimes think of the work of Christ as involving payment (Matt. 20.28; Mark 10.45). Yet it's not entirely clear what the payment is or to whom it is made. Social identity theory may shed some light on this: in his approach to the other, Jesus showed us that group solidarity can and must be achieved without increasing enmity towards outsiders, and he was crucified by the system for his pains. Something very like this understanding of the work of Christ is expressed in the letter to the Ephesians:

> But now in Christ Jesus you who once were far off have been brought near by the blood of Christ. For he is our peace; in his flesh he has made both groups into one and has broken down the dividing wall, that is, the hostility between us. and might reconcile both groups to God in one body through the cross, thus putting to death that hostility through it. So he came and proclaimed peace to you who were far off and peace to those who were near. (Ephesians 2.13–14, 16–17)

Notice too how in Matthew's and Mark's Gospels the boundary between the sacred and the profane is broken down at the moment of Jesus' death (Matt. 27.51; Mark 15.38; Luke 23.45), and how in John's Gospel, Jesus talks about his crucifixion as drawing *all* people to him (John 12.32). The consequences of Jesus' death and raising are that *all* can now be part of the in-group.

This was, of course, anticipated in Jesus' life and teaching. In Chapter 3 we noted Jesus' habit of spending time with 'undesirables' – those literally on the margins of the people of God because they were collaborating with Gentiles, especially their Roman overlords (Zacchaeus is an obvious example). Jesus' healing ministry is also notable in its focus on those with 'marginal' health conditions, in particular leprosy (Matt. 8.2 and parallels; Matt. 10.8; Luke 17.12), the case of the haemorrhaging woman (Matt. 9.20ff. and parallels), and the dissociation of identity seen in some demoniacs (Matt. 8.28 and parallels; Luke 4.33–35).

These individuals had symptoms that attacked the borders of their bodies and minds and, it has been argued, thus symbolized the threat to the borders of the nation posed by Roman occupation and gentile corruption (Douglas 1966). They themselves were consequently marginalized by both local custom and religious law. A particularly clear example is the demoniac of Mark 5 and Luke 8, who is both occupied by a *legion* and marginalized by his community. In drawing close to people like these and making physical contact, Jesus not only offered healing, but he himself suffered stigmatization.[7]

---

7 For a detailed consideration, see Collicutt 2009a, pp. 88–101.

> That evening they brought to him many who were possessed with demons; and he cast out the spirits with a word, and cured all who were sick. This was to fulfil what had been spoken through the prophet Isaiah, 'He took our infirmities and bore our diseases.' (Matt. 8.16–17)

In Chapters 3 and 6 we noted the transformative set of blessings that form Jesus' 'position statement' in the Sermon on the Mount. It is worth contrasting these with the corresponding 'position statement' at the beginning of the Hebrew Psalter. Both the Sermon on the Mount and Psalm 1 begin with 'blessed' (*makarios* in the Greek Old and New Testaments). However, while in Psalm 1 we have a description of identity that is established against the other (the 'wicked'), in the Sermon on the Mount identity is established by alignment towards God; consideration of the other plays no part in this. Indeed as we have seen, part of being blessed is to be a peacemaker – to reach out to the other. Moreover, we are instructed to love our enemies (Matt. 5.44; Luke 6.27, 35).

The new community that Jesus established is marked by aggregation around him rather than the policing of boundaries that separate those who are in from those who are out. A separation will indeed happen, but as part of a final judgement by God, not in the present life of the faithful (Matt. 13.24–30; 25.31–46), who are exhorted to refrain from this practice (Matt. 7.1; Luke 6.37). For the Christian there are to be no more in- and out-groups (hence Paul's anathema to circumcision).

What does all this mean for the Christian disciple now? For a start it suggests that we should reject the term 'non-Christian' as unchristian. It seems that if we are to be formed into the likeness of Christ we must, as individuals and communities, not only be open to the other in theory, but actively seek out the company of the other. Sherif's early research indicated that simply increasing familiarity with members of the out-group was a powerful force in challenging stereotypes and decreasing hostility. Mark's account of Jesus and the Syrophoenician woman depicts this rather nicely (Mark 7.24–30). Notice how Jesus is not presented here as uncritically open to the other from a position of strength, but as gradually and thoughtfully *opening* to the other in a situation where he would have felt under a degree of threat (Collicutt 2009a, pp. 26–37). This communicates an acute sense of the pain that can be involved in such transformative encounters; they are costly.

We need to be aware of who 'the other' is for us, and bear in mind the research findings indicating that religious folk are *more* not less prone to out-group suspicion and hostility. Perhaps our other is the secular world; perhaps it is other religions; most likely of all it is Christian traditions that differ from our own (1 Cor. 1.10–13). It may be that we despise these groups; it is more likely that we fear them. Intentionally spending time with our 'others', finding out what they actually believe (rather than our stereotypes of what they believe), collaborating with them on a piece of work that will benefit us both (Jay 1993), are all ways we can visit with and see them more clearly. The visiting needs to go beyond that of the tourist who marvels at the strangeness of the other, and become that of the pilgrim who sees points of similarity and is willing to learn from the other. This requires a certain way of thinking that involves the ability to shift perspective discussed in Chapter 6, but also a security in one's own perspective that makes it possible to inhabit the perspective of the other critically and without being overcome by fear (Savage and Liht 2008) – a willingness to accept the other as she is.

Seeing the person as she is: 'If I were you, I wouldn't start from here'

Getting beyond our stereotypes marks the first step in seeing the other. However, the process can be thrown off course by evaluative judgements. We may notice things that lead us to the conclusion that the other needs to change (usually to be more like us): we start to see, but then we judge. This is the opposite of the wondering mindful approach that we considered in Chapter 9, one of whose characteristics is intentional non-evaluation. It is instead the imposition of our agenda on the other.

Apart from anything else, this is simply rude. If I visit your home, discover more about your taste in interior décor and find it profoundly different from my own, it would nevertheless be most discourteous of me to advise you to change your furnishings. The love that is expressed through visiting is that of meeting the other fully where he is. This coming close to the other has been described as 'moral proximity' (Levinas 1981), an offering of the self with no expectation of anything in return. We shall explore this more fully when we consider compassion in Chapter 12; here we observe that this unconditional acceptance is a key feature of Jesus' visit to Zacchaeus. Jesus' entry to Zacchaeus' home causes outrage among the onlookers because Zacchaeus is a sinner (cf. Rom. 5.8); the implication is that Jesus should have required Zacchaeus to change his ways before crossing the threshold. Instead Zacchaeus appears to change his ways *in response to* Jesus' visit, not as a condition for it.

When Jesus sends out his disciples, he instructs them to enter a house with an open attitude and a message of peace (Matt. 10.12–13; Luke 10.5–6); the worthiness of the house depends on its response to this message rather than its starting state.

Jesus' message of peace must be communicated, but there can be a problem here. Our theological concepts and language can often be a barrier. Words such as 'gospel', 'sin', 'absolution', 'salvation', 'redemption', 'blood', 'sacrifice', 'resurrection', 'crucifixion' may not convey the peace we wish to offer, even to those familiar with Christian vocabulary. Where people of other faiths and none are involved, this language is simply meaningless, as it is for those who do not speak English or who have limited or no language due to cognitive impairment. It is then necessary to unpack the meaning of Christian peace into principles, forms of words or – crucially – actions that meet the human needs of the other where he is. We have a lovely example of this in Paul's speech to the Athenians at the *Areopagus* (Acts 17.22–28).

One way of doing this is to consider the deep existential bones of the gospel, the points at which it touches the big and personal questions of life mentioned in Chapter 6. This enables us to see the gospel as good news even when stripped of its religious trappings, and thus to preach peace to those who are 'far off', in a form with which they can connect.

My own perspective on this is that the core message of *shālôm* can be summed up by the phrase 'It's OK' (Collicutt 2012a). This seems to beg the question of what 'It' and 'OK' mean. Yet when a parent takes a frightened child in her arms and says 'It's OK', no further explanation is required; the implication is that all is well with the cosmos. To visit like Jesus is to communicate that all things are, or are in the process of becoming, OK, even in the midst of chaos and danger; this is the deep meaning of 'Peace be to this house.'

> And thus our good Lord answered to all the questions and doubts that I might make, saying full comfortably, 'I may make all things well, and I can make all things well, and I shall make all things well; and thou shalt see thyself that all manner of things shall be well.'
>
> Julian of Norwich (1342–1416)

Yet there remains the question of how a frightened child knows that it actually *is* OK. How do we communicate this? In everyday life the phrase 'It's OK' is often accompanied by 'I'm here' or 'It's me' (Matt. 14.27; Mark 6.50). This is the language of attachment (all is well because of the parent's presence), and it gives a profound sense of security. Jesus instructs that the words 'Peace be to this house' are uttered on arrival. They announce that the visitor is present, just as the angels announced peace to the world as a mark of the birth of Christ who is *Immanuel*, God with us. The gospel assures us that things are OK because God is with us: to visit like Jesus is to be fully present to the other and thus to show solidarity.

> I think most of the struggle I get from people who struggle – whether it's financially, losing their job, house, whatever – is that you feel like you're in those things apart from God. The greater tragedy they're dealing with is God's abandonment. And then they finally see that, no, God hasn't abandoned me, God is bigger than my joblessness. God's bigger than my cancer . . . When people live in that reality, even their own tragedies are not as significant because they're not alone.
>
> 'Warner' quoted by Lee, Poloma and Post 2013, p. 132

If we look at the way Jesus visits with people in the Gospel accounts, we see that his presence generally seems to open up options for change. This may involve physical or behavioural healing, a change of heart or a change of perspective on the situation – a way of seeing *how* things could be OK. A phrase that sums this up well is 'Things don't have to be this way.' The situation could be different, or I could look at it differently. A visitor always brings a fresh perspective with her, even as she respects the perspective of those she visits. Here we have the seeds of transformation: to visit like Jesus is thus to offer hope.

So whatever words or other ways of communicating we might use, the visitation of the other should convey peace through a sense of solidarity and hope. This is true of literal visits paid to people in their homes, in hospital or in prison, but also of metaphorical visits, where we reach out to those who, for whatever reason, seem a long way off from where we are (Nouwen 1975). We will touch and be touched by the other, emotionally, existentially, intellectually or, in some cases, physically.

Seeing potential

We saw in Chapters 5 and 8 that taking the trouble to be present with someone indicates that she is worth that trouble. To open up options indicates a belief that change and growth are possible in a place that might otherwise appear stuck. Turning up at someone's home with a hopeful attitude communicates a sense of expectation that she may rise to the occasion and at least offer her visitor a cup of tea. She ceases to be simply the object of concern and is invested with the potential for agency.

When Jesus visits Zacchaeus he starts where he is and loves him as he is, but there is a sense in which Zacchaeus is also seen for what he is capable of becoming. There is no question of Jesus forcing change upon him, simply of his opening up the possibility. By being seen to have sufficient faith[8] in Zacchaeus to visit him in his home, Jesus also shows that he expects Zacchaeus to respond by rising to the occasion; to become more fully the person God created him to be. There is an almost exact parallel with the Samaritan woman whom Jesus asks to host him by giving him a drink.[9] Jesus affirms this woman by entering into a serious conversation with her, and at the same time he makes it clear that he sees her and understands her situation fully. She in her turn responds by rising to the occasion and becoming a highly effective evangelist. Jesus doesn't tell her to do this; the manner in which he visits her enables her to discover this capacity herself. To see the potential in the other is to cherish her strengths, to invite her to arise (Mark 5.41): to visit like Jesus is thus to confer dignity.

Our visiting with others should then also take the form of subtle strength-spotting. We can offer encouragement by framing habitual behaviours as character strengths or aptitudes and naming them, so that the other can attend to them and nurture them if she is so minded. This doesn't entail telling untruths; it involves an intentional practice of directing our attention aright, so that we

---

8 There is a sense in which Christ's faith seems to be as important as that of the believer in the economy of salvation. The literal translation of Romans 3.22 is 'the righteousness of God through faith *of* Jesus Christ for all believing', indicating a mutual relationship of trust.

9 For more on the Samaritan woman, see Savage 2007 and Collicutt 2009a, pp. 79–87.

notice the positive, as discussed in Chapter 4, and recognize the fruit of the Spirit, even where they may be expressed unconventionally, as discussed in Chapter 10. We live in a society that appears to be constitutionally inattentive to the positive. Even the Passion narratives, so full of darkness and human failure, are relieved by several incidents of individuals exhibiting strengths of character and rising to the occasion, or at least doing what they could; yet we rarely notice this or recognize it for what it is. Part of having the mind of Christ is to see the signs of the kingdom in the behaviour of the people around us (Luke 17.21),[10] to see folk as not only created by him but as capable of rising with and through him – being literally 'up for it'. Instead of wishing people would fail less, we should wish that they could succeed more; instead of conveying the message 'You are not good enough', our attitude should be 'You are better than this' (Eph. 4.1).

Welcoming

The first Christmas after my mother died, our daughter was also absent from the family circle for the first time, visiting her prospective in-laws. I felt that this was going to be a difficult time, and so instead of sticking with my usual pattern of celebrating the festival, I decided to host a lunch party for some family and friends on Christmas Eve. I baked a meat pie, according to a recipe that had been one of my mother's specialities. I made lots of gravy and made sure we had a whole range of traditional pickles to go with it. I had managed to obtain some very good *crème de cassis* and so was able to serve some rather special *kir royales* to the adults. For dessert there was the best part of an enormous and rather synthetic yet wickedly delicious Betty Crocker chocolate fudge cake. As it was a bit rich, I served some sorbet as a healthier option. Finally, to cheer things up even further, I had bought some table sparklers and a box of little cards with topics for children's charades at great expense from Fortnum & Mason.

The gathering seemed to be successful. In particular the chocolate cake went down well. Everyone had a jolly time playing charades, pulling crackers and waving sparklers. Then I forgot all about it.

At Easter some of the children who had been at the Christmas party were due to come for tea. I remembered how successful the chocolate cake had been, so I thought I'd make it again, simply putting some confectionery eggs and a toy chick on the top to make it seasonal. One little boy, the son of a friend whose family had been going through quite a difficult time, arrived and ran straight into my kitchen. 'Hooray!', we heard him cry, 'It's there!' 'What's there?' I asked, 'The cake,' he replied, 'the cake you always make.'

Some months later I visited that little boy's family. His mother said she had something to show me. It was a diary that he had kept as a homework task. He had got a very good mark for one piece of work entitled 'My Christmas holidays'.

---

10 'Jesus . . . locates the kingdom "among you" (in Greek, *entos humōn*) . . . the kingdom is distributed among them, secretly at work in unexpected ways and in unexpected people, such as Nicodemus (John 3.1)' (Collicutt 2012b, p. 102).

This was a very sweetly misspelt but highly detailed account of the meal he had experienced with us on Christmas Eve. Nothing else about the holidays, including his Christmas presents, was mentioned. He wrote of the 'tasty pie with loads of gravy', the 'dilishus chocolate cake – you could have raspberry or lemon sorbet or squirty cream – they let me have all three'; 'there was lemonade for me'; 'afterwards we played a hilirius game of shirads'; 'the grown ups played too'; 'it was a good Christmas'.

His mother had been very moved by this piece of writing. She reflected that I had created a space for her son that he could hold in his memory whenever life became hard or chaos threatened to overwhelm him; a place where there will always be for him 'that cake you always make with raspberry AND lemon sorbets' – a place where things can be different:

> Say, is there Beauty yet to find?
> And Certainty? and Quiet kind?
> Deep meadows yet, for to forget
> The lies, and truths, and pain? . . . oh! yet
> Stands the Church clock at ten to three?
> And is there honey still for tea?
> Rupert Brooke (1897–15), from 'The Old Vicarage, Grantchester' (1912)

My immediate and unprepared response was that this is simply the nature of Christian ministry, something very familiar to those of us who lead worship, and especially those of us who preside at the Eucharist.

Enabling wonder

The Christian ministry of welcome is to a large extent about making a space and offering the means whereby that space can be transformed that into a place of hope. This is not exclusively the role of priests and other church leaders. I took a lot of trouble to set up my Christmas lunch party, but it could not have happened without the presence of others; the whole community is involved in the process of welcome. A focal point for this welcome was 'the cake you always make'. It seemed to stand for more than the delicious meal; somehow it carried the memories and feelings of a gathering of folk who were at peace with each other, sharing food and joy and with a special space and welcome for each person – including this particular child.

The nature of this kind of space, in terms of both its epistemological contours and the psychological conditions for entering it, has been explored at great length by psychoanalysts from the school known as 'object relations'. Object relations theory has much in common with attachment theory, but it comes from a different theoretical perspective and has some quite distinctive features, particularly with regard to the significance of symbols (for further details see Fonagy 2001). Probably the most famous object relations theorist is the British psychoanalyst Donald Winnicott (1896–1971), who is best known for the concepts of the 'good enough mother' (which we have already encountered) and the 'transitional object'. Some might think that the term 'transitional object' is a piece of unnecessary psychological jargon for the soft toys and comfort blankets that children of a certain age carry around, refuse to be parted from and will not under any circumstances permit to be washed. There is, however, more to Winnicott's concept of 'transitional' than this.

The transitional object is only one aspect of what Winnicott refers to as 'transitional phenomena'. These are modes of thinking and being that arise from the child's negotiation of the tensions between her inner psychological world, where her needs are met well enough by her good enough parent, and an outside world that cannot offer this warmth and responsiveness, and is unyielding or even hostile. Winnicott posits the existence of a 'third area of human living, neither inside the individual nor outside in the world of shared reality' (Winnicott 1971, p. 110). Objects become important here because of their potential to function as symbols that enable the child to enter this third area, referred to by Winnicott as 'transitional space'. This is an 'intermediate area of experience . . . in which the child invests external phenomena with dream meaning and feeling' (p. 51). For Winnicott, a blanket or soft toy – or indeed chocolate cake – may bring the inner and outer worlds together through the child's capacity for *symbolic* thinking; a transitional object is a symbol of the inner world that is carried into the outer world.

According to Winnicott this form of thinking continues in adult life and can be found wherever events or objects in the public sphere are infused with meaning from the inner psychological world. He writes, 'I am therefore studying the substance of illusion, that which is allowed to the infant, and which in adult life is inherent in art and religion' (p. 3). Here Winnicott introduces the term 'illusion' and places it in close proximity to 'religion', which some might find troubling. It is important therefore to understand that in this context 'illusion' does not mean 'imaginary' but something more like 'imag*inative*', a distinction that is usefully drawn by C. S. Lewis.[11]

The role of illusion and transitional space in the life of faith is explored more fully by the Dutch psychologist of religion Paul Pruyser (1916–87). Pruyser writes of three worlds: the 'autistic[12] world', the 'realistic world' and the 'illusionistic world', whose characteristics are summarized in Table 3.

Pruyser's point is that when we are doing religion we are most likely to be inhabiting the illusionistic (or transitional) world (1985, p. 63):

Through rituals, words, stories. or introspective disciplines, religion evokes those transitional psychological spaces, which continually reverberate with the affects of past object relations and are pregnant with the possibility of future forms of intuition and transformation. (Jones 2002, p. 84, commenting on Pruyser)

As Christians our faith is grounded in the real world of historical events, but we often 'do business' with this reality through the use of symbol and imagination. Pruyser suggests that a failure to recognize this has led to all sorts of problems

---

11 Letter to Eliza Marian Butler dated 25 September 1940.

12 'Autistic' here is used in its original technical sense to mean self-referential or self-absorbed.

Table 3.

Autistic world	Illusionistic world	Realistic world
• Omnipotent thinking • Hallucinatory entities • Private needs • Dreams • Internal objects	• Creative thinking • Imaginative entities • Cultural needs • Symbols • Transcendent objects, prefigured by the child's transitional object	• Reality testing • Actual entities • Factual needs • Signs and numerical indices • External objects

in the history of the Church, in particular around the interpretation of the Bible and understandings of the Eucharist. A failure even to recognize the existence of the illusionistic world also lies behind the 'new atheist' critique of religion: writers such as Richard Dawkins see that religion does not sit easily in the realistic world of science, mistakenly locate it in the autistic world and dismiss it as 'delusion'[13] (Dawkins 2006).

Winnicott clearly identifies transitional space and illusionistic thinking with play, a theme to which we have returned repeatedly throughout this book. We have observed that in order to play, one must feel safe (Zech. 8.5). We might think of Christian welcome as providing a space that is fit for play, and therefore fundamentally a safe space. This is a space in which creative wondering can flourish, bounded yet offering degrees of freedom; a space between the world of literal rational thought and escapist wish-fulfilment. Jerome Berryman, the founder of Godly Play, describes play as the place where we meet our Creator (1991, p. 17), a sanctified mode of being, a sacred space. It is a place of symbol and story. It is also perhaps a small space: our churches seem prone to either excessive rationalism or escapism, and our own thinking can flip between the two.

Transitional space is not some self-centred fantasy cut off from the rest of the world. Its nature is that, by bridging the inner and the outer, by its very liminality, it can create community, something Winnicott describes as a 'natural root of grouping among human beings' (1971, p. 3). When the people of God gather around the Lord's Table there is the capacity for this kind of space to be opened up. For the child of my story, his transitional space was a place where a healthy community could be envisaged and indeed inhabited. The key symbol that could unlock that space was the cake, whose baking had become ritualized – 'you always make it'.

Food, glorious food

In Chapter 9 I introduced Holman Hunt's painting *The Light of the World* and observed that to welcome Christ is essentially to open our minds and to wonder, so that our lives can be illuminated by his light. In the previous section of this

---

13 In classic Freudian thinking there is a difference between a delusion and an illusion. A delusion is a belief about reality that is held despite overwhelming evidence against it. An illusion is a belief driven by our psychological needs that may or may not be compatible with reality.

Chapter a connection between wonder and welcome has also emerged. Linking them both is, perhaps unexpectedly, the experience of eating. A chocolate cake welcomed a child into a wondering space. In Revelation 3.20 – the text depicted in Hunt's picture and inscribed upon its frame – Christ requests that the believer welcome him into a reciprocal relationship in which food is shared.

The point that Jesus of Nazareth ate and drank with people hardly needs to be laboured. Of all the aspects of his character, this one is arguably definitive; after all, it is in the breaking of bread that he is recognized by the disciples on the road to Emmaus. The feeding of the multitudes on a grassy bank is explicitly framed in terms of welcome (*apodechomai*) by Luke (9.14). It is one of the few incidents from the life of Jesus that is depicted in all four Gospels, and the significance of this should not be overlooked. The different evangelists take slightly different approaches to the telling of the story, but a picture of the welcome offered by Jesus shines through:

- All are welcome – men, women, children (Matt. 14.21; 15.38) and foreigners (Matt. 15.27).
- A situation that is thought to be intractable (Matt. 15.33 and parallels; Mark 6.37; John 6.7) is opened up to new possibilities.
- A heavenly perspective is brought to bear (Matt. 14.19 and parallels).
- Teaching, healing and feeding are intertwined with each other (Matt. 14.14; 15.30; Mark 6.34; Luke 9.11).
- Ordinary folk rise to the occasion and become agents not just recipients of grace (Matt. 14.16, 19; 15.36; Mark 6.41; Luke 9.13, 15; John 6.9). They thus *belong* to the community rather than merely being included in it.
- The space is a 'green pasture' (Matt. 14.19; Mark 6.39; John 6.10). This allusion to Psalm 23 evokes the image of God as the host who sets the table for his people and anoints their heads with oil (Ps. 23.5; Luke 7.46). There is imagination at work here.

The Christian who aspires to host like Jesus will need to bear all this in mind. Eating together is vitally important (Acts 2.42) and is not an optional part of the Christian life. Indeed, there is a long tradition in the Church of seeing hospitality as a Christian discipline. Paying attention to the physical environment into which we welcome people, making it a place of green pastures and still waters that invites wondering and play, should not be neglected (Sheldrake 2001). It should be a safe place, for just as we need to feel safe in order to play, we also need to feel safe in order to eat (Wolpe 1958).

Encouraging guests to contribute food, talents, clearing up and so on, leads to a sense of belonging; but taking responsibility by preparing for the feast attentively – setting the scene – is the role of the householder who invites people into his home or the minister who presides at Holy Communion. (Notice that while the risen Christ invites a contribution from the disciples to their shared breakfast on the shore, he has already lit a fire and prepared some food.) As we do all these things we both welcome Christ in our guests and participate with them in his welcome of us all.

Love bade me welcome: yet my soul drew back.
Guiltie of dust and sinne.
But quick-ey'd Love, observing me grow slack
From my first entrance in,
Drew nearer to me, sweetly questioning
If I lack'd anything.
A guest, I answer'd, worthy to be here:
Love said, You shall be he.
I the unkinde, ungrateful? Ah, my deare,
I cannot look on thee.
Love took my hand, and smiling did reply,
Who made the eyes but I?
Truth Lord, but I have marr'd them: let my shame
Go where it doth deserve.
And know you not, sayes Love, who bore the blame?
My deare, then I will serve.
You must sit down, sayes Love, and taste my meat:
So I did sit and eat.

George Herbert (1593–1633)

Exercises

1 Try and identify your in- and out-groups. Explore what it is that you find objectionable in your out-group (e.g. certain political ideas, social values, taste in worship music and so on). Try and find a way of spending time with someone from this group and hearing her backstory.

2 Try and articulate your own understanding of the 'deep existential bones' of the gospel. (You may especially wish to ponder the meaning of 'Peace be this house', which is used in many orders of service for ministry to the sick and housebound.) Work out ways you might communicate this understanding to someone who knows little about the Christian faith.

3 Study the teaching and practices of one of the world's great faiths, preferably including some contact with a person from that faith community. Notice the significant areas of commonality with Christianity and reflect on the feelings this evokes – encouragement? disquiet? a desire to rehearse difference?

Further reading

Haidt, J., 2012, *The Righteous Mind: Why Good People Are Divided by Politics and Religion*, London: Allen Lane.

Jones, J., 2002, *Terror and Transformation: The Ambiguity of Religion in Psychoanalytic Perspective*, Hove: Brunner-Routledge.

Nouwen, H., 2006, *With Open Hands*, Notre Dame, IN: Ave Maria Press.

Savage, S. and Boyd-MacMillan, E., 2007, *The Human Face of the Church: A Social Psychology and Pastoral Theology Resource for Pioneer and Traditional Ministry*, Norwich: Canterbury Press.

Volf, M., 1994, *Exclusion and Embrace: Theological Exploration of Identity, Otherness and Reconciliation*, Nashville, TN: Abingdon Press.

12

Compassion:
Seeing, Feeling, Doing

In the year that King Uzziah died, I saw the Lord sitting on a throne, high and lofty; and the hem of his robe filled the temple. Seraphs were in attendance above him; each had six wings: with two they covered their faces, and with two they covered their feet, and with two they flew. And one called to another and said: 'Holy, holy, holy is the Lord of hosts; the whole earth is full of his glory.' The pivots on the thresholds shook at the voices of those who called, and the house filled with smoke. And I said: 'Woe is me! I am lost, for I am a man of unclean lips, and I live among a people of unclean lips; yet my eyes have seen the King, the Lord of hosts!' Then one of the seraphs flew to me, holding a live coal that had been taken from the altar with a pair of tongs. The seraph touched my mouth with it and said: 'Now that this has touched your lips, your guilt has departed and your sin is blotted out.' Then I heard the voice of the Lord saying, 'Whom shall I send, and who will go for us?' And I said, 'Here am I; send me!'

Isaiah 6.1–8

Set me as a seal upon your heart, as a seal upon your arm; for love is strong as death, passion fierce as the grave. Its flashes are flashes of fire, a raging flame.
Many waters cannot quench love, neither can floods drown it. If one offered
for love all the wealth of his house, it would be utterly scorned.

Song of Solomon 8.6–7

'You shall love the Lord your God with all your heart, and with all your soul, and with all your mind.' This is the greatest and first commandment. And a second is like it: 'You shall love your neighbour as yourself.' On these two commandments hang all the law and the prophets.

Matthew 22.37b–40

Remember those who are in prison, as though you were in prison with them; those who are being tortured, as though you yourselves were being tortured.

Hebrews 13.3

In Matthew's and Mark's accounts of the feeding of the multitudes, Jesus is said to have 'had compassion' (*splanchnizomai*) on the crowds, the implication being that this was at least part of the motivation behind his subsequent actions. This should not surprise us because Christian hospitality and compassion are closely connected. For example, the unconditional welcome of the stranger, the estranged or the enemy is mediated by compassion in the stories of both the Prodigal Son (Luke 15.20) and the Good Samaritan (Luke 10.33–34).

Less obvious but equally important is the nature of Winnicott's transitional (or Pruyser's illusionistic) space. In the previous chapter I argued that the opening up of such a space, where it is natural for us to do business with God, is at the heart of Christian hospitality. The kind of thinking that is characteristic of this space is sometimes referred to as 'as if' or 'subjunctive'[1] thought (see e.g. Puett and Simon 2008). It is therefore interesting that this sort of thinking has been identified with the ability to envision hope for a better world – that 'things don't have to be this way' (recall p. 169). This ability, described by some as 'seeing beyond circumstances', seems to increase the capacity to persevere with compassionate humanitarian action in situations that look hopeless when viewed with more 'realism' (Lee and Poloma 2009). Here 'as if' wondering becomes positive 'what if?' solution-focused wondering. In terms of my example in Chapter 12, if I am able to imagine the world as a place where there is a possibility of eating chocolate cake with those I love, I will be more inclined to see the situations of those who are hungry and lonely as also having this potential and, other things being equal, I will be more inclined to try and help them.

'Seeing beyond circumstances' is about having a bigger vision, and is characteristic of the prophets of the Hebrew Bible, who again and again name social injustice and call for action to redress it. One of the marks of an authentic prophet is that s/he has experienced a heavenly vision that gives a radically new and authoritative perspective on what is happening on earth (see e.g. 1 Kings 22.19). The prophet then feels compelled to act by denouncing, encouraging or intervening directly in a situation. The passage from Isaiah 6 at the beginning of this chapter is a classic biblical example of how a heavenly vision can engender an awareness of a mismatch between it and the realities of earthly life, with a consequent compelling sense of the need to act and empowerment to do so. A very similar pattern is seen in the incident of Moses and the burning bush in Exodus 3, and there are several others. Indeed, Jesus' baptism, during which the heavens are opened to him (Matt. 3.16 and parallels), can also be understood in this way.

This emphasis on vision reconnects us with the ideas about insight and attention explored in Chapter 9; recall how Robert Runcie's noticing of a group of people expressed itself in his reaching out towards them. Compassion always begins with seeing aright; noticing how things are and having a vision for how they could be better.

In this chapter we will explore the nature of human compassion, the things that can and often do stifle it, and ways that it can be nurtured.

What is compassion?

The psychological study of compassion is fairly recent. This is because for many years research was dominated by the question of whether human beings are capable of any kind of truly disinterested altruistic behaviour at all. This is a slippery philosophical question, because however disinterested an action appears to be, one can nearly always come up with a way in which the agent benefits directly or indirectly from it (Mansbridge 1990). Even Jesus' decision to go to

---

1 In English grammar the subjunctive is defined as 'relating to or denoting a mood of verbs expressing what is imagined or wished or possible' (*Oxford English Dictionary*).

the cross is described in terms of deferred gratification in the New Testament (Heb. 12.2). If not being true to oneself is as aversive as I suggested in Chapter 2, then simply acting in conformity with one's character and ideals can be seen as self-serving, even if this involves laying down one's life for a stranger. All helping behaviour will make us feel at some level better about ourselves, the world or both. To be totally disinterested is to be a machine, not a human being. The philosophical question of disinterested altruism is therefore something of a red herring in the practical quest to establish conditions that will make people more likely to help than to harm each other.

A more useful question is the less morally loaded one of whether people engage in helping behaviour for certain secondary psychological benefits – such as public praise, the avoidance of disapproval and punishment, co-dependency,[2] building their own sense of self-esteem, the reduction of their distress at witnessing trauma – or through a primary psychological drive that makes helping others intrinsically rewarding. This is analogous to the question we considered in Chapter 5 as to whether children of a certain age stick close to their parents in order to get food or because of a primary proximity-seeking drive.

As the result of a series of studies conducted by Daniel Batson and his colleagues, it now seems reasonable to conclude that, while people often help others in order to obtain secondary psychological or even material benefits, there is also a strong drive to help for its own sake that is based on empathy for the suffering person (Batson 1991; Batson, Ahmad and Lishner 2009). Empathy is an emotional response to another based on the perception that this other is 'like me' in some crucial respect(s). There is also a third plausible motive for helping behaviour; it may arise from a principled stance, and thus be an aspect of meaning-making (Post 2003, p. 67) – one way that we craft the story of our lives.[3]

Batson and colleagues' identification of empathy as a primary human motive eventually led psychologists to consider the nature of compassion. This is a quality that is said to be highly valued by most faith traditions, though there are problems in establishing the comparability of the many words in different languages that come under the general umbrella of 'kindness' (to use the VIA term). There is also the question of whether compassion is better understood as an enduring character strength or a short-lived emotion.

The 'passion' in the English word compassion should give us a clue here: compassion is an emotion (Lazarus 1991, p. 289). It comes upon us unbidden (Vaillant 2008, p. 152). Where Jesus is described as 'having compassion' it is clearly an event; he has been seized by an emotion. A propensity to experience episodes of compassion may be a sign of an enduring disposition of loving-kindness. So in a loose way we might understand the Hebrew ḥesed as an attitude of loving-kindness that expresses itself in a propensity to show mercy (ḥāmal) and to experience the emotion of compassion (raḥămîm). In the New Testament there is a similar though not exact parallel in the relationship between chrēstos, an attitude of loving-kindness

---

2 Co-dependency is essentially an extreme need to be needed in particular relationship(s).

3 Recall from Chapter 5 that the shape of our stories tends to be 'redemptive'. The desire to make things come right may therefore be a part of this.

that expresses itself in a propensity to show mercy (*eleaō*), and to experience the emotion of compassion (*splanchnizomai*). Mercy and compassion occur together in the story of the Good Samaritan. The lawyer to whom Jesus tells the story appears to receive it as an account of a merciful *action* (Luke 10.37), but Jesus foregrounds the Samaritan's *feeling* of compassion (Luke 10.33).

Understanding that compassion is an emotion is important in elucidating both the nature of the divine and our own formation into the likeness of Christ. God did not become incarnate as a rational human being devoid of emotion, or for whom the emotional life was a distraction from his main purpose; emotion is central to the New Testament account of God's actions in the world in Christ. On this understanding God acts to save us not simply, or even primarily, because it is the right thing for him to do or from an attitude of goodwill and kindness. God incarnate is depicted as overcome with an intensely acute *feeling* that compels him to respond to our situation. In the two compassion stories from Luke's Gospel the protagonists who stand for God are said to come close to the person for whom they have compassion where he is and as he is (Luke 10.33; 15.20); the father of the Prodigal actually runs. This is passionately driven moral proximity, emotionally charged incarnation. It is the zeal of the LORD of hosts. If we are to be formed into Christ's likeness we must be careful not to despise or quench this passionate form of love (Rom. 12.11).

From a psychological point of view an emotion always has certain features: it is elicited by a particular type of event (e.g. fear is elicited by threat); it has a characteristic subjective feeling (e.g. fear involves a feeling of extreme vulnerability); it involves a particular bodily physiological response (e.g. fight–flight[4] arousal); it involves certain patterns of thinking (e.g. fear involves heightened vigilance for sources of danger); it is expressed in particular behaviour (e.g. fear is mainly expressed in freezing, avoidance or escape).

So what are the corresponding features of the emotion we call compassion?

Compassion is elicited by seeing another being harmed or suffering

While it may seem rather obvious that compassion is elicited by witnessing suffering, not everyone notices the plight of others for what it is. It is simply easier to see our own situation than it is to see the situation of others, so being in the vicinity of a suffering person may not be enough to elicit compassion. Even if we do notice, we may not feel compassion. It is sadly the case that noticing the pain of another may elicit pleasure, including sexual pleasure, or mirth

---

4 The fight–flight response was first identified by Walter Cannon in 1915. It describes the way the individual prepares for action by disengaging from ongoing behaviour and marshalling resources. Brain changes result in the release of noradrenaline and adrenaline into the bloodstream leading to increased heart and respiration rate; release of stored red blood cells from the spleen so that more oxygen is made available; release of sugars from liver so that more energy is made available; redistribution of the blood supply from the skin and abdominal organs to the brain and muscles – the 'action' organs; pupil dilation, enhancing vigilance; and an increased capacity of the blood to coagulate, thus enabling quicker healing of wounds.

(much slapstick and cartoon humour is based on this principle). The histori-cally ambivalent relationship between Christianity and humour has to a large part been the result of an awareness of the link between humour and cruelty (Collicutt and Gray 2012); after all, people laughed at Jesus on the cross. Seeing harm and suffering is necessary for compassion but it is not sufficient.

Feeling compassion is about being moved

The sorts of words people use to describe the feeling of compassion include 'sympathetic', 'tender', 'warm', 'soft-hearted', 'sorry for', 'touched', 'concerned for' and above all 'moved' (see Goetz, Keltner and Simon-Thomas 2010 for a review). This movement involves an orientation towards the other and an empathic placing of the self in her shoes; a drawing close to her culturally and mentally as well as behaviourally (Cassell 2009). There is also a movement or disturbance of equilibrium that is highly physical in quality, as we shall see; and a mix of feeling tones that may often include yearning and indignation centred on two core thoughts: 'poor thing' and 'something must be done!'. The feeling of compassion is antithetical to fear.

Compassion involves the guts

The word *splagchnizomai* literally means to feel in one's inmost parts (*splagchna*), the heart or the guts – hence the KJV's use of the phrases 'bowels of Christ' (Phil. 1.8) and 'if any bowels and mercies' (Phil. 2.1). The Hebrew *raḥămîm* is closely related to *reḥem*, which means womb. This is a deeply visceral emotion.

Investigations into the physiology of compassion are still in their infancy. However, the physiology of one aspect of compassion – tender-hearted care giving – is beginning to be understood. Not all responses to stress and chal-lenge show themselves in the high levels of physiological arousal that we associate with fight–flight. Recently an alternative pattern, characterized by low arousal, calming and affiliative behaviour, has been identified and labelled 'tend–befriend' (Taylor, Klein, Lewis, Gruenewald, Gurung and Updegraff 2000). Whereas fight–flight involves the release of the chemicals noradrenaline and adrenaline into the bloodstream, tend–befriend seems to involve the release of oxytocin.

Oxytocin is one of several chemicals that transmit messages between nerve cells in the brain (recall dopamine on p. 48). It is only found in mammals, and appears to be involved in nearly all aspects of maternal and pair-bonding behav-iour. However, oxytocin is unusual in that it has a dual role: it also circulates in the blood as a hormone, and here it is crucial to the processes of labour, child-birth and lactation (Wang 2005). It appears to have a deeply calming effect, lowering arousal levels, inhibiting any tendency to fight–flight and enhancing approach behaviour (Goetz, Keltner and Simon-Thomas 2010).

Oxytocin is not the only chemical involved in 'these subtle feelings that we humans call acceptance, nurturance, and love' (Panksepp 1998, p. 248). Also implicated are endogenous opioids[5] and the hormone prolactin (Panksepp, Nelson and Bekkedal 1997). While Oxytocin is only found in mammals, prolactin is found across the animal kingdom. In mammals, along with oxytocin, it is vital for lactation; in birds it is vital in stimulating broodiness and the feeding of young (Angelier and Chastel 2009).

We might pause here to consider the connection between the Hebrew words for compassion and womb. We might also recall that the compassionate Jesus described himself as a broody mother hen (Matt. 23.37; Luke 13.34). There is a deep physicality about tender-hearted care giving, and it seems to be a particularly maternal physicality. It involves a calm and calming movement towards the other that is incompatible with arousal and distress. Excessive distress is the enemy of compassion – something we will explore in more detail later in this chapter.

Compassion involves complex cognitive appraisals

Although tender-hearted caregiving is an important aspect of compassion, there is more to it than this. This is partly because compassion doesn't always show itself in nurturing behaviour (to be explored further below), and because compassion extends beyond those whom we might be expected to nurture (our own young) or help in other ways (our tribe). Here again there is a connection with Christian hospitality that crosses tribal boundaries.

When confronted by a suffering creature (I am using this term because compassion can encompass non-human animals), we go through a very rapid series of barely conscious cognitive appraisals (Goetz, Keltner and Simon-Thomas 2010):

- Is this creature kin, not kin, or an enemy?
- Does this creature deserve to suffer?
- Am I in a position to do anything that would help?
- How costly would it be for me to help?

It is in the appraisal of kinship that empathy, the ability to see and respond to another as if she were akin to me, is vital. It is this sort of appraisal that makes us more concerned about the factory farming of pigs, who are often said to be 'intelligent' (and hence akin to human beings), than the factory farming of salmon, who are said to be 'cold-blooded' (and therefore not akin to human beings). This also seems to be one of the ways mystical experiences connect with compassion. At first sight this seems odd, because surely such experiences lift our attention away from the mundane world? However, an aspect of many mystical experiences is a sense of unity with all things (recall the joining up of the dots in epiphanies considered in Chapter 6). This is something William James refers to as 'cosmic consciousness' (1902, p. 386), and has subsequently been termed 'extrovertive mysticism' (Stace 1960). This sense of connectedness with the universe means that all parts of it feel like kin. It facilitates empathy for the

---

5 These are another group of brain chemicals, the most famous of which are the endorphins.

other and thus compassion. Something of this sort appears to have been part of the story of Francis of Assisi (1181–1226).

> In all the poor, he, – himself the most Christlike of all poor men, – beheld the image of Christ, wherefore he judged that all things that were provided for himself, – were they even the necessaries of life, – should be given up unto any poor folk whom he met, and that not only as largesse, but even as if they were their own property . . . When he bethought him of the first beginning of all things, he was filled with a yet more overflowing charity, and would call the dumb animals, howsoever small, by the names of brother and sister, forasmuch as he recognized in them the same origin as in himself. Yet he loved with an especial warmth and tenderness those creatures that do set forth by the likeness of their nature the holy gentleness of Christ, and in the interpretation of Scripture are a type of Him. Oft-times he would buy back lambs that were being taken to be killed, in remembrance of that most gentle Lamb Who brooked to be brought unto the slaughter for the redemption of sinners.
>
> Bonaventure (1221–74) on Francis

It is empathy that enables us emotionally to stretch the boundaries of kinship so that we can extend care beyond our own kin, tribe and even species. Empathy requires a shift to the perspective of the other – walking a mile in his shoes – and so it is more than simply seeing a likeness between us. If I simply see the other as like me, I may project my needs on to him rather than see his needs, resulting in a deficient kind of caring (that may nevertheless be better than no caring, as in 'benevolent' forms of paternalism and colonialism). There is therefore a two-stage process at work in empathy: first I see a connection between myself and the other; second I actively inhibit my natural tendency to treat the other as a clone of myself (Decety and Hodges 2006, p. 105).

Our appraisal of deservingness will also influence our response to suffering. We may feel superior, satisfied or even amused when someone we judge to be feckless or selfish gets into difficulties, because we sense that some natural justice is working its way out. This is one reason we are more inclined to help children (and why so many charities feature children in their publicity); they are less likely to be the authors of their own suffering. Seeing children in need may also automatically trigger the release of oxytocin.

As we look on suffering we also appraise the scale of the problem and our capacity to rise to the occasion and impact upon it (this is where 'seeing beyond circumstances' seems to make a difference). The answers we come up with to these computations will influence whether we respond or let things be.

Finally we compute the risks to ourselves. Situations in which another is suffering may be dangerous for us also, as in the case of war or infectious fatal disease. This seems to be one of the factors in the story of the Good Samaritan; he was on a road frequented by muggers who had already attacked one person. Computing the balance between costs and benefits of helping will be experienced as conflict, sometimes to an intense degree. As we have seen, feelings of tender loving care and fear are naturally incompatible, so to give care when one is also experiencing fear is both sacrificial (and hence an aspect of agape love) and heroic.

Compassion always shows itself in helping action

Compassion is about doing something aimed at making someone else's bad situation better. If compassion doesn't show itself in action it is not really compassion: 'There are sentimental people whose heart goes out to the suffering while their legs and arms and shoulders remain inert' (Roberts 2007, p. 180).

The Gospels use compassion to signal imminent action: Jesus feels compassion and then teaches, heals or feeds; the Good Samaritan feels compassion and goes to the aid of the injured man; the father of the Prodigal feels compassion and runs to embrace him.

However, the type of helping action may vary. It may be largely nurturing and affiliative in character, in which case the 'tend–befriend' system will be heavily involved. Here characteristic caring behaviour involving gentle stroking touch, soft tone of voice and attentive gaze will be part of the response (Goetz, Keltner and Simon-Thomas 2010). There is clearly a strong connection with the comfort offered in attachment relationships here. Harlow's early experiments on monkeys, mentioned in Chapter 5, indicated that the experience of emotional nurture in infancy is necessary for adequate development of the ability to give adequate emotional nurture to one's own offspring in adulthood (see also 2 Cor. 1.3–4), and there is evidence that in human beings security of attachment predicts the ability to experience feelings of compassion (Mikulincer, Shaver, Gillath and Nitzberg 2005).

On the other hand, compassionate action may be more reparative in character, seeking to right wrongs through protest, in which case righteous anger and indignation may be part of the picture. A mix of these two responses of comfort and protest is characteristic of the Hebrew prophets, as it is of Jesus himself.

Things that stifle compassion

Not noticing

The most common reason for not noticing the plight of another is preoccupation – elaborative cognitive processing. It doesn't matter whether we are preoccupied with something worthy or something base; both will make us less attentive to what is happening around us.

A study that demonstrated this very clearly is known as the 'Good Samaritan Experiment' (Darley and Batson 1973). This involved 67 students at Princeton Theological Seminary. The students were asked to prepare a talk that would be given in another building. Half the students prepared a talk on the parable of the Good Samaritan and half prepared a talk on the career prospects for seminarians.

The students then set off to deliver their talk and were given a map to help them find their way. Half the students in each group were told that they would need to hurry, because they were running late. The route went past an alley where a man was slumped down, eyes closed and not moving. As each student went past him, he coughed and groaned once. The object of the experiment was to see which students would stop and offer help.

The findings are very informative. Overall only 40 per cent of the total sample stopped to offer help. The religious tradition or type of spirituality espoused by the student did not predict who would stop. The topic of the talk they were preparing did not predict who would stop. The only predictor was whether or not the student had been told to hurry. Those who were in a hurry were significantly less likely to stop; they were preoccupied with getting to their destination in time, engaged in highly goal-focused behaviour.

There was another interesting finding from this study. The stooge had been instructed to refuse help if offered. Among those students who stopped, some would not take no for an answer. These were students who scored higher on a measure of religious commitment. Students who scored higher on a measure of open-minded spirituality were more prepared to leave the man alone as requested. The first group appear to have offered help on the basis of a principled stance; the second group appear to have been nearer to a truly empathic response that enters the perspective of the other.

Sometimes we do not notice the suffering of others because we fail to read the signs. This may be a particular challenge for people with autism spectrum and related conditions or with other types of learning difficulty, who may need help in decoding the behaviour of others. However, this can affect us all, especially when the individual concerned is from a very different culture or has a disability that stops them expressing emotion in the conventional way. For example, people affected by Parkinson's disease will often have 'flat' facial expressions that do not indicate how they are feeling on the inside. The problem here is not a lack of sympathy or empathy on the part of the observer, but a difficulty in reading subtle and non-verbal cues.

Difficulty in being appropriately moved

It looks as if the instinct to respond by nurturing is stronger in females than males. This would make sense, given the important role of maternal hormones in this response.

> It is especially important to emphasize that the experience of motherhood is a powerful force in promoting future nurturance . . . The acquisition of nurturant behaviour leaves a seemingly indelible imprint on a creature's way of being in the world. (Panksepp 1998, p. 259)

There is no denying that women seem to be drawn to the 'caring' professions and that the pastoral care teams in churches seem to be dominated by women (though cultural factors may also contribute to this gender pattern). So it may be that some individuals are better biologically equipped than others to respond to suffering by caregiving. As we have seen, attachment history also appears to be relevant. Nevertheless, there is more than one way of doing compassion, and protest responses to suffering may be less dependent on biology and early experience than are nurturing responses. Moreover, the main obstacle to being moved by suffering appears to be the egocentric thinking and lack of empathy that can afflict *both* male and female, either habitually or under conditions of stress, rather than a deficiency in the tend–befriend response.

Empathy has sometimes been understood as a sharing of the perspective of the other that is so complete that we experience her emotions almost as if they were our own. In fact this kind of total emotional identification can inhibit compassion in some cases, and current understandings of empathy stress the need to maintain a clear distinction between the self and the other (see e.g. Decety and Jackson 2004; Nussbaum 1996). If we identify too strongly with the feelings of distress experienced by a suffering individual, we may become so overwhelmed that we are unable to help her. There is increasing evidence that experiencing sympathetic distress seems to work against compassion (Volling, Kolak and Kennedy 2009; Welp and Brown 2013). In the account of the raising of Lazarus a clear separation is made between Jesus' response to Mary's tears (John 11.33–35), where he is described as feeling both a kind of indignant compassion (*embrimaomai*) and distress (*tarassō*) expressed in weeping, and his move into helping mode (John 11.38–44), where there is only indignant compassion (*embrimaomai*).[6] Jesus thus moves from emotional identification with Mary to compassionate reparative action directed at Lazarus. While he is weeping with Mary he cannot help Lazarus.

Judgemental or defeatist appraisal style

Compassion will be stifled where an individual has a propensity to see others as different, and approaches the world with the assumption that people are usually to blame for their suffering (Rudolph, Roesch, Greitemeyer and Weiner 2004). This is the philosophy of Job's comforters (see e.g. Job 4.7).

Compassion will also be stifled if the situation seems intractable, so that nothing any individual or group can do could make a difference (compassion fatigue). Why bother to help one starving child if there are millions more who cannot be helped?

If I appraise myself as effectively helpless, with no personal or material resources at my disposal, I will be very unlikely to show compassion: 'I'd like to help but I can't even look after myself'; 'I'd like to give but I have nothing *to* give.'

Finally, if I appraise the situation as dangerous and myself as vulnerable, compassion will be stifled: 'I'd like to help but I daren't.'

---

6 The New Jerusalem Bible gives the best translation of this passage.

Compassionate action can lose its way

The main way compassionate nurturing can go wrong is in smothering the recipient with kindness that is either unwanted – as in the Good Samaritan Experiment – or not in his best interests. The main thing that can go wrong with reparative compassion is that the righteous anger or indignation that drives it can easily move from constructive to destructive and become focused on vengeance. This will be most likely in cultures that have a retributive understanding of justice, exemplified by but not limited to vendetta cultures.

Cultivating kindness: practising mercy and being open to compassion

Noticing

It should be clear that if the main obstacle to noticing the plight of others is preoccupation, then any practice that helps us disengage from elaborative cognitive processing should help us notice the need that is around us. The first step is having less stuff to worry about in the way of possessions (recall p. 35). The second step is sitting lightly to what we do have by cultivating the ability to disengage from worry in general.

Mindfulness is an obvious tool to invoke here. A very interesting recent study (Condon, Desbordes, Miller and DeSteno 2013) compared the practice of mindfulness meditation with an alternative approach called loving-kindness meditation (LKM), to see what effect each might have on helping behaviour. In contrast to the rather more neutral and open practice of mindfulness, loving-kindness meditation focuses on the intentional cultivation of positive feelings towards the self and others (Shapiro and Sahgal 2012). In a design reminiscent of the Good Samaritan Experiment, participants were given eight weeks' training in either mindfulness or LKM, and a third group were told that they were on a waiting list. Then all the participants were requested to attend an appointment in the psychology department, ostensibly for some cognitive tests as part of the study. While they were sitting in the waiting room, a stooge entered on crutches, with his foot bandaged and wincing in pain. The room had been set up so that all the chairs were occupied. The participants were observed for two minutes to see if they gave up their seat to the stooge.

The results showed that the participants who had undergone either type of meditation training were significantly more likely to give up their seats than those on a waiting list, but that LKM was no more effective than mindfulness in this regard. This is an important finding because, as with the Good Samaritan Experiment, it seems to indicate that it is *how* we think rather than *what* we are thinking about that is key when it comes to cultivating compassionate attentiveness.

Cultivating empathy

In addition to facilitating pro-social attentiveness, mindfulness also appears to be beneficial in the cultivation of empathy (Grepmair, Mitterlehner, Loew,

Bachler, Rother and Nickel 2007). One way that it may do this is through the establishment of a habit of self-compassion. Self-compassion is an attitude of care to oneself that is based simply on the fact that one is a member of the human race, not because one is special or deserving in some other way. It seems that being kind to myself may, paradoxically, make me more prepared to be kind to others. We should recall here that the second commandment requires each of us to love our neighbour *as our self*.

A recent study (Welp and Brown 2013) examined the relationship between self-compassion and intention to help a (fictitious) person in a stressful situation. The results suggest two ways self-compassion might enhance compassion for others. First, if I am kind to myself even when I know that I am at fault, my compassion for others is less likely to be stifled by the knowledge that they are responsible for their situation. Second, if I am kind to myself I am more likely to be emotionally resilient (Leary, Tate, Adams, Allen and Hancock 2007); I have come to terms with my own vulnerability, and I can be alongside those who are vulnerable without being overwhelmed by any distress they may be feeling – a very sophisticated form of empathy that puts me in a better position to help:

> I know viscerally and steadily that I am destined for death and subject to moral failure, and in one way or another I become reconciled to this fact. I get an emotionally clear view of myself in my darker aspect, and thus lay the groundwork for seeing as fellows those who are walking through the valley of the shadow of death . . . this process is encouraged by Christian hope. (Roberts 2007, p. 184)

This nuanced account of Christian self-compassion distinguishes it from simple and uncritical kindliness to self, which may not always result in compassion to others. One study indicates that males who are low on C (conscientiousness) but who score high on secular measures of self-compassion show *less* compassion towards others (Baker and McNulty 2011). For them kindness to self may have become complacency.

There are other ways to cultivate empathy that do not rely on mindfulness. Taking the trouble to find out more about the situation of another may help us to see her as akin to ourselves. In the poem 'Running orders' Lena Khalaf Tuffaha describes the hurried flight of a Palestinian resident from her home in Gaza that is about to be bombed. She enumerates the things that must be left behind: the wedding album, a child's favourite blanket, a teenager's almost complete college application. As I read that poem I felt much more strongly connected with the Palestinians in their current situation, because I had been helped to see beyond the television footage of bombed buildings and wounded bodies to 'people like me'. As already discussed in Chapter 6, this is why prayer letters are so helpful. They enable us to pray with empathy. The next stage of this discipline of cultivating empathy is, having achieved this deeper sense of connection with the other, intentionally to focus on and respect points of difference.

Christlike appraisal style: taking a principled theological stance

While finding out more about the other can help me to see that he is akin to me, the *reason* that a Christian might want to establish this connection is not primarily to cultivate empathy and so nurture compassion, good though this motive might be, but because we have been commanded to do so. Christian teaching can inform our semi-automatic appraisals of others, and it also requires us to bring these appraisals under the discipline of a principled stance. I may look at another person and naturally see her as different, even when I know something of her story; the gospel requires me to look again and to see her with the eyes of Christ.

The story of the Good Samaritan turns on the definition of 'neighbour' (Luke 10.29), and concludes with the words 'Go and do likewise' (Luke 10.37b). It is clear that Jesus' teaching expands the definition of kin and, as discussed at length in Chapter 11, is set against tribalism. The instruction to 'love your enemies' (Matt. 5.44; Luke 6.27, 35) takes this to its radical extreme.

The gospel is not just about the breaking down of barriers between different communities, but also about the establishment of a new community. So my relationship with other Christians, even where they may seem deeply 'other' or strange (indeed frankly weird!), is one of kinship. We are brothers and sisters and members of the body of Christ, bound to each other through the Spirit (John 11.17–26). Hospitality and compassion should be extended to all people, but there is a special place in our hearts for our Christian brothers and sisters (John 13.34–35).

There is also a special place for the suffering and marginalized. This is because Jesus seems to have had a special place in his heart for people in these situations. It is also because Jesus himself suffered and was marginalized, so there is a sense in which he is most characteristically present where people suffer and are marginalized (this is one way of understanding the story of the sheep and the goats in Matthew 25). Therefore in looking on the other the Christian is required not only to see her as 'akin to me' but also as 'akin to Christ', created in his image and redeemed through his suffering and marginalization.

Seeing the other as Christ also addresses our tendency to judge and blame, for we can hardly judge and blame Christ. The message of Job is that there is no simple relationship between suffering and sin, and this is explicitly confirmed by Jesus in John's account of the man born blind (John 9.2–3). The servant songs in Isaiah go further and open up the possibility of suffering as a mark of God's favour (e.g. Isa. 53). Again, it is clear from Jesus' teaching that judging others is not to be part of the Christian life (Matt. 5.45; Matt. 7.1 and Luke 6.37; Matt. 13.29–30).

Where the scale of suffering seems too big for us to make a difference, Jesus' teaching that God works spectacular transformation through very small things – such as five loaves and two fishes, a mustard seed, a pinch of salt or a spoonful of yeast – is there to encourage us to try (Matt. 14.17 and parallels and John 6.9; Matt. 13.31–32 and parallels; Matt. 5.13; Matt. 13.33 and Luke 13.21; Rom. 14.1–13).

Finally, Christian teaching assures us that we are not helpless and without resources, but can call on the power of God through the Spirit to support us in our attempts to help others (Isa. 40.28–31). We also have the example of Paul, who is at his strongest when he is weak (2 Cor. 12.9), and who 'can do all things through him who strengthens me' (Phil. 4.13); and of the widow praised by Jesus because she gave 'out of her poverty' (Mark 12.44 and Luke 21.4).[7] Even when there is personal danger, the sacrificial nature of a life that follows in the steps of Christ (Matt. 10.38; 16.24 and parallels; Matt. 10.22ff. and parallels and John 15) requires the Christian to press forward regardless, with the assurance that 'perfect love casts out fear' (1 John 4.18).

Seeing and doing leads to feeling

Compassion is an aspect of love, one that focuses on trying to make things better for the beloved. As we saw in Chapter 7, joy is another aspect of love, one that delights in the beloved. Just as we do not always, or even often, feel naturally joyful, we may not always feel compassionate. Just as the discipline of taking intentional delight in a person or situation may result in real feelings of joy, the decision to look at the other in the way demanded by Christ and to act in accordance with his command – to cultivate kindness by practising mercy – may lead in time to a genuine sense of solidarity and a genuine feeling of compassion (Roberts 2007, p. 196). We may not be able to cultivate compassion directly, but we can nurture the conditions for its emergence.

The Good Samaritan Experiment may seem discouraging, indicating as it does that engaging with this biblical story had a negligible impact on helping behaviour in a situation where compassionate attentiveness was required. However, the results of a series of more recent studies suggest that, where the attentional demands are less and the decisions more considered, exposure to religious material can positively influence helping behaviour such as charitable giving (Pichon, Boccato and Saroglou 2007; Shariff and Norenzayan 2007). Consciously focusing on the ethical teaching of our faith, reflecting on God's moral imperative that we are to love as he loves us, is a vital part of the process of Christian formation.

Elevation

Compassion leads us to do what we can, and often to go beyond our expectations and rise to the occasion. Being empowered to rise to the occasion is one of the benefits of being raised with Christ. The emotion of 'elevation' is thus likely to be relevant to this aspect of Christian formation. Elevation has been described as a warm, *uplifting* feeling that is a response to witnessing moral excellence in others (Haidt 2003).

---

7 It is noteworthy that humility seems to help compassion (La Bouff, Rowatt, Johnson, Tsang and McCullough Willerton 2012). Again, this seems to be about sitting light to what we have. See also Micah 6.8.

Elevation is elicited by acts of charity, gratitude, fidelity, generosity, or any other strong display of virtue. It leads to distinctive physical feelings; a feeling of 'dilation' or opening in the chest, combined with the feeling that one has been uplifted or 'elevated' in some way. It gives rise to a specific motivation or action tendency: emulation, the desire 'of doing charitable and grateful acts also.' . . . In sum, elevation is a response to acts of moral beauty in which we feel as though we have become (for a moment) less selfish, and we want to act accordingly. (Algoe and Haidt 2009, p. 106)

Notice the 'as though' phrase in the above quotation. It appears that elevation is one of those feelings that opens up previously unthought-of possibilities; an inhabitant of transitional space that invites us to wonder if *we* could do something like that. It is significant, then, that exploratory studies of elevation indicate that 'openness' is one of its distinctive features (Algoe and Haidt 2009). Research is also accumulating to suggest that elevation is not just a warm feeling, but leads to behaviour change (Schnall, Roper and Fessler 2010) and, perhaps most interesting of all, that it might stimulate the release of oxytocin (Silvers and Haidt 2008).

I say móre: the just man justices;
Keeps grace: thát keeps all his goings graces;
Acts in God's eye what in God's eye he is –
Chríst – for Christ plays in ten thousand places,
Lovely in limbs, and lovely in eyes not his
To the Father through the features of men's faces.

Gerard Manley Hopkins (1844–89)

This research offers us another angle on the cultivation of kindness: witnessing others acting with compassion will encourage us to rise to the occasion. It offers us a psychological model of being raised with Christ; the moral beauty of his life and death elevates those who have the eyes to see it. More practically, it tells us that if we want to open ourselves to compassion we should mix with compassionate people and listen to the stories of compassionate people. Reading the lives of the saints (in the broadest sense of that word), watching television programmes like *The Secret Millionaire*, finding out more about the work of frontline aid workers, helping out at a local voluntary agency, are all likely to expose us to the people and stories that will lift us up both emotionally and morally.

Visionary experiences: crisis and call

We have seen that the conditions for the emergence of compassion can be set by practising mindful attention; finding points of connection with the other by obtaining more information, while resisting the temptation to project my issues on to her; seeing her as Christ, while avoiding the temptation to idealize her;

meditating on Christian ethical teaching; practising mercy even when I don't feel particularly compassionate; spending time with inspirational compassionate people. However, there are times when compassion comes upon us uninvited. This is often in response to the sort of epiphanies we considered in Chapter 6. Here compassion seems more like a spiritual gift – a *charisma* – than a spiritual fruit.

Spiritual gifts (see e.g. 1 Cor. 12.4–11) are not the same as the fruit of the Spirit. They are given on a particular occasion to build up the body of the Church in a particular situation. We should all be cultivating spiritual fruit, but spiritual gifts come and go as the Spirit wills (John 3.8), and individuals cannot hold on to them. One spiritual gift is prophecy – extraordinary vision that is communicated for the good of the Church (and also the wider world).

A prophetic vision carries with it the sense of a direct encounter with the divine, but its authenticity is ultimately judged by its fruit (Matt. 7.20–23), which are characterized by love (1 Cor. 13.2). As we saw in Chapter 6 and will explore further in Chapter 15 epiphanies have a tendency to come at times of personal and community trauma or crisis. This is also true of prophetic visions (Lee, Poloma and Post 2013). They are a response to a problematic situation and they contain within them the seeds of a solution to that situation.

Prophetic visionaries often experience a sense of dissonance between their visions and the world around them, such that they want to make things right. Some of Jesus' apparent distress as he looked about him seems to have been the mismatch between what he saw and his vision of the kingdom of God. The words 'Your will be done, on earth as it is in heaven' (Matt. 6.10) can be understood as a heartfelt plea arising from this sense of dissonance.

In line with this, a large-scale survey carried out in the USA by Matthew Lee and Margaret Poloma showed that a sense of prophetic call, often mediated through mystical experience, was strongly associated with benevolent attitudes to other human beings and the giving of time and money to good causes. However, an even stronger predictor of these attitudes and behaviours was a sense of God's personal love, received through both extraordinary and more routine spiritual experiences (Lee and Poloma 2009). It seems that the biggest driver to go out and act benevolently towards other human beings is the experience of God's benevolence towards us (1 John 4.19). This is not the same as being elevated by seeing how much God loves the world; it is an overflowing of the love we have received into love for others. We do not simply follow the example of Jesus; we are filled with living water that gushes out so that others can drink of it (John 4.14; 7.38). This accounts for the sense of charismatic power to act that accompanies many visionary experiences.

Lee's and Poloma's study also demonstrated that the response to such charismatic experiences can take a number of forms. They divided these into three types: community service (outreach to people in need, such as volunteering at a foodbank); renewal or revival movements that re-envision the larger Church in line with a vision of the breaking in of God's kingdom; and social justice (taking action to address systemic social and political factors). The first of these two types of responses corresponds to what I have called nurturing compassion; the second and third correspond to what I have called reparative compassion. Lee and Poloma observe that in their USA sample socio-political action tended to be characteristic of those operating within a more liberal political culture, and initiating church renewal tended to be characteristic of those operating within a more politically conservative culture. This alerts us to the need to develop some self-awareness in relation to our own cultural influences. But it also reminds us, yet again, that there is more than one way of doing compassion.

Exercises

1 Read John 11, noticing the way that Jesus moves between approach and withdrawal, engagement and detachment, emotion and action. Look at the interplay of fear and love and try and connect with the general tone of danger and imminent crisis for Jesus himself. Reflect on why John tells us so much about Jesus' feelings and motives in this account.

2 Choose an area of social action with which that you have been meaning to get more involved but for which you haven't yet found time.
   - Get hold of some relevant literature and pray in an informed way about the issues.
   - Find some human stories and meditate on the connections between you and those involved.
   - Make a gift of money and or time to a project in this area.

Further reading

Brother Ramon, 2008, *Franciscan Spirituality: Following St Francis Today*, London: SPCK.

Germer, C., 2009, *The Mindful Path to Self-compassion: Freeing Yourself from Destructive Thoughts and Emotions*, New York: Guilford Press.

Gross, R. and Muck, T., 2003, *Christians Talk about Buddhist Meditation: Buddhists Talk about Christian Prayer*, London: Continuum.

Hughes, T. O., 2013, *The Compassion Quest*, London: SPCK.

Lee, M., Poloma, M. and Post, S., 2013, *The Heart of Religion: Spiritual Empowerment, Benevolence, and the Experience of God's Love*, New York: Oxford University Press.

Percy, E., 2014, *Mothering as a Metaphor for Ministry*, Farnham: Ashgate.

13

Not Retaliating:
Forgiveness and Repentance

In Christ God was reconciling the world to himself, not counting their trespasses against them, and entrusting the message of reconciliation to us.

2 Corinthians 5.19

You have heard that it was said, 'An eye for an eye and a tooth for a tooth.' But I say to you, Do not resist an evildoer. But if anyone strikes you on the right cheek, turn the other also; and if anyone wants to sue you and take your coat, give your cloak as well; and if anyone forces you to go one mile, go also the second mile.

Matthew 5.38–41

Whenever you stand praying, forgive, if you have anything against anyone; so that your Father in heaven may also forgive you your trespasses.

Mark 11.25

'If another member of the church sins against you, go and point out the fault when the two of you are alone. If the member listens to you, you have regained that one. But if you are not listened to, take one or two others along with you, so that every word may be confirmed by the evidence of two or three witnesses. If the member refuses to listen to them, tell it to the church; and if the offender refuses to listen even to the church, let such a one be to you as a Gentile and a tax-collector.' . . . Then Peter came and said to him, 'Lord, if another member of the church sins against me, how often should I forgive? As many as seven times?' Jesus said to him, 'Not seven times, but, I tell you, seventy-seven times.'

Matthew 18.15–17; 21–22

Embracing an attitude of non-retaliation is the most difficult and countercultural of all the principles of Christian discipleship, one of the demands of Jesus that renders him profoundly strange, if not frankly repellent, when seen from a human point of view. It makes some sort of sense for us to pursue humility, hospitality and kindness, even to the heroic extreme of giving up our lives for another person who is in need. But the idea of letting ourselves be treated as doormats – or worse, punch bags – by others who are out to exploit or abuse us goes against the grain. Paul identifies this feeling when he reflects, 'Indeed, rarely will anyone die for a righteous person – though perhaps for a good person someone might actually dare to die. But God proves his love for us in that while we still were sinners Christ died for us' (Rom. 5.7–8).

Paul's point is important; he is saying that the fact that God became incarnate in Christ, suffered and died a dreadful death shows us the extent of his love; but the fact that this death was at the hands of those he had come to help shows the *nature* of his love. It is radically open, unconditional and non-coercive. It is love that loves the beloved simply because he exists. While it recognizes and responds to lovable qualities in the beloved, it does not love him on account of these. It does not force itself upon him and so risks the pain of rejection and even abuse (Levinas 1981; Toner 1968).

This radical divine love is the context in which the principle of non-retaliation arises. We saw in Chapter 1 that our formation takes place in the context of the transformation of the whole created order (p. 4). A key aspect of this transformative process is God's reconciliation of all things to himself in Christ (Col. 1.20). This divine act of cosmic reconciliation is the context for the Christian's ministry of reconciliation, as the famous extract from 2 Corinthians that opens this chapter makes clear. Just as our compassion for others is a participation in the overflowing compassion of God for us, our reconciliation with those who have done us harm is a participation in something much bigger.

Reconciliation is about peace-making. The divine reconciliation described in Colossians 1.20 has been achieved by Christ 'making peace by the blood of his cross' (a supreme act of non-retaliation). This peace is the cosmic *shālôm* discussed in Chapters 10 and 11, whose bottom line is that 'It's OK'. It is peace within each person, peace between people of different races, ages and gender (Zech. 8), peace between different species (Isa. 11.6–9) and peace between the created order and its Creator.

There are several accounts of reconciliation between people in the Bible. Three of the most moving are the meeting of Esau and Jacob (Gen. 32—33), the story of the Prodigal Son (Luke 15.11–32) and the conversation between the risen Christ and Peter over breakfast on the lakeshore (John 21.15–19). In each of these accounts two people have become estranged because one has seriously transgressed against the other; there is an issue between two individuals. But in each case the wider community is also affected. Jacob has a large company of his tribe with him and even goes so far as to divide them into two groups in case the reconciliation goes horribly wrong (Gen. 32.7–8); the Prodigal Son has a brother, and a third of the story is devoted to his place in the family (Luke 15.25–32); the conversation between Jesus and Peter turns quickly to 'my sheep' – the wider Church (John 21.15–17). Like formation, reconciliation is a community, not a private, affair.

I have often wondered what happened in the hours, days and weeks after the joyful celebration with the fatted calf. Did the older brother go in and join the party? Did the younger brother mend his ways? Was the father able to regain his standing in the local community? Did they become one big happy family? We are not told. The story of Esau and Jacob gives us more information: there is a deeply emotional reconciliation between these brothers (perhaps a mix of joy and relief), but they go their separate ways. Being at peace did not mean that they had to live in each others' pockets; indeed, peaceful relations may have been difficult to maintain had they continued to be in close proximity. They appeared to have made a good farewell. The interchange between Jesus and Peter is bittersweet (John 21.17), and it is also a farewell; Jesus and Peter will separate, but Peter follows Jesus' way and is blessed by the coming of the Spirit. It seems that there can be different ways of doing reconciliation.

Within the regime of reconciliation that is the kingdom of God, the currency is repentance and forgiveness. Forgiveness expresses an attitude of non-retaliation, rather as compassion expresses an attitude of loving kindness. However, there is a significant difference between compassion and forgiveness: while compassion is an emotion, forgiveness is a *process* or a transaction. This has two implications: first, while we might feel inclined to forgive, we don't *feel* forgiveness in the way that we might be said to feel compassion; second, forgiveness is often bound up with repentance in both the one who forgives and the one who is forgiven. In this chapter we will look at the repentance–forgiveness process in some depth. As this is a book about psychology, the consideration will be primarily from a psychological rather than a moral philosophical point of view, and the focus will be on interpersonal forgiveness in individual relationships rather than larger-scale political processes (important though these are). We begin with the principle of non-retaliation.

No tit for tat

In Chapter 11 we saw that, according to social identity theory, one aspect of our sense of who we are is constituted in terms of our affiliation to a social group, a sense of belonging to a community. We saw that markers of group affiliation include the way we dress, the way we talk and the beliefs we espouse. Another marker of group affiliation is the ethical code to which we adhere (Taylor 1989). The degree to which an individual adheres to her group's rules for living is one of the things that determine her own felt sense of identity as a group member; it also acts as a signal to other group members, indicating the degree of her commitment to the group.

So when an individual transgresses her community code it will be in everyone's interests for things to be put right through restitutive action. It will be in the interests of any individuals who have been wronged to receive compensation, or at least formal public acknowledgment of the wrong that has been done them; it will be in the interests of the community to restore the status quo and consolidate its identity by the return of the erring member to the fold; it will be in the interests of the transgressor to ease tensions in her immediate interpersonal relationships and to consolidate her own sense of identity through an act of re-affiliation to the group.

Yet there also has to be an assurance of the trustworthiness of the offender and in particular her commitment, not just to her own self-interests but to the greater good of the group. This is where the biological idea of 'costly signalling' (Zahavi 1995) comes in: the restitution needs to be seen by the community to hurt the offender, physically, materially, financially or emotionally. This acts as a kind of guarantee of her sincerity and intention to mend her ways.

If the community is to be strengthened by this process, there must be some safeguards and limits placed on the degree of hurt inflicted on the offender. This is one reason that most cultures have a recognized judicial system with a set of sentence tariffs. One example of such tariffs can be found in the Law of Moses (e.g. Exod. 21.23ff.; Lev. 24.15ff.). Here the cost exacted by the punishment is exactly commensurate with the cost extracted by the offence. This allows a line to be drawn under disputes and guards against an escalation of offence and counter-offence.

A less formal type of costly signalling on the part of the offender would be an acknowledgment of personal responsibility and guilt, expressions of remorse and an – often grovelling – apology. This, together with a costly lowering of his position in the household, seems to be the restitutive action the Prodigal Son has in mind as he decides to return home (Luke 15.18–19). It is, after all, an option that is offered by his religious tradition (Lev. 26.40). Indeed, religious restitutive rituals, which often involve confession, sacrifice or public penance, have attracted a good deal of scrutiny from anthropologists with an interest in costly signalling (see e.g. Irons 2001; Slone and Van Slyke 2015), and some biblical scholars have used costly signalling as a lens through which to read certain New Testament texts (see e.g. Roitto 2012).

It seems plausible that these complex systems of costly but limited restitution for an offence help to keep communities stable by shoring up a sense of collective identity, and that this process can be particularly powerful in faith communities. However, as we saw in Chapter 11, the identity of a community is very often strengthened at the cost of hostility towards outsiders. The process of offence and restitution is likely to consolidate the ethical code of a community, enabling its code to become enmeshed with its identity. This has the effect that anyone whose lifestyle does not conform to the code becomes even more of an outsider – not just strange, but morally unacceptable (McCullough 2008; Van Tongeren, Burnette, O'Boyle, Worthington and Forsyth 2013).

This is one way of understanding the situation that Paul describes as living under the law, already discussed in the Introduction to Part 3. In his letter to the Galatians, Paul describes the law as like a teacher – literally a 'pedagogue' (Gal. 3.24) – that was previously in place to keep things under some sort of reasonable control. His point is that with the coming of Christ something radically different has happened; a new dispensation has arrived that is all about grace. This works its way out most obviously for Paul in terms of the breaking down of the barriers between Jew and gentile so that there are no more in- and out-groups (Gal. 3.28). But it can be seen more fundamentally in Jesus' teaching on non-retaliation in the Sermon on the Mount, set out in the second of our opening passages. Here Jesus takes the Law of Moses relating to sentence tariffs and sets himself against it.

The new dispensation is not about tit-for-tat justice. People are not required to make costly restitution in order to be forgiven. Whatever the precise mechanism of the saving work of God in Christ, the outcome is that the cost has been borne and costly signalling is no longer a prerequisite for mercy. The Prodigal Son's attempt at costly signalling is pre-empted by his father's embrace (Luke 15.20). In the new dispensation of grace, costly signalling has been replaced by faith.

All of this is expressed both in Jesus' teaching about non-retaliation and in the non-retaliative stance he took as his Passion unfolded. In his teaching he requires his followers to refrain from rendering evil for evil; essentially pointing out that two wrongs don't make a right. To make it clear that he is not talking about rolling over through fear of superior power, he instructs the disciple to seize the initiative; to offer his body to the bully, to offer his belongings to the thief, to offer his service to the imperial power. In an occupied country, where there was no expectation of justice for those who were weak and oppressed, this would have been the one certain way of taking back dignity and power. It helps us to understand Jesus' encouragement not to fear those who can kill the body but can do no harm to the soul (Matt. 10.28 and Luke 12.4). They cannot take from you what you freely offer; in offering up yourself you cease to become an object of abuse or exploitation and become an agent of grace.[1] Running through all of this is the paradoxical notion that non-retaliation and the forgiveness that can flow from it are about exerting power (see also Rom. 12.17–21).

In Matthew's Passion narrative Jesus emphasizes that he could call on legions of angels to fight on his behalf, but he chooses not to (Matt. 26.53). In Matthew's, Luke's and John's accounts he also rebukes his followers for attacking those who have come to arrest him (Matt. 26.53; Luke 22.50; John 18.11). In John's Gospel Jesus says very clearly that his life is not taken from him; he has chosen to give it and in doing so is exerting his power (John 10.8). As the Passion narrative unfolds, the reader is then able to understand that, while Jesus appears to be objectified and powerless, he is actually the supreme agent, moving towards the culmination of his work on earth. The deep irony of the situation is exquisitely drawn out in the dialogue with Pilate in chapters 18 and 19.

Jesus' call to embrace an attitude of non-retaliation, not rendering evil for evil, may trouble us. It certainly invites a number of pressing questions about how we should live it out in our current context, some of which we will explore shortly. Nevertheless, it cannot simply be ignored. It is not a minor quirky detail of his ethics. It is absolutely central to his identity and his understanding of what God was doing in reconciling all things to himself; and it sent him to the cross.

Forgiveness

As with humility, the forgiveness of the Christian is not a simple replication of divine forgiveness, but there is a connection between divine forgiveness and the calling of all Christians. Our forgiveness of others and the fact that we can dare to ask God for forgiveness (Matt. 6.12; Luke 11.4) arise in the context of divine reconciliation, a part of which is divine forgiveness. Rather than getting embroiled in the question of whether we forgive others *out of* a sense of being forgiven by God or instead have to forgive others *in order to* be forgiven by God, it is perhaps more helpful to think of forgiveness as something within which we are caught up, an eschatological event initiated by God into which we fall (Watts 2004, pp. 55–6), and in which we continue to live and move and have our being.

Watts, following Holloway (2002), suggests that one way divine and human forgiveness may differ is that, while divine forgiveness is utterly unconditional,

---

1 See de Certeau 1988 for a parallel modern analysis of the way in which people individualize mass culture and thus subvert it through conscious and unconscious 'tactics'.

the forgiveness of all but the most spiritually advanced Christian may need to be supported by restitution on the part of the offender. This appears to have been the case in the early church communities; the aspiration to forgiveness was high, but because human beings cannot read the hearts of their fellows, some acknowledgement of wrongdoing on the part of the offender seems to have been required (Matt. 5.23–25; Matt. 18.15–17 and Luke 17.3–4; 1 John 1.9), especially if the church community felt that it was forgiving with divine authority – something we will consider in more detail shortly.

The nature of forgiveness

But what is forgiveness? Many of the worries that people have about forgiveness rest upon misunderstandings of its nature. For example, it is sometimes understood to entail forgetting the offence, condoning the offence, excusing the offender, resuming or beginning a close personal relationship with the offender or developing positive feelings for the offender. In fact neither biblical nor psychological understandings of forgiveness involve these things.

> You should never hate yourself for hating others who do terrible things: the depth of your love is shown by the extent of your anger. However, when I talk of *forgiveness* I mean the belief that you can come out the other side a better person. A better person than the one being consumed by anger and hatred. Remaining in that state locks you in a state of victimhood, making you almost dependent on the perpetrator. If you can find it in yourself to forgive then you are no longer chained to the perpetrator.
>
> Desmond Tutu (2014)

The verb that is translated as 'forgive' in the New Testament is *aphiēmi*. Its most usual meaning is to let something go or to cancel a debt. Debts were a major issue in first-century Palestine. Land had been redistributed under the Roman administration, with the result that there was a great increase in the numbers of landless peasants. Agricultural practices changed so that workers who had traditionally been tenant farmers were instead hired by the day to work for richer, often absentee, landowners (Matt. 3.20). Money-lending at exorbitant rates became common. If the repayments could not be made, horrific penalties could be exacted (Matt. 18.34).[2] It is then not surprising that the dominant images used by Jesus to communicate the good news of God's kingdom were cancellation of debts and redemption from kidnap or slavery.

---

2 The first-century Hellenistic Jew, Philo, writes about some of the awful punishments meted out to debtors in Egypt in *De specialibus legis* (On individual laws) II.159–62, and it is possible that such practices had spread to Palestine (Theissen 1987, p. 204).

The New Testament understanding of forgiveness is thus less moral in tone than our contemporary popular understandings and more about the economy of liberation. This is exemplified in the wording of the Lord's Prayer, which is now generally received as referring to trespasses or sins but whose original emphasis, translated literally in the KJV, was on debt:

And forgive us our debts, as we forgive our debtors. (Matthew 6.12, KJV)

And forgive us our sins; for we also forgive every one that is indebted to us. (Luke 11.4a, KJV)

Current psychological approaches to forgiveness do not claim to tell us how people *should* forgive; they simply describe how people *do* forgive. Interestingly, they correspond in some respects to the New Testament accounts. Human forgiveness is understood primarily as a process, but its emotional aspects are also acknowledged. There is still much research to be done, but the current consensus is that the key features of forgiveness include:

- a recognition that one has been wronged;
- a voluntary decision to forego justifiable retribution;
- active communication of this decision to the offender, with the objective of restoring or establishing improved relations (Enright and Coyle 1998);
- the letting go of negative feelings towards the offender (Tangney, Fee, Reinsmith, Boone and Lee 1999, cited in Snyder and Lopez 2007, p. 280; McCullough, Fincham and Tsang 2003).

In order to recognize that I have been wronged I must have a sense that I have certain entitlements – that I am worth something – and it therefore matters if my entitlements are violated. That is, a healthy degree of self-esteem is necessary in order to be able to forgive. This assertion is moderately supported by empirical studies (see e.g. Wade, Worthington and Meyer 2005; Eaton, Struthers and Santelli 2006). It connects with the Christian's sense of being a beloved and esteemed child of God that we considered in Chapter 7 and is well exemplified in the account of the death of Stephen (Acts 7.60). Psychologically speaking, we can forgive if we feel loved.

Recognizing that I have been wronged is precisely *not* sweeping the offence under the carpet, saying 'It's nothing' or 'It doesn't matter', because I feel that perhaps I am nothing and I don't matter. If I understand that God took me sufficiently seriously to die for me, I am more likely to take offences against myself seriously. They are, after all, offences against Christ's own body. Of course, in the subtle social world in which we live, some discernment will often be required to determine whether an incident that has caused me distress really *is* an offence (recall the discussion on overreaction in Chapter 2); but simply denying it is not an option.

Having recognized the offence for what it is, either privately or publicly, I then make a free decision to let go what would reasonably expected to be my due. Unlike first-century Palestine, in the late-modern western world my due is likely to be largely psychological. I am entitled to be angry with the offender, to hate the offender, to bear a grudge, to be known as a victim, to have the moral high ground, to receive the sympathy of others and so on. My decision to relinquish these sorts of things must be voluntary (rather than, for example, arising out of a coercive relationship). This free decision then needs to be communicated to the offender in some way.

The way that the decision then translates into action is much more problematic for psychological dues than monetary dues; one cannot simply tear up angry feelings in the way one can tear up a bill. What seems clear from the psychological literature is that when people forgive they experience a decrease in negative feelings towards the offender over time, but they do not experience a comparable increase in positive feelings (McCullough, Fincham and Tsang 2003). This makes some sort of logical sense; forgiveness is about cancelling a debt, not giving a bonus payment. (We will consider the case of Zacchaeus and his fourfold repayment of debt in the next section.)

Influences on forgiveness

Forgiveness is more likely in cases where the desire to maintain a relationship with the offender takes precedence over the desire for self-protection. Thus it is seen more in the context of close, committed and interdependent relationships and collectivist cultures (one reason for its very great importance in the early church communities). It is seen less in situations where resources are scarce, and in individuals who have a very strong sense that they need to protect themselves. In line with this, certain personality characteristics appear to be associated with a difficulty in forgiving: narcissism, indicating an exaggerated sense of entitlement (Exline, Baumeister, Bushman, Campbell and Finkel 2004); high scores on those aspects of N that relate to anxiety, indicating an exaggerated sense of personal vulnerability (Brose, Rye, Lutz-Zois and Ross 2005); high scores on the aspects of N that relate to anger and hostility, indicating a high capacity to fuel a grudge by rumination (Maltby, Wood, Day, Kon, Colley and Linley 2008).

Other influences on forgiveness include the nature of the offence and the subsequent behaviour of the offender. Offences that shatter assumptions about the relationship with the offender or broader life existential issues are particularly difficult to forgive (Exline, Worthington, Hill and McCullough 2003). Everyday observation suggests that apologies and offers of restitution may make forgiveness more likely; however, there are not many systematic studies in this area. In one interesting laboratory study Witvliet and colleagues found that participants who imagined themselves as victims of a robbery were most likely to take a forgiving attitude if they imagined receiving both a strong apology and some restitution, rather less likely to do so if they imagined receiving only one or the other, and least likely if they imagined receiving only a weak apology. In these participants a more forgiving attitude was found to be correlated with physiological markers of relaxation, including lower heart rate and muscle tension (Witvliet, Worthington and Wade 2002).

Finally, degree of empathy for the offender is a strong predictor of forgiveness (Worthington 1998; Macaskill, Maltby and Day 2002). It appears that empathy has a role in forgiveness similar to its role in compassion; it reduces the social distance between the victim and the offender. If I can imagine pressures that might have led me to commit a similar offence and can then find signs of such pressures in the story of the offender, the task of forgiveness will be easier because the offence will *feel* less severe to me. This may look very like excusing the offender, but it is a psychological experience, not a moral judgement. The offence remains objectively the same; it is just psychologically easier to forgive.

Psychological costs and benefits of forgiving

There is an increasing body of research demonstrating an association between forgiveness and indicators of physical health and psychological well-being, such as blood pressure, self-reported physical symptoms and measures of anxiety, depression and hostility (see e.g. Worthington and Scherer 2004; Witvliet and McCullough 2007). Some caution needs to be applied in interpreting these findings because the direction of causation – if any – is not clear; instead of forgiveness making people more healthy, it could be that people who already have good emotional and physical health are in a better position to forgive. Nevertheless, there is at least one study that suggests that forgiveness has a causal role (Bono, McCullough and Root 2008).

The way that forgiveness might contribute to well-being is best understood in terms of its being a positive way of coping with adversity. Forgiveness breaks through the rumination on one's situation that can lead to a spiral of depression; it can be a kind of taking back of control that gives a sense of self-efficacy and dignity that comes with the non-retaliative stance promoted by Jesus; it is a healthy alternative to suppressing feelings by denial, alcohol or drug use; the skills involved in forgiving are likely to be useful in maintaining other relationships.

On the other hand, forgiveness is costly. It involves letting go of a grudge that may have become part of my story and my identity. Nevertheless, grudges are high maintenance; they need to be nursed, and this takes time and energy (Muraven and Baumeister 2000). So laying a grudge down may initially be very costly, but on balance it may turn out to be a relief.

Forgiveness also involves risk. I may appear weak and vulnerable if I forgive; or it may look as if I condone the actions of the offender, thus increasing the likelihood of his reoffending or of similar offences by others.[3] In this way I risk becoming morally tainted myself. These sorts of issues, relating to 'cheap grace' and its consequences, seem to be behind the older brother's criticism of his father's welcome of the Prodigal, and Paul's defensive approach to his imaginary interlocutors from the church in Rome (Rom. 3.8; 6.1).

It therefore seems that if I am to reap the benefits of forgiveness, I am likely to need support in managing the costs as I go through the process.

---

3 There is some preliminary evidence that forgiveness does not necessarily lead to repeat offending (Wallace, Exline and Baumeister 2008).

Repentance

In his teaching on prayer Jesus instructs his followers to forgive others (Matt. 6.12; Mark 11.25; Luke 11.4), not in order to gain the sorts of benefits described above, but in order to establish a context within which they can legitimately ask for forgiveness from their heavenly Father. This is something we might understand as 'repentance' (*metanoia*).

In Chapter 6 repentance was presented as a turning from a way of life that has gone off course in order to realign with God's way, and as something that happens continually throughout the Christian life. Seen in this light, repentance involves a good degree of self-awareness and a regular asking of the question 'Have I strayed off course?' As we saw in Chapter 7, repentance is also something that is nested within a secure parental relationship with our divine parent. We are already reconciled with God – that is why we can call him 'Father'. In the Lord's Prayer we do not confess a long list of sins in order to be reconciled with God; *out of the reconciliation that already exists* between God, ourselves and our brothers and sisters (expressed in our willingness to forgive them), we are entitled to ask God to cancel any debts we have accrued along the Christian way and to set us back on course.

Coming regularly to God in repentance is important, not only in keeping us on the right path, but also in resisting any temptation to judge or scapegoat others. In owning the way that I have strayed off course as an individual, and my complicity in the systemic sin of my community, nation and planet, I am also building empathy and hence a forgiving attitude in myself.

> To me three propositions seem self-evident. The first is that nothing can save the world but a general act of repentance in place of the present self-righteous insistence on the wickedness of others; for we have all sinned, and continue to sin most horribly. The second is that good treatment and not bad treatment makes men good. And the third is . . . that unless you treat a man well when he has treated you ill you just get nowhere, or rather you give further impetus to evil and head straight for human annihilation.
>
> Victor Gollancz (1893–1967)

The cultural analyst René Girard identifies scapegoating as the means by which communities manage systemic sin in the short term but perpetuate it in the long term. An individual or group is selected as a figure on to which the guilt of the whole community is loaded. This scapegoat[4] is then destroyed, expelled or contained, allowing the community to feel that it has dealt with its sin, but masking the fact that sin is something that is distributed throughout it. One reason

---

4 Despite the use of the word 'scapegoat' in the KJV translation, the psychosocial concept of scapegoating is quite distinct from the Day of Atonement ritual of Leviticus 16 (Douglas 2004, pp. 38–60).

Figure 20.

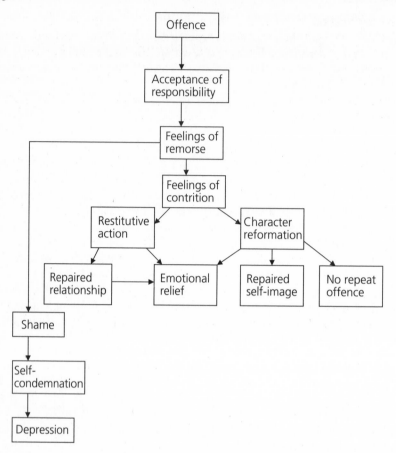

that this process works well in the short term is that the chosen scapegoat is highly plausible – a foreigner, a criminal, someone mentally troubled, a member of a demonized group (such as paedophiles). Girard argues that the crucifixion of Jesus was itself an act of scapegoating, but that because Jesus' innocence is clear and revealed unquestionably by his resurrection, God has acted in him to expose and repudiate the process of scapegoating once and for all (Girard 1977).

The story of the woman taken in adultery (John 8.3–11)[5] is a good illustration of Girard's analysis. An individual who has sinned becomes the focus of blame for the whole community, but Jesus suggests that each of her accusers examine his own conduct, and each finds himself to be guilty. The notion of systemic sin has several theological ramifications, but for our purposes the important issue is the need to examine our own hearts before we rush to blame others. We may also need to be attentive to the words of others to us as we do this (Matt. 18.15).

---

5 For more on scapegoating and the woman in adultery, see Collicutt 2009a, pp. 38–56.

Sometimes, of course, we are only too aware of our mistakes and transgressions against others and against God. However, self-awareness is just the first step in the process of repentance, which has the potential to go off track. The psychologist Julie Exline and her colleagues provide a helpful analysis (see e.g. Fisher and Exline 2010). This is summarized in Figure 20.

This model of repentance holds that the first step is to accept that I am responsible for an offence against another. With this acceptance of responsibility come feelings of remorse and then contrition, which lead in two positive directions. First, I will want to make things right, especially if the relationship is of value to me. If I am successful in any restitution I undertake, the relationship with the one I have hurt will be repaired. Second, I will learn from the experience, perhaps resolving to make some major changes in my life. If I am successful, my character will be reformed, I will think better of myself and I am unlikely to repeat the offence. Any success in my attempts at restitutive justice and character formation will result in relief of my feelings of remorse and contrition.

However, things can go wrong along the way. My attempts at restitutive justice and character formation may be inept or inappropriate. I am likely to need help and support in effecting them. Perhaps more fundamentally, I may never move beyond feelings of remorse to the feelings of contrition that can motivate change. Instead I may go down the path of self-condemnation that ends in depression. The key issue here appears to be shame, something we considered in the context of humility in Chapter 8. Shame makes us frightened to engage with the one we have wronged because of an overwhelming fear of rejection or condemnation. Consistent with this, at least one empirical study has found that *high* self-esteem, conscientiousness (C) and agreeableness (A) are associated with willingness to apologize and seek forgiveness. In contrast, narcissism and a sense of entitlement make apologizing and forgiveness-seeking less likely (Howell, Dopko, Turowski and Buro 2011), presumably because narcissism makes an individual much less likely to accept responsibility for the offence in the first place.

Some of us, because of our every-daily sins, hold not our promises nor keep we our cleanness that our Lord setteth us in, but fall oft-times into such wretchedness that shame it is to say it. And the beholding of this maketh us so sorry and so heavy, that scarce can we see any comfort. And this dismay we take sometime for a meekness – but it is a foul blindness and a weakness, and we cannot despise it as we do another sin that we know which cometh through lack of true judgement. And it is against truth; for of all the properties of the Blissful Trinity it is God's will that we have especially faithfulness and comfort in love; for love maketh might and wisdom meekness to us. For just as by the courtesy of God He forgetteth our sin after the time we ourselves repent, right so willeth He that we forgive our sin in regard to our stupid depression and our doubtful fears.

Julian of Norwich (1342–1416)

The dynamic in our experience of God's forgiveness is subtly but significantly different from that described above and is depicted in Figure 21.

Figure 21.

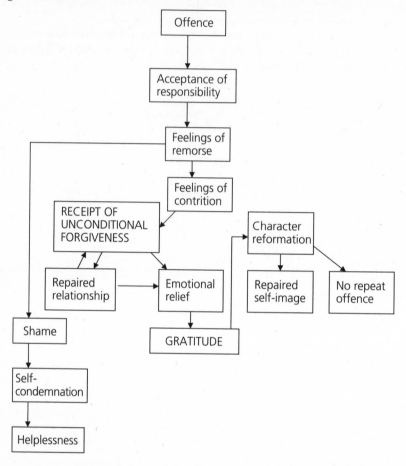

We might think of the route that leads to shame and self-condemnation as the route taken by Adam and Eve, as discussed in Chapter 8. The route that finds its expression in gratitude is that taken by Zacchaeus and the sinful woman of Luke 7. On this model of forgiveness, the reformation of character is not so much a resolve taken in the light of my horror at my own behaviour, but an expression of gratitude to the one who loves and accepts me just as I am. Because this is an experience of grace, the response is not a sense of relief and a mending of ways, but an extravagant outpouring – of cancelled debts in the case of Zacchaeus and expensive ointment in the case of the sinful woman.

This is also the model of forgiveness that is behind the story of the unmerciful servant (Matt. 18.23–35). If our experience of God's unconditional forgiveness is authentic, it should show itself in our capacity to forgive others, especially, as in this parable, in small things. If it does not, there is a sense in which we are liars; we are not participating in grace, we have taken God's forgiveness as our entitlement and are grasping it like a commodity.

Nevertheless, as already observed earlier in this chapter (pp. 198–9), the pattern of Christian forgiveness and repentance is likely to contain elements of both the human and the divine patterns described in this section.

Abuse and whistle-blowing

Feelings of shame or excessive guilt can, ironically, be exacerbated in certain faith traditions. Within Christianity the notion of the 'unforgivable sin'[6] has been particularly destructive. The rather disturbing finding of one study was that religious individuals who experienced suicidal thoughts readily applied the idea of the unforgivable sin to themselves (Exline, Yali and Sanderson 2000). Even more disturbingly, there are anecdotal reports that some individuals who have been abused by clergy have been told that the disclosure of such abuse is the unforgivable sin against the Holy Spirit.

This brings us to the question of abuse. There is a theoretical worry that the Christian requirement to forgive may play into the hands of abusers, and several stories of the survivors of abuse in church settings have confirmed this (Minister and Clergy Sexual Abuse Survivors (MACSAS) report 2011). In the past many women (and some men) were counselled to remain in abusive marriages on the basis of the Christian requirement to forgive.

Genuine forgiveness happens when we feel safe (or 'safe enough'), so forgiveness and safeguarding are closely related. As emphasized earlier in this chapter, forgiveness is essentially about the liberation of the weak by the strong. It is surely significant that the story of the unmerciful servant is told by Jesus to Peter, who will become the first pope. Running through the New Testament is a deep concern that Christian leaders do not abuse power. They are to behave as servants, and they are not to treat those in their care with cruelty. Paralleling Matthew's story of the unmerciful servant is Luke's story of the dissolute manager, who 'begins to beat the other slaves, men and women, and to eat and drink and get drunk' (Luke 12.45). Luke's Gospel is the one that is most clear about the unconditional forgiveness offered to all by God, but it also contains this warning for Christian leaders who abuse their power:

> The master of that slave will come on a day when he does not expect him and at an hour that he does not know, and will cut him in pieces, and put him with the unfaithful . . . From everyone to whom much has been given, much will be required; and from the one to whom much has been entrusted, even more will be demanded. (Luke 12.46, 48)

---

6 The nature of this sin is often described as enigmatic, but the context of Matthew 12.32 and Luke 12.10, indicate quite clearly that it is knowingly and intentionally to call that which is of God evil.

The mistake that the Church has repeatedly made across the centuries has been to require the weak to forgive the strong, when it should have been liberating the weak and supporting them to become strong. The colleagues of the servant who is being abused by his unmerciful creditor blow the whistle on him (Matt. 18.31). It seems then that there is more than one way of doing forgiveness:

> Sometimes our role is to stand in solidarity with those who are weak and abused, to stop the offence, to name the interpersonal debt and support the victim's move into a position of strength. (Collicutt 2012b, p. 174)

Being caught up in the forgiveness of God may at times mean repenting; at times forgiving; at times naming injustice and supporting the powerless; even sometimes overcoming a church culture of unthinking deference and setting ourselves in opposition to our leaders.

In very exceptional cases it is possible for a fully capable adult to remain in an abusive relationship, freely and intentionally embracing a Christlike attitude of non-retaliation and hence seizing moral power. However, such cases are extremely rare. The vast majority of adults and all children stay in abusive relationships, trying to keep the peace, tolerating or colluding with their own abuse, because they have no other option, real or perceived. They are trapped and afraid, emotionally or financially dependent on their abusers.

This is not the Christian way of forgiveness, though it is sometimes mistaken for it. Such people need help to escape from their abusers. Moreover, the act of forgiveness happens after the offence has been completed, not in its midst. (Notice that Jesus' words of forgiveness (Luke 23.34) are almost his last words on earth 'then' (*de*) – *after* the nails have been driven in.) If I am to achieve the first step in forgiveness – the recognition that an offence has been committed against me – I will at the very least need time and a safe place to process events. I will then need to be in a position of strength if I am to set what is due to me aside. This may take many years.

As a Christian, working out when I have been wronged, when I am in the wrong, whether I am in a position to forgive or instead need to find a physically and psychologically safe place to think through what has been happening, is an enormously complex task. I cannot go through it alone. I need the help of friends and advisors inside and outside the Church. Yet it is the church community, locally or more widely, that should have the most important role in supporting me (Worthington, Davis, Hook, Webb, Toussaint, Sandage, Gartner and Van Tongeren 2012), for 'If one member suffers, all suffer together with it' (1 Cor. 12.26a).

Cultivating interpersonal forgiveness

Allow time and space

We can't conjure up the forgiveness process to order. Almost by definition, if we have been deeply hurt, we will feel reluctant to forgive. Reaching a decision to forgive the offender will often require time and space, as discussed above. We may first need to do some work in looking after ourselves and becoming stronger. This is particularly true in the case of psychological trauma, which by its nature puts us through the event again and again by way of nightmares and flashbacks. For a person with these sorts of symptoms, in which the event is relived on a regular basis, the offence is not complete, and forgiveness may be almost impossible.[7] The first rule, then, is to take the pressure off ourselves and to resist any pressure from well-meaning others.

Talk through the offence in a supportive setting

Again, unless we can recall the offence without being overwhelmed by anger, hurt or anxiety, we are probably not ready to forgive. We need to have our story heard and our hurt acknowledged. Some sort of public acknowledgment – not necessarily by the offender – that an offence has occurred is a prerequisite for forgiveness (Matt. 18.16–17). Simply offering a confidential, non-judgemental listening ear, without encouraging the rehearsal of a grudge script, is something that we can all do for each other.[8]

Consider whistle-blowing

Sometimes the offence against us may be part of a pattern, and there is a risk that others may be hurt in a similar way. In these circumstances we need to take responsibility and share information with an appropriate authority. This can be daunting and potentially costly. We may not wish to get a name as a troublemaker or have to relive events by going through formal – even judicial – proceedings. Our instinct may be to try to forget. Nevertheless, with support from others, we may find it in our power to whistle-blow.

Focus on God's love

This may be hard to do in a situation of deep hurt, but recalling the good gifts of God in the past may help. Connecting with the suffering of Christ and his stance of non-retaliation may comfort, elevate and inspire. It will be important to reflect on Christ's command to forgive and what it may mean in these circumstances. If the time is not yet right for forgiveness, there is no point getting sidetracked into guilt. We will need to place our conflicting feelings in the hands of God.

---

7 Yet it may also be true that adopting a forgiving attitude can help with the processing of trauma (Schultz, Tallman and Altmaier 2010).

8 For a helpful analysis, see *Responding Well to Those Who Have Been Sexually Abused: Policy and Guidance for the Church of England*, London: Church House Publishing, 2011.

Try and find some points of connection with the offender

A full empathic understanding of the offender may be a tall order. People usually find it easier to forgive if they can see the offender as pitiful or in need of care (and conversely themselves as stronger). This isn't ideal, but it is a first step out of the victim position. If the offender is a stranger, finding out more of his story may be helpful. We have seen that an apology or some other attempt at restitution on the part of the offender makes us more inclined to forgive, but these may not be forthcoming. While the New Testament does not strictly require us to forgive unconditionally, it may be in our interests to do so in order to get on with our lives and indeed to conform more to the character of Christ.

Do not be too ambitious

Forgiveness is essentially a decision to adopt a particular attitude. Forgiving 'from the heart' (Matt. 18.35) refers to sincerity of motive, not intensity of emotion. We should aim to lay down our grudge, but we are not required to feel warmth towards the offender, and certainly not to return to an abusive relationship. The first and hardest step is the decision. This is significant and should be communicated to somebody else, perhaps in writing, and returned to from time to time. The rest of the process cannot be forced; I have heard it described as like stepping on to a train that may not leave the station for some time. We should pray and then leave the Spirit to do his work. If and when we are ready to communicate with the offender, let this be gracious in tone. It may be wise to do this in the presence of a trusted third party.

Cultivating repentance

A balanced self-awareness that rejoices in our strengths, but also acknowledges that each strength has a downside which will require attention, is important. We also need to be aware of repeated negative patterns or scripts within our lives, perhaps arising from childhood experiences, but also maintained simply out of habit. Some of us will be over-conscientious and obsessive about our shortcomings, in which case we may need to lighten up and turn our attention outwards. Keeping a journal, consulting a spiritual director, and in some instances counselling, are valuable in building the necessary self-awareness.

Some people find that making a formal confession once or twice a year – what is sometimes called the 'sacrament of reconciliation' – is a vital spiritual discipline for them. It may be particularly helpful for those of us who are constitutionally resistant to repentance (prone to shame or with a tendency to think we are special). This sort of confession should be seen not so much as a spring clean or dental scale and polish which sets us back where we were, but a reorientation on the right course that supports our continuing growth. Any actions required of us by our confessor should also be seen in this light.

Growing up (again)

'Who can forgive sins but God alone?' ask the scribes when Jesus pronounces for-giveness to the paralytic (Mark 2.7b). They are right to ask the question. There is not much about interpersonal forgiveness in the Hebrew Bible (Schimmel 2004), precisely because it is God who forgives. Jesus' response is to pronounce that 'the Son of Man has authority on earth to forgive sins' (Matt. 9.6 and par-allels). He is clearly referring to himself, but his words can also be understood as indicating that human beings have the capacity to grant interpersonal forgive-ness to each other in this earthly life. This is made more explicit in the giving of the Spirit in John's Gospel (20.23). While this text has often been understood to refer to the Eleven minus Thomas, it is actually 'the disciples' (v. 19), contrasted with a reference to 'the twelve' in v. 24, who are gathered together in the house, and it can thus be read as referring to the whole Christian community.

With the coming of Christ and the gift of the Spirit, human beings have come of age. Not only do we no longer need to hide from God in shame behind psy-chological fig leaves; not only do we no longer need to try to make restitution in order to be forgiven; not only are we now entitled to ask directly for divine forgiveness; we are entitled to forgive others. The call to forgive, which we so often see as burdensome, is in fact a divinely granted privilege. After all, 'To err is human, to forgive is divine.'[9]

Exercises

1 Consider a situation in your life where an offence has been committed but forgiveness has not been possible, perhaps because the perpetrator is dead, perhaps because the time is not right, perhaps because forgiveness feels too painful and difficult. Light a candle in a place of worship or some other special place, as a way of offering the situation up to God.

2 Explore in your imagination the days after the return of the Prodigal Son. Look at the situation from the point of view of the father and each of the two brothers. You may wish to do a piece of writing on this theme.

Further reading

Alison, J., 1997, *Living in the End Times: The Last Things Re-imagined*, London: SPCK.

Collicutt, J., 2012, *When You Pray: Daily Reflections for Lent and Easter on the Lord's Prayer*, Oxford: BRF, pp. 149–78.

McCullough, M., Pargament, K. and Thoresen, C., 2001, *Forgiveness: Theory, Research, and Practice*, New York: Guilford Press.

Monbourquette, J., 2000, *How to Forgive: A Step-by-step Guide*, London: Darton, Longman & Todd.

---

9 Alexander Pope (1711). *An Essay on Criticism*.

Pembroke, N., 2010, *Pastoral Care in Worship: Liturgy and Psychology in Dialogue*, London: T. & T. Clark, pp. 25–43.

Tutu, D. and Tutu, M., 2014, *The Book of Forgiving*, London: William Collins.

Watts, F. and Gulliford, L. (eds), 2004, *Forgiveness in Context: Theology and Psychology in Creative Dialogue*, London: T. & T. Clark.

14

Wisdom:
Inhabiting Uncertainty with Confidence

So when the woman saw that the tree was good for food, and that it was a delight to the eyes, and that the tree was to be desired to make one wise, she took of its fruit and ate.

Genesis 3.6a

And this is my prayer, that your love may overflow more and more with knowledge and full insight to help you to determine what is best, so that on the day of Christ you may be pure and blameless, having produced the harvest of righteousness that comes through Jesus Christ for the glory and praise of God.

Philippians 1.9–11

Always be ready to make your defence to anyone who demands from you an account of the hope that is in you.

1 Peter 3.15b

For my thoughts are not your thoughts, nor are your ways my ways, says the LORD.

Isaiah 55.8

For Jews demand signs and Greeks desire wisdom, but we proclaim Christ crucified, a stumbling block to Jews and foolishness to Gentiles, but to those who are the called, both Jews and Greeks, Christ the power of God and the wisdom of God.

1 Corinthians 1.22–24

Recently the teenage daughter of a friend told me that she had spent a whole day trying to think of ways of describing herself on her university application form. After much deliberation, she had come up with the adjective 'inquisitive'. In my opinion that was a really good choice, and I told her that I would definitely look positively on an applicant who described herself in those terms. Being inquisitive and curious – wanting to *know* – is a very basic human characteristic. It accounts for the compelling nature of whodunits. The fact that whodunits are not just compelling but also fun indicates curiosity's playful aspect; it is particularly characteristic of toddlers, who are often described as 'into everything' by exasperated parents. Curiosity is one of the character strengths in Peterson's and Seligman's VIA, most definitely seen as a positive human quality in their system. Yet, we are told, curiosity killed the cat. Curiosity drove Pandora to open her box and Eve to eat the fruit of the tree of knowledge of good and evil.

Eve's curiosity is laudable, but it ends in tears. As discussed in Chapters 7 and 8, the knowledge given by the fruit is a consciousness of self and of the nature of the world that brings with it fear and shame. This seems to indicate that the relationship between Adam, Eve and God is not yet one within which their new-found knowledge can do the human pair any good. They are rather like toddlers who play with electricity in the hope of wielding power, but end up burning their fingers. They need to explore such things when they are ready and within a relationship of love and care. But the relationship has now become damaged.[1] The irony is that in a way Adam and Eve get what they want; they are catapulted into the adult world of sex, reproduction, work and commerce, but the opportunity to play in the garden with their Creator is lost. They have, as it were, grown up prematurely.

Human beings continue to be inquisitive, and in the Hebrew Bible this has shown itself at its best as a yearning for wise understanding and a deep instinct that this is to be found through turning to God (Job 28.28; Ps. 111.10; Prov. 1.7; 9.10; 15.33; Isa. 11.2; Micah 6.9), perhaps reflecting a collective memory of Eden. Yet wisdom remains elusive, sometimes depicted as a hidden treasure that can only be accessed by esoteric practices or secret knowledge (Job 28), or as openly available but easily missed or too readily rejected (Prov. 8.2; 5.1–14), an issue we explored at length in Chapter 9.

With the coming of Christ comes an opportunity for human beings finally to grow up properly and attain true insight, and a promise that we can finally eat freely from the tree of life (Rev. 2.7). Jesus says, 'I do not call you servants any longer, because the servant does not know what the master is doing; but I have called you friends, because I have made known to you everything that I have heard from my Father' (John 15.15). This knowledge is now disclosed because there is a reconciled intimate and trusting relationship within which it can sit. Nevertheless, as with ancient Hebrew wisdom, this disclosure is not blatant and blanket. As we saw in Chapter 9, there is a subtle interplay between the natural human capacity for inquisitive wonder and the illumination shed by Christ.

In Part 3 of this book we have been looking at the cultivation of the fruit of the Spirit, the 'harvest of righteousness' of our second opening extract from Philippians 1. In this important passage Paul presents these fruit as growing out of a combination of love and 'knowledge with full insight to determine what is best'. This is a very good summary of the nature of wisdom, and the context makes it clear that Paul regards wisdom as at the heart of Christian formation, second only to love. This view, that to be formed is to be informed, is one I strongly endorse, and the present book has been written with it in mind throughout.

---

1 If one reads Genesis 3 with an open mind and as an isolated text, God ('ĕlōhîm) does not seem to come out of it well; his actions are not easy to comprehend. It is most helpfully read as an account of the psychology of human kind, as we have done in this book. If it is to be read theologically, it must be seen in the whole sweep of Scripture and the Judaeo-Christian tradition's understanding of God. The analytic psychologist Carl G. Jung (1875–1961) makes a bold, if disturbing, attempt at both approaches. He addresses the question of why the Hebrew Bible depicts God as at times showing what he describes as 'peculiar and double-faced behaviour', in his 1953 book, Answer to Job.

The starting point in Part 1 was Christ, as it always should be in any Christian endeavour; Part 2 was largely devoted to the issue of self-understanding, an important part of wisdom; Part 3 has addressed several themes that are central to wisdom, in particular having the humble mind of Christ in Chapter 8, developing insight in Chapter 9, and achieving an appropriate balance[2] in Chapter 10. Chapters 11, 12 and 13 dealt with some of the ethical demands that arise within the Christian life, all of which involve inhabiting alternative perspectives and, in the case of forgiveness, dealing with intricate ethical dilemmas. Finally, as the book draws towards its close, we address wisdom directly, starting to pull together many of the threads from earlier chapters.

It seems that of all the virtues, wisdom is the one that has the greatest claim to be universal across cultures (Dahlsgaard, Peterson and Seligman 2005). The understanding of wisdom and the emphasis on its different aspects does, however, appear to depend somewhat on the epistemology of a culture, and these have developed differently across the world and across history. The most sophisticated account of wisdom is arguably to be found in the Hebrew Bible, which presents wisdom (*ḥokmâ*) as an integrated form of different types of knowledge – practical and reflective – of the world, the self, and God (Fiddes 2013). Accordingly, this chapter is divided into sections that deal with a range of different ways and objects of knowing, before finally considering the limitations of human knowledge.

Knowing what

The psychologists Paul Baltes (1939–2006) and Ursula Staudinger, working within the framework of the Berlin Wisdom Paradigm, state the first aspect of wisdom to be 'rich factual knowledge' (Baltes and Staudinger 2000). This seems unarguable; trying to be wise without good knowledge of the facts is like trying to build bricks without straw. Having said that, it must be acknowledged that the concept of factual accuracy and its close relation 'truth' are problematic, especially in postmodern culture (recall Chapter 9). More congenial to the postmodern mind are the corresponding ideas of 'trustworthiness' and 'authenticity'. We want our bricks of wisdom to be built with the good straw of trustworthy and authentic information. We obtain this information in two ways: directly from our experience of events and indirectly from the accounts of others.

On the whole we are inclined to trust our own experience, though often we need to validate it by consulting with others, using questions of the form, 'Is it just me, or . . .?' However, we are naturally cautious about believing the accounts of others without some sort of additional guarantee of their trustworthiness and authenticity. (There is a parallel here with the difference between perceiving and believing drawn out in Chapter 9.) In this section we will briefly consider wisdom gleaned from direct life experience, and then four guarantees of trustworthiness and authenticity invoked within the Christian tradition:

---

2 Balance is the key component in at least one psychological model of wisdom (Sternberg 1998).

eyewitness testimony; institutional authority; science and rationality; and the mark of the Spirit.

Direct knowledge

Direct knowing involves a felt sense of certainty that is lacking from indirect knowing, and thus carries its own particular authority. This is a characteristic of 'implicational processing', something we touched on in Chapter 8 when considering the difference between head and heart knowledge in relation to self-esteem, and which is thought to be an important aspect of religious experience (Watts 2002, pp. 85–8). We are relying on this system when we say 'I can't say why, but I just don't trust him.'

> The 'implicational' system is distinguished by a lack of reliance on verbal aspects of communication, with a strong emphasis on affect and 'non-verbals' such as prosody, gesture, and facial expression. It generates high-level intuitive knowledge, often about significant evaluative aspects of social relationships, that is difficult to express in words, difficult to justify rationally, but highly compelling in quality. (Collicutt 2012c, p. 34)

Much wisdom is constructed from key individual or corporate life experiences, including epiphanies such as those discussed in Chapter 6 and the charismatic experiences discussed in Chapter 12. This accounts for the widespread cultural belief that the old are wiser than the young – they have had the chance to accrue more experiences. Indeed, some would argue that the young cannot be wise by definition. In Luke's wonderful account of the adolescent Jesus' visit to the temple, he is described as full of *sunesis* (intelligence and understanding) (2.47), but his growth into *sophia* (wisdom) takes place after his return home and is described as a gradual process that develops as he approaches adulthood (2.52). In line with this view, psychologists who study adolescents tend to talk of 'wisdom-related performance' rather than wisdom as such (Pasupathi, Staudinger and Baltes 2001; Staudinger and Pasupathi 2003). As we saw in Chapter 6, it is clear that there is a blossoming of this ability in adolescence. In contrast, the idea that simply getting older makes one wiser has not been supported empirically (Staudinger 1999), largely because the undoubted benefits of life experience appear to be counterbalanced by a decline in basic cognitive abilities from mid-life onwards. There is also the issue of what we *do* with our life experience, which we will consider towards the end of this chapter.

Indirect knowledge: the biblical witness

The New Testament is essentially to be read as a witness to the Christ event and its immediate aftermath. This is why the apostolic identity of the authors of its various books was such an important criterion for inclusion in the canon. It is also why Paul makes so much of his eyewitness encounter with the risen Christ (Gal. 1.11–16); it guarantees the authenticity of his teaching.

In proceeding to make mention of these things, I shall adopt, to com-mend my undertaking, the pattern of Luke the Evangelist, saying on my own account: 'Forasmuch as some have taken in hand,' to reduce into order for themselves the books termed apocryphal, and to mix them up with the divinely inspired Scripture, concerning which we have been fully persuaded, as they who from the beginning were eyewitnesses and ministers of the Word, delivered to the fathers; it seemed good to me also, having been urged thereto by true brethren, and having learned from the beginning, to set before you the books included in the Canon, and handed down, and accredited as Divine; to the end that any one who has fallen into error may condemn those who have led him astray; and that he who has continued steadfast in purity may again rejoice, having these things brought to his remembrance.

Festal Letter of Athanasius XXXIX 3. (367)

Bearing witness is an important theme in the New Testament (Acts 4.20). While Luke emphasizes that he has based his account of Jesus on eyewitness testimony (Luke 1.2), John insists that he and his community *are themselves* eyewitnesses and that what he writes is to be received as eyewitness testimony (John 1.14). The meaning of 'eyewitness' in the ancient world was somewhat different from our own rather passive and visual notion (Bauckham 2008). It seems to have involved 'being there' and having been part of things from the beginning, so that one can give an overall account of events placed in a meaningful narrative framework (Acts 1.20–21). As in our world, eyewitness testimony, especially from a number of collaborating sources (Mark 14.56, 59), carried authority and ensured that the information imparted was trustworthy.

The take-home message is that the Church understands the New Testament to be the trustworthy and authentic source of knowledge on which the Christian is to base her wisdom. As argued in the discussion of *Lectio Divina* in Chapter 9, it needs to be read in an informed way and in the context of the Hebrew Bible, but it is where we must start.

Indirect knowledge: institutional authority

The institutional authority of the churches, especially the Roman Catholic Church, as holders of a tradition passed on in an unbroken line from the first eyewitnesses, has historically been a mark of trustworthy and authentic informa-tion. The official decrees issued by councils, synods or popes are an example of a potential source of knowledge from which Christian wisdom might be built.

However, social hierarchies, such as the institutional churches, always have a vested interest in maintaining their structures and practices, and there is always a danger that they will construct 'legitimizing myths' (Sidanius and Pratto 1999).

These are teachings or narratives that support the status quo and the concentration of power with an élite, and whose trustworthiness as sources of wisdom are therefore potentially compromised. This concern is by no means unique to Roman Catholicism; Jesus was critical of something similar in the Judaism of his day (Matt. 15.6–9 and Mark 7.6–8), and within Christian Protestant culture there has always been a tendency to filter or squeeze biblical material, so that it supports certain highly valued tropes that seem to take on a life of their own.

Consistent with this, the work of philosophers such as John Austin (1911–60) and Ludwig Wittgenstein (1889–1951) has drawn our attention to the fact that language does not simply represent the way things are, but instead has a 'performative' function – it *does* something (Wittgenstein 1958; Austin 1962). One of the things it can do is to establish or consolidate power dynamics in a set of relationships by the way the speaker positions himself or frames a narrative. As we know only too well from the worlds of politics and the media, stories can be spun.[3]

This tells us that, starting with the construction of the biblical texts themselves, the narratives of the churches, plagued as they are by power struggles, should be approached using a 'hermeneutic of suspicion' (Ricoeur 1970). That is, they should be treated with respect and a willingness to learn, but also an awareness of the power games that may be unconsciously played out through them.[4] In a way this was the instinct of Protestant reformers such as the Bible translator William Tyndale (1494–1536), who is famously said to have asserted, 'If God spare my life, before very long I shall cause a plough boy to know the scriptures better than you do!' The Reformers wanted to by-pass what they saw as narratives driven by the self-interest of a church they no longer trusted, and give ordinary people trustworthy and authentic information so that they could discern *for themselves* how best to live.[5]

Indirect knowledge: scientific reports

This philosophy, so much part of the reformers' agenda, developed into the Enlightenment project, which rejected religious and political institutional interest in favour of rationalist and empiricist approaches to knowledge. It is out of this project that modern science has grown. The values of science are very similar to those of the Protestant Reformation (Harrison 2001); there is a desire for transparency and accessibility in the communication of information. Thus empirical scientific reports describe the methods and procedures used

---

3 The difference between the infancy narratives of Matthew and Luke are instructive here. In Matthew's version Mary is essentially an object (grammatically speaking); in Luke's version she is essentially an agent. The ratio of female to male agents is higher in Luke's infancy narrative (the difference is statistically significant). The power dynamics that emerge in the two accounts are quite different; they depend on the way the story is told.

4 There is also a large literature on this issue in relation to the writing of history in general (see e.g. Stone 1979).

5 Clearly a similar but distinctive motive lies behind liberation theology and postcolonial approaches to the Bible and church pronouncements (see e.g. Schüssler Fiorenza 2009).

in meticulous detail so that they can be replicated or disconfirmed by others; they report raw data, not simply the conclusions that have been reached; they report the process of reasoning to their conclusions and give consideration to alternative interpretations of their data and flaws in their procedure; the methods used are agreed to be trustworthy by the scientific community; and before the report is published, it is subjected to the scrutiny of independent blind peer reviewers. This is true for both quantitative and qualitative scientific research (Elliott, Fischer and Rennie 1999).

All of these things guard the trustworthiness and authenticity of the information conveyed in scientific reports, but they do not completely guarantee that it will be free from the influences of powerful groups. Nevertheless, published scientific reports are a good bet when gathering information on which to base wise decisions. (This is essentially the philosophy behind western medicine.) In this book I have cited scientific reports and also biblical texts quite extensively. This is precisely because I want the reader to see that my statements are for the most part supported by empirical research or the reflections of the first eyewitnesses to Christ and are thus to that extent trustworthy. The aim is also to offer the reader the opportunity to follow up the citations and draw her own conclusions on the matters discussed.

Indirect knowledge: the mark of the Spirit

In John's Gospel Jesus describes himself as 'the truth' (*alētheia*) and the Holy Spirit as 'the Spirit of truth' (John 14.6, 17; 15.26; 16.13), who will guide the faithful into the truth. In 1 Corinthians 12—14 Paul describes the ability to offer a word of knowledge (*gnōsis*) as one of the gifts of the Spirit which, as already discussed, are to be understood as special resources for 'a particular occasion to build up the body of the Church in a particular situation' (p. 192). As with prophetic visions, individuals sometimes have a certainty that words of knowledge – true insights on a situation – have been given them by God to share with others in the Church.

As with the Bible, tradition, and the claims of science, words of knowledge and reports of prophetic visions need to be approached critically with a hermeneutic of suspicion. There is always a danger that they will be used to advance the power of the speaker.[6] Indeed, Jesus himself warned his followers of this (Matt. 7.15).

Testing the trustworthiness and authenticity of words that claim to be directly from the Holy Spirit is the job of the church community within which they emerge (1 John 4.1). However, the process of testing is different from that in science; it is more intuitive, resting on implicational knowing, not easily articulated in rules and propositions. As always, the key principle is that

---

6 A noteworthy example is that of Mabel Barltop (1866–1934), the founder of the Panacea Society. Mabel (who became known as Octavia) was adept at automatic writing, which she and her followers understood to be a spiritual gift bringing direct revelations from God. However, the content of the writing was often uncannily convenient, for example being directed against rivals to her spiritual power base. For more details, see Shaw 2011.

such words are to be judged by their fruit; authentic spiritual gifts should bear good spiritual fruit. The great inspirational writings from two thousand years of Christian tradition – some of which have been quoted in text boxes in this book – often appeared on the edge of the received orthodoxy of their time but have been found with hindsight to yield a 'harvest of righteousness'.

One way of working out what such a harvest might look like in practice is to take what we know about the character of Christ as an evaluative framework. For example, using the characteristics of Christ that I set out in Chapter 3, and around which this book is organized, we might ask how a word of knowledge fits with the themes of divine intimacy for all; humility; awe, wonder and respect for the created world; balance; hospitality; compassion; non-retaliation and the liberation of the weak. Above all, as Paul makes clear, we should ask about love (1 Cor. 13.2).

This critical approach is a key aspect of spiritual discernment, and is necessary if we are to identify the trustworthy and authentic knowledge on which we can base life decisions. It is behind the call of the Reformers that the Church *semper reformanda est* – 'is always to be reformed' – through a critical balance between respect for its heritage and openness to the Spirit. It is there in Paul's exhortation to 'be transformed through the renewing of your minds, so that you may discern what is the will of God' (Rom. 12.2); for him the church *semper transformanda est*. It is there in Mary's questioning of Gabriel (Luke 1.34) and Jesus' questioning of his Father (Matt. 26.39 and parallels). It is noticeably absent from the behaviour of Adam and Eve.

Knowing where

Wisdom is about knowing where to look. This is something we considered in detail in Chapter 9, and need not be repeated here. It is, however, interesting to note that evolutionary biologists have advanced a theory for the wisdom attributed to the very old and the deference accorded them, suggesting that this is on account of their memory for where to look for hidden sources of food or safety in times of scarcity and danger (e.g. Henrich and Gil-White 2001).

It is also important to acknowledge the expansive nature of the search for wisdom (Fiddes 2013). It could be almost anywhere. So when Jesus talks of a field within which treasure is hidden (Matt. 13.44), he is perhaps referring to an area that is cosmic in scale. As if to confirm this, the first act of wisdom mentioned in the New Testament is that of the Magi, wise folk from the East who studied the heavens in their search for understanding, ancient astrophysicists or cosmologists (Matt. 2.1–12).

The Magi were fundamentally inquisitive. They also took an empirical approach. Not content to engage in theoretical speculation, they wanted to test their theory out, to go and see for themselves. They were apparently prepared to undergo hardship and massive expense in the process. Most important of all, they are depicted as open minded; willing to be responsive to events, to look somewhere unexpected, in a place not predicted by their theory.

Looking can be about searching for the location of wisdom, but it can also be about observing wisdom. The main way that we acquire wisdom is not through instruction (despite the best efforts of parents and the author of Proverbs), not through trial and error, but through close observation and copying (Rosenthal and Bandura 1978; Rizzolatti, Fadiga, Fogassi and Gallese 1996). I was amused recently when my husband, who had insisted for some time that we could not stream programmes from the internet on to our television set because it is not 'smart', proudly connected it to his laptop using an HDMI cable so that we could do so. When I asked him what had prompted him to do this very helpful thing, he said that, during a visit to our daughter's home some weeks previously, he had noticed our son-in-law doing this. He, an older man, had stumbled upon wisdom in a younger man, and he had quietly watched and learnt.

This example brings us to perhaps the most important aspect of wisdom: it concerns practical skill.

Knowing how

Baltes and Staudinger (2000) hold that, in addition to rich factual knowledge, there is a second main aspect of wisdom: 'rich procedural knowledge' or know-how. This fits well with the Hebrew Bible's understanding of wisdom as a skilled craft (Exod. 36.2, 8; 1 Chron. 22.15–16). There can be woodcraft, but there can also be political craft (Exod. 1.10). In fact there is a very wide range of physical and social crafts. For example, Aristotle's concept of *phronēsis* refers to craftsmanship of the highest order in the exercise of virtue and the making of moral judgements, and is a key aspect of his account of wisdom.[7]

From a more psychological perspective, the Berlin Wisdom Paradigm group define wisdom overall as 'expertise in the fundamental pragmatics of life' (Baltes and Smith 1990, p. 87). In a large series of studies they have explored the exercise of wisdom in several life domains, including life planning, making meaning out of life events and addressing existential life issues.

In order to assess wisdom-related performance the Berlin group devised a series of dilemmas, and used a highly structured and systematic procedure for rating the free verbal responses of individuals who had been presented with a selection of these dilemmas. As a result, the group came up with three themes that seem to be important in the bringing together of factual and procedural knowledge to make wise decisions:

- Contextualism across the lifespan and current situation: in order to make a wise decision you need to take the context into account.
- Relativism of values and priorities: in order to make a wise decision you need to be flexible and open with your value system, and to be able to entertain alternative perspectives.

---

7 In the Nichomachean Ethics, *phronēsis* acts as a counterpoint to *episteme* – reasoning and scientific understanding.

- Recognition and management of uncertainty: in order to make (and live with) a wise decision you need to acknowledge that it may involve risks and compromises, and that circumstances may change.

Having achieved a rich operational description of wisdom, the group has carried out a number of studies to investigate whether there are particular human characteristics that contribute to it. As might be expected, general intelligence, specifically the ability to reason at Piaget's formal operational level, plays a part. The Big Five (see Chapter 4) personality trait of openness (O) also seems to be relevant (Staudinger and Pasupathi 2003; Pasupathi and Staudinger 2003).

This is perhaps not surprising, in view of the fact that the group's definition of wisdom includes being open to other perspectives. Nevertheless, it should not be too readily dismissed. Researchers in psychology of religion have generally held the view that the Big Five do not change as a result of religious conversion; instead it is the life goals and orientation of the person that seem to change – see Paloutzian, Richardson and Rambo 1999, citing the example of Saul of Tarsus. To expand on this example, we might hazard a guess that Saul was high on C, low on E, low on A and high on N both before and after he became Paul; he simply became zealous for Christ rather than Judaism (Gal. 1.13–14). However, his hypothetical score on O doesn't fit this story so easily; he shows signs of having become radically open as his new faith developed (e.g. 1 Cor. 9.22). The research literature suggests that openness may be more malleable than the other personality traits; in my experience it seems to increase when people encounter Christ. The fact that it has been found to have a connection to wisdom is therefore intriguing. One biblical scholar puts it this way:

> Wisdom does not set absolute standards or norms. Wisdom does not fix life in place . . . Woman Wisdom opens up the world rather than closes it down; she is always ready to take new experiences into account, recognizing that God may be about new things for new times and places. (Fretheim 2012, p. 45)

Knowing who

The figure of 'Woman Wisdom' referred to above is to be found in the book of Proverbs in the Hebrew Bible and in the books of Ecclesiasticus and the Wisdom of Solomon in the Greek Old Testament. This brings to our attention another way of knowing. The wise person doesn't just know facts and where to find them, or skills and how to develop them; he knows who it is who holds or embodies wisdom. This is partly because, as we have seen, we learn wisdom best by being around the wise.

In all cultures individuals are seen as holders of wisdom. They are often female (see e.g. 1 Sam. 14). These people are usually understood to combine aspects of both intellect and character, and to show both general wisdom about life and personal wisdom about themselves (Mickler and Staudinger 2008). They are expected to express their wisdom in giving wise advice and counsel to others.

It seems that human beings have always had a tendency to see wisdom as located in a person. This goes beyond the understanding of all cognition as something embodied, an idea that is largely taken for granted in modern cognitive neuroscience (see e.g. Varela, Thompson and Rosch 1993). Rather, it is an intuitive understanding that wisdom by its nature is inseparable from the wise individual who exhibits it.

This has important implications. Wisdom is not *reducible* to the wise individual, so we are not to worship him (with one obvious exception). On the other hand, because of the interconnectedness of wisdom with the wise individual, it is fruitless to try and extract it from him and treat it as a commodity (Fiddes 2013, p. 351). This means that we can only truly learn wisdom through apprenticeship. The transmission of wisdom is relational. It is human to human because wisdom is essentially concerned with human dilemmas. Books, manuals, lectures and sermons will not do as substitutes. If we are to teach others wisdom, we need to concentrate on becoming wise ourselves and encourage others to watch and learn.

In a fascinating study that sheds light on this point, Staudinger and Baltes compared the performance of participants on a wisdom task under four conditions: they undertook the task alone and were required to give an immediate response; they discussed the task with a person of their choice before responding; they were instructed to engage in a mental dialogue about the task with a person of their choice as if that person were really present before responding; they were given some free time to think before responding. The results indicate that the two social conditions produced a significantly better performance on the task and, most intriguing of all, that the mental dialogue was as effective as the real dialogue (Staudinger and Baltes 2006).

We see from this that, while cultivating wisdom is a relational pursuit, our teacher does not have to be physically present; we can engage with him using our imagination. Perhaps, then, one of the ways the Spirit helps us in our weakness is by enabling us to engage imaginatively with the question 'What would Jesus do?' At a less exalted level, engaging with the stories of the great Christians of history, or those we have known but see no longer, is a significant part of the acquisition of this practical wisdom.

Despite the fact that people with high intellect and those who score high on O might have a bit of a head start in developing wisdom, the heartening evidence is that the most important thing is not intelligence or personality, but *training* in complex life pragmatics (Staudinger, Maciel, Smith and Baltes 1998), and that this training should be practical and apprentice-based (Smith, Staudinger and Baltes 1994). This approach can be summed up in Jesus' words, 'Follow me.' This call to formation through apprenticeship is still the fundamental call of the Christian. Now, however, without his physical presence, we follow Jesus through community memory and imagination guided by the Spirit, stepping into transitional space, invoking subjunctive thought (p. 178), and repeatedly returning to the question 'What *would* Jesus do?'

Knowing when

In Chapter 10 we considered the role of balance in the Christian life in some detail. We saw that the wise person strikes a balance between different modes of being: telic and paratelic; dwelling and seeking; work, rest and play; disciplined effort, mindful contemplation and engaged attentiveness. The wisdom also comes in knowing *when* to employ each mode of being – to read the signs of the times and be alert to the season (Eccl. 3.1).

An awareness of seasonality is a feature of older people, simply because they have seen many seasons and may use this experience to put things into perspective. They know that pain and passion must pass. As a result of their experience they have access to knowledge of when to plant and when to harvest, when to seize the moment and when to be patient. (Impatience is said to be the cardinal failing of the young, who do not have this perspective.) It is the mark of experienced practitioners that they can tolerate the anxiety associated with waiting or intentionally deciding to take a hands-off approach. It is the mark of a skilled practitioner to have an expert sense of timing and pace. There are lessons to be learnt not just from experienced individuals, but from the collective experience that is embodied in the history and culture of the social group.

Timing also relates to the setting of priorities and the balance between them. At one time a certain issue may have the highest priority; at another time it must cede to other issues. Working through the balance of priorities is one of the tasks of prayer, and priorities can also be thrown into the air at times of crisis. To look at things through the lens of crisis is to look eschatologically. This is the viewpoint from which much of the New Testament is written. Its priorities are for the 'now time' (*nun kairōi*) (Rom. 3.26). This helps us to understand Jesus' hard saying that 'you always have the poor with you, but you do not always have me' (Matt. 26.11; Mark 14.7; John 12.8). At the moment he says this – the threshold of his Passion – the ongoing needs of the poor, which should normally dominate, recede into the background.

Our difficulty is that our sense of the times has expanded beyond that of the New Testament writers, and it is not always easy to connect with their focused sense of urgency. We are aware that we live between the times, knowing that God's kingdom has been established with the raising of Christ, but still awaiting its ultimate fulfilment at his coming again. Christian wisdom for our time is of a particular kind that sees the things of this life as redeemed and in the process of transformation, but ourselves as agents in this process; that understands present realities as provisional, but can only guess at the time frame of this provisionality; that sees suffering and evil all around, but knows that good has triumphed and that ultimately 'God will wipe away every tear' (Rev. 7.17) – that things are now OK and not yet OK. Not only does the wise Christian have to work out how to turn the 'rules I aim to live by' (or Christlike virtues) into 'what I try to do' (or habits of life) taking her personality and situation into account, she also needs to read the signs of the times; to achieve not so much the lifespan contextualism of the Berlin Wisdom Paradigm, but the contextualism of an inaugurated eschatology.

This can be helped by an awareness of the historical context within which the great Christian spiritual classics emerged. Understanding that the message of Julian of Norwich that 'all shall be well' was received and shared over a millennium after the resurrection of Christ, in a society decimated by the black death, suffering the economic effects of a series of disastrous harvests and undergoing major political upheaval resulting in crippling taxation, helps us to envision wisdom for our times.

Knowing why

One of the domains identified by the Berlin Wisdom Paradigm in which wisdom can be displayed is that of making meaning out of life events. This is closely related to Dan McAdams' construal of personality as a story that gets told, considered in Chapter 5. We need to be able to build wise stories about ourselves and our communities that make sense of the things that happen, both good and bad, by placing them in a meaningful whole. These stories are constructed to help us know *why*, not just historically but teleologically. It is, for example, not enough for us to know that Jesus died because he got caught between two powerful interest groups in first-century Jerusalem, or even because it was God's will; we want to know what *purpose* it served.

An apparently insatiable desire to know why is characteristic of a certain phase of child development, and the explanation favoured by the child will be teleological rather than historical in form (Barrett and Burdett 2011; Kelemen 2004). We are, it seems, teleological creatures from our earliest years.

The stories we construct integrate our knowledge and experience, smoothing out the bumps, anomalies and niggles into a coherent and convincing-enough account. The process of constructing and consolidating such stories is one of cognitive assimilation (recall p. 86), and it is often deeply satisfying, especially if the events present something of a challenge. Perhaps the best example of this sort of process in the Bible is the letter to the Hebrews. This is a beautifully sophisticated and polished piece of work, written in arguably the best Greek to be found in the New Testament. It tells a story grounded in the history of God's people, using an understanding of the Levitical priesthood as the framework for making sense of the death of Jesus, smoothing out the bump of Jesus' parentage by resourcefully applying the idea of the 'priest after the order of Melchizedek' (Heb. 5.6). Hebrews is also, as we saw in Chapter 2, a highly teleological book. Its author uses the sense of God's purpose in Christ, together with the example of God's people through history, to instil a sense of purpose in his or her[8] intended audience. The story has the power to rouse them from the apathy or

---

8 The authorship of Hebrews is unknown, but it has traditionally been attributed to Apollos, other contenders being Prisca or Aquila.

apostasy into which they may have been sinking, to energize them and get them back on track. The story is true, but it could of course have been told in another way; its form was wisely crafted for a particular situation and purpose.

The passage from 1 Peter 3 at the beginning of this chapter exhorts its readers to be active in constructing their own story and ensuring that it is persuasive (the rhetorical mark of trustworthiness and authenticity). The Greek words used here, *apologia* and *logos*, are respectively rational and narrative in character. So this as an exhortation to be ready to give a reasoned argument to support the story you tell. This story is not a diverting tale told to pass the long winter evenings; it is the ground of your hope, the thing that makes you get up in the morning and keeps you going day by day, even if you are a Roman slave with a cruel and capricious master (1 Pet. 2.18–20). It is your 'why'.

The dimension of time is very evident here: there is an element of *always* being prepared to speak, assured of the assistance of the Spirit (Luke 12.12), because we do not know the day or the hour. My most surreal experience of this was when a Muslim junior doctor came to stitch me up in the delivery room after the birth of my first child. As he donned his surgical gloves, he told me that he had often wondered what the attraction of Christianity was, and he asked if I could explain the difference that it made in my life. So I did. This is an example of a life experience that taught me wisdom and allowed me for a while to participate in divine humour.

We might, then, think of Christian wisdom as showing itself in the construction of a persuasive, and thus authentic and trustworthy, account of our reason for living, so that others are drawn into the story (John 20.30–31). This is a story that will weave many themes and experiences together, and one that is continually developing, because the story of Jesus is not over yet, and the Spirit continues to work in us.

Living well with uncertainty: trauma, adversity and humour

It is pleasing to compose, tell or hear a good story. But at the end of the day, stories are human constructions; God is not a story (Murphy 2007). This is why, just as we settle into a story, God seems to have a habit of breaking in and messing it up. It is the pattern of the parables, unpleasing stories marked by ambiguity, incongruity and paradox (Crossan 1991), raising more questions than they answer, glorying in rather than smoothing out niggles and forcing us to move from assimilation into accommodation mode. It is there in the ancient Wisdom tradition of the Hebrew Bible: 'Behind the teachings of the wise men there lies, therefore, a profound conviction of the ambivalence of phenomena and events' (von Rad 1972, p. 111).

In Chapters 6 and 9 we saw that traumatic events and crises often form the backdrop to epiphanies, and that the nature of trauma is a breaking in that forces us to accommodate to a different sort of reality, one in which our previous certainties have been snatched away. This leads naturally to the question of the place of trauma and adversity in the development of wisdom.

> There cannot be wisdom without an encounter with the holy, with that which creates awe, and shakes the ordinary way of life and thought.
>
> Paul Tillich (1863–1965)

What evidence there is indicates that the experience of adversity can lead to wisdom (Wink and Helson 1997), but that it is what we do with that experience, rather than the adverse event itself, that is important. In a careful and large-scale prospective longitudinal study, the American psychologists Paul Wink and Michelle Dillon examined a sample of older adults to see what personal qualities and events in their earlier lives predicted their degree of spirituality. Spirituality was carefully operationalized to include not just ideas and beliefs but also practices, and assessed using a structured interview and questionnaires. Although this was a study of spirituality, the authors draw a close connection between this and wisdom (2002, p. 93). The study produced a number of interesting findings, the most relevant of which for this discussion is the relationship between adverse life events and spirituality in later life. Adverse events in early and mid adult life did not predict high degrees of spirituality in later life unless they were combined with something the authors term 'cognitive commitment' in early life. This is a measure of the tendency to evaluate situations in depth and with insight, and to think creatively (something rather like wisdom). Cognitive commitment on its own did not predict a high degree of spirituality in later life: it had to be combined with the experience of adversity. The authors conclude from this that 'spiritual development is particularly characteristic of individuals who possess the necessary psychological sensitivity and strength to be able to transform personal pain and sorrow into a deeper understanding of life's mysteries' (Wink and Dillon 2002, p. 93).

Shortly after the publication of this study, the British psychologist Alex Linley published a theoretical paper in which he explored the relationship between trauma, adversity and wisdom (Linley 2003). He presented an understanding of wisdom as *both* the process by which people engage with trauma and adversity in order to grow through it *and* the good outcome of that struggle. Thus we achieve wisdom through wisdom, rather like Paul's 'through faith for faith' (Rom. 1.17). We might think of wisdom helping us to accommodate our world view to events (wisdom as process) so that we reach a new view of the world that does it better justice – a wiser world view (wisdom as outcome) that will help us get on with our lives.

If we are to accommodate to adversity, rather than being destroyed by it, we need to face it without being overwhelmed. It seems that one way wisdom works to help here is by holding opposites in tension through paradox, stopping us from flipping into either despair or defensive denial, and enabling us to be *both* realistic and hopeful. As we have already seen, paradox is a characteristic of Jesus' parabolic teaching that points out that small is big, sadness is blessed, marginal is central, our enemy is our friend, loss is gain, the poor are rich. We might describe these ideas as absurd. Here we find a connection with humour (Collicutt and Gray 2012).

Humour rests on incongruity together with a sense of mastery. Like trauma, humour forces us to shift our perspective. It helps us to see large and dreadful things as small and ridiculous. We use it to cope with our fears and to live with suffering; indeed, it helps us snatch some dignity from situations that might otherwise be totally humiliating, such as my giving of my testimony in the delivery room. Over the centuries proverbs and jokes have been understood to be both carriers of the received wisdom and a means of challenging it. Absurdity has a special role in enabling us to inhabit meaninglessness without going mad. Humour is thus closely related to both wisdom and coping with adversity and, when used well, can enhance both.

In his review Linley draws out three dimensions of post-traumatic wisdom. The first dimension is the integration of emotion and cognition (something in which humour can play a big part), so that we do not retreat into intellectualizing our problems or drown in a sea of emotional excess, but instead achieve a kind of 'connected detachment' of the sort we discussed in Chapter 10.

The second dimension is the recognition and management of uncertainty in life. The wise person does not pretend that life is certain, but has found a way of remaining stable enough in the midst of good and bad, of being receptive to change rather than clinging to stability, of making plans but acknowledging that these will always be provisional.

The final dimension of post-traumatic wisdom is recognition and acceptance of human limitation; the realization that some things cannot be controlled, some problems cannot be solved and some issues will never be understood. This insight relates to a particular feature of the apophatic tradition mentioned in Chapter 9, whose emphasis is not so much human limitation but the inexhaustible and transcendent nature of the divine.

Trauma offers us a compelling glimpse of our finitude, a new humility and the insight that 'it's bigger than me' that can lead to a self-transcendence that shows itself in concern for others, as we saw in Chapter 12. Here is another fascinating connection with humour, which in Peterson's and Seligman's VIA is classified as a character strength that expresses *transcendence*. Somehow, when we are brought low by shock, awe or the realization that we are ridiculous, we are set free to rise above ourselves and reach out beyond ourselves.

Christ the wisdom of God

Linley's analysis of the relationship between trauma, adversity and wisdom is secular in content and was published in a prestigious secular academic journal, yet it seems to have tapped into the deep cross-shaped structure of the Christian gospel (Collicutt 2006). The natural contours of post-traumatic wisdom tell us that the deep structure of our world is cross shaped. Just as the natural order of seed time and harvest offers an insight into the work of the Spirit in transforming suffering and death to life (John 12.24; 16.21), so too does the natural order of the human response to trauma.

Everything that we have said about wisdom in this chapter finds its fulfilment in Christ, who is the way and the truth and the life (John 14.6). It is through the historical event of the incarnation that we are given trustworthy and authentic information about the nature of God; it is the teaching of Christ that shows where wisdom is to be found; it is by following Christ that we learn how to live wisely; it is in the person of Christ that wisdom is embodied, and in encounter with him that truth – not just trustworthiness and authenticity – is experienced; it is the time frame between Christ's raising and his coming again that sets the tempo for our wisdom; it is Christ's life story that helps us make wise sense of our lives. Above all, it is in the trauma and absurdity of Christ's shameful death that the secret of divine wisdom is revealed.

Exercises

1 Think critically about the Berlin Wisdom Paradigm's approach to wisdom, identifying its strengths and limitations. Construct your own definition of wisdom.

2 Identify mentors who have guided you in the past. Reflect on what it was about them that led you to trust their wisdom. Next time you face a dilemma, intentionally imagine their presence, discuss it with them, and see if this helps.

Further reading

Cameron, H., Reader, J., Slater, V. and Rowland, C., 2013, *Theological Reflection for Human Flourishing: Pastoral Practice and Public Theology*, London: SCM Press, especially Chapter 5.

Dennis, T., 1997, *Imagining God*, London: SPCK, especially first reflection, pp. 4–7.

Martin, R., 2006, *The Psychology of Humor: An Integrative Approach*, Burlington, MA: Academic Press.

Schüssler Fiorenza, E., 1994, *Jesus: Miriam's Child, Sophia's Prophet*, London: SCM Press, Part 3: The Power of Wisdom, pp. 131–87.

Shults, F. L., 2006b, 'Becoming wise', in F. L. Shults and S. Sandage (eds), *Transforming Spirituality: Integrating Theology and Psychology*, Grand Rapids, MI: Baker Academic, pp. 67–93.

Sternberg, R. and Jordan, J., 2005, *A Handbook of Wisdom: Psychological Perspectives*, New York: Cambridge University Press.

Williams, R., 2003a, *Silence and Honey Cakes: The Wisdom of the Desert*, Oxford: Lion.

15

Transformation:
Embracing the Pattern of the Cross

He called the crowd with his disciples, and said to them, 'If any want to become my followers, let them deny themselves and take up their cross and follow me. For those who want to save their life will lose it, and those who lose their life for my sake, and for the sake of the gospel, will save it.

Mark 8.34–35

Jesus said to Simon Peter . . . 'Feed my sheep. Very truly, I tell you, when you were younger, you used to fasten your own belt and to go wherever you wished. But when you grow old, you will stretch out your hands, and someone else will fasten a belt around you and take you where you do not wish to go.' (He said this to indicate the kind of death by which he would glorify God.) After this he said to him, 'Follow me.'

John 21.15; 17b–19

I will give you the treasures of darkness and riches hidden in secret places, so that you may know that it is I, the LORD, the God of Israel, who call you by your name.

Isaiah 45.3

Very truly, I tell you, unless a grain of wheat falls into the earth and dies, it remains just a single grain; but if it dies, it bears much fruit.

John 12.24

In the previous chapter we saw that many things contribute to wisdom. In order to cultivate wisdom about ourselves and the world, we need to adopt a critical mindset; keep an open mind; look at an issue from several different perspectives, enabling this by cultivating joy and other broaden-and-build emotions; employ implicational as well as propositional thinking; develop an awareness of timing; get involved in real-life dilemmas; stick close to people who are wise, watching and learning from them; try from time to time to join up the dots to make a whole story that we can share with others; accept not knowing and not being in control, using paradox and humour to make this tolerable.

Above all we need to be aligned with the transforming pattern of the cross. This is the last and most difficult lesson of Christian discipleship. When Jesus first calls people to follow him he doesn't talk about the cost. Indeed, in the call of Simon Peter and Andrew he makes a little joke, connecting their new calling with their current job and valuing their gifts as he does so (Matt. 4.19; Mark 1.17). But as their discipleship with Jesus advances, little by little he reveals the deep wisdom of the gospel, until at Caesarea Philippi he openly explains his destiny and goes on to call his disciples to follow the way of the cross after him – to watch and learn.

Post-traumatic growth and the way of the cross

As we have seen throughout Part 3 of this book, there is much in the Christian gospel that resonates with the positive psychology movement. This is hardly surprising given that the VIA draws heavily on the wisdom traditions of the great world faiths, including Christianity, and that *euangelion* means good news. Sometimes in the history of the Church the fact that the gospel is *good* news has been forgotten. Bringing the gospel into conversation with positive psychology is one very effective way of recovering this truth.

Nevertheless, positive psychology has not been without its critics (Held 2004; Lazarus 2003), some of whom have seen it as naïve and in denial of the darker side of human nature and experience. This is rather nicely illustrated by the final scene of the 1979 film *Monty Python's Life of Brian*.[1] As the title character hangs on a cross, his fellow crucifixion victims try to cheer him up by singing, 'Always look on the bright side of life',[2] a song that suggests that whistling or cracking a joke will sort everything out. Here ironic humour holds great wisdom, for surely there *is* no bright side to being slowly tortured to death due to a series of bizarre accidents (in the case of Brian) or for political expedience (in the case of Jesus)? However, there are perhaps clues, both in the title of the song and its humorous genre, that taking a different perspective might open up even this darkest of situations.

The field of post-traumatic growth, that has been touched on at several points in this book and discussed at more length in Chapter 6, is perhaps the one area of positive psychology that takes the dark side of human experience – if not nature – seriously. Its proponents acknowledge that while the pain of many dark situations can indeed be eased by taking an optimistic attitude, positively reframing them or even by denying their full seriousness, negative events also offer the potential for more radical personal transformation, but only when the darkness is fully entered and the horror fully undergone (Tedeschi and Calhoun 1995; 2004).

To expand, there seem to be five main ways people can respond psychologically to a traumatic event. The first is to break down and despair. The next three involve attempts to assimilate the event into the world view of the individual or community (Davis, Nolen-Hoeksema and Larson 1998): completely denying the event or its impact; distorting the event (e.g. by focusing on the benefits it has allegedly delivered); and changing the meaning of the event (e.g. investing an apparently random event with significance or purpose). The fifth response involves accommodating one's world view to the event, leading to a significant shift in perspective that can be summed up in the sentence, 'Things (me, the world, God) are not as I thought.'

---

1 Handmade Films.
2 E. Idle 1979.

These ways of responding are summarized in Table 4, which is a worked example in relation to the psychological threat posed by a serious illness such as a heart attack.

Table 4.

Psychological response	Schemas	Thoughts of harm
Despair	Shatter	'I'm seriously ill. I'm going to die. Life has no meaning. The future is hopeless.'
Denial	Assimilate	'I am not ill at all.'
Distortion	Assimilate	'I've made new friends in hospital.' 'Compared with other people on the ward, I have a minor health condition.'
Changing meaning	Assimilate	'God is testing me. I can learn endurance from this.' 'This is a wake-up call. If I change my diet and give up smoking I will recover.'
Personal transformation	Accommodate	'I'm seriously ill. So I'm not immune from harm; perhaps I need to get on and live my life with this in mind. I appreciate each day now, and my priorities may need to change.' 'Life with God is clearly not as easy and straightforward as I thought. Perhaps living with uncertainty is part of discipleship. I find I can connect with the writings of some of the mystics, and I see prayer from a different perspective now.'

The different ways of responding are not mutually exclusive: in the aftermath of a traumatic event an individual or community can go down a number of these pathways in succession or flip between them (Zoellner and Maercker 2006). Attempts to assimilate the event, such as denial, are not necessarily unhealthy. Indeed, they may be literally health-giving. For example, the health psychologist Shelley Taylor and her team have carried out a series of studies that indicate that 'looking on the bright side' of various health conditions – that is, invoking a certain amount of denial, or distorting the situation so that the positives are exaggerated – actually improves prognosis and shows itself in enhanced physiological markers (see e.g. Taylor and Brown 1994; Taylor, Kemeny, Reed, Bower and Gruenewald 2000). Nevertheless, there is evidence that psychological *maturity* – as distinct from well-being – is more strongly associated with accommodation to adverse events rather than assimilation of them (King 2001).

The psychologist of religion, Kenneth Pargament, has argued strongly that faith provides a framework within with responses to crisis may sit (Pargament

2001). Through its stories, teachings and rituals, faith offers resources for what he terms 'religious coping through conservation' (assimilating the events into one's faith perspective and enriching it) and 'religious coping through transformation' (accommodating one's faith perspective to the events, so that it is broken open and revised in their light).

Pargament's account of the ways that human beings attempt to make sense of crisis, trauma and adversity can be applied to the book of Job. Job's comforters largely invoke the assimilative conservation strategy of changing the meaning of Job's troubles, seeing them as punishment for some unknown sin (e.g. Job 4.7–8) or a spiritual discipline (e.g. Job 5.17–18), but Job challenges this by asserting his innocence (e.g. Job 9.15) and the inscrutability of God (e.g. Job 9.16–18). In contrast to his comforters, Job will undergo *transformation* in the light of events because he accommodates to them, helped along by an awe-inspiring encounter with God. At the end of the day, through the undergoing of all his pain and trauma, Job comes to a profound understanding that 'God is not as I thought' (Job 42.5).

A similar set of processes appear to be at work in the New Testament as it bears witness to the death and raising of Jesus. In fact bearing witness is one way that human beings deal with psychological trauma (Tal 1996), and there is no doubt that the Christ event was traumatic in a number of respects. First-century Jews just did not expect God to act in this sort of messy, self-emptying and humiliating way in order to save his people. The New Testament is full of attempts to make sense of the shocking events of the Passion and its aftermath, together with the fact that the majority of Palestinian Jews continued to reject Jesus as messiah even after he had been raised. There is much in the way of helpful assimilation into the prophecies of the Old Testament – a changing of the meaning of the crucifixion, so that it is seen not as a squalid and random murder, but as a significant and heroic act of self-sacrifice in line with the lives and teachings of the prophets (Collicutt 2006).[3]

Yet at the end of the day, accommodation has to be made to the deep wisdom of Christ, which shows us that in the light of the cross 'God is not as we thought' in all sorts of ways. This is summed up in Paul's famous assertion that 'God's foolishness is wiser than human wisdom' (1 Cor. 1.25a). Following from this, Paul is convinced that if we want to attain the well-being and wisdom of Christ, to be fully formed, we have in some sense to participate in the senseless confusion and pain of his Passion and death with him. We cannot simply squeeze the way of Christ into conformity with our preconceptions about the divine nature. Conservation will not do; our call is to be transformed.

Contemplation and embodiment

Such insight into the true wisdom of God seems to be discovered most frequently in an odd combination of contemplation – often mystical – with an exquisite

---

3 This is a particular feature of Matthew's Gospel. See also discussion of the letter to the Hebrews on p. 225.

awareness of the bodily nature of our transformation. This working out of the mystical in and through the body is something that is quite alien to the post-Enlightenment western mind that has become accustomed to thinking in terms of a split between things spiritual or mental and things physical or material. We are at last starting to discover a more holistic understanding of human spirituality and psychology through the increasing popularity of meditation practices that have arisen within the less dualistic cultures of the East. However, this embodied understanding has actually always been there in the western Christian pre-Enlightenment tradition, and needs to be recovered.

It begins with the Gospel accounts of the bodily nature of the risen Christ: here he is definitely *not* an immaterial apparition (Luke 14.37–43). Particular emphasis is placed on the nail holes in Christ's hands and feet and the spear wound in his side as identifying marks that connect his transformed body with the physical undergoing of the crucifixion. Paul has much to say about the bodily transformation of the Christian (1 Cor. 15.35ff.), though he struggles to express himself, so that his words on this have remained ambiguous if not impenetrable to many. More enlightening are his intriguing partial references to his own experiences of spiritual transformation. In 2 Corinthians 12 he alludes to his heavenly ascent, possibly within the tradition of Jewish *merkabah* mysticism (Scott 1996), and crucially links this with his mysterious 'thorn in the flesh' (2 Cor. 12.7). Elsewhere he states that he bears the marks of Jesus (*ta stigmata tou Iēsou*) on his body (Gal. 6.17). These stigmata are physical imprints, but the word 'stigma' reminds us that the marks of Jesus are also those of social exclusion and shame.

It seems that Paul's conviction that the wisdom of God is to be found in the crucified Christ came out of his mystical experiences, where he 'heard things that are not to be told' (2 Cor. 12.4). The physical rigours and difficulties of Paul's life, through which he developed that capacity to be 'content in all circumstances' (Phil. 4.11), so similar to Linley's 'recognition and management of life uncertainty', are set in a context of contemplative prayer and mystical insight.

Paul is not alone in this. Francis of Assisi is famous for developing stigmata in the context of mystical experience, played out in a life of self-emptying, poverty and compassionate action. Teresa of Ávila writes of the experience of being repeatedly pierced bodily and spiritually by a spear wielded by an angelic being,[4] emphasizing the paradox of the sweetness that this pain evoked. The experience seems to have arisen in the context of a mystical state evoked in part by rigorous bodily discipline. It played out in her passionate reformation of the Carmelite order, restoring it to its original vision of purity of life, prayer, asceticism and poverty. In seventeenth-century Spain this embrace of poverty would have been not so much an isolated spiritual discipline, but a political act of solidarity with the majority. Here again we see a link between mystical experience and social action. Following in Teresa's footsteps, John of the Cross, who experienced social exclusion, physical abuse and imprisonment, all against the background

---

4 *The Life of St Teresa of Jesus* (1565) XXIX, 17.

of the threat of the Inquisition, writes paradoxically of a wound of love and the finding of light in the deepest darkness.[5]

Both Teresa's spear and John's light penetrate. This word has clear sexual connotations, and it should be noted that the writings of these two Spanish mystics has an erotic quality. If anything, this is more marked in John's work. It is full of passionate longing, bittersweet love and tender physical attachment to his beloved Christ, the fruit of his detachment from voluntary desires discussed in Chapter 10. To note the erotic overtones here is not to reduce the spiritual to the sexual (and hence discredit it), but rather to draw out the deeply embodied aspect of such paradoxical experiences of joy through suffering, and of knowledge that is beyond our grasp but can yet be received as a gift in the midst of our unknowing.

> Oh, happy night that guided me,
> Oh, night more lovely than the dawn,
> Oh, night that joined Beloved with lover,
> Lover transformed in the Beloved!
>
> John of the Cross (1542–91)

A particular feature of Christ's wounding on the cross is that he was himself penetrated. Openings were made in his flesh, and these continue to function as emblems of the ways all sorts of boundaries are breached in Christ; they are places of risk and liminality. There is here a mysterious but strong connection with our own unsought wounding – physical and psychological – as the means by which we become open to new possibilities, to the acceptance of grace and thus to transformation:

> There has been an intense development of my spiritual life and finding direction. [The injury] has changed my life hugely – my priorities are so different. I've let go of things that were previously important and now seem worthless. Previously I had a low view of myself – and I still struggle with this. But despite my loss of ability and changed appearance, which is extremely difficult at times, I have got through it and it has enabled me to let other people in. (Research participant cited in Collicutt and Linley 2006, p. 771)

For Paul, the spiritual transformation of the Christian comes through her intentional appropriation of the wounding and death of Christ. It is the fruit of a conscious decision to undergo baptism (Rom. 6.3ff.), an action that involves the whole body, and is worked out in a transformed pattern of bodily life (Rom. 12.1).

As with Paul, the transforming power of the cross is a particular feature of the thought of Martin Luther (1483–1546), who at first glance is quite a different character from the monastic mystics considered above. Luther's theology of the cross was not, however, simply an intellectual system or ideology but, more profoundly, an expression of his own experience of contemplative prayer

---

5 *Dark Night of the Soul* and *Ascent of Mount Carmel*.

and radical transformation. His theology arose from his spirituality. Rowan Williams sums up Luther's position in words that could apply equally to his Spanish Catholic contemporaries:

> God is himself the great 'negative theologian' who shatters all our images by addressing us in the cross of Jesus. If we are looking for signs of God's authentic life, activity and presence, we shall find them only in their contradictories, in our own death and hell, as in Christ's. (Williams 1990, p. 149)

It seems then that there are different ways of doing Christian spirituality, but that in the end they all come back to the cross, to the transformation of wounding and death to glory and life.

If we want a love which will protect the *soul* from wounds we must love something other than *God*.

Simone Weil 1947, p. 62

Building resilience

Unfortunately this deepest of all truths about the Christian life is also the one that is most vulnerable to misinterpretation and misapplication. The seeming obsession with suffering, affliction and martyrdom of many of the spiritual giants in Christian history can come over as alien to us in our comfortable and affluent society. Their writings are historically distant and can seem to us – at least in places – morbid, escapist and masochistic: in short, dysfunctional. Perhaps they resonate more strongly with the experience of Christians living as minorities under violent regimes, in conflict zones or in areas of the developing world marked by low life expectancy. In the settled west they remain somewhat problematic.

One particular misinterpretation of the Christian understanding of transformation of suffering is the idea, to be found in some circles, that being damaged guarantees spiritual advancement or places one in a better position to help others. The notion of the 'wounded healer' is sometimes invoked in this context. However, the teaching of Jesus on this is quite clear; he has strong words to say about 'blind guides' (Matt. 15.14), and insists that to be able to help others one must first attend to oneself (Matt. 7.3–5). Justine Allain-Chapman puts her finger on the dangers inherent in the idea of the 'wounded healer' by suggesting that it can be a cover for the activities of the 'unhealed wounder' (Allain-Chapman 2012, p. 115). Jesus' wounds are not festering sores but imprints (*tupoi*) of his past suffering on his gloriously transformed body (John 20.25). Healers and pastors need to be wise, to have developed and to be continuing to develop wisdom through engaging with life experience that includes adversity, not to be chronically wounded. Wounded creatures tend to bite.

This is one reason for engaging with the contemporary western psychological literature on post-traumatic growth; it can help us to distinguish it from its counterfeits, and so support the process of spiritual discernment. Post-traumatic growth is not about the denial of suffering, looking on the bright side (even when this is healthy), wallowing in suffering, seeking out suffering for its own sake (sadomasochism), creating a spiritual culture whose discourse is all about suffering, or tolerating emotionally destructive or abusive environments. It's about the unexpected shattering of assumptions and their reconstruction into something unimaginably better. It's about a shifting of psychological tectonic plates and the consequent dissonances, stretches and strains. It is about a way of being that is always poised for departure.

> Old men ought to be explorers
> Here or there does not matter
> We must be still and still moving
> Into another intensity
> For a further union, a deeper communion
> Through the dark cold and the empty desolation,
>
> T. S. Eliot 1888–1965

Understanding something about post-traumatic growth can also help us get the point the great mystics were trying to make about the transformation of suffering so that we can appropriate it in a way that works for our time and culture.

As we saw in Chapter 14, there is a particular demand for us to work out how to live between the times, keeping a vibrant eschatological vision yet pacing ourselves for something more like a marathon than a sprint, and fully inhabiting our historical reality. In the developed west at least, this reality is not one of constant martyrdom. As discussed in Chapter 12, virtual and real visiting of places where acute suffering and deprivation are part of everyday life can help us get a handle on this perspective. But we also need to give some thought to the way we embrace adversity when it arises in our home setting, aiming to develop ways that will make us more likely to grow through it than be destroyed by it. In other words, we need to build stamina through developing resilience, especially if we are to minister effectively to others.

Resilience is the capacity to bounce back having received a knock (Lepore and Revenson 2006; Bensimon 2012). It means being flexible and emotionally grounded (Chapter 7). It means having good resources at one's disposal in the way of knowledge and practical and emotional support systems (Chapter 14). Resilience and stamina also depend on conserving energy. Here we are back with the image of the fit body. We use up energy when we try and keep up a front (Chapter 2), when we grasp too tightly (Chapter 8), when we work but take no rest or play (Chapter 10) and when we harbour grudges (Chapter 13). Personal authenticity, the ability to sit lightly, a disciplined rule of life and readiness to forgive will all help us to develop resilience.

We have also seen that there are several possible pathways through trauma and adversity. Resilience therefore involves that aspect of wisdom that discerns when to withdraw to marshal resources and when to advance; when to fight and when to fly; when to look on the bright side and when to gaze into the darkness. For this we need to know something about ourselves as well as the situation that faces us.

One aspect of this wisdom concerns holding an appropriate balance between the agony of Good Friday and the triumphant joy of Easter Sunday. Each of us is more naturally disposed to one than the other, and this is also a characteristic of different church cultures and theologies. Paying some attention to Holy Saturday has the potential to help us here. It is a place of as yet unresolved dissonance, of watching and waiting, poised between parting and reunion. Like a musical pause in a great orchestral score, like the evenings and mornings in the creation account of Genesis 1, Holy Saturday is there in the Christian story and preserved in the liturgical calendar for a reason. The way we inhabit this day liturgically, and the extent to which we incorporate its contours into our spiritual life, will influence our resilience; for it is about not rushing the process of transformation of trauma but instead tolerating delay, co-operating with God's timing and trusting that God is at work even when he seems to be absent.

> We must guard against this theological busyness and religious impatience which insists on anticipating the moment of fruiting of the eternal redemption through the temporal passion – a dragging forward that moment from Easter to Holy Saturday.
>
> Hans Urs von Balthasar (1905–88)

This message is especially important for Christians who are in positions of leadership or public ministry, for they have a particular need for resilience. It is something of which Jesus himself seems to have been well aware in his own ministerial team (Mark 6.31). The demands of church leadership can be multiple and constant (Proeschold-Bell, LeGrand, James, Wallace, Adams and Toole 2011), with blurring of boundaries between work and home (Morris and Blanton 1998), loneliness and isolation (Doolittle 2010), and the burden of unrealistic expectations (Weaver, Flannelly, Larson, Stapleton and Koenig 2002). Burnout is a well recognized problem in Christian leaders (Grosch and Olsen 2000).

It is therefore reassuring to find that a positive experience of prayer and confidence in praying in public are associated with signs of increased resilience in clergy (Turton and Francis 2007). Prayer is, of course, the powerhouse of every Christian, and without it we are running on empty. It helps us cope with adversity as we engage with the situation, reflect on it and offer both it and those involved, including ourselves, to God. But the way we do this turns out to be important.

We have already seen that faith can be construed as – though not reduced to – a way of coping with challenge and adversity. Kenneth Pargament and his colleagues have carried out numerous studies to examine the varied ways this happens. They have identified different ways that people of faith navigate through times of difficulty, which can be broadly divided into three types (Pargament, Smith, Koenig and Perez 1998). These are described as 'deferring' (passively waiting for God to sort out the situation); 'self-directing' (using one's own initiative without reference to God); and 'collaborative' (entering into a partnership with God to address the issue). The first attitude can be found in many of the psalms, where the psalmist calls out to God to intervene in situations or asks why he seems to be taking so long (e.g. Ps. 10; 24). The second attitude is more typical of contemporary secular western society. The third attitude – that of collaboration with God in working through the difficulty – has been found to be associated with self-reported post-traumatic growth, spiritual advancement, increased life satisfaction, self-esteem and physical and mental health indicators (Koenig, McCullough and Larson 2001; Ano and Vasconelles 2005).

Here we have some empirical evidence suggesting that approaching God in an adult-to-adult way, expecting to work with him rather than to be done to by him or to snatch the reins ourselves, results in both increased resilience and personal transformation. Back in Chapter 1, Christian formation was described as a process of co-operation between the human and the divine. We bring what we have, do what we can, with the expectation that God will receive it gladly and, through the Spirit, transform it to our good and his glory. In this book I have tried to do exactly this by bringing the insights of human psychology, limited though these may be, to the endeavour of Christian formation, trusting that God will use them too for the good of Christ's body, and thus further his mission in the world.

Pour upon the poverty of our love,
and the weakness of our praise,
the transforming fire of your presence.[6]

Exercises

1 Look back at a dark time in your life and try and identify what you learnt from it about:
   - yourself;
   - other people;
   - God.
2 Plan a way of keeping Holy Saturday that enables you to explore the spiritual discipline of being poised for a new departure and a new beginning.

---

6 © Archbishops' Council.

Further reading

Allain-Chapman, J., 2012, *Resilient Pastors: The Role of Adversity in Healing and Growth*, London: SPCK.

Frankl, V., 1959, *Man's Search for Meaning*, Boston, MA: Beacon Press.

Howells, E. and Tyler, P., 2010, *Sources of Transformation: Revitalising Christian Spirituality*, London: Continuum.

Lewis, A., 2003, *Between Cross and Resurrection: A Theology of Holy Saturday*, Grand Rapids, MI: Eerdmans.

Tedeschi, R. and Calhoun. L., 1995, *Trauma and Transformation: Growing in the Aftermath of Suffering*, Thousand Oaks, CA: Sage.

Williams, R., 1990, *The Wound of Knowledge*, London: Darton, Longman & Todd.

Bibliography

Aberson, C., Healy, M. and Romero, V., 2000, 'Ingroup bias and self-esteem: a meta-analysis', *Personality and Social Psychology Review* 4, pp. 157–73.

Adam, D., 2012, *Occasions for Alleluia*, London: SPCK.

Ainsworth, M., 1967, *Infancy in Uganda: Infant Care and the Growth of Love*, Baltimore, MD: Johns Hopkins University Press.

Ainsworth, M., 1993, 'Attachments and other affectional bonds across the life cycle', in C. M. Parkes, J. Stevenson-Hinde and P. Marris (eds), *Attachment Across the Life Cycle*, London: Routledge, pp. 33–51.

Ainsworth, M., Blehar, M., Waters, E. and Wall, S., 1978, *Patterns of Attachment: A Psychological Study of the Strange Situation*, Hillsdale, NJ: Erlbaum.

Algoe, S. and Haidt, J., 2009, 'Witnessing excellence in action: the "other-praising" emotions of elevation, gratitude, and admiration', *The Journal of Positive Psychology* 4, pp. 105–27.

Alison, J., 1997, *Living in the End Times: The Last Things Re-imagined*, London: SPCK.

Allain-Chapman, J., 2012, *Resilient Pastors: The Role of Adversity in Healing and Growth*, London: SPCK.

Allport, G., 1954, *The Nature of Prejudice*, Cambridge: Addison-Wesley.

Allport, G., 1961, *Pattern and Growth in Personality*, New York: Holt.

Angelier, F. and Chastel, O., 2009, 'Stress, prolactin and parental investment in birds: a review', *General and Comparative Endocrinology* 163, pp. 142–8.

Ano, G. and Vasconcelles, E., 2005, 'Religious coping and psychological adaptation to stress: a meta-analysis', *Journal of Clinical Psychology* 61, pp. 1–20.

Apter, M. J., 2001, *Motivational Styles in Everyday Life: A Guide to Reversal Theory*, Washington, DC: American Psychological Association.

Arbib, M., 1991, 'Interaction of multiple representations of space in the brain', in J. Paillard (ed.), *Brain and Space*, Oxford: Oxford University Press, pp. 379–403.

Aristotle, 1980, *Nichomachean Ethics*, tr. D. Ross, Oxford: Oxford University Press.

Austin, J., 1962, *How to Do Things with Words: The William James Lectures delivered at Harvard University in 1955*, Oxford: Clarendon Press.

Baer, R., Smith, G., Lykins, E., Button, D., Krietemeyer, J., Sauer, S., Walsh, E., Duggan, D., Williams, M., 2008, 'Construct validity of the Five Facet Mindfulness Questionnaire in meditating and nonmeditating samples', *Assessment* 15, pp. 329–42.

Baker, L. and McNulty, J., 2011, 'Self-compassion and relationship maintenance: the moderating roles of conscientiousness and gender', *Journal of Personality and Social Psychology* 100, pp. 853–73.

Balcetis, E. and Dunning, D., 2006, 'See what you want to see: motivational influences on visual perception', *Journal of Personality and Social Psychology* 91, pp. 612–25.

Ball, D., 1996, *'I Am' in John's Gospel*, Sheffield: Continuum.

Baltes, P. and Smith, J., 1990, 'Towards a psychology of wisdom and its ontogenesis', in R. Sternberg (ed.), *Wisdom: Its Nature, Origins, and Development*, Cambridge: Cambridge University Press, pp. 87–120.

Baltes, P. and Staudinger, U., 2000, 'Wisdom: the orchestration of mind and virtue toward human excellence', *American Psychologist* 55, pp. 122–36.

Bandura, A., 1997, *Self-efficacy: The Exercise of Control*, London: W. H. Freeman.

Bar-Haim, Y., Lamy, D., Pergamin, L., Bakermans-Kranenburg, M. and van Ijzendoorn, M., 2007, 'Threat-related attentional bias in anxious and nonanxious individuals: a meta-analytic study', *Psychological Bulletin* 133, pp. 1–24.

Barr, J., 1988, 'Abbā isn't daddy', *Journal of Theological Studies* 39, pp. 8–47.

Barr, J., 1993, *Biblical Faith and Natural Theology*, New York: Oxford University Press.

Barrett, J. and Burdett, E., 2011, 'The cognitive science of religion', *The Psychologist* 24, pp. 252–5.

Barrington-Ward, S., 2007, *The Jesus Prayer*, Oxford: Bible Reading Fellowship.

Barton, J., 1999, *Love Unknown: Meditations on the Death and Resurrection of Jesus*, Oxford: Fairacres.

Barton, S., 2013, *Joy in the New Testament*, Cambridge: Grove Books.

Bash, A. and Bash, M., 2004, 'Early Christian thinking', in F. Watts and L. Gulliford (eds), *Forgiveness in Context: Theology and Psychology in Creative Dialogue*, London: T. & T. Clark, pp. 29–49.

Batson, C. D., 1991, *The Altruism Question: Toward a Social-psychological Answer*, Hillsdale, NJ: Lawrence Erlbaum.

Batson, C. D., Ahmad, N., Lishner, D., 2009, 'Empathy and altruism', in C. Snyder and S. Lopez (eds), *The Oxford Handbook of Positive Psychology*, New York: Oxford University Press, pp. 417–26.

Batson, C. D., Schoenrade, P. and Ventis, W. L., 1993, *Religion and the Individual: A Social-psychological Perspective*, New York: Oxford University Press.

Batten, M. and Oltjenbruns, K., 1999, 'Adolescent sibling bereavement as a catalyst for spiritual development', *Death Studies* 23, pp. 529–46.

Bauckham, R., 2008, *Jesus and the Eyewitness: The Gospels as Eyewitness Testimonies*, Grand Rapids, MI: Eerdmans.

Baumeister, R., 1992, *Meanings of Life*, New York: Guilford.

Baumeister, R., Bratslavsky, E., Finkenauer, C. and Vohs, K., 2001, 'Bad is stronger than good', *Review of General Psychology* 5, pp. 323–70.

Baumeister, R. and Muraven, M., 1996, 'Identity as adaptation to social, cultural, and historical context', *Journal of Adolescence* 19, pp. 405–16.

Beier, M., 2010, 'The deadly search for God: absolute aggression in the heritage of the Bible', in D. Daschke and A. Kille (eds), *A Cry Instead of Justice: The Bible and Cultures of Violence in Psychological Perspective*, London: T. & T. Clark, pp. 131–55.

Bennet, M. and Hacker, P., 2003, *Philosophical Foundations of Neuroscience*, Oxford: Blackwell.

Bennett, Z., 2013, *Using the Bible in Practical Theology*, Farnham: Ashgate.

Bensimon, M., 2012, 'Elaboration on the association between trauma, PTSD and post-traumatic growth: the role of trait resilience', *Personality and Individual Differences* 52, pp. 782–7.

Berne, E., 1964, *Games People Play: The Basic Handbook of Transactional Analysis*, New York: Ballantine Books.

Berryman, J., 1991, *Godly Play: An Imaginative Approach to Religious Education*, San Francisco, CA: Harper.

Berryman, J., 2002, *The Complete Guide to Godly Play, Volume 3*, Denver, CO: Living the Good News.

Bloos, I. and O'Connor, T., 2002, 'Ancient and mediaeval labyrinth and contemporary narrative therapy: how do they fit?', *Pastoral Psychology* 50, pp. 219–30.

Boden, M., 1985, 'Wonder and understanding', *Zygon* 20, pp. 391–400.

Bono, G., McCullough, M. and Root L., 2008, 'Forgiveness, feeling connected to others, and well-being: two longitudinal studies', *Personality and Social Psychology Bulletin* 34, pp. 182–95.

Borke, H., 1975, 'Piaget's mountain's revisited: changes in the egocentric landscape', *Developmental Psychology* 11, pp. 240–3.

Bowlby, J., 1951, *Maternal Care and Mental Health*, Geneva: World Health Organization Monograph.

Bowlby, J., 1959, 'Separation anxiety', *International Journal of Psychoanalysts* 61, pp. 1–25.

Bowlby, J., 1969, 1973, 1980, *Attachment and Loss*, 3 volumes, New York: Basic Books.

Bowlby, J., 1988, *A Secure Base: Clinical Applications of Attachment Theory*, London: Tavistock.

Bowlby, J., 2005, *The Making and Breaking of Affectional Bonds*, London: Routledge.

Brewer, M. and Gardner, W., 1996, 'Who is this "we"? Levels of collective identity and self-representations', *Journal of Personality and Social Psychology* 71, pp. 83–93.

Brose, L., Rye, M., Lutz-Zois, C. and Ross, S., 2005, 'Forgiveness and personality traits', *Personality and Individual Differences* 39, pp. 35–46.

Brother Ramon, 2008, *Franciscan Spirituality: Following St Francis Today*, London: SPCK.

Brueggemann, W., 2002, *Spirituality of the Psalms*, Minneapolis, MN: Augsburg Fortress.

Brueggemann, W., 2007, *Praying the Psalms: Engaging Scripture and the Life of the Spirit*, Eugene, OR: Cascade Books.

Brueggemann, W., 2014, *Sabbath as Resistance*, Louisville, KY: Westminster John Knox Press.

Bruner, J., 1990, *Acts of Meaning*, Cambridge, MA: Harvard University Press.

Bryant, F. and Veroff, J., 2007, *Savoring: A New Model of Positive Experience*, Mahwah, NJ: Lawrence Erlbaum.

Buchanan, M., 2006, *The Rest of God: Restoring Your Soul by Restoring Sabbath*, Nashville, TN: Thomas Nelson.

Cain, S., 2013, *Quiet: The Power of Introverts in a World that Can't Stop Talking*, London: Penguin.

Cameron, H., Reader, J., Slater, V. and Rowland, C., 2013, *Theological Reflection for Human Flourishing: Pastoral Practice and Public Theology*, London: SCM Press.

Cannon, W., 1915, *Bodily Changes in Pain, Hunger, Fear and Rage: An Account of Recent Researches into the Function of Emotional Excitement*, New York: Appleton.

Capps, D., 2000, *Jesus: A Psychological Biography*, St Louis, MO: Chalice Press.

Carmichael, K., 2003, *Sin and Forgiveness: New Responses in a Changing World*, Aldershot: Ashgate.

Carson, T., 2013, 'Ignatius, gratitude and positive psychology: does Ignatian gratitude develop subjective well-being?', *The Way* 52, pp. 7–19.

Carver, C. and Scheier, M., 1990, 'Origins and functions of positive and negative affect: a control-process view', *Psychological Review* 97, pp. 19–35.

Carver, C. and Scheier, M., 1998, *On the Self-regulation of Behavior*, Cambridge: Cambridge University Press.

Case, R. and Okamoto, Y., 1996, 'The role of central conceptual structures in the development of children's thought', *Monograph of the Society for Research in Child Development* 61, pp. v–265.

Cassell, E., 2009, 'Compassion', in C. Snyder and S. Lopez (eds), *The Oxford Handbook of Positive Psychology*, New York: Oxford University Press, pp. 393–404.

Cassidy, J., 2008, 'The nature of the child's ties', in J. Cassidy and P. Shaver (eds), *Handbook of Attachment: Theory, Research, and Clinical Applications*, New York: Guilford, pp. 3–22.

Chan, M., 2012, 'A biblical lexicon of happiness', in B. Strawn (ed.), *The Bible and the Pursuit of Happiness*, New York: Oxford University Press, pp. 323–70.

Charry, E., 1997, *By the Renewing of Your Minds: The Pastoral Function of Christian Doctrine*, Oxford: Oxford University Press.

Charry, E., 2012, 'The necessity of divine happiness', in B. Strawn (ed.), *The Bible and the Pursuit of Happiness*, New York: Oxford University Press, pp. 229–47.

Cherry, S., 2010, *Barefoot Disciple: Walking the Way of Passionate Humility*, London: Continuum.

College, E. and Walsh, J., 1978, *Guigo II's Ladder of Monks and Twelve Meditations*, London: Mowbray.

Collicutt, J., 2006, 'Post-traumatic growth and the origins of early Christianity', *Mental Health, Religion and Culture* 9, pp. 291–306.

Collicutt, J., 2008a, 'Discernment and the psychology of perception', in A. McGrath, *The Open Secret: The Renewal of Natural Theology*, Oxford: Blackwell, pp. 80–110.

Collicutt, J., 2008b, 'Face to faith column', *The Guardian*, Saturday 31st May.

Collicutt, J., 2008c, 'The mystery of the kingdom: Jesus of Nazareth and the natural realm', in A. McGrath, *The Open Secret: A New Vision for Natural Theology*, Oxford: Blackwell, pp. 117–25.

Collicutt, J., 2009a, *Jesus and the Gospel Women*, London: SPCK.

Collicutt, J., 2009b, 'Word', in A. Richards and P. Privett (eds), *Through the Eyes of a Child*, London: Church House Publishing.

Collicutt, J., 2011a, 'Psychology, religion and spirituality', *The Psychologist* 24, pp. 250–1.

Collicutt, J., 2011b, 'Posttraumatic growth, spirituality, and acquired brain injury', *Brain Impairment* 12, pp. 82–92.

Collicutt, J., 2012a, 'Ethical issues in dementia care', *Crucible*, pp. 7–17.

Collicutt, J., 2012b, *When You Pray: Daily Reflections for Lent and Easter on the Lord's Prayer*, Oxford: Bible Reading Fellowship.

Collicutt, J., 2012c, 'Bringing the academic discipline of psychology to bear on the study of the Bible', *Journal of Theological Studies* 63, pp. 1–48.

Collicutt, J. and Gray, A., 2012, '"A merry heart doeth good like a medicine": humour, religion and wellbeing', *Mental Health, Religion and Culture*, pp. 759–78.

Collicutt, J. and Linley, P. A., 2006, 'Post-traumatic growth in acquired brain injury: a preliminary small scale study', *Brain Injury* 20, pp. 767–73.

Condon, P., Desbordes, G., Miller, W. and DeSteno, D., 2013, 'Meditation increases compassionate responses to suffering', *Psychological Science*, doi:10.1177/0956797613485603.

Cook, C., 2004, 'Addiction and spirituality', *Addiction* 99, pp. 539–51.

Costa, P. and McCrae, R., 1992, *NEO PI-R Professional Manual*, Odessa, FL: Psychological Assessment Resources, Inc.

Coyle, A., 2011, 'Critical responses to faith development theory: a useful agenda for change?', *Archive for the Psychology of Religion* 33, pp. 281–98.

Crocker, J. and Park, L., 2004, 'The costly pursuit of self-esteem', *Psychological Bulletin* 130, pp. 392–414.

Crossan, J. D., 1991, *The Historical Jesus: The Life of a Mediterranean Jewish Peasant*, San Francisco: HarperCollins.

Crossan, J. D., 2008, *Cliffs of Fall: Paradox and Polyvalence in the Parables of Jesus*, Eugene, OR: Wipf & Stock.

Csikszentmihalyi, I. S., 1988, 'Flow in a historical context: the case of the Jesuits', in M. and I. S. Csikszentmihalyi (eds), *Optimal Experience; Psychological Studies of Flow in Consciousness*, Cambridge: Cambridge University Press, pp. 232–48.

Csikszentmihalyi, M., 1975, *Beyond Boredom and Anxiety*, San Francisco, CA: Jossey-Bass.

Csikszentmihalyi, M., 1988, 'The Flow Experience and its significance for human psychology', in M. Csikszentmihalyi and I. S. Csikszentmihalyi (eds), *Optimal Experience: Psychological Studies of Flow in Consciousness*, Cambridge: Cambridge University Press, pp. 15–35.

Csikszentmihalyi, M., 1990, *Flow: The Psychology of Optimal Experience*, New York: Harper & Row.

Csikszentmihalyi, M., Abuhamdeh, S. and Nakamura, J., 2005, 'Flow', in A. Elliot and C. Dweck (eds), *Handbook of Competence and Motivation*, New York: Guilford Press, pp. 598–608.

Dahlsgaard, K., Peterson, C. and Seligman, M., 2005, 'Shared virtues: the convergence of valued human strengths across culture and history', *Review of General Psychology* 9, pp. 203–13.

Darley, J. and Batson, C. D., 1973, '"From Jerusalem to Jericho": a study of situational and dispositional variables in helping behaviour', *Journal of Personality and Social Psychology* 27, pp. 100–8.

Davies, S., 1995, *Jesus the Healer: Possession, Trance, and the Origins of Christianity*, New York: Continuum.

Davis, C. G., Nolen-Hoeksema, S. and Larson, J., 1998, 'Making sense of loss and benefiting from the experience: two construals of meaning', *Journal of Personality and Social Psychology* 75, pp. 561–74.

Dawkins, R., 2006, *The God Delusion*, London: Random House.

Deane-Drummond, C., 2006, *Wonder and Wisdom: Conversations in Science, Spirituality and Theology*, London: Darton, Longman & Todd.

Dearing, R. and Tangney, J., 2006, *Shame and Guilt*, New York: Guilford.

de Certeau, M., 1988, *The Practice of Everyday Life*, Berkeley, CA: University of California Press.

Decety, J. and Hodges, S., 2006, 'The social neuroscience of empathy', in P. van Lange (ed.), *Bridging Social Psychology: Benefits of Transdisciplinary Approaches*, Mahwah, NJ: Erlbaum, pp. 103–9.

Decety, J. and Jackson, P., 2004, 'The functional architecture of human empathy', *Behavioral and Cognitive Neuroscience Reviews* 3, pp. 71–100.

Dennis, T., 1997, *Imagining God*, London: SPCK.

Diener, E., 2000, 'Subjective well-being: the science of happiness and a proposal for a national index', *American Psychologist* 55, pp. 34–43.

Doolittle, B., 2010, 'The impact of behaviors upon burnout among parish-based clergy', *Journal of Religion and Health* 49, pp. 88–95.

Douglas, M., 1966, *Purity and Danger*, London: Routledge & Kegan Paul.

Douglas, M., 2004, *Jacob's Tears*, Oxford: Oxford University Press.

Drury, J., 2000, 'Ruskin's way: *tout a fait comme un oiseau*', in S. Collini, R. Whitmore and B. Young (eds), *History, Religion, and Culture: British Intellectual History 1750–1950*, Cambridge: Cambridge University Press, pp. 156–76.

Duff, J. and Collicutt McGrath, J., 2006, *Meeting Jesus: Human Responses to a Yearning God*, London: SPCK.

Eaton, J., Struthers, C. W. and Santelli, A., 2006, 'Dispositional and state forgiveness: the role of self-esteem, need for structure, and narcissism', *Personality and Individual Differences* 41, pp. 371–80.

Edwards, K. and Hall, T., 2003, 'Illusory spiritual health: the role of defensiveness in understanding and assessing spiritual health', in T. Hall and E. McMinn (eds), *Spiritual Formation, Counseling and Psychotherapy*, Hauppauge, NY: Nova Scotis Publishers.

Ekman, P., 1992, 'Are there basic emotions?', *Psychological Review* 99, pp. 550–3.

Eliot, T. S., 1943, *Four Quartets*, San Diego, CA: Harcourt.

Elliott, R. Fischer, C. and Rennie, D., 1999, 'Evolving guidelines for publication of qual-itative research studies in psychology and related fields', *British Journal of Clinical Psychology* 38, pp. 215–29.

Emmons, R., 2003, *The Psychology of Ultimate Concerns*, New York: Guilford.

Emmons, R. and McCullough, M., 2003, 'Counting blessings versus burdens: an experi-mental investigation of gratitude and subjective well-being in daily life', *Journal of Personality and Social Psychology* 84, pp. 377–89.

Enright, R. and Coyle, C., 1998, 'Researching the process model of forgiveness within psychological interventions', in E. Worthington (ed.), *Dimensions of Forgiveness*, Pennsylvania, PA: Templeton Press, pp. 139–61.

Esler, P., 2000, 'Jesus and the reduction of intergroup conflict: the parable of the Good Samaritan in the light of social identity theory', *Biblical Interpretation* 8, pp. 325–57.

Exline, J., Yali, A. and Sanderson, W., 2000, 'Guilt, discord, and alienation: the role of religious strain in depression and suicidality', *Journal of Clinical Psychology* 56, pp. 1481–96.

Exline, J., Baumeister, R., Bushman, B., Campbell, W. and Finkel, E., 2004, 'Too proud to let go: narcissistic entitlement as a barrier to forgiveness', *Journal of Personality and Social Psychology* 87, pp. 894–912.

Exline, J., Worthington, E., Hill, P. and McCullough, M., 2003, 'Forgiveness and jus-tice: a research agenda for social and personality psychology', *Personality and Social Psychology Review* 7, pp. 337–48.

Eysenck, H., 1967, *The Biological Basis of Personality*, Springfield, IL: Charles C. Thomas.

Eysenck, H., 1990, 'Genetic and environmental contributions to individual differences: the three major dimensions of personality', *Journal of Personality* 58, pp. 245–62.

Farb, N., Segal, Z., Mayberg, H., Bean, J., McKeon, D., Fatima, Z. and Anderson, A., 2007, 'Attending to the present: mindfulness meditation reveals distinct neural modes of self-reference', *Social, Cognitive and Affective Neuroscience* 2, pp. 313–22.

Fennell, M., 2009, *Overcoming Low Self-esteem: A Self-help Guide Using Cognitive Behavioural Techniques*, London: Robinson.

Fiddes, P., 2013, *Seeing the World and Knowing God: Hebrew Wisdom and Christian Doctrine in a Late-modern Context*, Oxford: Oxford University Press.

Finlay, L. and Gough, B., 2003, *Reflexivity: A Practical Guide for Researchers in Health and Social Sciences*, Oxford: Blackwell.

Fischer, K. and Bidell, T., 1998, 'Dynamic psychologies of development structures in action and thought', in W. Damon and R. Lerner (eds), *Handbook of Child Psychology, Volume 1: Theoretical models of human development*, New York: Wiley, pp. 467–561.

Fisher, M. and Exline, J., 2010, 'Moving toward self-forgiveness: removing barriers related to shame, guilt, and regret', *Social and Personality Psychology Compass* 4, pp. 548–58.

Fonagy, P., 2001, *Attachment Theory and Psychoanalysis*, London: Karnac Books.

Francis, L., Penson, A. and Jones, S., 2001, 'Psychological types of male and female bible college students in England', *Mental Health, Religion and Culture* 4, pp. 23–32.

Francis, L. and Rodger, R., 1994, 'The influence of personality on clergy role priori-tization, role influences, conflict and dissatisfaction with ministry', *Personality and Individual Differences* 16, pp. 947–57.

Frankl, V., 1959, *Man's Search for Meaning*, Boston, MA: Beacon Press.

Fredrickson, B., 2001, 'The role of positive emotions in positive psychology: the broaden-and-build theory of positive emotions', *American Psychologist* 56, pp. 218–26.

Fredrickson, B., 2004, 'The broaden-and-build theory of positive emotions', *Philosophical Transactions of the Royal Society B: Biological Sciences* 359, pp. 1367–77.

Fretheim, T., 2012, 'God, creation, and the pursuit of happiness', in B. Strawn (ed.), *The Bible and the Pursuit of Happiness*, New York: Oxford University Press, pp. 33–56.

Freud, S., 1928, *The Future of an Illusion*, tr. W. D. Robson-Scott, London: Hogarth Press.

Frijda, N., 1994, 'Emotions are functional most of the time', in P. Ekman and R. Davidson (eds), *The Nature of Emotion: Fundamental Questions*, New York: Oxford University Press, pp. 112–22.

Furnham, A., 1996, 'The big five versus the big four: the relationship between the Myers-Briggs Type Indicator (MTBI) and the NEO-PI five factor model of personality', *Personality and Individual Differences* 21, pp. 303–7.

Gallagher, T., 2006, *The Examen Prayer: Ignatian Wisdom for Our Lives Today*, New York: Crossroad.

Germer, C., 2009, *The Mindful Path to Self-compassion: Freeing Yourself from Destructive Thoughts and Emotions*, New York: Guilford Press.

Goetz, J., Keltner, D. and Simon-Thomas, E., 2010, 'Compassion: an evolutionary analysis and empirical review', *Psychological Bulletin* 136, pp. 351–74.

Girard, R., 1977, *Violence and the Sacred*, Baltimore, MD: Johns Hopkins University Press.

Granqvist, P., Mikulincer, M. and Shaver, P., 2010, 'Religion as attachment: normative processes and individual differences', *Personality and Social Psychology Review* 14, pp. 49–59.

Gradus, J., Qin, P., Lincoln, A., Miller, M., Lawler, E., Sørensen, H. T. and Lash, T., 2010, 'Posttraumatic stress disorder and completed suicide', *American Journal of Epidemiology* 171, pp. 721–7.

Graf, P. and Masson, M., 2013, *Implicit Memory: New Directions in Cognition, Development, and Neuropsychology*, Hove: Psychology Press.

Gray, J. A., 1982, *The Neuropsychology of Anxiety*, Oxford, Oxford University Press.

Grepmair, L., Mitterlehner, F., Loew, T., Bachler, E., Rother, W. and Nickel, M., 2007, 'Promoting mindfulness in psychotherapists in training influences the treatment results of their patients: a randomized, double-blind, controlled study', *Psychotherapy and Psychosomatics* 76, pp. 332–8.

Grosch, W. and Olsen, D., 2000, 'Clergy burnout: an integrative approach', *Journal of Clinical Psychology* 56, pp. 619–32.

Gross, R. and Muck, T., 2003, *Christians Talk about Buddhist Meditation: Buddhists Talk about Christian Prayer*, London: Continuum.

Grossman, P., Niemann, L., Schmidt, S. and Walach, H., 2004, 'Mindfulness-based stress reduction and health benefits: a meta-analysis', *Journal of Psychosomatic Research* 57, pp. 35–43.

Haidt, J., 2003, 'The moral emotions', in R. Davidson, K. Scherer and H. Goldsmith (eds), *Handbook of Affective Sciences*, Oxford: Oxford University Press, pp. 852–70.

Haidt, J., 2012, *The Righteous Mind: Why Good People Are Divided by Politics and Religion*, London: Allen Lane.

Hardt, J. and Rutter, M., 2004, 'Validity of adult retrospective reports of adverse childhood experiences: review of the evidence', *Journal of Child Psychology and Psychiatry* 45, pp. 260–73.

Hardy, A., 1979, *The Spiritual Nature of Man: A Study of Contemporary Religious Experience*, Oxford: Clarendon Press.

Harlow, H., 1958, 'The nature of love', *American Psychologist* 13, pp. 673–85.

Harris, T., Brown, G. and Bifulco, A., 1990, 'Depression and situational helplessness/mastery in a sample selected to study childhood parental loss', *Journal of Affective Disorders* 20, pp. 27–41.

Harrison, P., 2001, *The Bible, Protestantism, and the Rise of Natural Science*, Oxford: Oxford University Press.

Harter, S., 2012, 'Emerging selves during childhood and adolescence', in M. Leary and J. P. Tangney (eds), *Handbook of Self and Identity*, New York: Guilford, pp. 680–716.

Hawks, S., 2004, 'Spiritual wellness, holistic health, and the practice of health education', *American Journal of Health Education* 35, pp. 11–18.

Hay, D., 2006, *Something There: The Biology of the Human Spirit*, London: Darton, Longman & Todd.

Hay, D. with Nye, R., 2006, *The Spirit of the Child*, London: Jessica Kingsley.

Heine, S., Lehman, D., Markus, H. and Kitayama, S., 1999, 'Is there a universal need for positive self-regard?', *Psychological Review* 106, pp. 766–94.

Held, B., 2004, 'The negative side of positive psychology', *Journal of Humanistic Psychology* 44, pp. 9–46.

Hemsley, D., 2005, 'The development of a cognitive model of schizophrenia: placing it in context', *Neuroscience and Behavioral Reviews* 29, pp. 977–88.

Henrich, J. and Gil-White, F., 2001, 'The evolution of prestige: freely conferred deference as a mechanism for enhancing the benefits of cultural transmission', *Evolution and Human Behavior* 22, pp. 165–96.

Holloway, R., 2002, *On Forgiveness: How Can We Forgive the Unforgivable?*, Edinburgh: Canongate.

Holmes, J., 2001, *The Search for the Secure Base: Attachment Theory and Psychotherapy*, London: Routledge.

Hood, R., 1977, 'Eliciting mystical states of consciousness with semistructured nature experiences', *Journal for the Scientific Study of Religion* 17, pp. 278–87.

Hood, R., 1992, 'Sin and guilt in faith traditions: issues for self-esteem', in J. Schumaker (ed.), *Religion and Mental Health*, New York: Oxford University Press, pp. 110–21.

Hood, R., Hill, P. and Spilka, B., 2009, *The Psychology of Religion: An Empirical Approach*, New York: Guilford.

Horn, J., 1996, *Mystical Healing: The Psychological and Spiritual Power of the Ignatian Spiritual Exercises*, New York: Crossroad.

Horrell, D., 2002, '"Becoming Christian": solidifying identity and content', in A. Blasi, J. Duhaime and P.-A. Turcotte (eds), *Handbook of Early Christianity: Social Science Approaches*, Walnut Creek, CA: Alta Mira Press, pp. 309–35.

Howell, A., Dopko, R., Turowski, J. and Buro, K., 2011, 'The disposition to apologise', *Personality and Individual Differences* 51, pp. 509–14.

Howells, E. and Tyler, P., 2010, *Sources of Transformation: Revitalising Christian Spirituality*, London: Continuum.

Hughes, G., 2008, *God of Surprises*, London: Darton, Longman & Todd.

Hughes, T. O., 2013, *The Compassion Quest*, London: SPCK.

Hunsberger, B. and Jackson, L., 2005, 'Religion, meaning, and prejudice', *Journal of Social Issues* 61, pp. 807–26.

Ignatius of Loyola, 1996, *Personal Writings*, tr. J. Munitiz and P. Endean, London: Penguin.

Ingalls Wilder, L., 1941, *Little Town on the Prairie*, New York: Harper.

Inhelder, B. and Piaget, J., 1958, *The Growth of Logical Thinking from Childhood to Adolescence*, London: Routledge & Kegan Paul.

Irons, W., 2001, 'Religion as a hard-to-fake sign of commitment', in R. Nesse (ed.), *The Evolution of Commitment*, New York: Russell Sage Foundation, pp. 292–309.

James, W., 1902, *The Varieties of Religious Experience*, New York: Longmans, Green & Co.

Janoff-Bulman, R., 1992, *Shattered Assumptions: Towards a New Psychology of Trauma*, New York: The Free Press.

Jay, J., 1993, 'Realistic Group Conflict Theory: a Review and Evaluation of the Theoretical and Empirical Literature', *Psychological Record* 43, pp. 395–415.

Jenkins, S., 1998, *Windows into Heaven: The Icons and Spirituality of Russia*, Oxford: Lion.

Jewell, A., 2011, *Spirituality and Personhood in Dementia*, London: Jessica Kingsley.

Johnson, E., 2010, *Psychology and Christianity: Five Views*, Downers Grove, IL: InterVarsity Press.

Jones, D. and Francis, L., 1992, 'Personality profiles of Methodist ministers in England', *Psychological Reports* 70, p. 538.

Jones, J., 1995, *Affects as Process: An Inquiry into the Centrality of Affect in Psychological Life*, London: Routledge.

Jones, J., 2002, *Terror and Transformation: The Ambiguity of Religion in Psychoanalytic Perspective*, Hove: Brunner-Routledge.

Jones, J., 2008, *Blood that Cries out from the Earth: The Psychology of Religious Terrorism*, Oxford: Oxford University Press.

Jonte-Pace, D. and Parsons, W. B., 2001, *Religion and Psychology: Mapping the Terrain*, London and New York: Routledge.

Jose, P., Lim, B. and Bryant, F., 2012, 'Does savoring increase happiness? A daily diary study', *The Journal of Positive Psychology* 7, pp. 176–87.

Joseph, S., 2009, 'Growth following adversity: positive psychological perspectives on posttraumatic stress', *Psychological Topics* 18, pp. 35–344.

Julius, H., Beetz, A., Turner, D., Kotrschal, K. and Uvnäs-Moberg, K., 2013, *Attachment to Pets: An Integrative View of Human-Animal Relationships with Implications for Therapeutic Practice*, Cambridge, MA: Hogrefe.

Jung, C. G., 1954, *Answer to Job*, London: Routledge & Kegan Paul.

Kabat-Zinn, J., 1982, 'An outpatient program in behavioral medicine for chronic pain patients based on the practice of mindfulness meditation: theoretical considerations and preliminary results', *General Hospital Psychiatry* 4, pp. 33–47.

Kagan, J., 2013, *The Human Spark: The Science of Human Development*, New York: Basic Books.

Kelemen, D., 2004, 'Are children "intuitive theists"? Reasoning about purpose and design in nature', *Psychological Science* 15, pp. 295–301.

Kellenberger, J., 2012, *Dying to Self and Detachment*, Farnham: Ashgate.

Keltner, D. and Haidt, 2003, 'Approaching awe, a moral, spiritual, and aesthetic emotion', *Cognition and Emotion* 17, pp. 297–314.

Kempster, P. and Alty, J., 2008, 'John Ruskin's relapsing encephalopathy', *Brain* 131, pp. 2520–5.

Kerns, K., 2008, 'Attachment in middle childhood', in J. Cassidy and P. Shaver (eds), *Handbook of Attachment: Theory, Research, and Clinical Applications*, New York: Guilford, pp. 366–82.

Kernis, M., 2003, 'Toward a conceptualization of optimal self-esteem', *Psychological Inquiry* 14, pp. 1–26.

Kille, D. A., 2004, '"The Bible made me do it!" Text, interpretation and violence', in J. H. Ellens (ed.), *The Destructive Power of Religion*, Volume 1, Westport, CT: Praeger, pp. 60–2.

King, L., 2001, 'The hard road to the good life: the happy, mature person', *Journal of Humanistic Psychology* 41, pp. 51–72.

Kirkpatrick, L., 1992, 'An attachment-theory approach to the psychology of religion', *The International Journal for Psychology of Religion* 2, pp. 3–28.

Kirkpatrick, L., 2004, *Attachment, Evolution, and the Psychology of Religion*, New York: Guilford.

Koenig, H., McCullough, M. and Larson, D., 2001, *Handbook of Religion and Health*, New York: Oxford University Press.

LaBouff, J., Rowatt, W., Johnson, M., Tsang, J.-A. and McCullough Willerton, G., 2012, 'Humble persons are more helpful than less humble persons. Evidence from three studies', *The Journal of Positive Psychology* 7, pp. 16–29.

Lambert, M., Stillman, T. and Fincham, F., 2013, 'Autobiographical narratives of spiritual experiences: solitude, tragedy, and the absence of materialism', *The Journal of Positive Psychology* 8, pp. 273–9.

Lazarus, R., 1991, *Emotion and Adaptation*, Oxford: Oxford University Press.

Lazarus, R., 2003, 'Does the positive psychology movement have legs?', *Psychological Inquiry* 14, pp. 93–109.

Leary, M., Tate, E., Adams, C., Allen, A. and Hancock, J., 2007, 'Self-compassion and reactions to unpleasant self-relevant events: the implications of treating oneself kindly', *Journal of Personality and Social Psychology* 47, pp. 748–55.

Lee, M. and Poloma, M., 2009, *A Sociological Study of the Great Commandment in Pentecostalism: The Practice of Godly Love or Benevolent Service*, New York: Edwin Mellen.

Lee, M., Poloma, M. and Post, S., 2013, *The Heart of Religion: Spiritual Empowerment, Benevolence, and the Experience of God's Love*, New York: Oxford University Press.

Leigh, J., Bowen, S. and Marlatt, G., 2005, 'Spirituality, mindfulness and substance abuse', *Addictive Behaviors* 30, pp. 1335–41.

Lepore, S. and Revenson, T., 2006, 'Relationships between posttraumatic growth and resilience: recovery, resistance, and reconfiguration', in L. Calhoun and R. Tedeschi (eds), *Handbook of Posttraumatic Growth: Research and Practice*, New York: Lawrence Erlbaum, pp. 24–46.

Levinas, E., 1981, *Otherwise Than Being*, Pittsburgh, PA: Duquesne University Press.

Lewis, A., 2003, *Between Cross and Resurrection: A Theology of Holy Saturday*, Grand Rapids, MI: Eerdmans.

Lewis, C. S., 1940, 'Letter to Eliza Marian Butler, 25 September 1940', in W. Hooper (ed.), *The Collected Letters of C. S. Lewis*, San Francisco: HarperOne, pp. 444–6 (2004).

Lewis, C. S., 1960, *The Four Loves*, London: Geoffrey Bles.

Lewis, C. S., 2009, *The Horse and His Boy*, London: Harper Collins.

Linley, P. A., 2003, 'Positive adaptation to trauma: wisdom as both process and outcome', *Journal of Traumatic Stress* 16, pp. 601–10.

Linley, P. A., 2008, *Average to A+: Realising Strengths in Yourself and Others*, Warwick: CAPP Press.

Linley, P. A. and Joseph, S., 2004, 'Positive change following trauma and adversity: a review', *Journal of Traumatic Stress* 17, pp. 11–21.

Loder, J., 1989, *The Transforming Moment*, Colorado Springs, CO: Helmers & Howard.

Loehlin, J., McCrae, R., Costa, P. and John, O., 1998, 'Heritabilities of common and measure-specific components of big five personality factors', *Journal of Research in Personality* 32, pp. 431–53.

McAdams, D., 1996, 'Personality, modernity, and the storied self: a contemporary framework for studying persons', *Psychological Inquiry* 7, pp. 295–321.

McAdams, D., 2006, *The Redemptive Self: Stories Americans Live By*, New York: Oxford University Press.

McAdams, D. and Pals, J., 2006, 'A new big five: fundamental principles for an integrative science of personality', *American Psychologist* 61, pp. 204–17.

McAfee Brown, R., 1988, *Spirituality and Liberation: Overcoming the Great Fallacy*, Philadelphia: Westminster John Knox Press.

Macaskill, A., Maltby, J. and Day, L., 2002, 'Forgiveness of self and others and emotional empathy', *The Journal of Social Psychology* 142, pp. 663–5.

McCrae, R. and Costa, P., 1990, *Personality in Adulthood*, New York: Guilford Press.

McCrae, R., Costa, P., Del Pilar, G., Rolland, J-P. and Parker, W., 1998, 'Cross-cultural assessment of the five-factor model: the revised NEO-PI', *Cross-cultural Psychology* 29, pp. 171–88.

McCullough, M., 2008, *Beyond Revenge: The Evolution of the Forgiveness Instinct*, San Francisco: Jossey-Bass.

McCullough, M., Fincham, F. and Tsang, J., 2003, 'Forgiveness, forbearance, and time: the temporal unfolding of transgression-related interpersonal motivations', *Journal of Personality and Social Psychology* 84, pp. 540–57.

McCullough, M., Pargament, K. and Thoresen, C., 2001, *Forgiveness: Theory, Research, and Practice*, New York: Guilford Press.

McGrath, A., 2008, 'The open secret: the ambiguity of nature', in A. McGrath, *The Open Secret: A New Vision for Natural Theology*, Oxford: Blackwell, pp. 115–39.

McGrath, A., 2009, *Heresy: A History of Defending the Truth*, New York: Harper Collins.

McGrath, A. and Collicutt, J., 2008, 'A Christian approach to natural theology', in A. McGrath, *The Open Secret: A New Vision for Natural Theology*, Oxford: Blackwell, pp. 171–217.

McGrath, J. and Adams, L., 1999, 'Patient-centred goal planning: a systemic psychological therapy?', *Topics in Stroke Rehabilitation* 6, pp. 43–50.

McGrath, J. and McGrath, A., [1992] 2001, *Self-esteem: The Cross and Christian Confidence*, Leicester: InterVarsity Press.

McIntyre, A., 2007, *After Virtue: A study in Moral Theory*, Notre Dame, IN: University of Notre Dame Press.

MACSAS, 2011, *The Stones Cry Out: Survey Report*, www.macsas.org.uk/MACSAS_SurveyReportMay2011.pdf.

Main, M. and Solomon, J., 1986, 'Discovery of an insecure-disorganized/disoriented attachment pattern', in T. Brazelton and M. Yogman (eds), *Affective Development in Infancy*, Westport, CT: Ablex Publishing, pp. 95–124.

Maltby, J., Wood, A., Day, L., Kon, T., Colley, P. and Linley, P. A., 2008, 'Personality predictors of levels of forgiveness two and a half years after the transgression', *Journal of Research in Personality* 42, pp. 1088–94.

Mann, M., Hosman, C., Schaalma, H. and de Vries, K., 2003, 'Self-esteem in a broad-spectrum approach for mental health promotion', *Health Education Research* 9, pp. 357–72.

Mansbridge, J., 1990, *Beyond Self-interest*, Chicago, IL: University of Chicago Press.

Martin, R., 2006, *The Psychology of Humor: An Integrative Approach*, Burlington, MA: Academic Press.

Meggitt, J. J., 2007, 'The madness of King Jesus', *Journal for the Study of the New Testament* 29, pp. 379–413.

Memmott, A., 2009, *Positive About Autism Newsletter*, http://www.positiveaboutautism.co.uk/attachments/Ann_Memmott.pdf.

Mickler, C. and Staudinger, U., 2008, 'Personal wisdom: validation and age-related differences of a performance measure', *Psychology and Aging* 23, pp. 787–99.

Mikulincer, M. and Shaver, P., 2004, 'Security-based self-representations in adulthood: contents and processes', in W. Rhodes and J. Simpson (eds), *Adult Attachment: Theory, Research, and Clinical Implications*, New York: Guilford Press, pp. 159–205.

Mikulincer, M., Shaver, P., Gillath, O. and Nitzberg, R., 2005, 'Attachment, caregiving, and altruism: boosting attachment security increases compassion and helping', *Journal of Personality and Social Psychology* 89, pp. 817–39.

Milgram, S., 1965, 'Some Conditions of obedience and disobedience to authority', *Human Relations* 18, pp. 57–76.

Miller, J., 1992, *In the Throe of Wonder: Intimations of the Sacred in a Postmodern World*, Albany, NY: State University of New York Press.

Miller, W. and C'de Baca, J., 1994/2001, *Quantum Change: When Epiphanies and Sudden Insights Transform Ordinary Lives*, New York: Guildford.

Miller, W. and C'de Baca, J., 1994, 'Quantum change: toward a psychology of transformation', in T. Heatherton and J. Lee (eds), *Can Personality Change?*, Washington, DC: American Psychological Association, pp. 253–80.

Mischel, W., 1968, *Personality and Assessment*, New York: Wiley.

Mischel, W. and Shoda, Y., 1995, 'A cognitive-affective system theory of personality: reconceptualizing situations, dispositions, dynamics, and invariance in personality structure', *Psychological Review* 102, pp. 246–68.

Moltmann, J., 1992, *The Spirit of Life*, Minneapolis, MN: Fortress Press.

Monbourquette, J., 2000, *How to Forgive: A Step-by-step Guide*, London: Darton, Longman & Todd.

Moore, A., 2010, 'Should Christians do natural theology?', *Scottish Journal of Theology* 63, pp. 127–45.

Morris, M. and Blanton, P., 1998, 'Predictors of family functioning among clergy and spouses: influences of social context and perceptions of work-related stressors', *Journal of Child and Family Studies* 7, pp. 27–41.

Muraven, M. and Baumeister, R., 2000, 'Self-regulation and depletion of limited resources: does self-control resemble a muscle?', *Psychological Bulletin* 126, pp. 247–59.

Murphy, F., 2007, *God is Not a Story: Realism Revisited*, Oxford: Oxford University Press.

Nakamura, J. and Csikszentmihalyi, M., 2002, 'The concept of flow', in C. Snyder and S. Lopez (eds), *Handbook of Positive Psychology*, New York: Oxford University Press, pp. 89–103.

National Institute for Health and Clinical Excellence (NICE), 2009, 'Depression: the treatment and management of depression in adults', *NICE Clinical Guideline 90*, London: NHS.

Nelstrop, L., Magill, K. and Onishi, B., 2009, *Christian Mysticism: An Introduction to Contemporary Theoretical Approaches*, Farnham: Ashgate.

Newsom, C., 2012, 'Positive psychology and ancient Israelite wisdom', in B. Strawn (ed.), *The Bible and the Pursuit of Happiness*, New York: Oxford University Press, pp. 117–35.

Niemiec, R., 2013, *Mindfulness and Character Strengths: A Practical Guide to Flourishing*, Göttingen: Hogrefe.

Nouwen, H., 1975, *Reaching Out: The Three Movements of the Spiritual Life*, Garden City, NY: Doubleday.

Nouwen, H., 1994, *The Return of the Prodigal Son: A Story of Homecoming*, London: Darton, Longman & Todd.

Nouwen, H., 1997, *Bread for the Journey*, London: Darton, Longman & Todd.

Nouwen, H., 2006, *With Open Hands*, Notre Dame, IN: Ave Maria Press.

Nussbaum, M., 1996, 'Compassion: the basic social emotion', *Social Philosophy and Policy* 13, pp. 27–58.

Oakes, L., 1997, *Prophetic Charisma: The Psychology of Revolutionary Religious Leaders*, Syracuse, NY: Syracuse University Press.

O'Brien, K., 2011, *The Ignatian Adventure: Experiencing the Spiritual Exercises of Saint Ignatius Loyola in Daily Life*, Chicago, IL: Loyola Press.

O'Donahue, J., 2007, *Benedictus: A Book of Blessings*, New York: Bantam Press.

Otto, R., 1958, *The Idea of the Holy*, tr. J. W. Harvey, Oxford: Oxford University Press.

Otway, L. and Vignoles, V., 2006, 'Narcissism and childhood recollections: a quantitative test of psychoanalytic predictions', *Personality and Social Psychology Bulletin* 32, pp. 104–16.

Painter, C. V., 2012, *Lectio Divina: The Sacred Art*, London: SPCK.

Paloutzian, R., Richardson, J. and Rambo, L., 1999, 'Religious conversion and personality change', *Journal of Personality* 67, pp. 1047–79.

Panksepp, J., 1986, 'The anatomy of emotions', in Plutchik, R. and Kellerman, H. (eds), *Emotion: Theory, Research and Experience*, Volume III, New York, Academic Press.

Panksepp, J., 1998, *Affective Neuroscience: The Foundations of Human and Animal Emotions*, New York: Oxford University Press.

Panksepp, J. and Burgdorf, J., 2003, '"Laughing" rats and the evolutionary antecedents of human joy?', *Physiology and Behavior* 79, pp. 533–47.

Panksepp, J. and Biven, L., 2012, *The Archaeology of Mind: Neuroevolutionary Origins of Human Emotions*, New York: Norton.

Panksepp, J., Nelson, E. and Bekkedal, M., 1997, 'Brain systems for the meditation of social separation-distress and social-reward: evolutionary antecedents and neuropeptide intermediaries', *Annals of the New York Academy of Science* 807, pp. 78–100.

Pargament, K., 1996, 'Religious Methods of Coping: sources for the Conservation and Transformation of Significance', in E. Shafranske (ed.), *Religion and the Clinical Practice of Psychology*, Washington, DC: American Psychological Association, pp. 215–35.

Pargament, K., 1999, 'The psychology of religion and spirituality? Yes and no', *International Journal for the Psychology of Religion* 9, pp. 3–16.

Pargament, K., 2001, *The Psychology of Religion and Coping*, New York: Guilford.

Pargament, K., Koenig, H. and Perez, L., 2000, 'The many methods of religious coping: development and initial validation of the RCOPE', *Journal of Clinical Psychology* 56, pp. 519–43.

Pargament, K., Smith, B., Koenig, H. and Perez, L., 1998, 'Patterns of positive and negative religious coping with major life stressors', *Journal for the Scientific Study of Religion* 37, pp. 710–24.

Park, N., Peterson, C. and Seligman, M., 2006, 'Character strengths in fifty-four nations and fifty US states', *The Journal of Positive Psychology* 1, pp. 118–29.

Parkes, C. M., 2010, *Bereavement: Studies of Grief in Adult Life*, London: Penguin.

Pasupathi, M., 2001, 'The social construction of the personal past and its implications for adult development', *Psychological Bulletin* 127, pp. 651–72.

Pasupathi, M. and Staudinger, U., 2003, 'Do advanced moral reasoners also show wisdom? Linking moral reasoning and wisdom-related judgement', *International Journal of Behavioral Development* 25, pp. 401–15.

Pasupathi, M., Staudinger, U. and Baltes, P., 2001, 'Seeds of wisdom: adolescents' knowledge and judgment about difficult life problems', *Developmental Psychology* 37, pp. 351–61.

Pattison, S., 2001, *Shame: Theory, Therapy, Theology*, Cambridge: Cambridge University Press.

Pawelski, J., 2007, *The Dynamic Individualism of William James*, Albany, NY: State University of New York Press.

Pembroke, N., 2010, *Pastoral Care in Worship: Liturgy and Psychology in Dialogue*, London: T. & T. Clark, pp. 25–43.

Pepping, C., O'Donovan, A. and Davis, P., 2013, 'The positive effects of mindfulness on self-esteem', *The Journal of Positive Psychology* 8, pp. 376–86.

Percy, E., 2014, *Mothering as a Metaphor for Ministry*, Farnham: Ashgate.

Peterson, C., Maier, S. and Seligman, M., 1995, *Learned Helplessness: A Theory for the Age of Personal Control*, New York: Oxford University Press.

Peterson, C. and Seligman, M., 2004, *Character Strengths and Virtues: A Handbook and Classification*, New York: Oxford University Press.

Peterson, C. and Park, N., 2009, 'Classifying and measuring strengths of character', in Lopez and Snyder (eds), *Oxford Handbook of Positive Psychology*, New York: Oxford University Press, pp. 25–34.

Peterson, C., Park, N., Hall, N. and Seligman, M., 2009, 'Zest and work', *Journal of Organizational Behavior* 30, pp. 161–72,

Phillips, D., 1965, *The Concept of Prayer*, Oxford: Blackwell.

Piaget, J. and Inhelder, B., 1948/1956, *La representation de l'espace chez l'enfant/The child's conception of space*, Paris: Presses Universitaires de France/ London: Routledge & Kegan Paul.

Pichon, I., Boccato, G. and Saroglou, V., 2007, 'Nonconscious influences of religion on prosociality: a priming study', *European Journal of Social Psychology* 37, pp. 1032–45.

Piedmont, R., Williams, J. and Ciarrochi, J., 1997, 'Personality correlates of one's image of Jesus', *Journal of Psychology and Theology* 25, pp. 364–73.

Plante, T., 2012, *Religion, Spirituality, and Positive Psychology: Understanding the Psychological Fruits of Faith*, Santa Barbara, CA: Praeger.

Popper, K., 1963, *Conjectures and Refutations: The Growth of Scientific Knowledge*, London: Routledge & Kegan Paul.

Posner, M., 1980, 'Orienting of attention', *Quarterly Journal of Experimental Psychology* 32, pp. 3–25.

Post, S., 2003, *Unlimited Love: Altruism, Compassion, and Service*, Philadelphia, PA: Templeton Foundation Press.

Premack, D., 1959, 'Toward empirical behavior laws: I. Positive reinforcement', *Psychological Review* 66, pp. 219–33.

Procter, A. and Procter, E., 2012, *Encountering Depression: Frequently Asked Questions Answered for Christians*, London: SPCK.

Proeschold-Bell, R., LeGrand, S., James, J., Wallace, A., Adams, C. and Toole, D., 2011, 'A theoretical model of the holistic health of United Methodist clergy', *Journal of Religion and Health* 50, pp. 700–20.

Pruyser, P., 1985, 'Forms and functions of the imagination in religion', *Bulletin of the Menninger Clinic* 49, pp. 353–70.

Puett, M. and Simon, B., 2008, *Ritual and Its Consequences*, New York: Oxford University Press.

Ramel, W., Goldin, P., Carmona, P. and McQuaid, J., 2004, 'The effects of mindfulness meditation on cognitive processes and affect in patients with past depression', *Cognitive Therapy and Research* 28, pp. 433–55.

Ramsey, M., 2008, *The Christian Priest Today*, London: SPCK.

Ricoeur, P., 1967, *The Symbolism of Evil*, Boston, MA: Beacon Press.

Ricoeur, P., 1970, *Freud and Philosophy: An Essay on Interpretation*, New Haven, CT: Yale University Press.

Rizzolatti, G., Fadiga, L., Fogassi, L. and Gallese, V., 1996, 'Premotor cortex and the recognition of motor actions', *Cognitive Brain Research* 3, pp. 131–41.

Rizzuto, A-M., 1979, *The Birth of the Living God: A Psychoanalytic Study*, Chicago, IL: Chicago University Press.

Roberts, R., 2004, 'The blessings of gratitude: a conceptual analysis', in R. Emmons and M. McCullough (eds), *The Psychology of Gratitude*, New York: Oxford University Press, pp. 58–78.

Roberts, R., 2007, *Spiritual Emotions: A Psychology of Christian Virtues*, Grand Rapids, MI: Eerdmans.

Robertson, J. and Robertson, J., 1989, *Separation in the Very Young*, London: Free Association Press.

Roitto, R., 2012, 'Practices of confession, intercession, and forgiveness in 1 John 1.9; 5.16', *New Testament Studies* 58, pp. 235–53.

Rosenthal, T. and Bandura, A., 1978, 'Psychological modelling: theory and practice', in S. Garfield and A. Bergin (eds), *Handbook of Psychotherapy and Behaviour Change*, New York: Wiley, pp. 621–58.

Rosmarin, D., Pirutinsky, S., Cohen, A., Galler, Y. and Krumrei, E., 2011, 'Grateful to God or just plain grateful? A comparison of religious and general gratitude', *The Journal of Positive Psychology* 6, pp. 389–96.

Rothbart, M., Ahadi, S. and Evans, D., 2000, 'Temperament and personality: origins and outcomes', *Journal of Personality and Social Psychology* 78, pp. 122–35.

Roukema-Koning, B., 2007, 'Prayer as a psychological phenomenon: proposal of concepts contributing to theory and research', paper presented at the *International Conference in Spirituality*, Prague, Czech Republic.

Royzman, E., Cassidy, K. and Baron, J., 2003, 'I know you know: epistemic egocentrism in children and adults', *Review of General Psychology* 7, pp. 38–65.

Rozin, P. and Royzman, E., 2001, 'Negativity bias, negativity dominance, and contagion', *Personality and Social Psychology Review* 5, pp. 296–320.

Ruch, W., 1993, 'Exhilaration and humor', in M. Lewis and J. M. Haviland (eds), *The Handbook of Emotion*, New York: Guilford, pp. 605–16.

Rudolph, U., Roesch, S., Greitemeyer, T. and Weiner, B., 2004, 'A meta-analytic review of help giving and aggression from an attributional perspective: contributions to a general theory of motivation', *Cognition and Emotion* 18, pp. 815–48.

Rumsey, P., 2003, 'The Liturgy of the Hours: are we biologically programmed?', *New Blackfriars* 84, 462–72.

Rumsey, P., 2008, 'Liturgy, time, and the politics of redemption', *International Journal of Systematic Theology* 10, pp. 356–8.

Ruskin, J., 1860, *Modern Painters V*, London: Smith, Elder & Co.

Ruskin, J., 1894, *Letters addressed to a college friend during the years 1840–1845*, London: George Allen.

Ruskin, J., 1907, *Praeterita Volume II*, London: George Allen.

Sacks, O., 2011, *The Man who Mistook His Wife for a Hat*, London: Picador.

Salter, M. D., 1940, *An Evaluation of Adjustment based upon the Concept of Security*, Toronto: University of Toronto Press.

Sandage, S., 2006, 'Spirituality and human development', in F. L. Shults and S. Sandage (eds), *Transforming Spirituality: Integrating Theology and Psychology*, Grand Rapids, MI: Baker Academic, pp. 153–86.

Sandage, S., 2012, 'The transformation of happiness', in B. Strawn (ed.), *The Bible and the Pursuit of Happiness*, New York: Oxford University Press, pp. 263–86.

Savage, S., 2007, 'Healing encounters', in F. Watts (ed.), *Jesus and Psychology*, London: Darton, Longman & Todd, pp. 44–61.

Savage, S. and Boyd-MacMillan, E., 2007, *The Human Face of the Church: A Social Psychology and Pastoral Theology Resource for Pioneer and Traditional Ministry*, Norwich: Canterbury Press.

Savage, S. and Liht, J., 2008, 'Mapping fundamentalisms: the psychology of religion as a sub discipline in the prevention of religiously motivated violence', *The Archive for the Psychology of Religion* 30, pp. 75–91.

Savage, S. and Boyd-MacMillan, E., 2010, *Conflict in Relationships: At Home, at Work, in Life: Understand It, Overcome It*, Oxford: Lion.

Scheepers, P., Gijsberts, M. and Hello, E., 2002, 'Religiosity and prejudice against ethnic minorities in Europe: cross-national tests on a controversial relationship', *Review of Religious Research* 43, pp. 242–65.

Schimmel, S., 2004, 'Interpersonal forgiveness and repentance in Judaism', in F. Watts and L. Gulliford (eds), *Forgiveness in Context: Theology and Psychology in Creative Dialogue*, London: T. & T. Clark, pp. 11–28.

Schmemann, A., 1963, *For the Life of the World*, New York: St Vladimir's Seminary Press.

Schnall, S., Roper, S. and Fessler, D., 2010, 'Elevation leads to altruistic behaviour', *Psychological Science* 21, pp. 315–20.

Schore, A., 2001, 'Effects of a secure attachment relationship on right brain development, affect regulation, and infant mental health', *Infant Mental Health Journal* 22, pp. 7–66.

Schultz, J., Tallman, B. and Altmaier, E., 2010, 'Pathways to posttraumatic growth: the contributions of forgiveness and importance of religion and spirituality', *Psychology of Religion and Spirituality* 2, pp. 104–14.

Schüssler Fiorenza, E., 1994, *Jesus: Miriam's Child, Sophia's Prophet*, London: SCM Press.

Schüssler Fiorenza, E., 2009, *Democratizing Biblical Studies: Towards an Emancipatory Educational Space*, Louisville, KY: Westminster John Knox Press.

Scott, J., 1996, 'The triumph of God in 2 Corinthians 2:14: additional evidence of merkabah mysticism in Paul', *New Testament Studies* 42, pp. 260–81.

Segal, Z., Williams, J. M. G. and Teasdale, J., 2013, *Mindfulness-based Cognitive Therapy for Depression*, New York: Guilford.

Seligman, M., 1999, 'The president's address', *American Psychologist* 54, pp. 559–62.

Seligman, M., 2002, *Authentic Happiness: Using the New Positive Psychology to Realize Your Potential for Lasting Fulfillment*, New York: The Free Press.

Seligman, M., Parks, A. and Steen, T., 2004, 'A balance psychology and a full life', *Philosophical Transactions of the Royal Society of London* 359, pp. 1379–81.

Selvam, S. G., 2013, 'Towards religious spirituality: a multidimensional matrix for religion and spirituality', *Journal for the Study of Religions and Ideologies* 12, pp. 129–52.

Selvam, S. G. and Collicutt, J., 2012, 'The ubiquity of character strengths in African Traditional Religion: a thematic analysis', in H-H. Knoop and A. Delle Fave (eds), *Well-being and Cultures: Perspectives from Positive Psychology*, New York: Springer, pp. 83–102.

Shapiro, D., 1980, *Meditation: Self-Regulation Strategy and Altered State of Consciousness*, New York: Aldine.

Shapiro, S. and Sahgal, M., 2012, 'Loving-kindness', in T. Plante (ed.), *Religion, Spirituality, and Positive Psychology*, Santa Barbara, CA: Praeger.

Shariff, A. and Norenzayan, A., 2007, 'God is watching you: supernatural agent concepts increase prosocial behaviour in an anonymous economic game', *Psychological Science* 18, pp. 803–9.

Shaw, J., 2011, *Octavia, Daughter of God: The Story of a Female Messiah and her Followers*, London: Jonathan Cape.

Sheldon, K. and Elliot, A., 1999, 'Goal striving, need satisfaction, and longitudinal well-being: the self-concordance model', *Journal of Personality and Social Psychology* 76, pp. 482–97.

Sheldon, K. and Kasser, T., 1995, 'Coherence and congruence: two aspects of personality integration', *Journal of Personality and Social Psychology* 68, pp. 531–43.

Sheldrake, P., 2001, *Spaces for the Sacred: Place, Memory and Identity*, Baltimore, MD: Johns Hopkins University Press.

Sherif, M., Harvey, O., White, B. J., Hood, W. and Sherif, C., 1988, *The Robbers Cave Experiment: Intergroup Conflict and Cooperation*, Middletown, CT: Wesleyan University Press.

Shin, D., 1999, 'Some light on Origen: scripture as sacrament', *Worship* 73, pp. 399–425.

Shiota, M., Keltner, D. and Mossman, A., 2007, 'The nature of awe: elicitors, appraisals, and effects on self-concept', *Cognition and Emotion* 21, pp. 944–63.

Shults, F. L., 2006, 'Becoming just', in F. L. Shults and S. Sandage (eds), *Transforming Spirituality: Integrating Theology and Psychology*, Grand Rapids, MI: Baker Academic, pp. 94–122.

Shults, F. L., 2006a, 'Reforming pneumatology', in F. L. Shults and S. Sandage (eds), *Transforming Spirituality: Integrating Theology and Psychology*, Grand Rapids, MI: Baker Academic, pp. 39–66.

Shults, F. L., 2006b, 'Becoming wise', in F. L. Shults and S. Sandage (eds), *Transforming Spirituality: Integrating Theology and Psychology*, Grand Rapids, MI: Baker Academic.

Shults, F. L. and Sandage, S. (eds), 2006, *Transforming Spirituality: Integrating Theology and Psychology*, Grand Rapids, MI: Baker Academic, Introduction, pp. 34–5.

Sidanius, M. and Pratto, F., 1999, *Social Dominance: An Intergroup Theory of Social Hierarchy and Oppression*, Cambridge: Cambridge University Press.

Siegel, D., 2007, 'Mindfulness training and neural integration: differentiation of distinct streams of awareness and the cultivation of well-being', *Social, Cognitive and Affective Neuroscience* 2, pp. 259–63.

Siegert, R., McPherson, K. and Taylor, W., 2004, 'Toward a cognitive-affective model of goal setting in rehabilitation: is self-regulation theory a key step?', *Disability and Rehabilitation* 26, pp. 1175–83.

Silf, M., 1998, *Landmarks: Exploration of Ignatian Spirituality*, London: Darton, Longman & Todd.

Silf, M., 2001, *Wayfaring: A Gospel Journey into Life*, London: Darton, Longman & Todd.

Silvers, J. and Haidt, J., 2008, 'Moral elevation can induce nursing', *Emotion* 8, pp. 291–95.

Singer, J. and Salvoley, P., 1993, *The Remembered Self: Emotion and Memory in Personality*, New York: The Free Press.

Sirgy, M. J. and Wu, J., 2009, 'The pleasant life, the engaged life and the meaningful life: what about the balanced life?', *Journal of Happiness Studies* 10, pp. 183–96.

Slone, D. J. and Van Slyke, J., 2015, *The Attraction of Religion: A New Evolutionary Psychology of Religion*, London: Bloomsbury Academic.

Smith, J., Staudinger, U. and Baltes, P., 1994, 'Occupational settings facilitating wisdom-related knowledge: the sample case of clinical psychologists', *Journal of Consulting and Clinical Psychology* 62, pp. 989–99.

Snyder, C. and Lopez, S., 2007, *Positive Psychology: The Scientific and Practical Explorations of Human Strengths*, Thousand Oaks, CA: Sage.

Soldz, S. and Vaillant, G., 1999, 'The big five personality traits and the life course: a 45-year longitudinal study', *Journal of Research in Personality* 33, pp. 208–32.

Srivastava, S., John, O., Gosling, S. and Potter, J., 2003, 'Development of personality in early and middle adulthood: set like plaster or persistent change?', *Journal of Personality and Social Psychology* 84, pp. 1041–53.

Stace, W., 1960, *Mysticism and Philosophy*, Philadelphia, PA: Lippincott.

Staudinger, U., 1999, 'Older and wiser? Integrating results on the relationship between age and wisdom-related performance', *International Journal of Behavioral Development* 23, pp. 641–64.

Staudinger, U., Maciel, A., Smith, J. and Baltes, P., 1998, 'What predicts wisdom-related performance? A first look at personality, intelligence, and facilitative experiential contexts', *European Journal of Personality* 12, pp. 1–7.

Staudinger, U. and Pasupathi, M., 2003, 'Correlates of wisdom-related performance in adolescence and adulthood: age-graded differences in "paths" toward desirable development', *Journal of Research on Adolescence* 13, pp. 239–68.

Staudinger, U. and Baltes, P., 2006, 'Interactive minds: a facilitative setting for wisdom-related performance?', *Journal of Personality and Social Psychology* 71, pp. 746–62.

Steger, M., Hicks, B., Kashdan, T., Krueger, R. and Bouchard, T., 2007, 'Genetic and environmental influences on the positive traits of the values in action classification, and biometric covariance with normal personality', *Journal of Research in Personality* 41, pp. 524–39.

Sternberg, R., 1998, 'A balance theory of wisdom', *Review of General Psychology* 2, pp. 347–65.

Sternberg, R. and Jordan, J., 2005, *A Handbook of Wisdom: Psychological Perspectives*, New York: Cambridge University Press.

Stone, L., 1979, 'The Revival of narrative: reflections on a new old history', *Past and Present* 85, pp. 3–24.

Tajfel, H., 1970, 'Experiments in intergroup discrimination', *Scientific American* 223, pp. 96–102.

Tajfel, H. and Turner, J. C., 1979, 'An integrative theory of intergroup conflict', in W. G. Austin and S. Worchel (eds), *The Social Psychology of Intergroup Relations*, Monterey, CA: Brooks-Cole, pp. 33–47.

Tal, K., 1996, *Worlds of Hurt: Reading the Literature of Trauma*, Cambridge: Cambridge University Press.

Tangney, J. P., 2000, 'Humility: theoretical perspectives, empirical findings and directions for future research', *Journal of Social and Clinical Psychology* 19, pp. 70–82.

Tangney, J. P., Fee, R., Reinsmith, C., Boone, A. and Lee, N., 1999, 'Assessing individual differences in the propensity to forgive', paper presented at the annual meeting of the American Psychological Association, Boston, MA.

Taylor, C., 1989, *Sources of the Self: The Making of Modern Identity*, Cambridge: Cambridge University Press.

Taylor, S. and Brown, J., 1994, 'Positive illusions and well-being revisited: separating fact from fiction', *Psychological Bulletin* 116, pp. 21–17.

Taylor, S., Kemeny, M., Reed, G., Bower, J. and Gruenewald, T., 2000, 'Psychological resources, positive illusions and health', *American Psychologist* 55, pp. 99–109.

Taylor, S., Klein, L., Lewis, B., Gruenewald, T., Gurung, R. and Updegraff, J., 2000, 'Biobehavioral responses to stress in females: tend-and-befriend, not fight-or-flight', *Psychological Review* 107, pp. 411–29.

Teasdale, J. and Barnard, P., 1993, *Affect, Cognition and Change: Re-modelling Depressive Thought*, Hove: Lawrence Erlbaum.

Tedeschi, R. and Calhoun, L., 1995, *Trauma and Transformation: Growing in the Aftermath of Suffering*, Thousand Oaks, CA: Sage.

Tedeschi, R. and Calhoun, L., 2004, 'Posttraumatic growth: conceptual foundations and empirical evidence', *Psychological Inquiry* 15, pp. 1–18.

Theissen, G., 1987, *The Shadow of the Galilean: The Quest of the Historical Jesus in Narrative Form*, London: SCM Press.

Thomas, A. and Chess, S., 1977, *Temperament and Development*, New York: Brunner/Mazel.

Thomas, A., Chess, S., Birch, H., Herzig, M. and Korn, S., 1963, *Behavioral Individuality in Early Childhood*, New York: New York University Press.

Thompson, J. and Thompson, R., 2012, *Mindful Ministry: Creative, Theological and Practical Perspectives*, London: SCM Press.

Tomkins, S., 1987, 'Script theory', in J. Aronoff, A. Robin and R. Zucker (eds), *The Emergence of Personality*, New York: Springer, pp. 147–216.

Tomlin, G., 2009, *Spiritual Fitness*, London: Continuum.

Toner, J., 1968, *The Experience of Love*, Washington, DC: Corpus Books.

Tucker, J. B., 2011, *You Belong to Christ: Paul and the Formation of Social Identity in 1 Corinthians 1–4*, Eugene, OR: Pickwick.

Turton, D. and Francis, L., 2007, 'The relationship between attitude toward prayer and professional burnout among Anglican parochial clergy in England: are praying clergy healthier clergy?', *Mental Health, Religion, and Culture* 10, pp. 61–74.

Tutu, D. and Tutu, M., 2014, *The Book of Forgiving*, London: William Collins.

Vaillant, G., 2008, *Spiritual Evolution: A Scientific Defense of Faith*, New York: Harmony.

van den Boom, D., 1994, 'The influence of temperament and mothering on attachment and exploration: an experimental manipulation of sensitive responsiveness among lower-class mothers with irritable infants', *Child Development* 65, pp. 1457–77.

van der Hart, W. and Waller, R., 2011, *The Worry Book: Finding a Path to Freedom*, Nottingham: InterVarsity Press.

van der Horst, F., LeRoy, H. and van der Veer, R., 2008, '"When strangers meet": John Bowlby and Harry Harlow on attachment behavior', *Integrative Psychology and Behavioral Science* 42, pp. 370–88.

van Os, B., 2007, 'Psychological method and the historical Jesus: the contribution of psychobiography', *Theological Studies* 63, pp. 327–46.

Van Tongeren, D., Burnette, J., O'Boyle, E., Worthington, E. and Forsyth, D., 2013, 'A meta-analysis of intergroup forgiveness', *The Journal of Positive Psychology* 9, pp. 81–95.

Vanstone, W., 1977, *Love's Endeavour, Love's Expense*, London: Darton, Longman & Todd.

Vanstone, W., 1982, *The Stature of Waiting*, London: Darton, Longman & Todd.

Varela, F., Thompson, E. and Rosch, E., 1993, 'The embodied mind: cognitive science and human experience', Cambridge, MA: MIT Press.

Verduyn, P. and Brans, K., 2011, 'The relationship between extraversion, neuroticism, and aspects of trait affect', *Personality and Individual Differences* 52, pp. 664–69.

Vinkhuyzen, A., van der Shuis, S., Posthuma, D. and Boomsma, D., 2009, 'The heritability of aptitude and exceptional talent across different dimensions in adolescents and young adults', *Behavior Genetics* 39, pp. 380–92.

Volf, M., 1994, *Exclusion and Embrace: Theological Exploration of Identity, Otherness and Reconciliation*, Nashville, TN: Abingdon Press.

Volling, B., Kolak, A. and Kennedy, D., 2009, 'Empathy and compassionate love in early childhood: development and family influence', in B. Fehr, S. Sprecher and L. Underwood (eds), *The Science of Compassionate Love: Theory, Research, and Applications*, Malden, MA: Wiley Blackwell, pp. 161–200.

von Rad, G., 1972, *Wisdom in Israel*, London: SCM Press.

Wade, N., Worthington, E. and Meyer, J., 2005, 'But do they work? A meta-analysis of group interventions to promote forgiveness', in E. Worthington (ed.), *Handbook of Forgiveness*, New York: Brunner-Routledge, pp. 423–39.

Wallace, H., Exline, J. and Baumeister, R., 2008, 'Interpersonal consequences of forgiveness: does forgiveness deter or encourage repeat offenses?', *Journal of Experimental Social Psychology* 44, pp. 453–60.

Wang, S., 2005, 'A conceptual framework for integrating research related to the physiology of compassion and the wisdom of Buddhist teachings', in P. Gilbert (ed.), *Compassion: Conceptualisations, Research and Use in Psychotherapy*, London: Routledge, pp. 75–120.

Wansbrough, H., 2010, *The Use and Abuse of the Bible: A Brief History of Biblical Interpretation*, London: T. & T. Clark.

Ward, B., 1975, *Selections from Sayings of the Desert Fathers*, Kalamazoo, MI: Cistercian Publications.

Ware, K., 2000, *The Inner Kingdom*, Crestwood, NY: St Vladimir's Seminary Press.

Watts, F., 2001, 'Prayer and psychology', in F. Watts (ed.), *Perspectives on Prayer*, London: SPCK, pp. 39–51.

Watts, F., 2002, *Theology and Psychology*, Aldershot: Ashgate.

Watts, F., 2004, 'Christian theology', in F. Watts and L. Gulliford (eds), *Forgiveness in Context: Theology and Psychology in Creative Dialogue*, London: T. & T. Clark, pp. 50–68.

Watts, F. and Williams, M., 1988, *The Psychology of Religious Knowing*, Cambridge: Cambridge University Press.

Weaver, A., Flannelly, K., Larson, D., Stapleton, C. and Koenig, H., 2002, 'Mental health issues among clergy and other religious professionals: a review of research', *The Journal of Pastoral Care and Counseling* 56, pp. 393–403.

Weber, R., Tamborini, R., Westcott-Baker, A. and Kantor, B., 2009, 'Theorizing flow and media enjoyment as cognitive synchronization of attentional and reward networks', *Communication Theory* 19, pp. 397–422.

Welch, S., 2011, *Every Place is Holy Ground: Prayer Journeys through Familiar Places*, Norwich: Canterbury Press.

Welch, S., 2013, *Walking the Labyrinth: A Spiritual Practice Guide*, Norwich: Canterbury Press.

Welp, L. and C. Brown, 2013, 'Self-compassion, empathy, and helping intentions', *The Journal of Positive Psychology* 9, pp. 54–65.

Wesley, John, Entry for 24 May 1738; *Journals and Diaries*, ed. W. Reginald Ward and Richard P. Heitzenrater, Nashville, TN: Abingdon, 1988, vol. 1, pp. 249–50.

Williams, M., Kabat-Zinn, J., Teasdale, J. and Zindel, S., 2007, *The Mindful Way through Depression*, New York: Guilford.

Williams, C., Richards, P. and Whitton, I., 2002, *I'm Not Supposed to Feel Like This: A Christian Approach to Depression and Anxiety*, London: Hodder & Stoughton.

Williams, R., 1982, *Resurrection: Interpreting the Easter Gospel*, London: Darton, Longman & Todd.

Williams, R., 1990, *The Wound of Knowledge*, London: Darton, Longman & Todd.

Williams, R., 2003, *The Dwelling of the Light: Praying with Icons of Christ*, Norwich: Canterbury Press.

Williams, R., 2003a, *Silence and Honey Cakes: The Wisdom of the Desert*, Oxford: Lion.

Willard, D., 1988, *The Spirit of the Disciplines: Understanding how God Changes Lives*, New York: Harper Collins.

Wimmer, H. and Permer, J., 1983, Beliefs about beliefs: representations and constraining function of wrong beliefs in young children's understanding of deception', *Cognition* 13, pp. 103–28.

Wink, P. and Helson, 1997, 'Practical and transcendent wisdom: their nature and some longitudinal findings', *Journal of Adult Development* 4, pp. 1–15.

Wink, P. and Dillon, M., 2002, 'Spiritual development across the adult life course: findings from a longitudinal study', *Journal of Adult Development* 9, pp. 79–94.

Winnicott, D., 1957, *The Child, the Family, and the Outside World*, London: Tavistock.

Winnicott, D., 1971, *Playing and Reality*, Middlesex: Penguin.

Wittgenstein, L., 1958, *The Blue and Brown Books*, New York: Harper Collins.

Witvliet, C., Worthington, E. and Wade, N., 2002, 'Victims' heart rate and facial EMG responses to receiving an apology and restitution', *Psychophysiology* 39, p. 588.

Witvliet, C. and McCullough, M., 2007, 'Forgiveness and health: a review and theoretical exploration of emotion pathways', in S. Post (ed.), *Altruism and Health: Perspectives from Empirical Research*, New York: Oxford University Press, pp. 259–76.

Wolpe, J., 1958, *Psychotherapy by Reciprocal Inhibition*, Redwood City, CA: Stanford University Press.

Worthington, E., 1998, 'An empathy-humility-commitment model of forgiveness applied within family dyads', *Journal of Family Therapy* 20, pp. 59–76.

Worthington, E., 2007, *Humility: The Quiet Virtue*, Philadelphia, PA: Templeton Press.

Worthington, E. and Scherer, M., 2004, 'Forgiveness is an emotion-focused coping strategy that can reduce health risks and promote health resilience: theory, review, and hypotheses', *Psychology and Health* 19, pp. 385–405.

Worthington, E., Davis, D., Hook, J., Webb, J., Toussaint, L., Sandage, S., Gartner, A. and Van Tongeren, D., 2012, 'Forgiveness', in T. Plante (ed.), *Religion, Spirituality, and Positive Psychology*, Santa Barbara, CA: Praeger, pp. 63–78.

Wright, N. T., 2010, *Virtue Reborn*, London: SPCK.

Wuthnow, R., 2000, *After Heaven: Spirituality in America since the 1950s*, Berkeley, CA: University of California Press.

Zagano, P. and Gillespie, C. K., 2006, 'Ignatian Spirituality and Positive Psychology', *The Way* 45, pp. 41–58.

Zahavi, A., 1995, 'Altruism as handicap: the limitations of kin selection and reciprocity', *Journal of Avian Biology* 26, pp. 1–3.

Zoellner, T. and Maercker, A., 2006, 'Posttraumatic growth in clinical psychology: a critical review and introduction of a two-component model', *Clinical Psychology Review* 26, pp. 626–35.

Sources for Boxed Quotations

Chapter 1

Irenaeus of Lyon, *Against heresies*, IV.xx.7, translation, 1867, *Anti-Nicene Christian Library*, Edinburgh: T & T Clark.

Maximus the Confessor, *The Church's Mystagogy*, in Berthold, G., 1985, *Maximus the Confessor: Selected Writings*, Mahwah, NJ: Paulist Press, p. 212.

Meister Eckhart, Sermon 10 of 'Selected German Sermons', in Davies, O., 1994, *Selected Writings by Meister Eckhart*, London: Penguin, p. 144.

Chapter 2

Merton, T., 1969, *My Argument with the Gestapo*, New York: New Directions, pp. 160–1.

Ruskin, J., 1849, *The Seven Lamps of Architecture*, London: Smith, Elder, & Company, p. 137.

Chapter 3

Thomas à Kempis, *The Imitation of Christ*, translated by Croft, A. and Bolton, H., 1940, Milwaukee, WI: Bruce Publishing Company, p. 1.

Williams, R., 1990, *The Wound of Knowledge*, London: Darton, Longman & Todd, p. 181.

Chapter 4

Butler, J., 1749, 'Upon Humane Nature', in *Fifteen Sermons Preached at the Rolls Chapel*, London: James & John Knapton, pp. 1–43.

Willard, D., 2006, *The Great Omission: Reclaiming Jesus' Essential Teachings on Discipleship*, Oxford: Monarch, p. 34.

Chapter 5

Augustine of Hippo, *Confessions*, X.xvii.26, translated by Chadwick, H., 1991, Oxford: Oxford University Press.

Therese of Lisieux (attributed, but source is anecdotal). This translation cited in Foley, M., 2000, *The Love that Keeps us Sane: Living the Little Way of St. Therese of Lisieux*, Mahway, NJ: Paulist Press, p. 54.

Chapter 6

Bunyan, J., 1678, *The Pilgrim's Progress*, London: Nathaniel Ponder, p. 19.

St. Patrick's Breastplate, translated by Alexander, C. F., 1889, *Hymns Ancient and Modern*, London: William Clowes.

Weil, S., 1952, *Waiting on God*, London: Fontana, p. 57.

Chapter 7

Athanasius of Alexandria, *Against the Heathen*, I.ii.2, trans. Thomson, R., 1971, Oxford: Clarendon Press.

Lewis, C. S., 1950, *The Lion, the Witch and the Wardrobe*, London: Geoffrey Bles, pp. 150-1. The Lion, the Witch and the Wardrobe by C. S. Lewis copyright © C.S. Lewis Pte. Ltd. 1950. Extract reprinted with permission.

Richard of Chichester (attributed). This version is based on one in Bullock-Webster, G., 1913, *The Churchman's Prayer Manual*, London: SPCK.

Traherne, T., 'Rapture', in Margoiouth, H., 1958, *Thomas Traherne: Centuries, Poems, and Thanksgivings, II*, Oxford: Oxford University Press, p. 30.

Chapter 8

Benedict of Nursia, *Rule*, lvii, translated by B. Verheyen, 1949, Atchison, KS: Abbey Student Press, p. 71.

Ignatius of Loyola, 1536, Letter of 18th June to Teresa Rejedell, translated by Munitiz, J. and Endean, P., 1996, *Saint Ignatius of Loyola: Personal Writings*, London: Penguin, p. 130.

Traherne, T. 'A Sober View of Dr. Twisses his Considerations', in Ross, J., 2005, *The Works of Thomas Traherne I*, Cambridge: D.S. Brewer, p. 119.

Chapter 9

Blake, W., 'Auguries of innocence', in Erdman, D., 1980, *The Complete Poetry and Prose of William Blake*, Berkeley, CA: University of California Press, p. 490.

Herbert, G., 1633, 'The Elixir', in *The Temple, Sacred Poems and Private Ejaculations*, Cambridge: Thomas Buck and Roger Daniel.

Hugh of St. Victor, 'De tribus diebus 4', in Eruditiones Didascalicae (*Migne Patrologia Patrologia Latina* 176 814B), Vatican Observatory translation: http://www.vaticanobser vatory.org/vo-news/news-archive/98-news-archive/the-two-books/518-the-two-books retrieved 20.8.14.

Meister Eckhart, German Sermon 6, translated by Walshe, M. O'C., 1979, *Meister Eckhart: Sermons and Treatises, I*, London: Watkins, p. 67.

Chapter 10

Benedict of Nursia, *Rule*, xlviii, translated by B. Verheyen, 1949, Atchison, KS: Abbey Student Press, p. 62.

Fanthorpe, U. A., 2010, 'Atlas' in *U A Fanthorpe, New and Collected Poems*, London: Enitharmon Press, p. 335. Reproduced with permission.

John of the Cross, Ascent of Mount Carmel. XI ii, translated by Peers, A. E., 1935, London: Burns & Oates, p. 49.

Liddell, E. ascribed in script by Colin Welland, 1981, *Chariots of Fire*, Goldrest Films.

Traherne, T., 'Wonder', in Margoiouth, H., 1958, *Thomas Traherne: Centuries, Poems, and Thanksgivings, II*, Oxford: Oxford University Press, p. 8.

Chapter 11

Benedict of Nursia, *Rule*, liii, translated by B. Verheyen, 1949, Atchison, KS: Abbey Student Press, p. 59.

Herbert, G., 1633, 'Love', in *The Temple, Sacred Poems and Private Ejaculations*, Cambridge: Thomas Buck and Roger Daniel.

Julian of Norwich, *Revelations of Divine Love* (Short Text), translated by Spearing, E., 1998, London: Penguin, p. 23.

'Warner' research participant quoted in Lee, M., Poloma, M. and Post, S., 2013, *The Heart of Religion: Spiritual Empowerment, Benevolence, and the Experience of God's Love*, New York: Oxford University Press, p. 132.

Chapter 12

Bonaventure, *The Life of Saint Francis*, VII. Vi, translated by Gurney Salter, E., 1904, London: J.M. Dent, p. 85.

Manley Hopkins, G., 1918, 'As kingfishers catch fire', in Bridges, R., 1918, *Poems of Gerard Manley Hopkins*, London: Humphrey Milford, p. 129.

Chapter 13

Gollancz, V., 1947, *In Darkest Germany*, Chicago, ILL: H. Regnery Company, p. 19.

Julian of Norwich, *Revelations of Divine Love* (Short Text), translated by Franklin Chambers, P. F., 1951, *Juliana of Norwich: An Appreciation and an Anthology*, London: Gollancz.

Tutu, D., 2010. *The forgiveness project*, http://theforgivenessproject.com/stories/desmond-tutu-south-africa/ retrieved 27.8.14.

Chapter 14

Athanasius of Alexandria, *Festal Letter* XXXIX.iii., translated by Thomson, R., 1971, Oxford: Clarendon Press.

Tillich, P., *The Eternal Now*, 1963, New York: Scribner, p. 168.

Chpter 15

Eliot, T. S., 1940, 'East Coker', in *Four Quartets*, London: Faber & Faber, reproduced with permission.

John of the Cross, 'The dark night of the soul', translated by Peers, A. E., 1935, London: Burns & Oates, p. 17.

Von Balthasaar, H. U., 1996, *Mysterium Paschale: The mystery of Easter*, translated by Nicholls, A., Grand Rapids, MI: Eerdmans, p. 179.

Weil, S., 1947, la Pesanteur et la Grâce', translated by Crauford, E., 1952, *Gravity and Grace*, London: Routledge & Kegan Paul, p. 62.

Index of Bible References

Genesis

1.26–27	59
1.26	97
2	156
2.7	3fn
3	69, 100, 214fn1
3.1	100
3.6	213
3.10	100
32–33	195
32.7–8	195
32.24–30	106

Exodus

1.10	221
3	178
3.3	79
3.6	31
3.14	97
21.23ff	197
33	7
36.2	221

Leviticus

24.15ff	197
26.40	197

Deuteronomy

10.19	161

Judges

12.5–6	163fn5

1 Samuel

3	136
14	222

1 Kings

18	125
19.11–12	125
22.19	178

1 Chronicles

22.15–16	221

Job

4.7	186
4.7–8	233
5.17–18	233
28	214
28.28	214
42.3	129
42.5	233
42.5–6	129

Psalms

1.1	166
1.3	13
2.9	3
8	124
8.3–4	135
10	239
17.8	62
22.1–2	62
23.4	62
23.5	174
27.5	69
89.26	69
110.10	214
139.14	114

Proverbs

1.7	214
5.1–14	214

8 105

8.2	214
8.30	105
8.31	106
9.10	214
15.33	214
24.13–14	142

Ecclesiastes

3.1	224
3.3	40

Song of Solomon

8.6–7	177

Isaiah

6	135
6.1–8	177
6.5	31
6.10	80
11.2	214
11.6–9	195
40.28–31	190
41.25	3
45.3	230
53	189
53.2–3	140
55.8	213
64.17–25	153

Jeremiah

6.14	154
18.6–7	3

Amos

7.14–15	54

Micah		7.13	79	13.44	105, 220
6.8	190fn7	7.14	29, 79	14.13	36
6.9	214	7.15	41, 219	14.14	38, 174
		7.16	27	14.16	174
Zechariah		7.20	27	14.17	189
8	153, 195	7.20–23	192	14.19	174
8.5	173	8.2	38fn4, 165	14.21	174
		8.8	37	14.23	36
Matthew		8.10	38, 80	14.27	168
2.1–12	220	8.11	38	15.4	36
3.13–17	31	8.16–17	166	15.6–9	218
3.16	178	8.20	37	15.14	236
3.17	117	8.22	36	15.15–21	38
3.20	199	8.28	165	15.21	36
4.5–6	117	9.2	80	15.27	174
4.12	36	9.6	39, 211	15.28	80
4.19	230	9.10	37	15.32	38
5.3–11	78	9.20ff	165	15.32–38	38
5.4–6	39	9.22	80	15.33	174
5.9	153	9.29	80	16.1	35, 125
5.12	110	9.36	38	16.2–3	125
5.13	189	10.8	165	16.17	132
5.23–25	199	10.12–13	167	16.20	110
5.31–32	39	10.15	80	16.21–23	29
5.38–42	40	10.22ff	190	16.22	35
5.44	166, 189	10.28	198	16.22–23	117
5.44–47	38	10.34ff	154	16.23	132
5.45	34, 189	10.37	36	16.24–25	59, 111
5.46–47	161	10.38	190	17.1–18	36
5.48	13, 14, 15	10.39	41	18.15	204
6.1–18	151	10.40–41	17	18.15–17	194, 199
6.3	95	11.4–6	125	18.16–17	209
6.7–8	107	11.19	37, 146	18.18	39
6.9	31	11.28	112	18.20	10
6.10	192	12.7–12	156	18.21–22	194
6.12	198, 200, 203	12.11–12	39	18.23–25	206
6.12–14	39	12.29	47	18.31	208
6.19	35	12.32	207fn6	18.34	199
6.23	110	12.46–47	35	18.35	210
6.25	35	12.46–50	98	19.20	15
6.25–32	107	12.48–50	36	19.3	35
6.26	125	13.2	35	19.5	68
6.28	35, 125	13.10–13	126	19.16	131
6.31	125	13.15	80	19.19	36
6.33–34	125	13.20	105	19.20–21	15
7.1	137, 166, 189	13.24–30	137,166	20.20–21	35
7.3–5	236	13.29–30	189	20.25–27	34
7.7–11	107	13.31–32	9, 11, 189	20.28	33, 165
7.11	127	13.33	189	20.34	38

21.7	36	7.6–8	218	4.42	36
21.12	40	7.10	36	5.8	31
21.23	35	7.11–13	39	5.17	35
21.35–37	141	7.24–30	166	6.32	161
22	80	8.1–9	38	6.27	166, 189
22.16–32	35	8.2	38	6.27–36	38
22.37–40	177	8.17–18	34	6.35	166, 189
23.23	39	8.24	83	6.36	32
23.27	100	8.34–35	230	6.37	137, 166, 189
23.37	69, 182	8.35	120	7	206
25	189	9.35	34	7.6	37
25.18	116	10.7–8	68	7.9	38
25.24–25	59, 116	10.21	38	7.13	38
25.31–46	166	10.32	29	7.22–23	125
25.38	161	10.35–37	35	7.34	37, 146
25.40	11, 139	10.45	33, 165	7.39	152
26.11	224	11.25	32, 107, 194, 203	7.44–46	37
26.37	38	12.29–30	47	7.46	174
26.39	109, 220	12.40	39	7.47	152
26.41	6fn5	12.44	190	7.48	39
26.46	110	14.7	224	7.50	80
26.52–56	40	14.8	152	8	165
26.53	198	14.27	38	8.45	35
27.51	165	14.35	40	8.46	35
28.8	105	14.36	109	9.10	36
		14.48–49	40	9.11	174
Mark		14.56	217	9.13	174
1.17	230	14.59	217	9.14	36, 174
1.35	36	15.38	165	9.18	36
2.1–12	139			9.51	79
2.4	35	**Luke**		9.58	37
2.7	211	1.2	217	9.60	36
2.11	139	1.14	105	10.1–11	160
3.5	38	1.34	220	10.5–6	167
3.9	35	1.35	6	10.7	37
3.21–22	144	1.38	6	10.21–22	105
4.19	35	1.48	118fn3	10.25–37	38
4.30–32	11	1.52	118fn3	10.29	189
5	165	1.68	37	10.31–34	79
5.41	169	2.9	31	10.33	180
6.6	38	2.12	125	10.33–34	177
6.31	238	2.14	153	10.37	180, 189
6.34	38, 174	2.41–50	101	10.38	37, 161
6.37	174	2.47	216	10.41	35
6.39	174	2.48	35	10.42	161
6.41	174	2.49	85	11.2	32, 97
6.46	36	2.52	216	11.4	198, 200, 203
6.50	168	4.18	6	11.11–13	107
7.2	36	4.33–35	165	11.13	127

11.27–28	6	19.9–10	160	6.66	29
11.42	39	20.47	39	7.1	36
12.4	198	21.4	190	7.1–5	35
12.6	47	21.34	35	7.38	192
12.10	207fn6	22.15	38, 146	8	32
12.12	226	22.19	37	8.1–11	35
12.22	8, 35	22.26	34	8.3–11	204
12.22–30	107	22.27	33	8.12	126
12.26	3.9	22.42	109	8.23	206
12.30	3.5	22.44	38	8.56	105
12.45	207	22.49–53	40	8.59	36
12.46	207	22.50	198	9	83
12.48	207	23.34	208	9.2–3	189
13.1–3	127	23.45	165	10.4–5	69
13.4	34	24.13–36	76	10.7	126
13.8	13	24.30–31	37	10.8	198
13.15–16	39	24.35	37	10.11	126
13.21	189	24.41	105	10.17–18	40
13.29	38	24.52	105	10.24	35
13.31	100			11.5–6	145
13.34	69	**John**		11.14–15	145
14.12–14	161	1.9	128, 199	11.17–26	189
14.20	36	1.12	105	11.21	35
14.26	36	1.14	7, 128,	11.25	41
14.37–43	234		160, 217	11.32	35
15.1–2	37	1.18	98, 128	11.33	38
15.6	105	1.39	160	11.33–35	186
15.8	131	2.3–4	35	11.33–38	145
15.9	105	2.4	40	11.38	38
15.11–32	195	2.11	126	11.38–44	186
15.15	69	2.14–15	40	11.41–42	145
15.16–17	21	3.1	170fn10	11.54	36
15.17	74	3.1–8	80	12.8	224
15.17–18	23	3.8	192	12.21	29
15.18–19	197	3.29	105	12.21–28	8
15.20	177, 180, 197	4	161	12.24	34, 126,
15.25–32	195	4.1–3	36		230, 228
15.32	41, 105	4.10	126	12.24–25	41
16.1–9	127	4.14	192	12.27	38, 40
17.3–4	199	4.36	105	12.32	165
17.4	80	4.48	135	13.1–17	34
17.12	165	5.20	31	13.15	34, 113
17.19	80	5.39	127	13.21	38
17.21	170	6.7	174	13.34–35	189
18.3–8	127	6.9	174, 189	14.5–6	29
18.11–12	82, 115	6.10	174	14.6	219, 229
18.13	26	6.15	34, 36	14.9	7
18.20	36	6.24–26	35	14.10–13	31
19.5	139	6.35	126	14.17	6, 219
19.5–6	160	6.51	41	14.27	154

15	9, 190
15.1	126
15.4–5	13
15.5	69
15.10–11	105
15.15	110, 152, 214
15.26	6, 219
16.13	6, 219
16.23	107
16.20–24	110
16.21	34, 228
16.22	105
17.15–16	144
17.23	11
18.4–11	40
18.11	198
19.26–27	36
19.30	15
20.3–8	47
20.17	32
20.20	105
20.23	39, 211
20.25	236
20.30–31	226
21.9–13	160
21.12	37, 38
21.15	230
21.15–19	39, 195
21.17	195
21.17–19	230

Acts

1.20–21	217
2.1	10
2.42	174
3.19	79
3.26	79
4.20	217
5.41	110
6.3	160fn1
6.15	8
7.60	40, 200
8.22	79
9.5	11
11.23	105
14.17	103
15.3	105
15.19	79
17.22–28	127, 167
26.20	79

Romans

1.3	99
1.17	227
1.20	127
3.8	202
3.21–24	56
3.22	169fn8
3.26	224
5.2	107
5.6–8	102
5.7–8	194
5.8	118fn3, 152, 167
6.1	202
6.3	235
7.11–13	165
8	6
8.1	118fn3
8.10	10
8.15	32
8.15–16	97
8.17	111
8.19–21	4
8.27	82
8.29	29
8.31	103
8.35	103
8.37–39	103
9.17–24	3
9.33	118fn3
10.11	118fn3
12.1	235
12.2	13, 220
12.3–5	122
12.11	180
12.13	37, 160
12.15	105
12.17	40
12.17–21	198
14.17	153
16.19	105

1 Corinthians

1.10–13	166
1.20	155
1.24	41, 105, 110
2.6	41
6.9	5
9.22	222
9.24–27	14
11.24	37

12.3	26
12.4–6	7
12.4–11	192
12.7	9
12.14–20	142
12.15	105
12.26	208
13.2	192, 220
13.4–7	152
13.6	105
13.10	35
13.12	35, 135
15.21	94
15.20	29
15.23	29
15.35ff	234
15.45	94
16.7	105

2 Corinthians

1.3–4	184
1.24	105
3.2	4
3.17–18	3
4.4–6	7
5.19	194
6.12	110
7.7	105
8.2	110
12	234
12.4	234
12.7	234
12.9	15, 190
12.21	79
13.9	105

Galatians

1.11–16	216
1.13–14	222
2.20	10
3.5	93
3.24	93, 197
3.28	197
4.3–6	104
4.6	32, 97
4.9	80
4.9–10	156
4.19	3
5.16–20	108
5.16–23	93

5.22	13, 112, 151	4.11–13	142	13.1–2	160
6.2	142	4.13	190	13.2	37
6.17	234			13.3	177
		Colossians			
Ephesians		1.17	153	**James**	
1.5	8	1.20	153, 195	1.2	110
1.9	8	1.24	110	3.5–10	109
2.13–14	165	1.25	7		
2.16–17	165	2.5	105	**1 Peter**	
4.1	170	3.1–2	23	1.6	110
4.1–2	112	3.5–17	108	1.8	110
4.15–16	13	3.14	22, 112	2.18–20	226
4.16	112, 150			2.23	40
4.17–32	108	**1 Thessalonians**		3.9	40
		5.15	40	3.15	213
Philippians		5.18	78	4.12–13	110
1.8	181				
1.9–11	213	**2 Thessalonians**		**1 John**	
1.11	13	2.14	8	4.1	219
2.1	181			4.4	105
2.4	121, 139	**2 Timothy**		4.18	118, 190
2.5–8	112	1.4	105	4.19	192
2.6–11	113				
2.13	8	**Hebrews**		**2 John**	
2.15	8	1.3	7	1.12	103
2.17	110	2.10	15, 110		
2.18	105	2.11	118fn3	**Revelation**	
2.28	105	2.11–14	97	2.7	214
2.29	105	2.16–17	97	3.19	136
3.13–14	23	5.6	225	3.20	160, 174
3.21	118fn3	7.25	82	7.17	224
4.1	105	12.1	108	21.1–4	153
4.10–13	110	12.2	29, 105, 118fn3, 12.3		
4.11	234	12.12	15		

Index of Names and Subjects

Note: Page numbers in *italics* denote quotations in text boxes.

abuse 207–8
Adam and Eve *see* Eden (Garden of)
addictions 108
adolescence 85
adversity 226–8
agapē 152
Ainsworth, Mary 63, 65–6, 68, 103, 105
Allain-Chapman, Justine 236
Allport, Gordon 164
apophatic tradition 134
Apter, Michael 36
aptitudes 54–5
Athanasius of Alexandria 98, 217
attachment theory 63–72
Augustine of Hippo 73
Austin, John 218
authority, in the churches 217–18
autism 155
awe 132–3

balance 142–58, 224
Baltes, Paul 215, 221, 223
Balthasar, Hans Urs von *238*
Barltrop, Mabel (Octavia) 219fn6
Batson, Daniel 179
Benedict of Nursia *123, 143, 161*
Berlin Wisdom Paradigm 215, 221, 225
Berryman, Jerome 173
Blake, William *127*
blessings 140, 166
boasting 115
body of Christ 10–11, 23, 189
body as metaphor for community 13–14, 23
Bonaventure *183*
Bowlby, John 63–5, 67, 68
bravery 55
Brooke, Rupert 171

Bunyan, John 79
Butler, Joseph 60

Calhoun, Lawrence 86–7
Cannon, Walter 180fn4
Carver, Charles 16, 18, 20
C'de Baca, Janet 84–5
character strengths 57–60
Charry, Ellen 24
child development 81, 86
childhood memories 62
Christian formation 3–14
communion service 26
community 8–10
compassion 38–9, 177–93
contemplation 25–6, 137–8, 233–6
contemplative prayer 82–3
conversion 70–1, 79–80
cooperation 6–7
costly signaling 196–7
courage 55
cowardice 55
creation 127–8
Crossan, John Dominic 37
Csikszentmihalyi, Mihaly 148
curiosity 213–14

detachment 143–5
Dillon, Michelle 227
discernment 27
discipleship 6
dwelling 157–8

E (personality trait) 49, 51–2, 146, 153, 154
eating and drinking 37–8
Eckhart, Meister *10, 133*
Eden (Garden of) 55, 100, 123
ego 120–1

egocentricity 81
elevation 190–1
Eliot, T. S. 237
email
 care over 109
 etiquette 18
embodiment 233–6
Emmaus Road 76–7, 85, 87
empathy 183–8
engagement 147–50
epiphanies 82–7
Esau and Jacob 195
eschatology 36
Eucharist 26, 173
eudaimonia 145–6
Examen 74
extraversion 48–9
eyewitnesses 216–17

faith
 and attachment 69
 development 80
 as insight 128
 as a journey 77
 justification by 118fn4
 telic nature of 15
 and turning 80–3
Fall, the 55, 100, 127
family, demands of 35–6
Fanthorpe, U. A. *152*
feelings 20
fight-flight response 180–1
flow 147–51
food, and Jesus 173–4
forgiveness 39–40, 107–8, 198–211
 and health 202
formation 3–14
Francis of Assisi 183, 234
Fredrickson, Barbara 147
fruit 13, 26–7
 of the Spirit 94, 150–3

Girard, René 203–4
glory of God 7–8
goals 15–17, 20, 27
God
 at work in the world 34
 as Father 31–2, 70, 97–111
 generosity of 147
 as Holy Other 97

love 117–19
 as safe haven 70, 102
Gollancz, Victor *203*
good life, the 145–6
Good Samaritan Experiment 184–5,
 190
Good Samaritan (parable) 189
Gospels 24–5, 30
grace of God 147
gratitude 78, 82
 letters 88
growth, Christian 13–28
growth (personal) 76–88
Guigo II 138
guilt 118

Haidt, Jonathan 132
happiness 103
hedonia 145–6
Herbert, George *127*
hesychasm 137–8
Holy Communion 26
Holy Spirit *see* Spirit of God
Hopkins, Gerard Manley 191
hospitality 37–8, 51, 160–75, 177
Hugh of St Victor *126*
humility 112–24, 190fn7
humour 123, 228
Hunt, William Holman viii, 135, 174

identity markers 163–5
idleness 143
Ignatius of Loyola 25, 74, *116*, 151
illusion 172–3
incarnation 24
intercessory prayer 81–2
internal working models (IWM) 67–8,
 102, 125
Irenaeus of Lyons 8
Isaiah 177, 178, 189

James, William 84–5, 132
Jesus
 adolescent visit to Temple 216
 agony 8, 38, 109–10
 compassion 38–9, 179
 crucifixion 231, 233, 235
 demands on his time 35–6
 eating and drinking 37, 173–4, 177
 forgives Peter 195

healing ministry 165
hospitality 37–8
incarnation 24, 29
intimacy with his Father 31–2
and the Law (Torah) 39
as light of the world viii
non-retaliation 39–40
as our brother 98–9
passion 198, 233
resurrection body 234
and the Samaritan woman 169
as Son of God 33–4
spends time with the socially undesirable
   165
teaching 23, 34, 40–1, 126, 189, 203,
   227
temptation 32–3, 117
visiting people 167–70
wisdom 40–1, 228–9
wounds 236
see also mind of Christ
Jesus Prayer 25–6, 82, 138
Job 233
John of the Cross 144, 234–5, 235
Joseph and Mary 101
journals, spiritual 158
joy 103–5, 110, 152–3
Julian of Norwich 168, 205, 225
Jung, Carl G. 214fn1
justification by faith 118fn4

Kabat-Zim, Jon 136–7
kairos 40
Kekulé, August 85
Keltner, Dacher 132
kingdom of God 9
Kirkpatrick, Lee 68–70, 101

Law (Torah) 39, 196–7
Lazarus, raising of 186
lectio divina 138–9
Lee, Matthew 192–3
Lewis, C. S. 106, 152, 172
liberation 6–7
Liddell, Eric 148, 151
life, as a journey 79
life in the Spirit, vs life under the law
   93–4
Linley, Alex 227–8
Lord's Prayer 97–111

Lord's Supper 26
Lorenz, Konrad 64
love
   as Christian virtue 112
   four types 152
   of God 117–119
loving-kindness meditation 187
Luther, Martin 235–6

McAdams, Dan 73
Magi 220
Makarios the Great 137
Mary (mother of Jesus) 6, 101
Mass 26
maturity 14–15
Maximus the Confessor 11
meditation 137, 187
memory 73
Merton, Thomas 16
Milgram, Stanley 53fn5
Miller, William 84–5
mind of Christ 112–24
mindfulness 95, 136–7, 138, 150
   meditation 187
Mischel, Walter 53
mustard seed (parable) 9, 12
mystical experience 84–5, 132–3, 192–3,
   233–6
   and compassion 182

N (personality trait) 49
narcissism 117
natural theology 34, 126–8
neighbor, Jesus' teaching on 189
nepsis 139
neuroticism 49, 55
Niemiec, Ryan 61
non-retaliation 194–211
numinous, the 31

Origen 138
Original Sin 56, 123
Otto, Rudolf 31

parables 126, 226
   see also Prodigal Son
paradox 227
paralysed man (in Mark's gospel) 139
Pargament, Kenneth 95, 232–3, 239
Patrick (Saint) 88

Paul (Saint), personality traits 222
Pawelski, James 83
peace 153–4
  preaching 167–70
  reconciliation 195
Pentecost 10
perception 128–32
perfection 14
  personality 20–1
personal identity 16
personality
  incoherent 21
  integrated 20–1, 35–6
  traits 47–60, 222
Peter (Saint), forgiven by Jesus 195
Peterson, Christopher 56–9
Piaget, Jean 81, 86
play 173
pleasure 103, 145–6
Poloma, Margaret 192–3
Popper, Karl 135
positive psychology 231
post-traumatic growth 87, 231–3
potter/clay imagery 3–4
prayer 25–6, 207, 238
  as attention 77–8
  contemplative 82–3
  in Gethsemane 109–10
  intercessory 81–2
  as work 106
  see also Jesus Prayer; Lord's Prayer
preaching peace 167–70
prejudice, and religion 164
presence of God 31
pride 115
Prodigal Son (parable) 23, 69, 74, 97, 195, 197
prophets 178, 192
Pruyser, Paul 172–3
psychoanalysis 63
psychology 45–6

quantal change 84

reconciliation 195
religion, and prejudice 164
religious spiritualty 95
repentance 203–7, 210
resilience 236–9
rest 143, 156

retreat 36
Richard of Chichester 99
Rizzuto, Ana-Naria 109
Robertson, James 64
Rothbart, Mary 48
Royzman, Edward 55
Rozin, Paul 55
Runcie, Robert 140, 178
Ruskin, John 21, 133–4

Sabbath 156
Samaritan woman 169
Sandage, Steven 96
savouring life 146–7
scapegoating 203–4
Scheier, Michael 16, 18, 20
schemas 72, 85–6
Schmemann, Alexander 26
science 218–19
Scriven, Joseph 71
seeking 157–8
self-compassion 188
self-esteem 67, 114–17, 163, 205
self-worth see self-esteem
Seligman, Martin 53, 56–9, 60, 145, 147
separation 64–6, 69
Sermon on the Mount 24, 78, 166
shame 117–18, 123–4
Sheldon, Kennon 21
Sherif, Carolyn and Muzafer 162, 166
signs 125–6
sin 55–6
  and suffering 189
  unforgivable 207
  see also Original Sin
skills 54–5
Skinner, B. F. 148
social identity theory 163–5
social justice 10
Spirit of God
  cooperation with 6–7
  as liberator 6
  as transformer 4–5
  see also life in the Spirit; Pentecost
spiritual gifts 192
spiritual journals 158
spirituality
  and adversity 227
  meanings of 5
  religious 95

Staudinger, Ursula 215, 221, 223
stereotyping 172
stories 72–4
suffering 110
 response to 182–4
 and sin 189
 transformation of 236–7
 see also trauma

Tajfel, Henri 162–3
Taylor, Shelley 232
Tedeschi, Richard 86–7
telic faith 15, 36
temperament 47–60
Teresa of Ávila 144, 234
thanksgiving 78, 82
 letters 88
theōsis 11
Thérèse of Lisieux 69
Thomas à Kempis 42
Thomas, R. S. 146
Tillich, Paul 227
Traherne, Thomas, *104, 123, 149*
transformation 4, 41, 230–9
transitional phenomena 172
transitional space 173
trauma 86–7, 132fn4, 226–8
 responses to 232–3
truth 215, 219
 in encounter with Christ 229
 and the Holy Spirit 6, 219
 and mystical experiences 84
 and paradox 41
truth-telling 154
Tuffaha, Lena Khalaf 188

Turner, John 163
Turner, Joseph 134
turning 80–3
Tutu, Desmond *199*
Tyndale, William 218

unforgivable sin 207
uplifting feelings 190–1

Value in Action (VIA) 56–60
Vanstone, W. H. 150
visionary experiences 191–3
visiting 160–70
visual perception 128–32

watchfulness 139
Watts, F. 198–9
Weil, Simone 77, 236
welcoming 161, 170–5
whistle-blowing 209
Wilder, Laura Ingalls 95
Willard, Dallas 5, *59*
Williams, Rowan *30*
 on Luther 236
Wink, Paul 227
Winnicott, Donald 171–2
wisdom 40–1, 213–29
Wittgenstein, Ludwig 218
Witvliet, C. 201
wonder 135–6
 enabling 171–3
worry 35, 136

Zacchaeus 167, 169
zest 146–7